Dreams of Speech and Violence

Dreams of Speech and Violence

The Art of the Short Story in Canada and New Zealand

W.H. NEW

UNIVERSITY OF TORONTO PRESS
Toronto Buffalo London

©University of Toronto Press 1987
Toronto Buffalo London
Printed in Canada
Reprinted in 2018
ISBN 0-8020-5663-6
ISBN 978-1-4875-8183-1 (paper)

Printed on acid-free paper

Canadian Cataloguing in Publication Data

New, W. H. (William Herbert), 1938–
   Dreams of speech and violence

   Includes bibliographical references and index.
   ISBN 0-8020-5663-6

   1. Short stories, Canadian (English) – History and
criticism. 2. Short stories, New Zealand – History
and criticism. 3. Literature, Comparative – Canadian
(English) and New Zealand. 4. Literature,
Comparative – New Zealand and Canadian (English).
I. Title.

PS8097.N49N49 1987   823'.01'09   C86-094730-0
PR9185.3.N49 1987

This book has been published with the help of
a grant from the Canadian Federation for the Humanities,
using funds provided by the Social Sciences and
Humanities Research Council of Canada.

For Jack and Dianne Hodgins, in Canada

For Campbell and Sue Ross, in New Zealand

Contents

Preface / ix
Acknowledgments / xiii

PART ONE: STORY AND THEORY

1 Canada, New Zealand, and the Genre of the Short Story / 3

PART TWO: STORY AND HISTORY

2 Canada: Story and History / 29

  D.C. Scott's Revolution, 1820–1920 / 29
  Country, War, and City, 1890–1940 / 48
  The Tensions between Story and Word, 1930–1980 / 79

3 New Zealand: Story and History / 113

  The Transformations of Kathleen Beauchamp, 1860–1920 / 114
  Frank Sargeson & Sons, 1900–1970 / 137
  The Match with Homogeneity, 1940–1980 / 153

PART THREE: STORY AND STRUCTURE

4 Altering Cycles: Duncan Campbell Scott's *In the Village of Viger* / 177

5 No Longer Living There: Margaret Laurence's *A Bird in the House* / 187

6 Pronouns and Propositions: Alice Munro's *Something I've Been Meaning to Tell You* / 201

7 Pronouncing Silence: Katherine Mansfield's 'At the Bay' / 211

8 Saying Speech: Frank Sargeson's 'Conversation with My Uncle' and Patricia Grace's 'A Way of Talking' / 221

9 Unsaying Memory: Maurice Duggan's 'Along Rideout Road that Summer' / 229

PART FOUR: EPILOGUE

10 In other words, that is to say, so to speak / 239

Appendix: Short Story Terminology / 247

Notes / 255

Index / 287

Preface

The subject of this book is the art of the short story in Canada and New Zealand, and the form the book takes is an implicit reflexive comment upon this subject. Both the art form and the book employ systems of fracture – sequentially (as is characteristic of the story form in Canada) and internally framed within a given text (as is typical in New Zealand). The plurality of approaches asks that a single version of the story not be accepted as the whole story, and asks, too, that the reader not impose conventional notions of 'wholeness' or 'unity' (or conventional 'universal' definitions of 'story' and 'nationhood') upon the art of short fiction as writers in these two societies have practised it.

Why the short story? And why Canada and New Zealand? Apart from the intrinsic interest of the form and the two societies, the similarity of the challenge that English-language writers in these two countries have faced presents an instructive opportunity for comparative commentary. Both societies have committed themselves historically to evolutionary or orderly development ('peace, order, and good government' was Canada's founding principle), yet both literatures are riddled with violence – as a direct subject, and as a verbal process. Why the paradox, and what does it imply?

To answer these questions requires some feeling for the history of the two societies and the cultural attitudes that have been generated in each. To a significant degree the societies see themselves in terms that derive from elsewhere. Celebrating their own roots, they simultaneously have felt 'marginalized' by the culturally powerful presence of their British heritage and their nearest neighbour (the United States, Australia). These neighbours and forebears, moreover – at least to anglophone Canada and pakeha New Zealand – even appear to speak the same language, framing or containing their own manner of expression. But is it the same? For writers, that is a fundamental question. Whether language expresses a culture or expresses an individual sensibility, how independent is the culture or the writer whose language is controlled from without? Alternatively, how do writers and societies claim language as their own?

Repeatedly, writers in Canada and New Zealand have declared their desire to tell 'real' stories. While this notion begins in documentary, it changes its impulse as the societies also change. Characteristically, writers in these two societies tell their stories by indirect means: the 'sub-version' proving more 'real' than the surface narrative – more 'dream,' perhaps, than 'documentary' – and 'sub-version' itself being a process of speech and form as well as a product of political will. The open, broken forms of the short story, that is, constitute a generic opportunity for authentic speech. The story turns marginality to its own purpose. Obliqueness and discontinuity sound verbal alternatives to the closed values of the status quo.

Louise Cotnoir's remarks at the 'Women and Words' conference in Vancouver in 1983 specify how marginality affects language. She writes as a woman, she says, and in particular as a québécoise, twice removed from conventional power inside Canada – the extra dimensions of marginality intensifying the general cultural experience out of which she writes: 'When I begin writing a text I must first rethink the social, political, and cultural space in which I move towards somewhere else. In a sense, we are all "thieves of language" because we read reality and we write it as terrorists.' Where then does power come from in a marginalized culture? From borrowing, emulating, and so appearing to join the power structure of the dominant society? Or from fidelity to the things that matter locally and personally, resisting the temptations of dominance and in time reshaping the character of the culture at large? The challenge is to use the existing language, even if it is the voice of a dominant 'other' – and yet speak through it: to disrupt (or do 'violence' to) the codes and forms of the dominant language in order to reclaim speech for oneself.

The theory section of this book shows how conventional theories of short fiction impose a dominant set of expectations (of 'wholeness,' 'unity,' 'nation') on literary form, expectations that are not necessarily applicable outside the society to which they were first applied. The history section – using Canada and New Zealand as examples – traces the processes of change that have allowed two literatures to move away from the dominance of received cultural forms, and that have consequently allowed speech through forms of fracture. The section on structure looks at representative examples of Canadian serial composition and New Zealand story-framing, in order to demonstrate in detail some of the strategies of indirect form. The Canadian examples illustrate the effects of cumulative arrangement, shifting motif, and reiterated rhetorical structure; the New Zealand examples illustrate the effects of framed silence, oral gesture, and the masks of memoir and articulate memory. The book then spirals to its conclusions – in open epilogue rather than formal closure – directing the reader outward into the ongoing processes of pattern, story, and change.

Acknowledgments

I should like to express my appreciation to the University of British Columbia and to the Social Sciences and Humanities Research Council of Canada, who helped support this research, and to the many students and colleagues to whom I am indebted for constructive advice and criticism. In particular I wish to thank Neil Besner, for his helpful research assistance in the early stages of the Canadian half of this project; Carole Gerson, for sharing her insights into nineteenth-century fiction; Laurie Ricou and Eva-Marie Kröller, for reading the manuscript and offering valuable comments; and many others in Canada and New Zealand, for giving of their time to talk about short fiction with me: Peter Alcock, K.O. Arvidson, Tony Bellette, Clark Blaise, Bill Broughton, Ray Copland, Wystan Curnow, Margaret Dalziel, Patrick Evans, Lawrence Jones, Bill Manhire, David Norton, W.H. Oliver, Brian Opie, Vincent O'Sullivan, Bill Pearson, Peter Simpson, Karl Stead, Donald Stephens, J.R. (Tim) Struthers, Audrey Thomas, John Thomson, Reg Tye, and Lydia Wevers. I appreciate the generosity of Roger Robinson and the Victoria University of Wellington, for inviting me to share in departmental life, and for providing me with study space while I was in New Zealand; of Irene Johnston and Lindsay Buick-Constable, for their courtesy; of Janet Horney, J.E. Traue, and the Alexander Turnbull Library for their kindness, and for giving me access to the research collection of the New Zealand national library; and of Joan Sandilands, Anne Yandle, and the staff of the Special Collections and Inter-Library Loan Divisions of the University of British Columbia, for their continuing assistance. I wish also to thank my family, for their support; Beverly Westbrook and Doreen Todhunter, who typed the manuscript; and my editors, Gerry Hallowell and Jean Wilson.

'Pronouns and Propositions' first appeared in slightly different form in *Open Letter*, and I am indebted to the editor, Frank Davey, for permission to reprint it in this new context. A few of the other ideas raised in this book first appeared in reviews in *Pilgrims, Islands, Landfall, Canadian Literature*, and the *New Zealand Listener*.

The mind will not be succoured by images of the forest or be thrilled by evocations of the ocean breaking on a tropical beach without being satisfied about the meaning of things. *Man's world is a world of meaning. It tolerates ambiguity, contradiction, madness, or confusion, but not lack of meaning. The very silence is populated by signs* (Octavio Paz). The mind has a quarrel with reality, having for generations rejected definitions of it while seeking, with the craving of an addict, one more new interpretation. (Zulfikar Ghose, *The Fiction of Reality*)

PART ONE
STORY AND THEORY

1 Canada, New Zealand, and the Genre of the Short Story

This book is a set of theoretical, historical and analytical inquiries into the growth and practice of the short story in Canada and New Zealand. Even to call it a 'set' of inquiries is to describe some of the paradoxes that accompany the topic – paradoxes that derive both from the particular literary form and from the particular societies in question. For the subject is fluid and plural, evading simplistic codifications, whereas any 'set' or 'fix' upon it is likely to impose limits that edge both art and culture rigidly. The form of this book – deliberately varied in order to talk about fragmented form – is an attempt to give fluid shape to a subject that is continuously undergoing change.

I do not intend to try to demonstrate the 'distinctiveness' of either Canadian or New Zealand literature. I take it as a given fact that Canada and New Zealand are independent and different societies whose literature is rooted in their peoples' experience; I also take it as axiomatic that there is no one theme or form that can be wheeled out on demand to define these differences and so categorize once and for all what Canadian or New Zealand literature is, or may do. At the same time, it is possible to observe what Canadian and New Zealand writers have done, one of which is to produce over the last hundred years a quite remarkable body of short fiction. Observably, these bodies of fiction differ both from each other and from the stories that have connected into national traditions elsewhere. In what ways this is so, how these separate traditions have grown, and how individual writers have shaped quite separate literary territories within these traditions are questions which occupy the rest of this book. But there are other preliminary questions to ask, which probe the nature and function of the short story form itself and its relevance to Canadian and New Zealand culture.

Theories of the short story began to develop in the nineteenth century, when Edgar Allan Poe championed the cause of a literary work that could be read at a single sitting;[1] his concern was to celebrate the force of a unity of tone in a narrative tale, a unity that could not logically be sustained at length.

Later critics and writers were to add their comments on the form in due course – either because they practised it or because they rejected it: there have been enthusiasts on both sides. But though there has in total been relatively little theoretical commentary on the short story genre, most of it has been curiously restrictive about matters of shape and value (most commentary, as Mary Louise Pratt has ably observed, has perceived a hierarchical relation between the short story and the novel, and despite Poe dismissed the short story as an artistically 'lesser' form).[2] And because of its preconceptions (more political and more restrictive than it often realizes) most commentary does not adequately apply to the practice of the short story outside America, England, and continental Europe. To understand the art of the short story in Canada and New Zealand, therefore, requires the critic first of all to appreciate the limitations of existing theoretical attempts to describe the genre as a whole.

The single most influential commentator on the form during the later nineteenth century, Brander Matthews, was indirectly responsible for much of this ambivalence about short fiction. By isolating a series of particular features which he said were requisites of the short story ('brevity,' 'ingenious originality,' 'unity,' 'compression,' 'action,' 'logical structure,' and if possible 'fantasy'), he inadvertently outlined a formula for the design of mechanical fiction.[3] And many writers promptly followed it. Books on 'how to write the short story' almost rivalled short stories themselves in number.[4] With the emergence of a healthy magazine trade in Philadelphia, Boston, and New York (*Saturday Evening Post* began in 1821; *Harper's* in 1850; *Atlantic* in 1857; *Century Magazine* in 1870; *Scribner's* in 1887), and hence an American outlet for all qualitative levels of story, mass market short stories grew in number and came for many people to epitomize the whole form.

Yet there came to be many artists working with the form between 1850 and 1940 – innovating with it, shaping the form to their own ends in all parts of the world: Chekhov, Turgenev, de Maupassant in Russia and France; Stevenson, Hardy, Kipling, Conrad, Wells, Jacobs, Coppard, Bowen, and Pritchett in the United Kingdom; Joyce, O'Flaherty, and O'Connor in Ireland; Hawthorne, James, Wharton, Garland, Freeman, O. Henry, Jewett, Aiken, Anderson, Hemingway, Fitzgerald, and Faulkner in the United States; Lawson in Australia; Machado de Assis in Brazil; Mansfield and Sargeson in New Zealand; Scott, Roberts, and Callaghan in Canada; and more besides them. Typically, they did not allow the magazine formulae to circumscribe their imaginations, and enough readers recognized the fact to justify the publication of scores of anthologies and several surveys and descriptive histories of

5   Canada, New Zealand, and the Short Story

the rise of short fiction, notably those by Fred Lewis Pattee, H.E. Bates, and later T.O. Beachcroft, William Peden, and Walter Allen.[5]

Several writers in their turn became commentators on the form as well as practitioners of it – Frank O'Connor in an important, personal book called *The Lonely Voice*.[6] More common were article-length analyses of particular stories and particular writers. And occasionally there would appear works which furthered the sophisticated reflections on the nature of what by the twentieth century could be claimed as a separate literary genre; among these are B.M. Eikhenbaum's 'O. Henry and the Theory of the Short Story,' the formalist essays of Tzvetan Todorov, Forrest L. Ingram's *Representative Short Story Cycles of the Twentieth Century*, Ian Reid's *The Short Story*, Helmut Bonheim's *The Narrative Modes*, and essays like those by Mary Louise Pratt and Suzanne Ferguson. Susan Lohafer's revisionist *Coming to Terms with the Short Story* appeared in 1983, and Clare Hanson's *Short Stories & Short Fictions, 1880–1980* in 1985.[7]

This catalogue constitutes the general picture. But it also disguises what has been its mass effect: the criticism's cumulative and presumptive appeal to certain localized norms of authority. Reading through these works it is possible to trace the shifts in respectability that the short story suffered; it is possible to see, too, how cultural biases affect each commentator's approach. For example, the Russian and French critics develop systems of literary analysis that are rooted in an understanding of language (and therefore of culture) as a coherent system. Bates and Allen, the British, take panoptic views which presume a linear tradition of fiction with its roots in Britain and British cultural history, and for Hanson the pivotal writer is Kipling; the American critics generalize from American examples to the practice of the genre as a whole anywhere; O'Connor, the Irishman, claims the short story as a new form for people who find themselves on the periphery of a metropolitan culture; Bonheim, the German, seeks categories of classification. Lohafer clearly and importantly provides an alternative procedure of response, exploring the processes of reading and writing stories by means of an instructive taxonomy of sentence form: her terms include 'density,' or the complexity of syntactic structure; 'intensity,' or the complexity of diction and echoic association; 'linearity,' or plot sequence; 'spatiality,' or dimensions of length; and 'rhythms of closure.' Yet with two significant exceptions her examples are American, and her approach does not take openly into account the contextual social restraints upon linguistic choices. Among the general theorists, it is in particular Reid (a New Zealander working in Australia) and Pratt (a Canadian working in the United States) who draw attention to the different impulses and patterns in still other English-language societies in the modern world. The patterns that begin to emerge indicate other assumptions on the part of twentieth-century critics as well.

Critical commentary on the short story, that is, repeatedly derives from one of three general premises: (1) that the short story can be formally defined, (2) that history explains the genre, and (3) that the genre derives from (and portrays) the cultural structure of society. Hence, although all critics appear to ask versions of the same question – seeking explanations of the external shape, the internal features, and the implicit or explicit function of the literary artifact – in practice the filter on their question makes it appear that there are three kinds of critic: those who categorize the story by the formal and thematic elements within it (or equate the story with its patterns and motifs), those who seek a literary tradition – often 'the' tradition – within which to read a story, and those who interpret only within the writer's political context. All reveal by the questions they ask of any writer or story their expectations of the genre.

Definition by Form (Length)

Consider, for example, attempts to define the story by its basic length. The general premise of the judgmental distinction between the short story and the novel involves a complex tripartite equation between length, complexity (or sophistication), and value – an equation that does not sustain analysis. Many long works are unsophisticated, many short ones complex, many texts (both short and long) of great consequence or none at all. The distinction by length that worked for nineteenth-century writers also clearly changed as time passed. Poe praised a work that could be read at a single sitting, but how long is that? There are different degrees of concentration and patience. Henry James observed that it was a general rule, established by practice, that the magazine tale be no longer than 8,000 words and no shorter than 6,000.[8] Yet any devotee of Hemingway or Sargeson knows that in the twentieth century short stories diminished further in size, sometimes to a page or less, and sometimes expanded (Sargeson's works range from about 500 words to about 32,000). How long must a story be to be a story? And how long can it be and still be 'short'? Such questions may be to no purpose. (Ian Reid quotes Claude Brémond to the effect that every story must be three elements long, involving two events in conflict and requiring a third for resolution, but this formula says nothing about physical dimensions, and anyway introduces a supplementary notion: the Aristotelian one, of the integral unity of a tripartite structure.)[9] Particular external pressures have dictated length in some cases (magazine editorial policy, column type-size); payment on a per-page basis seems to have sometimes extended stories beyond their natural limits; in still other cases, length is dictated internally, by the demands of the particular narrative and the artistic skill of its creator in shaping words to a specific end.

Definition by Form (Technique)

The variety of identifiable internal features of short fiction turns up questions of similar amorphousness and magnitude. Because identifiable, such features are open to description; open to description, however, they become susceptible to classification and implicit regulation, as though the elements were the requisite ingredients of a recipe, and a story concoctable from them. To describe what *plot* is, or how a *dénouement* functions, or who an *antagonist* parries may, that is, be valuable contributions to theory and to pedagogical method, and yet have relatively little to do with practice; describing how they work in practice may illuminate particular works and yet not advance theory.

But to turn such descriptions into codifications adds a quite different problematic dimension to the two processes we call reading and writing. When readers read, they commonly seek immediate entertainment first – responding to narrative thrust, vicarious adventure, titillation-on-demand – and only later (or with experience) come to appreciate how the effects result from verbal craftsmanship. Yet writers, who even more than readers appreciate the difficulty of crafting words effectively, do not (unless they are deliberately playing verbal games) write with technique uppermost in their minds. They are aware of people and events and relationships, and they reach for the words to animate these people, events, and relationships, on the page; they do not, except in exercise, approach matters the other way round, seeking relationships to illustrate techniques. Yet handbooks about writing – what in West Africa are known as 'how-for-do' books[10] – often imply by the structure they adopt that the mastery of a methodology equates with a mastery of the craft of short fiction. Once again the equation is reductive, almost casually minimalizing the sophistication of the art and ignoring its fundamental need for intelligence more than for imitative facility, or for that much-vaunted criterion of artistic quality: sincerity.

Any one of the elementary guidebooks – many of which, by virtue of their clarity, do have value for the novice writer – offers a sampling of this categorical approach to methodology which the mature artist has outgrown. The table of contents of Rust Hills's *Writing in General and the Short Story in Particular: An Informal Textbook*, for example, is one of the more recent, more personal, and more discursive of these works, and because more discursive more theoretical and less hard-edged. Yet the fifty-nine chapter titles none the less indicate the process of thinking-by-category about the process of creation; here is a selection of a dozen:

Character and Action
Loss of the Last Chance to Change
Enhancing the Interaction of Character and Plot
Techniques of Foreshadowing
Tension and Anticipation
Types of Character
The Stress Situation
Scenes
Plot Structure
Point-of-View Methods
Setting
Theme[11]

Each of these (and each of the other forty-seven subjects) is of course fit subject for inquiry, and Hills's book attempts to avoid formulaic writing by trying to get the reader to distinguish between mechanical and inventive applications of the terms and techniques under discussion. Indeed, its clarity makes it more useful to the apprentice reader and writer than any of the subjective essays by writers themselves, which appear to identify only luminescent vagaries as the essence of the short story writer's art: 'beauty and passion and truth' (Eudora Welty's term, for example),[12] or 'necessariness' (Elizabeth Bowen),[13] 'the real writing ... will be the individual' (William Carlos Williams),[14] 'a Will o'the Wisp chased hopefully' (Sean O'Faolain).[15] Yet the limitation of the how-for-do book is always the line between advice and practice, between the description of creation and the act of creating. Whatever the virtues of any system of classification, those people who write good stories repeatedly write their way out of genre, into a text – out of a system, into territory that the next critic will attempt to codify through a new set of combinations.

Definition by Form (Type)

This impulse to produce a taxonomy of art shows up also in the related endeavour to produce a consistent glossary of literary terms for the short story. In concept such a project seems laudable, yet once again practice instructs us in the dangerous presumption of hard-edged definition; walking the difficult ground between simplistic clarity and solipsistic obfuscation, artists reject the control implied by a narrow rein on 'meaning.' Just as they have varied the form by loosening the 'prescribed' limit on length, they have written their way into different arrangements and emphases, all of which alter the shades of meaning we can attach to the available terms of critical description. People who define by words can still not contain by words. And critics have not been able to agree on precise meanings for the terms they use largely because, struggling with the variety of literary practice, they have used the terms in different ways.

There has emerged a vocabulary of more than a hundred terms that bear upon the critical description of short fiction, not all of them in common currency, but all interrelating. Careful commentators like Ian Reid, Gerald Gillespie, and Graham Good have observed[16] that the terms frequently overlap and are frequently inexact. Part of the point of listing such terms in Appendix I is to illustrate this inexactness of formal description; part is to indicate the widespread adaptation of some forms and yet the recurrent need from culture to culture to devise a name for a form which has developed in any one particular society. The comments beside each term do not constitute 'definitions'; they are deliberately brief, and are to be taken as notes towards the interpretation of critical practice rather than as closed limits on critical use. Nor is the list exhaustive; there are numerous tributary forms not named here (such as riddle, proverb, aphorism, adage, lyric, drama, satire, song), and there are common terms that attempt to elucidate authors' various thematic and formal emphases (such as 'realist,' 'magic realist,' 'modern,' 'postmodern,' 'naturalist,' or 'slice-of-life'). As with the listed terms, these vary imprecisely in practice, as time and fashion dictate.

Several of these forms of classification derive from structural anthropology and folk-tale analysis, such as that established by Stith Thompson.[17] Thompson's division of fictional tales into particular types – Animal Tales, Folk Tales (a category which includes tales both of magic and of romantic imagination), Jokes and Anecdotes, and Formula Tales (ie, those which are memory games, or those which build suspensefully but close with a shouted 'Boo!' rather than with a plotline dénouement) – focuses the further complications of this process, complications that subsequent folklorists have had to try to root out. In any division by method and motif, categories overlap, variations occur both from place to place and through time (as old stories are re-rooted in new surroundings),[18] and 'true stories' (historical legends) blend with wholly invented ones. By this system, however, historical change and the individuality of an artist's style alike constitute descriptive subsets of differentiation, rather than the main elements of modal discrimination, which are form and formal function. The plot patterns that are repeated from tale to tale, time to time, culture to culture (a devil stranger enters the village; a married couple quarrels; a fool misunderstands the world around him; a hero descends and rises again; a woman meets a beast; the world goes on a voyage) matter more to the scheme of classification than does the social relevance or the aesthetic efficacy of the particular tale-telling.

Definition by History

For other commentators the reverse is true. Aesthetic immediacy, social message, historical insight: these become the main criteria for weighing value or classifying type. And consequently there is a large body of inquiry into the short story's historical antecedents, its historical relevance to the novel, the compass of its tradition, and the prospect for its accomplishment. One encounters the same terminology as before; but the interpretation is different, as is the set of relationships that is established as a context for understanding.

The commonest metaphors for any account of the short story's change through time are the river-with-tributaries and the genealogical tree. The function of both is the same: to account for a network of cross-connections ('fertilization,' 'pollination,' 'branches') and at the same time to assert a linearity of descent ('main trunk,' 'main flow,' 'mainstream,' 'main channel') from past to present. Perhaps inevitably, the versions of inheritance vary. One version takes the short story back to Poe, who is credited with more or less inventing the form; another sees it as one of the latest in a series of forms that derive from the impulse-to-tell-stories that has always been a human characteristic, and which in other times produced stories in verse or fable, parables of wisdom, dramas of circumstance, myths of experience, and narratives of picaresque and serial adventure. A third sees these same forms (parable, fable, myth, dramatic scene) and others as well (sketch, essay, anecdote, yarn) as tributary forms, all leading to the evolution of an identifiable genre; a fourth sees the short story as a result of a deterioration of larger forms, a fragmentation of some 'whole' ur-form. And different versions date the short story's 'coming-of-age' at different times – with Hawthorne, Flaubert, Chekhov, James, Joyce, Mansfield, Hemingway, the 'realistic' social commentators of the 1930s, or the postmodernist Borgesian ironists of the 1960s. to ask if any one is 'right' is only to invite another question for an answer: 'is any one not right?' Once again the variety is all.

This is not to deny what this kind of historical patterning can add to our understanding of what the short story is and does; it is only to guard against failing to perceive the limitations that any particular set of historical linkages will impose on interpretation. In this regard it is useful to place this temporal process of definition beside the spatial process of charting categories. In some sense Robert Scholes alludes to both processes when (comparing systems of linking with systems of framing) he advances a theory that basic to human desire is a belief in the possibility of a holistic system; both Marxism and structuralism, he suggests, are theories of unification, demonstrable of this desire (at least in the twentieth century) for coherence, for an integrative way of seeing the world.[19] It is a belief that lies behind many theories of short fiction. The 'categorical' approach is a system of framing, the 'historical' approach a system of linking – the 'unity' deriving in the one sense by containing the variety, the other by declaring a common root, source, or system of kinship.

In any event, to look more closely at historical connections and declarations of antecedents is to touch on other principles of connection and the desire for connection. Implicitly, rooting the short story in the nineteenth century is to declare it to be without antecedents, or at least (for an American body of commentary) without antecedents in English literature and therefore in England. For much American commentary, such 'newness' of form is what legitimizes it.[20] But in England the reverse is true; to seek roots in folk narrative or medieval saints' lives or sixteenth-century picaresque prose is to declare the short story to be legitimate because it is old and has the force of a continuous tradition behind it. Thus the implicit message is as much political and attitudinal as it is aesthetic and linguistic. Yet the overt justification for making or denying a connection with the past is usually verbal and formal, hiding its political dimension. Criticism speaks of the Swiftean ironies, the picaresque structure, the Johnsonian wit, the Theophrastian character types of nineteenth- and twentieth-century writers, imputing (and sometimes tracing) direct connections between writers, connections which derive from education, reading, political persuasion, or some other form of indirect contact. If 'influence' is intangible by nature, then (within this process of argument) formal likeness gives it a tangible basis. But the corollary is more complex still, for it reverts upon itself, the implicit argument running like this: because form carries meaning and gives shape to themes that rest abstract until they are made concrete by language, form becomes a way of discussing theme; hence observations of a formal tradition become arguments for a thematic tradition, out of which derive many critical declarations of cultural coherence, national identity, moral right, and political cause.

Whatever the attractions of such conclusions, historical commentary has virtues of quite another kind, virtues descriptive and documentary, which can justify much analytic commentary by according it its contextual reverberations. Names, dates, sequences of events: these it can establish or confirm; it can identify contemporary allusions; it can offer clues to buttress an interpretative suggestion. But once historical criticism moves to questions of cause and effect, it enters the critical territory of the imagination, where logical possibility must pair with associative sensitivity – the linear connecting with the lateral – if the results are to be instructive. Once again the historical approach gives rise to political implications. To presume a linear tradition, or one linear tradition, for the short story is to use a temporal scheme to limit the political (that is, to limit the partly spatial or regional) elements that affect the short story's compass. Yet to limit by region is to accept a form of geo-historical determinism that excludes any account of influence and impact from outside.

Definition by Cultural Origin

Such exclusivity is precisely the problem that cultural commentators on the short story must try to avoid.[21] Finding recurrent characteristics in a given nation's literature and then declaring them to be nationally distinctive is one kind of gesture that repeatedly traps cultural critics; generalizing to the entire genre (or to all literature) from common practice in any one society is the inverse face of the same impulse. The former appears to result from a narrowing of the spatial scale on which the short story genre is placed, concurrently with an expansion of the historical one. The reverse process (narrowing the historical and expanding the spatial) produces the latter process: a system of commentary that chooses either not to notice sociocultural distinctions (that is to say, the commentary which generally emphasizes formal topoi) or else to impose one version of history or one set of historical relationships panoptically upon the entire practice of the genre.

One should not be surprised that differences from language to language produce different effects; we are dealing here with a tautology: the sound system, the structure, the stylistic effects that any one language can achieve depend upon the sound system and structure it possesses, the sense of style that its current fashion approves. Yet these same differences apply within languages as well as between them, and though (for example) linguistic geographies of English abound, there are relatively few inquiries into the ways in which regional variations in English speech sounds, vocabulary, and style at once shape variations in the multiple English literatures of the world and articulate the cultural preoccupations, attitudes, and values of different English-speaking societies.

Part of the ambivalence perhaps derives from the implications read into the word 'regional.' For some commentators it means 'variation' from a norm which is identified (or presumed to exist) at a cultural 'centre' (which many accept as London or New York). My own western Canadian cultural bias perhaps shows when I reject this assumption and identify 'region' as one of a plural set of variations (a set which includes as regions of the whole such places as 'London,' 'New York,' 'Boston,' 'Toronto,' 'Los Angeles,' 'Calcutta,' 'Sydney,' or wherever else that has been identified from time to time as a 'centre'). To do so is, however, to illustrate my point: to extrapolate from one variation to the others is presumptuous. My bias will distort as much as others do, particularly historically. As the French political analyst Siegfried noted, after his visit to New Zealand in 1904, there is an acute distinction between actuality and aspiration, between power and image:

Each country has its artistic and literary centre, which prides itself on being the capital of civilization. Boston tries to be the Athens of the United States; and Toronto, the Boston of Canada. To preserve our sense of proportion and to remind ourselves that we are on a small stage, we may say that Christchurch aspires to be the Toronto of New Zealand.[22]

It may be that the nineteenth-century United States did regard Boston as a 'centre.' Translated to another stage, it certainly seems clear that in England the difference between provinces and metropolis has functioned politically as well as attitudinally — that whatever their local character, the provinces have seen themselves, at least as far as taste and power go, as outreaches of a metropolitan London. Extrapolated still further, this principle explains why one of the marks of a colonial society within the British or French empires was the degree to which it accepted the metropolitan standards of the 'parent' culture. But each of these examples is specific to a place and time, not a general truth. To appreciate these distinctions is to begin to understand why cultural theories of the short story depend on culturally-locked notions of the function of language and the equally locally-rooted assumptions about the organizational structure of society. And what this observation emphasizes once again is that cultural theories about the short story's origins are more likely to be valid for a single community than they are for the genre at large. It may be that the historical theories in English criticism, which claim for the short story a linear tradition that takes it back to the exemplum and beyond, are in fact disguised cultural theories. So may formal theories be. In one of the most articulate schemes of formal classification, for example, Helmut Bonheim refers to his methodology as unmistakeably 'Teutonic,'[23] which suggests that the angle of perspective has as influential an effect on interpretation (and on the system of definition) as does the body of material being perceived — or perhaps more that the critical scheme illuminates the cultural frame of the perceiver as much as it does the works under consideration.

American commentary produces still other kinds of example, much of it containing excessive claims for the distinctive American characteristics of short fiction. Sometimes there is an implicit nationalism at work, as when Poe claims that it is as Americans that his readers should be proud of Hawthorne, or when Richard Kostelanetz prominently quotes Frank O'Connor to the effect that the short story is an American 'national art form'; sometimes the claim is more open and enthusiastic, as when Bret Harte claims the

Americanness of the humorous tale or Heather McClave declares that it 'would not be too startling to say that the ... short story is virtually an American form'; sometimes the national pattern is presumed as the norm, as when Mary Rohrberger defines the short story closely, as a form which 'derives from the romantic tradition,' and categorizes other work that doesn't fit her scheme as mere 'simple narrative.'[24]

When Robert Marler and Fred Lewis Pattee inquire into the history of the American story in the nineteenth century, they both convincingly observe transformations taking place that result in a kind of short fiction they approve, and they both emerge with theories of the cultural interconnection between national character and story form; accepted at face value, the two theories would appear to run counter to each other, yet ultimately they are both theories of the literary effectiveness of speech. Focusing on the work of the 1850s, Marler observes how the American 'short story' as an identifiable genre emerged when the romantic impulses of the 'tale' form gave way to the 'story's' techniques of 'realism'; using Northrop Frye's distinction, he shows how during this period character *types* (redolent with psychological implications and therefore 'archetypes,' but still general figures, locally ungrounded) gave way to characters-with-*personae* (ie, individualized human beings wearing complex masks). And Pattee argues, basing his comments on the Twain-Harte-Garland-local-colour-story[26] chain of developments, that the American voice is to be heard in the *anecdotal* (ie, 'spoken') patterns of the short story, which derive from American humour, full of dialect, exaggeration, and tall tale fun. Pattee stresses speech, Marler the transformation of speech (the tale as a *told form*) into a complex written genre. The question is not whether the distinctive American story is either realistic and written or authentic and oral (or indeed, whether the orality of humour marks a story as American, a conclusion not to be granted), but whether it is possible to trace the emerging compatibility of source, form, and culture.

Any investigation of historical antecedents and change will produce paradoxes, and attempts to erase them will only falsify the kind of cultural and generic development that does take place. For example, for all the independence and occasional isolationism of American writing, one of the writers who has been claimed as a 'father' of this native American humorous tradition was the Nova Scotia judge and cultural commentator Thomas Chandler Haliburton,[27] who was not native to the United States and was in fundamental respects politically opposed to it. His *Clockmaker* sketches of the 1820s (continuing for several years after) recorded the dialect anecdotes and reflections (the 'sayings and doings') of an itinerant Yankee clock pedlar in the country of the Bluenoses. Within Canada, Haliburton's books continue to be read for their conservative politics; but it was his character's successful

15   Canada, New Zealand, and the Short Story

individualism that appealed to American readers, and hence it was for a conservative position of quite a different stamp that Haliburton (or at least Haliburton's form) became absorbed into American literary tradition.

Comparably, no more critical consistency exists between terminology and practice than exists between a cultural tradition and its sources. Washington Irving, for example, referred to his stories both as 'sketches' and as 'tales,' yet subsequent commentary has distinguished sharply between these terms, largely asserting the sketch to be a *static* form, and the tale a *dynamic* one.[28] By implication this distinction dismisses the sketch out of hand and claims two things: first that 'dynamism' is good, and second that it is 'American.' Dynamism comes to be seen as a characteristic of the American short story because the American story is seen as a written adaptation of speech forms. By definition, the speech forms were local. But then the hidden equation affects the critical generalization, and the art of the short story *in toto* comes to be seen as a direct development from tale-telling and anecdotal formulae.

Applying elsewhere, even sweepingly, this equation between speech and story, we can see its limitations as a general theory. In Australia, for example, there existed an anecdotal humour which in the 1890s (in the work of Henry Lawson, C.J. Dennis, Steele Rudd, and others of the so-called *Bulletin* School) resulted in anecdotal fiction; but the kind of general transformation that Pattee and Marler collectively note in the United States, shaping anecdotal tale into realistic story, was not to be the Australian pattern; in fact the major shift in the shape of the Australian short story was not to occur until the 1970s, when the *Bulletin* pattern (followed by E.O. Schlunke, Alan Marshall, and others, well into the twentieth century) was to give way, apparently suddenly, not to the realistic tale but to the Borgesian metafictions of writers like Michael Wilding, Frank Moorhouse, and Murray Bail.[29] In another way, English-language writers in modern West Africa (Chinua Achebe, for example) have also drawn on oral tradition, in this case on folk-tale and the syntactic patterns of proverbial utterance, but their tales are markedly different in form and function from those in the nineteenth-century United States; indeed, in Africa the dynamism derives more from the fact of orality than (as in America) from the particulars of the vocabulary of speech. South African writing provides another variation on the use of formal pattern, for the repeated appearance of fables and allegorical forms (as in the work of Nadine Gordimer, Richard Rive, Alex La Guma, and Christopher Hope) appears to relate to South Africa's particular political experience, and anecdote is submerged in the force of political implication; it is not the telling, but the form of telling, that matters, and is 'dynamic.'

In Canada and New Zealand, where local idiom and local attitude differ yet again, there were less strong traditions of indigenous English-language folk-tale than in the United States and Australia, and anecdotal patterns less apparent in the fiction that was produced. Yet the absence or flatness of anecdote in these two societies does not mean that the stories which did emerge there are lifeless. Whether consequently or only simultaneously, it is the form that telling takes, more than the particular local speech vocabulary, that shapes meaning in Canadian and New Zealand prose and gives it its vitality. The point is that an explanation of a formal cultural connection in one society does not transplant automatically to another. In each society there has been a separate cultural adaptation of literary form. Hence when in his classic essay the Russian formalist Boris Eikhenbaum declared that the short story, which is 'fundamental,' derives from anecdote, and that the novel, which is 'syncretic,' derives from history and travel, he was not producing a formal definition so much as he was making a fundamentally arbitrary distinction – arbitrary because culture-closed. Perhaps accurately referring to travel *narrative* (another form of history), his distinction is disputed by the existence, character, and function of the travel *sketch*. But not in the United States, where the 'sketch,' despite Irving's ambivalence about the term, fell in fact from favour. In the U.S. the narrative tale took over as the dominant basic form, and the terms of theory appeared to develop into a culture-closed system.

How then can one open it? How can one determine a means of assessing the accomplishment of writers who have written outside the patterns that American and English writers have used? Logically, one should not expect American or English rhetorical patterns to be universal ones, yet that is precisely what much criticism has implicitly assumed. In other words, to presume that Canadian or Australian or New Zealand patterns would not be different is to fail to conceive of the possibility of working alternatives, alternatives of working cultural pattern and of functionally different narrative modes to those in currency in, say, England or America. And not to perceive that the patterns are different is to misread the writers, granting them a kind of honorary English or American citizenship only to find that they wear such literary citizenship oddly, and that their stories are either exotics (therefore 'curious' or 'quaint' exceptions to the 'general' rule) or merely ill-handled versions of the short story form *as it is identified and defined in England or the United States.* Yet consciously to seek such alternative patterns is seldom to find wholly unfamiliar constituent parts (hence the prevalent but misleading illusion of *familiarity* that stories from other cultures often give us, and the consequent danger of imposing skewed expectations upon them); it is, rather, to see in operation a separate process of reassembling literary fragments into art. The fragments may be substantially the same from country to country, but the balance will be different, reflecting the different priorities of particular writers in their separate social context. Such writers (and cultures) display

17 Canada, New Zealand, and the Short Story

their quality and independence neither by refusing to meet international levels of standard nor by pretending their cultural freedom from external influence. But they will never achieve quality or independence if they mistake international levels of standard for a universal set of 'international standards' and so surrender passively to imitation.

The Presumptions of Critical Language

Each of the theoretical approaches that critics have taken towards an understanding of the short story form – by formal definition, by history, by cultural context – is implicitly an appeal to authority and an appeal for order. Seeking to elevate the short story's reputation, whether consciously or unconsciously, the critics have attached the genre to the classics (through an appeal to the continuity of history), to patriotism (through cultural identification), and to science (through systems of classification reminiscent of nineteenth-century botany). Each process does more than merely claim authority, of course – it illuminates the art form itself, the dimensions of the artist's imagination, and the critic's frame of reference – but appealing to tradition, appealing to nationalism, and placing faith in taxonomies alike tend to impose an order upon a fluid form and a fluid body of material. Part of the explanation for the marked tensions in short story theory derives from exactly this difficulty: the language of each process as received is difficult to apply beyond the system or the examples for which it has been developed, yet the assumptions behind the language live on as though they were axiomatic, only to contort subsequent criticism. What has happened is that the terms of judgment, defined within a particular context, have been implicitly defined for local use even though their users may not realize the restrictiveness involved; but they behave as though they were universally true. Terms that were born to describe conventions thus turn into critical dogma, into presumed 'axioms' that criticism must struggle to reconstruct if it is to free the perception of art from the constraints of conventional horizons.

Consider, for example, the kinds of association that are ordinarily built into several of the words that have already been required in these pages: *magazine, book, sketch, fragment, colony*. A colony is not only dependent on another society's metropolitan centre but is presumed by definition to be incapable of developing metropolitan centres of its own; a sketch is declared to be 'static' (though Ian Reid has shown how this is inexact).[30] A magazine has become a functional and popular vehicle for art – hence somehow, seemingly, a less than respectable one, a form of corruption that has taken a high art and brought it low, though many magazines have served art well. A book, by contrast, comes away as an act of artistic respectability, and there follows a seductive but illogical syllogism: 'novels' are 'books,' 'books' are substantial, therefore 'novels' must be a high artistic achievement, though once again we know that many books are nothing of the kind. A 'book,' moreover, is claimed as a 'complete' unit, an 'autonomous' text[31] – explicitly pointing to the fact that the short story, as physically published, is usually only one element in a larger collection of some sort (anthology, magazine, miscellany), and implicitly suggesting that it is therefore of lesser substance than a 'book / novel' and incapable itself of expressing the 'wholeness' which mankind desires.

Sorting out the net of assumptions here is much more complex than simply saying it is not a universal truth. What is immediately striking is how nineteenth-century the assumptions are, in particular the belief that the 'book' constitutes the acme of wholeness. An inquiry into publishing history quickly reveals how, though miscellanies had been printed from early on, the notion of the 'book' as a unified artistic unit developed in the eighteenth-century, partly in response to the development of copyright law, and is at least partly responsible for the emergence of the novel.[32] The novel, too, then, is a relatively recent historical development; and while in the eighteenth and nineteenth centuries it often (as a 'unit') spread over two or more volumes, in the twentieth century it has often been shorter than what one volume might contain and has appeared in magazine format. Whether or not as readers we accept that the novel depicts reality, that it is ever able to do so 'realistically,' or that it is even capable of representing (as *Middlemarch* and *The Scarlet Letter* are said to do) a 'whole society,' is more a matter of interpretive convention than of establishable fact.

But whether or not 'mankind' seeks 'wholeness' is a question of faith and psychological security. Certainly many twentieth-century writers do not seek to represent wholeness at all, and do not feel their art diminished by that fact.[33] The relativity of 'wholeness' is what is in question. For twentieth-century artists (in any medium) 'wholeness' has seldom been a characteristic of the social environment; it has had to be equivalent with the measure of understanding or insight that existed at any given moment – or in other words with whatever 'fragment' of insight time and change might allow. Nadine Gordimer writes:

Each of us has a thousand lives and a novel gives a character only one. *For the sake of the form*. The novelist may juggle about with chronology and throw narrative overboard; all the time his characters have the reader by the hand, there is a consistency of relationship throughout the experience that cannot and does not convey the quality of human life, where contact is more like the flash of fireflies, in and out, now here, now there, in darkness. Short-story writers see by the light of the flash;

19 Canada, New Zealand, and the Short Story

theirs is the art of the only thing one can be sure of – the present moment. Ideally, they have learned to do without explanation of what went before, and what happens beyond this point. How the characters will appear, think, behave, comprehend, tomorrow or at any other time in their lives, is irrelevant. A discrete moment of truth is aimed at – not *the* moment of truth, because the short story doesn't deal in cumulatives.[34]

It is not the short story writer alone who can perceive this way. Poets, dramatists, novelists: all in the twentieth century have sought a means to render such glimpses of experience; it is a factor of time perhaps even more than of genre, and of shared ways of interpreting common human experience. To appreciate the impact of this shift – from notions of nineteenth-century imperial nationalism to twentieth-century cultural independence, from nineteenth-century scientific holism to twentieth-century relativity, from nineteenth-century assumptions about linear development to twentieth-century observations of atomic plurality and random association – is to begin as well to reclaim the word 'fragment' from its simple pejorative aura. The difference we need to be aware of is the difference between a shard of a broken whole, usually static, and an atom in a set of related though perhaps different atoms, usually in flux – which coincidentally redefines the nature of the 'wholeness' that exists to be understood or claimed. And it is here that we circle back to the set of concurrent events in history and art that led towards the separate growth of the short story in Canada and New Zealand in the nineteenth century.

Canada, New Zealand, and the Short Story Form

I have been dealing with approaches both to the short story as a genre and to the cultural biases that affect the interpretation of reality (and hence the reader's response to the function and achievement of any art form that presumes to represent reality). Implicitly I have also been concerned with different ways of interpreting history, a distinction that must now be made somewhat more precise. Charting change and development (alterations not necessarily equivalent), history both traces and interprets verifiable facts; at the edges of interpretation are the historiographical theories that suggest why change takes place at all and how to understand it. New World historians in particular have been concerned with disputing the notion that history is a linear juggernaut and that all that happens in societies which European imperial expansion has established is whatever European tradition dictates. Frederick Jackson Turner's 'frontier thesis'[35] – that on the United States' leading edge of expansion, old values and old hierarchies broke down, resulting in a (democratic) reappraisal and restructuring of the community as a whole – was a theory long found attractive, until it became difficult to locate the frontier. It was in large part succeeded by Louis Hartz's 'fragmentation thesis,' *The Founding of New Societies*,[36] whereby it was possible to see each of several New World societies (Canada, the U.S., New Zealand, South Africa, Australia) as fragments of a particular European culture, different from each other (as from the parent culture) because of the time of formation, the reasons for formation, the geographical demands, and the cultural mixes and pressures of each new society. The theory is one which helps us appreciate the kinds of split affinity (between egalitarian independent-mindedness and colonial identification-by-imperial-connection) which divided and reshaped the old British dominions / nascent Commonwealth nations during the latter years of the nineteenth century and the first decades of the twentieth.[37] And it is in this period that, fastening further on detail, the short story in Canada and New Zealand came to take on its characteristic forms.

It was a period when newspapers and magazines were developing (Paul Rutherford documents how in Canada a split developed between the educative and the entertaining functions of the papers by the end of the 1870s);[38] when Canadians were publishing in American magazines and New Zealanders in Australian ones; when Canada was effectively divided between British and American copyright zones, which in practice limited both the Canadian literary market and the size of the local publishing industry; when both Canada and New Zealand were early shaping a politically and culturally united society out of trading post and agricultural economies; and when a stable and upwardly aspiring, largely Protestant, deeply Scots-influenced middle class was setting the mores of the new world. In both societies educated women were influential on the literary scene during the nineteenth century (eg, Susanna Moodie, Anna Jameson, Sara Jeannette Duncan, Mrs J.E. Aylmer, Lady Barker, Blanche Baughan), though (despite the granting of female suffrage in New Zealand in 1893) women still exerted little direct political power. And by the 1890s, when Duncan Campbell Scott and Katherine Mansfield, those most important of the early shapers of the short story in each society, were producing their first books and sketches, there was already a substantial body of writing and a growing local tradition behind them.

Prominent among the kinds of prose being attempted in the two countries were five types or patterns: documentary accounts of things seen and life lived; political and religious essays; romantic fictions made out of the conventional trappings that were borrowed from other traditions (oriental tales, tales of court, historical adventures); romantic fictions set in local landscapes (often a cross between the authentic and the stereotypical, depending on the author's experience); and dialect attempts (usually comic in intention) to record various kinds of character and 'low life' within the social structure. Many of these efforts were intended for a foreign audience rather than a local one, or at least for a 'home' audience, which was often not thought of as 'foreign.' But several of the patterns came together in the newspaper serials of Maritime Canada and in the form of fictional miscellany, or *Rahmenerzählung*, which characterized the shape of some Canadian and much early New Zealand prose publication.

At the same time as writers were seeking an appropriate literary form for the stories they wanted to tell, there was a determined effort in both societies to find a literary means of coming to terms with the specifics of the local experience. Initially it was a matter of faithfully recording the empirical facts of the environment, and the efforts for a long time were substantially the same in both places, so that with the exception of details (Indian or Maori, maple or pohutukawa, moose or kiwi, the trapline or the sheep station, the bush or the backblocks) the writing could exchange places without altering particularly in texture. Yet by World War I, the two cultures – and the two literatures – would be markedly different, and writers had by then begun to document the nuances of voice and attitude that were to mark their separateness as a culture as well as to record the specifics of flora and fauna that marked their separateness of territory. This documentary impulse was at least as strong as any narrative one, and in Canada especially it has remained so, affecting the shape of film and poetry as well as that of prose.[39] In much recent Canadian writing it has meant that narrative is often used for documentary purposes, that exposition is buried in narrative form, as in the novels of Hugh MacLennan, and that the essay has become predominantly an art of personal narrative. In much earlier prose in both societies it was the sketch which provided the available documentary form. In Canada and New Zealand the sketch thus became highly influential in shaping short prose, and it is to the sketch (rather than to local humorous anecdote, folk-tale, romantic tale, exemplum, or dramatic scene) that we look for the early signs of the indigenous short story.

Because the sketch was so voguish a form in the papers and magazines of the eighteenth and nineteenth centuries – one finds scores of them in such eminent (and widespread) magazines as the *Edinburgh* and *Fortnightly* reviews, for example – it is helpful to understand the term by the meaning it held for the generations who wrote it. A sketch was short; it stressed the sensorily perceptible; it emerged at a time when the new sciences were declaring the need to collect and record observable data, and equating such data with 'truth'; hence it came to communicate the 'factual' rather than the 'fictional' and therefore to be a form which implicitly countered the idealizing or escapist impulses of conventional art.[40] *Stewart's Quarterly* in the 1860s was using the terms 'pen photographs' and 'mental photographs' to describe the sketch, stressing the attractions of the documentary. By the end of the nineteenth century, as the writers of the useful survey articles of the state-of-the-art 1911 edition of the *Encyclopaedia Britannica* were to reveal, the meaning had slightly shifted: 'Though used of literary composition, as for a short slightly constructed play, or a rapid delineation in works of an event or character, the term is chiefly used [in art, to put an] immediate impression [on paper].'[41] There are four issues raised here that need emphasizing. Throughout the history of the sketch, the central element the form has required is a sense of *immediacy*; the writer is (or the reader infers that the writer is) *present as an observer*. But what can the observer see, and how? From observing *scenery and types* at the beginning of the nineteenth century, the writer is allowed by the end to observe *characters and events*. And as these narrative elements creep into the 'neutral' observer's form, neutrality disappears. 'Impression' takes over as the accompaniment to 'immediacy,'[42] and the force of the observer / narrator's point-of-view comes to be felt in the nature of the communication that takes place.

To overlay this brief history of a form on the general social history of Canada and New Zealand at this same time is to perceive how the shifts in literary direction acquire a particular kind of social resonance. For as the writers in the new societies attempted to make literature out of their own experience they faced three problems of story-telling: whose story to tell, whom to tell it to, how to tell it. Deciding to tell their own story meant for colonial writers that they had to enter into combat both with the stereotypes about their own society and with the conventional methods and expectations (established elsewhere) that codified 'international' standards in art. Deciding to speak to their own people meant that, though they sometimes still had to explain the experience of one part of the country to another, they could also begin to depend on a shared body of knowledge, a shared sense of values, and a shared language (meaning tone and cadence as well as syntax and vocabulary), which would be decoded or taken from the page in the same spirit it was placed there. Developing a language was not to be a fixed accomplishment of the nineteenth century; as late as Eli Mandel, Robert Kroetsch, and Patricia Grace, writers were still trying to articulate a speech that would accurately, adequately communicate a national, regional, ethnic, or gender-free experience. But out of writers' cumulative efforts to speak a literature that was germane to the local culture, fiction itself came to embody the particular shaping values of the new society.

We are dealing once again here both with a problem of expression and with a problem of interpretation or reaction, which becomes acute when a set of readers or a foreign culture is invited to assess the articulate accomplishment of another society, a society that is not merely foreign but is also in some sense in the very act of becoming foreign, of breaking away (either politically or literarily) from the world that is or has been the reader's own. Understanding the points of change becomes vital, but appreciating the need for such changes, and their significance (no matter how fine), and their implications within the new cultural history and idiom, may well be among the most difficult leaps demanded of the sociocritical imagination.

In the 1911 version of the *Encyclopaedia Britannica* there was, for example, no mention of literature in the entry on New Zealand, though there were substantive comments on political history, mining, geology, the flora, and the manufacturing industries. By implication as well as by direct statement, therefore, the entry is a qualitative judgment of what was thought to be important about New Zealand. Externally perhaps more than internally, New Zealand was seen to be a source of *matériel*, a set of observable scenes, even a crucible of political experiment, but not a seat of culture. Yet that there should have been a culture emerge from this period testifies to the existence of a cultural ferment of some sort. The challenge is to see in it not merely a collection of colonial imitations, by definition qualitatively less fine than the masterworks of the metropolis, but also the beginning attempts to reshape the language and forms of literature to the needs of the new society.

In some new societies the clearest evidence of a new 'language' for literature was a tangibly different 'English' vocabulary. Out of the slang of the new social mix, out of the need to find names for the elements and experiences in the new society that were not known in the old one, and out of the new social structures (democratic, egalitarian, ethnic, republican, racially mixed, restratified, 'real'), there could develop a new vitality of speech.[43] This process observably took place in Australia and the United States, in Walt Whitman's much-vaunted 'barbaric yawp,' Joseph Furphy's equally celebrated 'temper: democratic; bias: offensively Australian,'[44] and in the worlds of the socially representative novel to which Australian and American writers turned their minds. In other societies, Canada and New Zealand among them, English vocabulary did not on the surface much alter from that in England. There were some regionalisms developed, especially in Newfoundland, and there were several borrowings from Maori, Inuit, and indigenous Indian tongues, and there was a marked influence of Americanisms, particularly during the twentieth century. But much in the new society, though different from the Old, was renamed with the old words, creating problems not for communicating in the new society, where the words (like 'Indian') were understood in their local paradigm, but for adequately communicating the resonances and associations of the new society to a readership schooled in the same words with different echoes. In these societies it was thus not vocabulary which altered but the tonal modulation which carried the vocabulary and the formal shape it took. Writers found themselves, in a sense, by 'deconstructing' the only language they had, using their own words against their own words, in order to carry by subtext and undertow what on the surface seemed ordinary, familiar, and calm. In such worlds, it is scarcely surprising that irony should become so forceful (and a recurrent tonal literary device); nor should readers fail to appreciate that it is not just twentieth-century fashion which has led Canadian and New Zealand writers to use untrustworthy narrators and indirect modes of discourse. In Canada and New Zealand, to come at this question yet another way, the 'sketch' stopped being a 'static' form because it was charged with the tension between the observing mind and the documentary language of observation. The mistake of those critics who find the sketch merely static is to have mistaken an absence of narrative plot for a lack of narrative vitality; the vitality exists in another guise, in the tension held creatively between language and form.

What remains to be said is that in these two societies, the short story is one of the most central of these cultural adaptations of literary form. Nowhere else within the Commonwealth have the *major* English-language prose writers of the society been so *consistently* drawn to write in the genre; nowhere else has the novel figured so tangentially (until recently) among the major fictional accomplishments. But on the whole this accomplishment has been read as a literary failure – a failure to develop an identifiable society and 'therefore' a failure to produce the 'great' national (ie, nineteenth-century) fictional art form, the novel – and hence it has gone largely unrecognized for the innovative skills short story writers at their best display.

Thus Dan Davin – at home one of New Zealand's most highly regarded short story writers, who went on to become (in London) one of Oxford University Press's chief editors – could write in an introduction to an influential anthology of New Zealand short stories, that while 'it may be legitimate to look for something that would suggest a specifically New Zealand contribution' to the short story form, 'Nothing of the kind seems to offer itself.'[45] But in this context it can be seen to be an answer to the wrong question. Muriel Bradbrook was closer to observing the accomplishment of New Zealand short story writers when she declared several years later that

The maturity of a literature depends on the discovery of a characteristic form – not a theme nor a vocabulary, but an approach. Sharp contrast of certainty in uncertainty that issues in the short story has given a voice to the islands. The islands are part of the strange vulnerable community of the Pacific. [Since Hiroshima] ... remoteness has become exposure.[46]

Sensitive to the issue of form, this statement none the less remains an outsider's view of what constitutes strangeness and vulnerability; fundamentally an adaptation of Frank O'Connor's notion of the short story being the 'lonely voice' of a peripheral people, it identifies one kind of isolation (distance from metropolitan Europe) with another (human loneliness) which is only one of several constituent elements in the social patterns for which art finds words. Admittedly this sense of being distant from England ('Home') is a pervasive attitude among some New Zealanders, and is not to be held a European perspective alone: but it is also an attitude in flux, as the notion 'periphery' itself continues to change.

Given the other face of the Fragmentation Theory — that different kinds of self-containment and self-awareness will emerge in the new societies that derive from any initial (or cumulative set of) migrant movements — it is inevitable that there will emerge in different societies apparently different representations of the human condition. Perhaps what is more surprising is how commonly held certain values are and how recurrent from place to place the themes and the imagery prove to be.[47] Yet with the variations in cultural experience from place to place, the themes and imagery vary in the cultural resonances they carry: 'freedom' within America's black community or among Australia's 'Sydney-side Saxons' occupies a different position in the people's social preoccupation, for example, than it does in New Zealand, where 'fairness' is a social watchword of greater magnitude; imagery involving the luminous yellow desert light is more locally grounded in Australia and South Africa than in, say, eastern Canada; and in the north and West of Canada, the image of desert (Arctic barrens, prairie droughtland) acquires quite other associations, involves cold rather than heat and (as far as the prairies are concerned) historical circumstance rather than geographic barrier. But literary form, as surely as theme and image, is a means of voicing these differences in cultural attitude and cultural priority. To inquire into the history and practice of the short story in Canada and New Zealand is, then, to explore in part the separate shifting tensions between individual artistic commitment and an unfolding social context, tensions which the internal fragments of New Zealand fiction and the serial fragments that have come to be so characteristic of prose in Canada help to articulate.

PART TWO
STORY AND HISTORY

2 **Canada:** Story and History

It is possible to claim that a chain of connections links Thomas Chandler Haliburton's sketches in the 1820s to English-Canadian stories of the present day. The links involve Susanna Moodie's 1850s sketches of the backwoods, the Quebec stories of D.C. Scott, animal tales, satiric squibs, urban documentaries, and personal meditations. But while this chain of names roughly describes an outline of an argument to follow, it contains too many assumptions and sweeping connections to be satisfactory as an argument in itself. All it declares, in fact, is a simple historical sequence. That one group of writers should succeed another in time demonstrates nothing about continuity of form – or of indebtedness, reaction, rejection, progress, or simple differences in mode and skill. Yet there are continuities. They are plural rather than singular (the notion of a single-link chain imposing a faulty metaphor on the society's literary history). And there has developed a cumulative literary tradition through the shifting strategies of English-Canadian short story form. I propose to discuss these developments by means of three central topics – D.C. Scott's Revolution, Country, War, and City, and The Tension between Story and Word.

D.C. Scott's Revolution, 1820–1920

To speak in the same breath of Revolution and Duncan Campbell Scott (1862–1947) is, of course, a deliberate paradox. Scott was a conservative man, a civil servant, a man committed to the connections between literature in Canada and literature in Britain, a man consequently committed to the aesthetic force of tradition. In his presidential address to the Royal Society of Canada in 1922 he could declare that 'the poetry of our generation is wayward and discomforting, full of experiment that seems to lead nowhither, bitter with the turbulence of an uncertain and ominous time,' and that from it 'we may turn ... for refreshment to those earlier days when society appears to us to have been simpler, when there were seers who made clear the paths of life and adorned them with beauty.' But of equal importance to his quest for beauty here is his concurrent recognition of the turbulence in contemporary art and life; poetry of an earlier age may provide refreshment, but he recognizes that it does so by providing a kind of escape from the present, and he acknowledges that 'modernity is not a fad, it is the feeling for actuality.' Further, this actuality may be discomforting precisely because it does not allow relaxation, for either the reader or the writer, because

The desire of creative minds everywhere is to express the age in terms of the age, and by intuition to flash light into the future. Revolt is essential to progress, not necessarily the revolt of violence, but always the revolt that questions the established past and puts it to the proof, that finds the old forms outworn and invents new forms for new matters.[1]

Scott's own poetry demonstrates this theory only sporadically, as when he effectively breaks out of standard rhythmic patterns in 'At the Cedars' or challenges the conventions of historical psychology in 'At Gull Lake: August, 1810.' In some respects the nature of his formal revolution is clearest in his prose, though it was not immediately recognized as the innovation it was. As S.L. Dragland has observed,[2] anthologists from Knister in 1928 to Pacey in 1947 and Rimanelli and Ruberto in 1966 have acknowledged that Scott stands out technically from his contemporaries and forerunners; but as late as the second edition of the *Literary History of Canada* (1976), critics would also classify Scott's *In the Village of Viger* (1896) simply as one of a number of late nineteenth-century collections of 'bucolic' local colour sketches. To understand why this contradiction has persisted one has to delve briefly back into the narratives, tales, and sketches that preceded Scott, and to weigh the impact that writers like Moodie and Haliburton had on Canadian prose style. To do so is to begin to understand the simultaneous impact of conventions of critical expectation.

I use these three words — *narratives*, *sketches*, and *tales* — in order to indicate not so much a wide range in the art of the nineteenth-century Canadian story-telling as a fluidity in the kind of prose people wrote and in the terms they used to name it. And I use the term *prose*, rather than *fiction*, because narrative, sketch, and tale characterized descriptions of documentary record as well as of imaginative invention. And it was the documentary element that underpinned Canadian colonial writing. Repeatedly, story and history, fictional narrative and documentary narrative, tale and sketch overlap. Writers wrote a story (and readers read it) — even in its sentimental and sensational forms, those staples of the time — with an eye for its

Truth-with-a-capital-T. Since Truth took both moral and empirical forms, it was possible to read documentary as moral adventure, and adventure as moral documentary. Out of the consequent blurring of generic demarcations emerges some of the most arresting writing of the age.

The work that Susanna Moodie published from the 1820s to mid-century is a case in point. In *Roughing It in the Bush* (1852), Mrs Moodie assembled, in revised form, a number of sketches that she (and in a minor way, her husband, J.W. Dunbar Moodie) had earlier written about their life as settlers in the 1830s near Cobourg. She wrote them clearly for didactic reasons, of two sorts: in part to warn English gentlemen not to try to settle in Canada, because of the incompatibility between the trials of the country and their station and education, and in part (only inferentially acknowledging the contradiction) to document the moral uplift that Nature allows a person under stressful circumstances. Even more clearly, she wrote for economic reasons: the *Literary Garland*, newly established in Montreal, had promised her payment, and she contributed sketches and tales regularly to this journal from 1839 until it folded in 1851. Contributions she had earlier sent to the Philadelphia journal *North American Review* failed to bring recompense, and for want of funds to pay for her manuscripts to reach the frontier with the United States, she did not manage to reach other American journals which had expressed interest in her contributing.[3] If by expressing such an interest in selling to the Americans she appears to countermand her various sharp critiques of Americans in *Roughing It in the Bush*, it is important to recognize another more fundamental point: that economic and ethical motives were not in conflict. Want of a moral education, not money, Mrs Moodie was to assert in 1847 in her own periodical, *The Victoria Magazine*,[4] was the only real barrier between classes; but this is an argument she proffers while still acknowledging that Canada is fortunate to be a land of plenty. A moral education in Canada thus allowed its possessor to use with discretion the natural 'plenty' he or she enjoyed.

Pointedly, to suffer deprivation with moral insight was an experience she personally learned from but did not choose to continue to bear, hence she put the education to use by marketing her moral compositions as she could. Given this perspective, it is not surprising that a work like *Roughing It in the Bush* should be a mixed assemblage of anecdotes, pious reflections, conventional descriptions, and exemplary scenes ('It is not my intention to give a regular history of our residence in the bush,' she wrote, 'but merely to present to my readers such events as may serve to illustrate a life in the woods').[5] The difficulties arise when we attempt to assess the mix – either to locate an order in it (and a purpose for the 'illustrations') or to acknowledge its disorder and fragmentariness.

For the *book* of sketches is not of a piece, whether of form, quality, or even authorship, and while the central topic remains Mrs Moodie herself, even then a shift in mode ('to diversify my subject and make it as amusing as possible,' she writes in her introduction to the third edition in 1854)[6] interrupts the unity of narrative in order better to achieve the character of the miscellany. Language, too, is uneven. While her linguistic and attitudinal conventions – a stereotypical, class-biased dialect humour and a descriptive (and by this time out-of-fashion) vocabulary that overly relies on the words 'melancholy,' 'picturesque,' and 'sublime' – frequently get in the way of an exact visual evocation of place, she none the less manages to portray character and event, as she had intended, with some liveliness.

This distinction is important. Paradoxically, it was the language of stereotypical *fiction* which led her into her problems with the language of scene, and the language of the *sketch* which took her towards the vitality of portraiture. This holds true primarily while she deals with experience – when she moved into romantic fiction, as she did in her serialized tales and later novels, she employed a stilted style which derived from historical romance and the Protestant tracts of her youth, which she aimed at an English market she had long since left behind, and which English critics were in time to castigate and dismiss. She recognized the problem she had with specificity; in an 1853 letter to Richard Bentley she observes: 'There is a want of Individuality in my writings, which I feel and lament, but cannot remedy' ... A scene or picture strikes me as a whole, but I can never enter into details.'[7] (One might contrast with this difficulty the extraordinarily exact sense of detail which one finds in her sister Catharine Parr Traill's accounts of similar backwoods experiences at this same time.)

Yet she also implicitly defended her literary practice when at the beginning of *Rachel Wilde*, the novel she published serially in *The Victoria Magazine* in 1848, she asserted, 'Fiction, however wild and fanciful, / Is but the copy memory draws from truth; / 'Tis not in human genius to create; / The mind is but a mirror, which reflects / Realities that are ... '[8] In turn, these 'realities' are the fragmentary embodiments of a larger truth which in her terms it is one goal of human life to comprehend. 'Ah, poverty!' she cries at one point in *Roughing It in the Bush*, 'thou art a hard taskmaster, but in thy soul-ennobling school I have received more god-like lessons, have learned more sublime truths, than ever I acquired in the smooth highways of the world!'[9] Such a passage demonstrates all the weakness of her didactic impulse to generalization; behind it, however, remain the realities she transposed into this attenuated register of speech, and which in the portraits of the people of her acquaintance in the backwoods – characters she called Betty Fye, Old Satan, and the Little Stumpy Man, among others – she realizes with greater precision, through the vigour of recorded speech and dramatized action. In other words, she makes narrative out of observed event but moral sentiment out of the imaginative fictions of her own meditation, however much a mirror to reality she might claim them to be. Indeed it is the functional moral sentiment, rather than the empirical observation, which in her romantic fiction comes to constitute reality. In part she even claims it to be so in her personal narrative as well, but we no longer accept these claims at face value, for in her attempts at documentary she takes on the techniques of story-telling and (in *Roughing It in the Bush*, at least, and to the eye of the contemporary critic) the role of narrator and the guise of a persona. As the shift occurs, character and the pressures of empirical reality take over as the dominant centre of interest in her work.

As Carl Ballstadt and Michael Peterman have separately observed, one reason for Mrs Moodie's success in animating the sketch form (and perhaps for animating it more than she did the conventional modes of tale-telling) lay in her admiration and imitation of the Berkshire sketches of Mary Russell Mitford, whom she read in the 1820s and who (by one of those intricate intercontinental gestures that have so affected the course of modern literary history) was in turn influenced by the 1818 *Sketch Book* of Washington Irving. Indeed, at one point (31 July 1829), Moodie (still Susanna Strickland) wrote to Mitford:

I had always ranked Miss Mitford as one of the first of our female writers, and though my knowledge of your writing was entirely confined to the sketches in the annuals, and to some extracts from the 'Foscari,' these were sufficient to make me feel the deepest interest in your name, and even to rejoice in the success that ever attended the publication of your works. But when you condescended to place me in the rank with yourself, all my ambitious feelings rose up in arms against me, till, ashamed of my vanity and presumption, I stood abashed in my own eyes, and felt truly ashamed of being so deeply enamoured with a title I did not deserve, and I felt that that insatiable thirst for fame was not only a weak but a criminal passion, which, if indulged, might waken in my breast those feelings of envy and emulation which I abhor, and which never fail to debase a generous mind; conscious, too, that I had employed those abilities with which heaven had endowed me, doubtless for a wise and useful purpose, entirely for my own amusement, without any wish to benefit or improve my fellow-creatures, I resolved to give up my pursuit of fame, withdraw entirely from the scene of action, and, under another name, devote my talents to the service of my God.[11]

In a subsequent letter responding directly to a sketch in Mitford's *Our Village*, Moodie provides the beginnings of a sketch herself, noting that her brother Samuel 'gives me such superb descriptions of Canadian scenery that I often long to accept his invitation to join him, and to traverse the country with him ... ' The implication is, 'pen in hand.' But when life gave her the opportunity to travel, the literary results would be less fanciful and more earnest than she had anticipated.

There are several threads of English-Canadian literary history thus made clear by Mrs Moodie's day: (1) the importance of the documentary sketch; (2) the prevalence of a Protestant moral ethic (which in its strictest forms itself confirmed the precedence of 'history' over 'story,' ostensible 'truth' over ostensible 'lie'); (3) a concurrent political conservatism and desire to take cultural advantage of the near American market; (4) the appeal of the miscellany as a literary entertainment; (5) the increasing rootedness of literature in regional experience (despite various writers' aspirations to the English sentimental conventions of the recent past); and (6) the widespread availability of local journals and newspapers which themselves served as monthly miscellanies of literature and politics, and as outlets for stories and poems by local authors. But what sorts of stories and poems? Some were society romances; some, following on the explorers' journals, were the tales and observations of travellers through other parts of the continent or other parts of the world, often sketches of Empire; some were legends; and some were adventures. Many, like the sketches William Kirby published in the 1860s, later grew into historical fictions, as did *The Golden Dog* (1877). The Moodies themselves, editing *The Victoria Magazine*, deliberately devised an acceptance policy that would 'eschew all party feelings, banish from the pages of the Victoria, all subjects, however interesting, that might lead to angry discussion.' They contrived, instead, to encourage a taste for moral piety and romantic convention:

The hope of inducing a taste for polite literature among the working classes; for we are no respectors of persons, the mental improvement of the masses being the object nearest to our hearts, first stimulated us to accept the editorship of the Magazine. We joyfully hailed it as a medium through which the talent of the country could freely circulate to the community; and we have been a little disappointed that so few have offered the aid of their pens in carrying out the desired object.[13]

What they did include was their own work, and Agnes Strickland's, and 'the beautiful poems from the chaste and elegant pen of R.A.P. of Cobourg' which 'would not have disgraced the pages of any periodical.'

Yet as with those later benefactors who thought that the establishment of Workers' Institute libraries would produce a universal (ie, educated class) taste, they were mistaken in their audience. Writing in the preface to her novel *Mark Hurdlestone* in 1853, Mrs Moodie reflected that Canadians as a group were 'more practical than imaginative. Romantic tales and poetry would meet with less favour in their eyes than a good political article from their newspapers'[14] – the works that would appeal were exactly the sort of thing, in other words, that she chose to omit from *The Victoria Magazine*. We are dealing here not just with a political decision, but also with a question about literary form. Intellectually elevating the abstract convention over the particular detail, Mrs Moodie mistook the source that gave the documentary sketch (and the narrative that grew out of it) its power. Her audience in Canada was apparently more hungry for local detail, and found it in political argument. Indeed, over time, the (loosely defined) 'political' journals were to find less and less room for literature. That still left the *form* of literary communication in question: if received, romantic conventions were deemed inadequate, where were adequate words and literary structures to come from? For some people the answer to this question was social and geographic: the United States. For some it lay in an appreciation of indigenous cultures and in the retelling of legend and folk-tale, which had some play in James Le Moine's miscellany *Maple Leaves*, but was not to gather much momentum until the 1890s. For others it lay in aspirations to an urbane cosmopolitanism. For others still, an answer was to be found in control over voice and literary speech, and in a different kind of manipulation of the narrative sketch.

A different contribution to the growth of sketch forms in nineteenth-century Canada was provided by writers like Thomas McCulloch and Thomas Chandler Haliburton. For them, writing in the Maritimes between the 1820s and 1850s, there was nothing incompatible between the narrative sketch and political and moral comment. The sixteen 'letters' of the ironically and allegorically named Mephibosheth Stepsure, which the Scots-born Presbyterian minister McCulloch published serially in the *Acadian Recorder* in 1821 and 1822, take on a 'real-life' epistolary form in the context of a political journal, yet clearly they are fictions through and through, narrative structures which use an allseeing, apparently naïve observer-narrator to document the moral limitations and material excesses of Nova Scotia life.

The jurist and political historian Haliburton, the more innovative and influential stylist of the two, also used fiction for documentary purposes, though in his 'sayings and doings of Sam Slick' he relied more on anecdote than on descriptive sketch, a fact which ultimately curtailed their direct influence in Canada. Sam Slick stories ran for several years serially in Joseph Howe's paper *The Novascotian*, starting in 1835, and were later collected in eleven volumes (the three series of *The Clockmaker*, 1836, 1838, 1840; the two series of *The Attaché*, 1843, 1844; *Sam Slick's Wise Saws and Modern Instances*, 1853, which was cast as a set of anecdotal letters, though the other books are presented as recorded conversation; and *Nature and Human Nature*, 1855). They went through a hundred printings in the the nineteenth century alone, and circulated widely to France, Germany, England, and the United States. Indeed, as a figure of amusement (more, that is, than as a figure of social reform, which was Haliburton's local political intent) Sam probably had greater impact outside Nova Scotia than within.

As far as caricature is concerned, Haliburton's influence is also extra-national. Although one can draw connections between Haliburton's story-telling and that of Leacock in the early twentieth century, that is, most parallels between the two writers are spurious; Haliburton's main influence through the character of Sam Slick (the humour of regional dialect and hyperbolic anecdote) was on American writers, from Seba Smith in the 1830s through Artemus Ward to Mark Twain. It is his political conservatism and his determination to control voice that links Haliburton with Leacock – not method – but by Leacock's time the nature of the voice to be controlled was different, revealing the marked change in both Canadian society and Canadian literary mode that had occurred in the intervening decades.

Yet the Sam Slick stories remain relevant to a history of short fiction in Canada for several reasons. They tell of the force of particular observation of detail (made evident by the power of Sam-the-character's analysis of human behaviour as well as by the inventiveness of metaphor which characterizes his speech); they tell – though less directly – of Haliburton's increasing desire, as he continued to publish his Sam Slick stories, to alter his perspective towards his two chief characters. Sam, the crass, garrulous, jingoistic Yankee clock pedlar, loses neither his garrulity nor his ego as he variously leaves the peddling circuit, becomes an American attaché at the Court of St James, a fisheries commissioner, and a private citizen travelling, but he acquires (perhaps it indicates Haliburton's weariness with Slick as a device, rather than any progress in dimension of characterization) greater perspective towards himself and greater relaxation in his amusement at others. Sam's chief foil and subsequent friend, an anonymous English-born Squire, turns by later books (when Haliburton aims his satiric eye at England as directly as at Nova Scotia and the '*U*-nited States'), into a Nova Scotia native named Squire Thomas Poker, gentleman, a person less eager to challenge Sam than to be the passive vehicle that records Sam's presence and actions. At the end of the second series of *The Attaché*, Haliburton steps squarely in fact into the Squire's role; what separate voice the Squire had possessed disappears at this point into an authorial apologia:

It must not be supposed that I have recorded, like Boswell, all Mr Slick's conversations. I have selected only such parts as suited my object. Neither *The Clockmaker* nor *The*

Attaché were ever designed as books of travels, but to portray character; to give practical lessons in morals and politics; to expose hypocrisy; to uphold the connection between the parent country and the colonies; to develop the resources of the province; to enforce just claims of my countrymen; to discountenance agitation; to strengthen the union between Church and State; and to foster and excite a love for our own form of government and a preference of it over all others.[15]

The point is clear. But what interests us about the Sam Slick stories is not the typing of character which tells us of Haliburton's political purpose (Haliburton's indicative names – Slick, Flint, Snob, Dummkopf – are not far removed from McCulloch's Drab, Drone, Tipple, M'Cackle, and Trotabout) but the manner of story-*telling*. For Haliburton the sketch comes alive not as memoir or scene-painting but as a process of witty narration: of descriptive analysis through told event, of monologue spiked with analogy and metaphor.

Any number of anecdotes (particularly those in the first *Clockmaker* series) demonstrate Sam's (hence Haliburton's) skill as a raconteur; as he rides alongside the Squire and demonstrates his sales pitch, his biases, his patriotic enthusiasm, his guileful estimate of women, and his low opinions of British class and Bluenose lethargy in matters economic and political, Sam can, as a passage in *Nature and Human Nature* puts it, exchange brag for brag.[16] When the Squire seems to better him by dismissing the clawed eagle as an estimable national symbol, Sam turns the argument around to better the Squire at his own game, offering the owl as an appropriate emblem for Nova Scotia, 'and the motto, "he sleeps all the days of his life".'[17] And Sam captivates by turn of phrase in order to capture by turn of argument. Haliburton's control over the apparently garrulous 'literary dialect' (Walter Avis's term)[18] that Sam speaks shows that while the author makes no attempt to reproduce accurately a particular regional speech pattern (and does not, like Moodie, use dialect pejoratively, to dismiss a character by the departure of his speech from 'educated standard'), he can turn the form of dialect into inventive aphorism.

As R.E. Watters notes,[19] Haliburton is now credited with an extraordinary number of phrases that, once (and perhaps still) vivid, are now so familiar as to lurk at the edges of cliché: *upper crust, stick-in-the-mud, as quick as a wink, conniption fit, six of one and half a dozen of the other, as large as life and twice as natural, the early bird gets the worm, a nod is as good as a wink to a blind horse*, and many more. Such phrases then had a powerful individualizing force. '"I knew you",' says the Squire to Sam when the two meet up again in *Nature and Human Nature*, '"the moment I heard your voice, and if I had not recognized that, I should have known your talk".' To which Sam replies: '"That's because I'm a Yankee, sir ... no two on us look alike or talk alike; but bein' free and enlightened citizens, we jist talk as we please".'[20]

The satire cuts in various ways: against American self-centredness, against the stratification implicit in *British* speech, perhaps even by this time against the now 'Canadian' (ie, Nova Scotian) Squire's infatuation with the Yankee. By 1855 as dissatisfied with the liberal reforms in Nova Scotia as in 1835 he had been dissatisfied with the then status quo, Haliburton can find a distinguishing voice for the Yankee all right, but can never quite evoke a satisfactory 'Canadian' one. For one thing, as another of his books, *The Old Judge* (1849; the early chapters were published in *Fraser's Magazine* in 1846–7) was to stress, the British North American provinces were disparate and dissimilar. For another, as the preface to *The Old Judge* goes on, the typical Bluenoser was recognizable (though the term applied initially to the Loyalist émigré it gradually encompassed all Nova Scotians), but he shared his speech with others:

The accent of the Blue Nose is provincial, inclining more to Yankee than to English, his utterance rapid, and his conversation liberally garnished with American phraseology, and much enlivened with dry humour. From the diversity of trades of which he knows something, and the variety of occupations in which he has been at one time or another engaged, he uses indiscriminately the technical terms of all, in a manner that would often puzzle a stranger to pronounce whether he was a landsman or sailor, a farmer, mechanic, lumberer, or fisherman. These characteristics are more or less common to the people of New Brunswick, Prince Edward Island, and Cape Breton, and the scene of these sketches might perhaps to a very great extent be laid, with equal propriety, in those places [as] in Nova Scotia. But to Upper and Lower they are not applicable.[21]

It was a voice which the Tory Haliburton could never wholly identify. The authorial character, moreover, Sam Slick's Squire Poker, is neutrally formal; he is fascinated by the vernacular he does not possess, yet not particularly granted power or individuality by the formality, the inherited standards, which he does.

For Haliburton, as for Sam, there is something strikingly important about such individuality; it comes up again and again in these works as a political motif and as a literary one as well, reminding us once more that the literary mode served a social function. Most striking of all in some ways are the occasions in *The Attaché* (reiterated in *Nature and Human Nature*) when Sam comes close to a literary critique, for there we have an ironically told but not intrinsically ironic internal commentary on Haliburton's own method. In the later book Sam chastises Poker – using speech as a metaphor for political action – for not speaking out distinctively:

Now, if it was you who had done your country this sarvice, you'd 'a spoke as mealy-mouthed of it as if butter wouldn't melt in it. 'I flatter myself,' you'd 'a said, 'I had some leetle small share in it. I've lent my feeble aid: I've contributed my poor mite,' and so on, and looked as meek and felt as proud as a Pharisee. Now, that's not my way. I holds up the mirror whether, when folks see themselves in it, they see me there or not. The value of a glass is its truth. And where colonists have suffered is from false reports: ignorance and misrepresentation. There ain't a word said of 'em that can be depended on ... British travellers distort things ... They land at Halifax, where they see the fust contrast atween Europe and America, and that contrast ain't favourable, for the town is dingy-lookin' and wants paint, and the land round it is poor and stony. But that is enough; so they set down and abuse the whole country, stock and fluke, and write as wise about it as if they'd see'd it all instead of overlookin' one mile from the deck.[22]

In the earlier book, Sam puts a case that more closely concerns literary mode itself:

If you expect to paint them English, as you have Bluenoses and us, you'll pull your line up without a fish oftener than you are a-thinkin' on; that's the reason all our folks has failed. Rush's book is jist molasses and water – not quite so sweet as 'lasses and not quite so good as water, but a spilin' o' both. And why? His pictur' was of polished life, where there is no natur'. Washin'ton Irvin's book is like a Dutch paintin': it's good because it's faithful; the mop has the right number of yarns, and each yarn has the right number of twists (although he mistook the mop of the grandfather for the mop of the man of the present day) and the pewter plates are on the kitchen dresser, and the other leetle notions are all there. He's done the most that could be done for 'em; but the painter desarves more praise than the subject.

'Why is it every man's sketches of America takes? Do you s'pose it's the sketches? No. Do you reckon it's the interest we create? No. Is it our grand experiments? No. They don't care a brass button for us, or our country or experiments neither. What is it then? It's because they are sketches of natur'. Natur' in every grade and every variety of form; from the silver plate and silver fork, to the finger and huntin's knife. Our artificials, Britishers laugh at: they are bad copies, that's a fact; I give them up. Let 'em laugh and be darned; but I stick to my natur', and I stump 'em to produce the like.

'Oh, Squire, if you ever sketch me, for goodness gracious sake, don't sketch me as an Attaché to our embassy, with the legation button on the coat ... Don't do that; but paint me in my old wagon to Nova Scotia, with Old Clay afore me, you by my side, a seegar in my mouth, and natur' all round me.'[23]

Clearly it is advice Haliburton implicitly gave himself, then followed; much of Haliburton's vitality derives from his sensory clarity.

But as *The Old Judge* makes clear (it is a book in which Sam Slick is mentioned only parenthetically), story-telling involves pacing as well as a matter of particulars. We receive further literary advice from a Slick-like character, a fit, able farm manager named Stephen Richardson, who is cast at once as a droll clown and a sharply worded, story-telling, insightful judge of society's manners and values. After listening through one singularly drifting anecdote at one point, Stephen bursts forth:

'Why, man alive, it's no story at all, or else you don't know how to tell it. You might as well call half an apple a whole apple. If you cut off a dog's tail, it's a dog still, do you see? or dock a horse, there is the horse left to the fore, and, perhaps, looking all the better of it. But a story is like a snake, all tail from the head; and if you cut there, you don't strike the tail off, but cut the head off. You knock the life out of it at oncest – kill it as dead as a herring. Your story is like a broken needle, it has got no point; or like an axe without an edge, as dull as a hoe. Take my advice, my old moose-misser, and the very next time you are axed to sing a song, or spin a yarn, choose the first. It's better to sing a ditty that has no tune, than to tell a story that has no fun.'

'Why how would you have me tell it?' said the discomfited stranger.

'You might as well,' rejoined Stephen, 'ask me what I say when I say nothing, as to ask me how to tell a story that is no story. If I was to be so bold as to offer my advice, I should say tell it short, this way –

'"Once upon a time, when pigs were swine, and turkeys chewed tobacco, and little birds built their nests in old men's beards, a youngster that had no beard went out a hunting. He thought he could shoot, but couldn't, for he fired at a cariboo and missed it; was frightened to see the tracks of wild beasts instead of tame ones in the woods; ate for his supper what he neither killed nor cooked; got the nightmare; fancied he saw three hungry wolves, woke up and found but one, and that was himself." Now, there is the hair and head, body and bones, and sum and substance of your everlasting "long story".'[24]

Coming to a close this way, this particular story in the collection works more as metafiction than as fiction – reminding us that Haliburton was as concerned with the shape of his writing as with the shape of his society *because he wanted both to come to a point*. Whether he established his point by homily, analogy, anecdote, or tale, he persistently drew a social message out of recorded fact and observed behaviour, making his narrative scenes resonate with comment on colonial policy, educational practice, agricultural economy, trade, religion, law, the military, superstition, prejudice, manners, and other features of the society around him. At his least *fictionally* successful, as in 'Colonial Government' or 'The First Settlers,' he most abandons narrative form and formulates his message as bald historical statement. But what *The Old Judge* does as a whole is establish Haliburton's literary interest in formal variety and demonstrate, as the Sam Slick stories do not, his organization of a group of story forms to a unified, coherent end: that of analysing the impact of Lord Durham's notion of 'responsible government' on the traditional patterns of life, both constitutional and moral, in Nova Scotia – a fact which makes 'Colonial Government' (the final so-called story in the book) in some respects not an aberrant form but simply a closing homily writ large.

Subtitled 'Life in a Colony,' *The Old Judge* takes the form of a series of stories told over many weeks, stories told by and to an Englishman who comes to North America to travel and so to learn about the character and quality of colonial living conditions. The main narrators besides the traveller are a retired judge named Sandford and his nephew Barclay, Tory in their attitudes and essentially indistinguishable from the Englishman in the way they tell stories; Stephen Richardson, whose five related stories, told over several days at an inn during a storm, are positioned at the heart of the total twenty; and occasional figures (Zeb Hunt, John Thompson, Captain Smith), whose tales are retold within the context of the other narrator's performances. In all, the stories – to the contemporary reader, uneven in pacing and interest – tell of such subjects as the social aspirations of the rustic, the gulling of the greedy, the limitations of 'professional' people, and the superstitions of village-dwellers. But the main interest of the work is the way it exemplifies mid-nineteenth-century experimentation with the short story form.

The Old Judge is a *Rahmenerzählung*, a unified miscellany made up of the variety of forms that was then coming into fashion. There is, for example, a comic anecdote ('How Many Fins Has a Cod?'), a satiric comedy of manners ('Asking a Governor to Dine'), a meditative essay on mutability, with illustrative anecdote ('The Tombstones'), a character ('The Old Admiral and the Old General'), extracts from an historic journal ('The First Settlers'), a vernacular sketch ('Merrimakings'), a mystery ('The Schoolmaster'), a sentimental tale ('The Lone House'), a ghost story ('Judge Beler's Ghost'), a legend ('Seeing the Devil'), an animal tale about tale-telling ('A Long Night and a Long Story'), a tall tale ('A Pippin'), a melodramatic romance-adventure ('Horse-shoe Cove'), a descriptive sketch ('The Seasons'), a transformation tale ('The Witch of Inky Dell'), and a history ('Colonial Government'). The pervasive humour of the book derives from conventional rhetorical techniques – pun, hyperbole, meiosis, zeugma (as when we are told the Governor is 'all things to all men – a hand for all, a word for all, and a fig for all')[25] – and from dialect and situation (the misunderstandings of the deaf treated recurrently as a source of comedy). But neither the substantial unity of tone nor the political argument common to all the stories translates into a wholly fluid narrative. The motivations that lead into various stories are frequently arbitrary ('While discoursing on this subject with the Judge, he told me the following interesting story, illustrative of this sort of isolated life and of the habits of lone settlers in the wilderness',[26] and the failure to differentiate lexically among narrators (Stephen excepted) means that the narrator's point of view is of little consequence as a measure of each narrative itself: Sandford and Barclay are simply bodiless devices to suggest the occasion for speech. But the very fact of linking the stories suggests the literary possibility of constructing a unified work out of a shaped miscellany of fragments. It was D.C. Scott's revolutionary' accomplishment, later in the century, to take the sketch and conventions of tale and do precisely that.

The work in question was *In the Village of Viger* (1896), but it was neither the first work of prose Scott published nor an easy or direct step from *The Old Judge*. Indeed, society verse, religious tract, political treatise, racist joke, melodrama of love, and Indian romance (making ample use of the stereotypes of noble and warrior savage, and mixing them up with gothic exaggerations of the horrors of French Catholicism) were the stuff of magazine contributions for the greater part of the last half of the nineteenth century. The new French 'realism' was critically (or more exactly, morally) anathema, to the point that fiction itself was deemed an unworthy enterprise. In 1893, J.G. Bourinot fulminated:

I do not for one depreciate the influence of good fiction on the minds of a reading community like ours; it is inevitable that a busy people, and especially women distracted with household cares, should always find that relief in this branch of literature which no other reading can give them; and if the novel has then become a necessity of the times in which we live, at all events I hope Canadians, who may soon venture into the field, will study the better models, endeavour to infuse some originality into their creations and plots, and not bring the Canadian fiction of the future to that low level to which the school of realism in France, and in a minor degree in England and the United States, would degrade the novel and story of every-day life. To my mind it goes without saying that a history written with that fidelity to original authorities, that picturesqueness of narration, that philosophic insight into the motives and plans of statesmen, that study and comprehension of the character and life of a people, which should constitute the features of a great work of this class, – that such a history has assuredly a much deeper and more useful purpose in the culture and education of the world than any work of fiction can possibly have even when animated by a lofty genius.[27]

In practice, Sabine Baring-Gould was more the current model for writers of short fiction than was Zola, but change was coming, and coming from the United States rather than from Europe.

As the 'Confederation Group' began to publish in the 1880s – those writers with a fresh eye for the realities of the new Dominion – they took advantage, as Mrs Moodie had been unable to do, of the burgeoning American magazine market. Canadian writers appeared in the *Atlantic, Century Magazine*, the *North American Review, Scribner's Monthly* – as well as in Toronto periodicals like *The Week*, which briefly under Roberts' editorship flourished from 1883 to 1896, and *The Canadian Magazine* (1893-1939), which editorially fostered patriotism and mutual understanding. Canadian writers became journalists abroad and editors at home: Edward Thomson with the Toronto *Globe* and the Boston *Youths' Companion*, Norman Duncan with the New York *Evening Post*, Marjory MacMurchy with the *Canada Educational Monthly*, C.A. Fraser with the *Montreal Star*, Robert Barr (who published as 'Luke Sharp') with the *Globe*, the *Detroit Free Press*, and then with Jerome K. Jerome on the *Idler*. Canadian names like Roberts, Bliss Carman, Gilbert Parker, and later Ernest Thompson Seton became familiar in the United States just as American names like Harriet Beecher Stowe, Bret Harte, and William Dean Howells became familiar in Canada. But it seems fair to say that literary *influence* went all one way – North. Canadian writing in the United States was essentially an appeal to American taste for romantic tale and provincial stereotype. And Canadian writing in England remained a curiosity. An able writer like Susie Frances Harrison wrote with ironic humour of life in New York, but argued – in the title sketch of *Crowded Out & Other Sketches* (1886), notably – that the colonial writer was never truly recognized abroad, and would not be acknowledged in England until the English establishment accepted Canada's independent history as a viable cultural alternative. Such a conclusion, however, remained an aspiration rather than a reality, for politics and literature alike.

Whatever the temperature of Canadian nationalist sentiment – and writers like Graeme Mercer Adam were pleading in *The Week* that attention be paid to Canadian writers for patriotic reasons, arguing that aesthetic standards would follow native interest – the border to the United States was open. Sara Jeannette Duncan worked in the mid-1880s as an editorial writer for the *Washington Post*, for example, and distinguished herself as a critic by early recognizing the literary virtues of Henry James (and a decade later Joseph Conrad); but she also recognized about Canada the parochial twin dangers of self-deprecation and self-magnification and the consequent vulnerability of Canadians to American attitudes. 'Once Canadian minds are thoroughly impregnated with American matter,' she wrote in 1887, of the prominence of American books and magazines in the mass of Canadian homes, 'American methods, in their own work, will not be hard to trace.'[28] Yet she is somewhat ambivalent about what this means, wanting political distinctiveness but literary reform. In an essay in *The Week* in 1886, she satirizes the romantic indulgence that inhibits Canadian literary expectation and practice:

We are still an eminently unliterary people.
   Another Canadian summer has waxed and waned; mysterious in our forests, idyllic in our gardens, ineffably gracious upon our mountains. Another year of our national existence has rounded into the golden fulness of its harvest time. The yellow leaves of another September are blowing about our streets; since last we watched their harlequin dance to dusty death a cycle has come and gone. And still the exercise of hope and faith – charity we never had – continue to constitute the sum of our literary endeavour. We are conscious of not having been born in time to produce an epic poet or a dramatist; but still in vain do we scan the west for the lyrist, the east for the novelist whose appearing we may not unreasonably expect. Our bard is still loath to leave his Olympian pleasures; our artisan in fiction is busy with the human product of some other sphere.
   And we look blankly at each other at every new and vain adjustment of the telescope to the barren literary horizon, and question 'Why?' And our American cousins with an indifferent wonder, and a curious glance at our census returns, make the same interrogatory; whereupon one of them tarries in Montreal for three days, ascertains, and prints in *Harper's Magazine* that it is our arctic temperature! And in England, if our sterile national library excites any comment at all, it is only a semi-contemptuous opinion that it is all that might be expected of 'colonials.'[29]

At the same time she disputes American and English deterministic explanations of such literary torpor ('climate' and 'colonialism'). The problem, she makes clear, is a failure of aesthetic taste and imaginative talent, not of weather; and in another essay she goes on about the need to reform literary method, a statement that was as applicable to short fiction in 1887 as it was to the novel:

In fiction, that literary department that knows only the limits of human nature, there is the greatest change. All orthodoxy is gone out of it. It does not matter in the least whether there is a heroine or not, and if there is her ultimate fate is of no consequence whatever ... The novel of to-day may be written to show the culminative action of a passion, to work out an ethical problem of every-day occurrence, to give body and form to a sensation of the finest or of the coarsest kind, for almost any reason which can be shown to have a connection with the course of human life, and the development of human character ... The old rules by which any habitual novel reader could prophesy truly at the third chapter how the story would 'come out' are disregarded, the well-worn incidents discarded, the *sine qua nons* audaciously done without. Fiction has become a law unto itself, and its field has broadened with the assumption.

The practical spirit of the age has subtler, farther-reaching influences than we dream of. It requires simplicity in the art of the pen for readier apprehension in a busy time. Even the sciences appear divested of their old formalism and swagger. It demands sensation by the shortest nerve route. It has decided for light upon some practical subjects through plain window panes to the partial exclusion of stained glass embellished with saints and symbols. It asks, in short, that adaptation of method to matter which is so obscure yet so important a factor in all literary work.[30]

Meanwhile, in the United States, Sarah Orne Jewett was publishing serially in the 1880s, and Hamlin Garland's *Main-Travelled Roads* appeared in 1891. Such was the groundwork for D.C. Scott.

Yet Scott's first publications – stories in *Scribner's*, *Massey's Magazine*, and the *Dominion Illustrated Monthly* in the 1880s and 1890s – varied between somewhat overwritten formula tales (which Scott never subsequently collected) and several of the carefully pruned Viger stories which by about 1893 he had shaped into book form. Indeed, the stylistic contrast between the two groups of stories is perhaps the most striking of the surface distinctions. The Viger stories are restrained almost to the point of neutrality, and open tersely:

It was too true that that the city was growing rapidly. ('The Little Milliner')
It was an evening early in May. ('No. 68 Rue Alfred de Musset')
There was a house on the outskirts of Viger called, by courtesy, the Seigniory. ('The Tragedy of the Seigniory')[31]

But the other stories, like 'The Ducharmes of the Baskatonge' and 'The Triumph of Marie Laviolette,' open in adjectival profusion:

In the heart of a northern wilderness, on the shore of an unnamed lake, stands the ruin of a small hut ... In the dark corners spectral weeds and ferns die longing for the sun. The winter wind, untamed out of the north, charges against its crumbling walls and drives the sifted snow, hissing like steam, across the surface of the lake. The haunts of man seem as far away as the stars that throb faintly in the lonely vastness of the summer sky. The silence that dwells forever in the waste places of the world is shaken by unheeded storms and the muffled cries of life in the gloom of the immense forests that darken beneath her brooding wings. ('The Ducharmes of the Baskatonge')[32]

We cannot justifiably claim a geodeterministic distinction operating on the style here (ie, claim that the style shows how Viger, the town, is 'simple' and 'ordered,' and the wilderness 'dense' with its own profusion); nor does the animate world of Nature in the early stories ever adequately cross the corridor between pathetic fallacy and symbolism. This is not a symbolic landscape Scott has created for the Ducharmes, but a romantic precursor of one, a landscape in which nature mirrors human action – corresponds to it – but does not represent it.

The action that the landscape mirrors, moreover, while occasionally punctuated by an ironic aside or a sharp detail of observation or conversation, is predominantly melodramatic. 'The Ducharmes of the Baskatonge,' indirectly and inversely anticipating Scott's later and much stronger poem 'At the Cedars,' concerns a man who saves his brother from danger on the rapids and in the woods, then courts the woman his brother loves, then lives happily ever after when his brother sacrifices himself for the sake of the fraternal bond. Cast into the past, the story takes on the guise of a legend of heroic action; all is written more to satisfy a taste for grand gestures than out of any commitment to their credibility. The most dynamic part of the story occurs not in the Ducharmes' pledges of brotherhood but in the riverside drama of collective speech, when 'The crowd ran along the bank shouting wildly: "Get into the eddy!" – "Ducharme!" – "Ducharme!" – "Strike into the eddy, or you'll go over!" – "My God!" – "Catch the boom!" – "Strike in!" – "We'll pull you out!"'[33] Here the vocabulary and pacing are of a different order, emphasizing the passion of ordinary action rather than its theatre. What the passage also illustrates is Scott's greater skill with nuance than with plot; his dramas reside in narrative sketch rather than in narrative tale, and every time he moves towards plotted narrative he achieves melodramatic posture instead.

The beginning of the best of the uncollected stories – 'John Scantleberry,' a story about a tailor who almost commits murder to free himself from the clutches of a moneylender, but is saved from his own violence by the man's fateful heart attack – demonstrates a parallel ambivalence about the function of the story to follow. It reads:

There was something so peculiarly unprofessional about the painting and wording of John Scantleberry's sign that a passer-by would usually carry away some remembrance of it. It was so because John Scantleberry was a tailor, not a painter. He had elaborated the wording and arrangement of his sign with much thought, and when he produced his conception the result was unusual and quaint. Ignoring the existing literature of sign writers, the legend which he chose to describe his employment embodies in an obscure way the peculiar cast of his personality. This would not be evident until a close observation had been rewarded by some glimpse of his character, and therefore to the majority of persons this secret in the wording would remain forever hidden.[34]

The sign itself read '"John Scantleberry, working merchant tailor, a great speciality of pantaloons",' and showed an elf-sized pair of trousers. The paragraph asks us, on the surface, to respond either to straight information (the sign is 'unprofessional,' so we should expect unprofessional conduct: the dream of murder) or to something symbolic and semiotic in the sign itself; yet what 'secret' there is appears to lie in vocabulary more than in symbol: a 'scantle' or 'scantling' is a 'small portion,' 'tailor' suggests 'cutter,' 'pantaloons' derive from the Italian 'mask-wearer,' Pantaleone. More ominous, perhaps, 'to scantle' means 'to make scarce,' which is precisely what this mask-wearing cutter was going to do with the moneylender. In gentler form, it is also what (by retiring from his trade) he subsequently does to himself. But how functional is all this annotation? Clearly the mask Scantleberry wears is that of reclusiveness and passivity when in fact he harbours an extraordinary impulse to violence.

In an age of Wildean and Stevensonian stories, such dualities of personality were not uncommon subjects for fiction,[35] but once again the focus with Scott's story is on the mixed narrative impulse. What it appears the author is attempting is another tale: a plotted story of intrigue and mystery – yet we cannot accept it at this level: there is no suspense, no palpable action, no realized sense of evil in the villain of the piece. What Scott achieves, by contrast, is another modification of the sketch of character, this time making the drama internal, and requiring the form of language itself, more than the intricate twists of intrigue and adventure, to establish the tensions of narrative. It is as though, by experimenting with short story forms, Scott sought a language to deal with reality more than he sought a subject for fiction – subjects lay around him, and reality lay in the wilderness of documentable behaviour, which the techniques of romantic tale-telling could only make grandiloquent and so distort.

Scott spoke later of the 'wilderness of natural accent.'[36] By this he did not mean the comic vernacular of a Sam Slick, the sardonic vernacular of a Stephen Richardson, or the localizing dialect of Old Country settlers (which he himself handled so badly in 'The Stratagem of Terrance O'Halloran' in 1904); he meant the unmelodic line of ordinary speech, the directness of statement, which could none the less carry a multiplicity of perspectives, hint at dreams and aspirations that surface conditions might belie. He meant the speech that could hide from view, and yet express, such horrors that the heart might wish or flee from, the mind at once conceive and condemn. Bringing the conventions of mystery, sentimental tale, character, legend, and landscape sketch together he made *In the Village of Viger* (1896) into a linked series that would explore precisely these masks and multiplicities: such dimensions as made simplicity into an eloquent style also gave literary form to the social realities which experience taught to be true.

My concern here is to assert that Scott's experimentation with the effects of literary form meant that *In the Village of Viger* was functioning not simply as an evocation of 'local colour.' Its intent was not merely to describe a region's particularities for the education or amusement of a readership elsewhere; it was rather, through the cumulative medium of regional particulars, to dramatize the author's own perception of a society on the point of ethical change. The drama of such alteration required not falsification in romance but its own brand of natural speech wilderness. Hence in other people's hands the local colour story remained an ornamentation of reality; as the *Literary History of Canada* puts it, including Scott among a group of regionalists:

Most of these writers [on French Canada] were visitors to the *habitant* scenes they told about. Their tone is bucolic, as if they are remembering with some quiet pleasure the village scene and the people with whom they had spent some pleasant hours while on a vacation. The sentiment is marked, but not usually heavy; the humour and pathos equally light.[37]

But in Scott's hands the sketch came to *embody* story, to find irony in real life, and through it convey an implied narrative of attitudinal and social change which carried more than regional reverberations.

Country, War, and City, 1890–1940

It might have been anticipated that Scott would go on from his formal innovations with the Viger stories to greater and greater strengths. He had his critical enthusiasts — Bernard Muddiman, for instance, asserted in 1914 that there was 'no page in Canadian prose so perfect as the conclusion' to 'Sedan'[38] — and indeed, Scott's best individual story, 'Labrie's Wife,' along with several other strikingly shaped and anti-stereotypical stories of Indian and trader life in the 'North Woods' were to appear in journals and newspaper supplements like the Christmas *Globe* and *The Canadian Magazine* in the early years of the new century. 'Labrie's Wife' is an early triumph of indirect narrative, turning the fragmentary entries in the narrator's journal into an implicit and triangular story of frustrated passion that is most psychologically revealing about the unconsciously limited narrator himself. The use of the journal form reiterates that early impulse to adapt documentary form to fictional purposes, and there are hints (in the existence of another 'diary' story, 'The Vain Shadow') that Scott's imagination was working through this form towards another shaped and unified series of fragmented revelations. (Muddiman was looking forward to the presentation of these 'mordant little tragedies' in 'volume form,' noting about *In the Village of Viger* that the 'collected stories have a bewitching grace, that is ... deeper than mere prettiness').[39] But such was not to be.

When Scott's only two subsequent volumes of stories appeared, one (*The Witching of Elspie*, 1923) was a straightforward gathering of the two diary stories, the title legend, and nine other works, to no common purpose or effect; and the other (*The Circle of Affection*, 1947) was simply an anthology of several heretofore uncollected poems and essays, along with ten stories both early and late. Negatively asking why a different development did not take place is a barren critical inquiry, however tantalizing the question is. But we get some hint of why Scott's formal accomplishment was not immediately imitated, and why other forms for some years did become fashionable, by considering the Protestant mindset and the historical desires that underlay the critical language (even Muddiman's) of the first two decades of the twentieth century.

Essentially what Scott had done was to find a way of maintaining the separateness of the fragmentary units within the overall composite structure; but in the socially rooted criticism of the time, fragmentation was anathema, and a steadfast unity was all. That such 'unity' had its problems in reality does not need arguing here; the attitudinal godchild of the Anglo-Saxon Empire, it was an idea — as articles in *The Canadian Magazine* repeatedly and variously reveal — that had its basis in language, class, gender, and race.[40] By such arguments, the pre-eminent 'race' was 'English,' as the Empire's existence proved; 'Canadian literature' was and would be no more than a subset of literature in England, following tradition to find quality; and the educated classes would set the tone of political, social, aesthetic, and ethical decisions. All this was to change after World War I, when English models seemed no longer to be so attractive or so relevant to local conditions; then *The Canadian Magazine* began to publish articles on the social adaptation and material success of 'New Canadians.'[41]

But between 1895 and 1920, conventions ruled, and they ruled even in the face of empirical arguments against them. The growth and development of the Canadian Nation was a recurrent topic; the scenery and the literary contributions of the regions furnished repeated subjects for descriptive surveys and sketches; but on the whole such discoveries simply confirmed expectations: Canadian history was ransacked for distinguished accomplishments and heroes on English models, 'Canadian Girls' were complimented for their intelligence and beauty,[42] and Canadian nature was seen as the stuff that engendered literary pathos, masculine adventure, and Christian (meaning Protestant) probity. One should not discount casually the force of such values; but my concern here is with their literary ramifications, which encouraged moral message at the expense of verbal craft, and had the effect of educating a generation of readers to equate literary value with sentimental cliché. In effect people thereby learned to discount the relevance of literature to the changing political fabric of the times – or, put another way, to assert its relevance and quality only to the degree that it confirmed the political imagination's status quo.

Hence when an editorial on 'Diffuseness' appeared in *The Canadian Magazine* in 1897, its literary message developed out of a moral stance that reflected on society as a whole:

One lack among Canadian writers is the absence of a definite, steadily pursued aim. When they write they produce something, but it may be a poem, a novel, a short story, a history, or a political pamphlet ...

Charles G.D. Roberts ... has published two volumes of verse, a volume of tales for boys, a history of Canada, the first of a series of three novels, and a Canadian guide book. Then the question naturally arises, 'Is Roberts a poet, a historian, a novelist, or a literary hack?' ...

To ensure success a man should have but one vocation ... Young Canadians who desire to shine in literature would do well to take this matter into their serious consideration. Tenacity of purpose – which many Canadians lack – should be cultivated. A definite, single aim should be created, and pursued relentlessly, fiercely and untiringly.[43]

While the passivity with which purpose and aim were to be arrived at perhaps bears some scrutiny, the editorial writer's greater concern here is obvious: diversity is unacceptable, because it is not classifiable. Order mattered most of all, and literature that confirmed the presence of system and the existence of order, through the declaration of religion, or the assertion of society's endurance, or the discovery of natural law, was deemed intrinsically better than that which bruited change. Although Roberts, Scott, Grant Allen, and other writers continued to try their hand at various genres, such generic variation soon mattered little; Scott continued to hold aloof from stereotype, but Roberts, Ralph Connor, and the other more popular writers of these years were soon shaping tales to ends that confirmed the existence of a systematic universe – confirmed it, moreover, by their very celebration of nature, males, and Protestants. Against such a fashion, the suffragist stories of Nellie McClung were going to have a more immediate effect than were the psychological sketches of D.C. Scott.

Indeed, Scott's very independence from fashion constituted a critical problem, which Muddiman, for example, solved by using the language of fashion to reclaim him: to Muddiman, the Viger stories are French-Canadian 'vignettes' about the 'fall of some noble element in commonplace hearts.' And, 'like broken rose petals about a garden doorway,' they 'tell us of a world of perfect colour and perfume within.'[44] Scott thus became the best of the French Canada vignette writers rather than an innovator with form and attitude, and any potential threat to critical order was avoided. In the same way, an anonymous 1914 review of a work by the minor writer Hulbert Footner could begin by observing that 'His sense of the dramatic is not overrefined, because at timed his incidents become melodramatic,' but then go on to say that 'one should remember ... that he writes about a country and a class of people whose life and character is made up of melodrama.' In any event the melodrama is 'thrilling and picturesque.'[45] There appears almost a critical refusal to admit a departure from a received perspective; in such a climate, melodrama would persist and continue to be explained away, and Catholic French Canada would continue to be seen as a fit setting for sentimental primitivism but not for a new realism or a new genre.

In 1900, Errol Bouchette attacked this fallacy of Quebec, first of all by detailing literary practice:

It describes a quiet, law-abiding, but backward and even fossilized people, whose quaint manners and customs, for ages unchanged, are of special interest to the poet and writer of fiction, and whose dreamy existence reminds one of certain old towns of central Europe ... where it appears to the traveller that the world has stood still.[46]

But, he adds, however emotionally captivating such pastoral freshness might be, it is none the less ahistorical. Despite such assertions, the conventional stories created the more dominant image; even the stories which Louis Fréchette rendered into English (*Christmas in French Canada*, 1899, a collection of fourteen adventures and sentimental tales in which he consciously attempted 'to bring back to life some picturesque types of yore')[47] conveyed the impression of rural inoffensiveness, and were, one suspects, popular in English Canada at the time for much the same class-related reason that Pauline Johnson's Indian stories were popular a few years later: less because of any quality they possessed than because they showed that the authors could use English (indeed, it appears Johnson made quite calculated use of her Indian ancestry in order to win such public applause).[48] Simply put, their use of the form of the tale allowed the perpetuation of unrealistic assumptions about the social reality they portrayed. Like the dialect verse of William Henry Drummond which was so popular in English Canada for so many years, or the dialect stories of James Edward Le Rossignol, William McLennan, and Gilbert Parker, their effect was to focus attention on a people by making them look picturesque and quaint. 'Rural' became 'regional' became 'peripheral' became 'irrelevant' — a series of attitudinal changes which centralized and concentrated power over fashion. As Allan Douglas Brodie observed in 1895:

The English vernacular of our French-Canadian brothers has received a good deal of attention within the last few years, and, to use the words of Major J.P. Edwards, late editor of the now defunct *Dominion Illustrated Monthly*, 'Mr McLennan's setting has invested it with a pathos which is marvellously attractive.'[49]

The paradoxes here are clear: the assertion of brotherhood is immediately countered by the alienating effect of setting; the attractiveness of difference is governed by the author's implicit presumption that the difference underscores a 'natural' social order. That is, French-Canadian and Indian 'brothers' to the 'English'-Canadian were not attitudinally equals in this unified society, and the anglophone presumptions about a single Canadian nationhood depended on the identification of the minority peoples as habitant and noble *types*, belonging to a rural past and therefore literarily romantic, hence twice removed from the political future.

Critics praised such romances in terms that allowed them vast claims on history, civilization, imagination, and muscular experience all at once. E.J. Hathaway wrote in 1910 that

Canada seems now to be coming into her own as a field for the work of the romanticist. Her picturesque history of more than three hundred years, so successfully woven into literature by Parkman, and embroidered with all the wealth of his imagination, lies open to the world. The storied archives of old Acadia and New France are giving up their treasures of history, heroism, adventure, legend and tradition. Even the prairie districts of the West, and the mining camps of the mountains and the far North, are yielding a wealth of romance in tales of frontier life among the settlers, ranchers, miners and adventurers along the outer fringes of civilisation.[50]

It seemed that the tale, in practice, was a form for all reasons. In Fréchette's and Johnson's hands, for example, it took on the character of fable and legend. For Lucy Maud Montgomery, it was the didactic medium of stories for children.[51] For others, it was a form of incident or fantasy, as in the lively Labrador stories of Frederick William Wallace reprinted from *Adventure Magazine* in *The Shack Locker: Yarns of the Deep Sea Fishing Fleets*, 1916 (tales as varied, ostensibly, as the leftover food in the forecastle cupboard, but all designed to show bravery and fellowship), or Ernest S. Kirkpatrick's *Tales of the St John River and Other Stories*, 1904, which is full of ghosts, mad action, and sentimental memories of rural childhood. Most commonly of all, the tale at the turn of the century grew in length and experienced an extraordinary resurgence as a narrative religious tract.

An unsystematic search for examples yields titles such as these: *Neville Truman, the Pioneer Preacher: A Tale of the War of 1812* (W.H. Withrow, 1880), *Barbara Heck: A Tale of Early Methodism in America* (W.H. Withrow, 1895), *Black Rock: A Tale of the Selkirks* (Ralph Connor, 1898), *The Sky Pilot: A Tale of the Foothills* (Ralph Connor, 1899), *The Frontiersman: A Tale of the Yukon* (Hiram Cody, 1910), *The Measure of a Man: A Tale of the Big Woods* (Norman Duncan, 1911), *Tales of the Labrador* (Wilfred Grenfell, 1916), *The Preacher of Cedar Mountain: A Tale of the Open Country* (Ernest Thompson Seton, 1917). All of these were a far cry from the coquetry of A.S. Holmes's *Belinda; or, The Rivals: A Tale of Real Life*, which appeared in 1843. Yet both the social satire of mid-century and the proselytizing romances of fifty years later claimed to represent 'real life.' For Connor, Grenfell, and the others, real life consisted of the workings of the Christian spirit, and because the spirit endowed strength on the believer, what better setting than a wilderness frontier to demonstrate the masculine virtues of faith and work? Region thus became a spiritual metaphor, the setting for adventure, and the language of the tale was designed to elevate the enterprise of physical labour into the 'higher' endeavour of spiritual application.

But for other writers still, the tale was simply a way to embroider history. Madge MacBeth, for example, adapted stories of Thuggee from Meadows Taylor; M. Appleby, in *Told by the Innkeeper* (1927), sets an innkeeper down in rural B.C. and has him tell six connected stories, ostensibly taken from life, about the Boer War — and coincidentally about ghosts and a mad housekeeper; and Arthur H. Scaife, as 'Kim Bilir,' produced stories of the British military, Turks, and pashas, first for the Victoria *Province* (a weekly that Scaife edited) and then in book form as *Gemini and Lesser Lights* (1895). Gilbert Parker, in his 1900 volume *The Lane that Had No Turning and Other Associated Tales Concerning the People of Pontiac, Together with Certain 'parables of provinces,'* goes so far as to speak of his collection, in his prefatory letter to Laurier, as a '"bundle of life"'[52] — but the six parables, possibly Parker's best work, are conscious fantasies, not life recorded in any mimetically recognizable fashion, and the problem with the historical romances of Pontiac is that Parker's heightened language, instead of elevating the characters' responses as it was supposed to do, makes them sound maudlin and their emotions false. Unhappily, these stories of adventure and entanglement often led directly into emotional cliché at precisely the moments they were designed to stir and engage, as in Cecil Logsdail:

Under the spell of his seductive verse, Infelise forgot all her anger, and like one hypnotized, saw only the constant object of her day dreams in the dark-eyed Spaniard before her[53]

or in C.C. Farr:

Next morning they awoke refreshed, and, fortified by an excellent breakfast, they again donned their snowshoes, and turning their faces to the north, trudged bravely on.[54]

At such points language severs any effective connection it has with sensibility and reads like parody instead of drama. 'Real life' escapes its reach; so do history and regional accuracy; and in the religious tales even the moral commitment comes to seem suspect because the language and the narrative form serve the showmanship of theatre more readily than they do the expression of experience. The effort to elevate intrudes upon the moral intention, leaving the reader aloof and aside.

Yet the need to elevate language persisted in Canadian writing for some time, in part because Latinate generalizations and emotive diction were deemed fashionable, in part because they were deemed appropriate to spiritual aspiration. There appears to have been a socially related reason as well, one which stemmed from the wish to find a language commensurate with the size, space, and grandeur of the nation's physical territory. Yet this literary effort to contend with the natural wilderness — sketches of British Columbia, the North, and the new provinces of Alberta and Saskatchewan were a common feature in magazines during the early 1900s — was occurring at the same time as another literary movement was attempting to assert the sophistication of the cities; the one group was transforming the wilderness regions into imaginative territories of conflict and struggle, the other converting urban social behaviour into a region of repartee. And with the sentimental conventions of the romantic tale as a constant backdrop, it is scarcely an exaggeration to see Canadian literary history until World War II as a record of the interconnections between these two modes of perception; as a record, that is, of writers' cumulative search for a local and contemporary manner of expression, and of their abandonment of elevated vocabulary in favour of laconic idiom and the artifice of indirect form.

One can see something of this development by looking at it retrospectively, through the filter of the anthologies of the 1920s and 1930s, which provide something of a guide to shifts in style and expectation. They are of different kinds. J.L. Rutledge's 1937 edition of *Selected Short Stories*, for example, the third selection from *The Canadian Magazine*, merely indicated the degree to which the magazine had after 1925 altered its character and determined —

like the *Star Weekly* and *Maclean's* – to appeal to a domestic market more eager for escape than for artistry. (One 1932 story in *The Canadian Magazine* tells all by its title alone: 'She was a Cheap Little Thing and He a Handsome Lad in a Big, Fair, Surly Fashion and all He Wanted was Someone who Could Scrub and Cook so What Could you Expect From Such a Marriage.' The answer: love.)

Two other anthologies indicate the emergence of something that might be called a 'canon' of early Canadian short fiction. Raymond Knister's *Canadian Short Stories* (1928), dedicated to Duncan Campbell Scott and asserting that *In the Village of Viger*, despite its 'unobtrusive influence,' 'stands out ... as the most satisfyingly individual contribution to the Canadian short story'[55] – gathered Merrill Denison, Norman Duncan, Gilbert Parker, Marjorie Pickthall, E.W. Thomson, C.G.D. Roberts, Mazo de la Roche, D.C. Scott, Thomas Murtha, Leslie McFarlane (who went on to greater fame as the ghost writer of the Hardy Boys novels), Morley Callaghan, and others. Knister celebrates the 'realistic' as it was emerging from the imitative stage, a view of the growth of literature that has nudged its way into critical dogma. Looking at the stories, however, we have to hear this term 'real' in the context of all those romance writers who asserted their own claim to portraying 'real life.' May Lamberton Becker's American collection, *Golden Tales of Canada* (1938), more openly reveals the limitations of its bias and is therefore now easier to dismiss: 'The charm of Canadian literature,' the editor writes, ' ... wherever English is read, is largely due to its romantic reassurance that in an over-crowded world, wide and wonderful spaces yet remain.' Moreover, the 'stories in this collection, like those in the five regional anthologies that have preceded it, bring back an America that has ceased to be.'[56]

Desirous of their own independence, and firm in the belief in their own sophistication, Canadian writers and critics by 1940 were unlikely to bend easily to this identification of Canada as a charming backwater of the United States, but Becker's statement draws attention both to the persistence of rural romance in Canadian writing and to the force of national perspective as a gauge of significance and accuracy. What Becker says about Canada is, after all, just a more general version of what Canadian critics at the turn of the century were saying about habitants and Indians. And the attitude persisted in literary practice. When Harry James Smith's *Cape Breton Tales* appeared in 1920 it was marketed (in Boston) as a collection about 'simple pastoral people;'[57] and when Grace McLeod Rogers penned her *Stories of the Land of Evangeline* ('tales of Old Acadie') in 1923, they were full of caskets of gold, flashing eyes, brave spirits, and adjectivally overwhelmed sentences like these from 'The Hunchback of Port Royal': 'Mindful of the fresh vernal energy, and taking the wholesome salt breath of the flood in deep-drawn respirations, was a broad breasted, tall man, walking leisurely along the crooked path that led from the Settlement up Lequille River, to Port Royal. He was keen-eyed, firm-faced, and compact of build – a French Catholic priest ...'[58] Comparable sentimental romance continued in Paul Wallace's *The Twist* (1923), Martha Eugenie Perry's *The Girl in the Silk Dress* (1931), and Mazo de la Roche's *The Sacred Bullock* (1939). Small wonder that such a body of fiction should be found more charming – 'golden tales' – than realistic.

Yet the further point is still to be made: the writers collected in Becker's anthology were not Smith and Rogers but the familiar Denison, Duncan, Parker, Pickthall, Thomson, Grey Owl, Connor, and half a dozen others. The question is multifold: what were these writers doing that in Canada they should be considered signs of a new realism? why should such writers – like Carman, Pickthall, Drummond, and Robert Service in verse – continue to be thought of as 'characteristic' Canadian voices in school textbooks well into the 1950s? why did the counter-tradition of urban wit – as represented by Robert Barr, Grant Allen, and Albert Hickman – not survive? and what did Knister and Callaghan subsequently do that would reshape sketch and story form yet again? The answers involve an image of self and nation that was being consciously cultivated, and the kinds of transition that took place in that seminal period between the early 1890s and the end of World War I.

Barr's *In a Steamer Chair* (1892), Allen's *An African Millionaire* (1897), and Hickman's *Canadian Nights* (1914) form a trio of sorts, with Barr – the least successful of the three – still capable of Wildean conceits. '"I am glad to find that I am in the majority",' says one character, discussing Howells, James, and chutney, '"even in the matter of ignorance".'[59] But Barr's solemn comedies – of romances between the naïve and the articulate, gamesmanship among the low and the highborn – scarcely reach beyond anecdote and do not survive their time. Characters called Plodkins and Cupples are pre-Leacockian stereotypes, of the sort that Leacock himself satirized. And a story like 'The Man Who Was Not on the Passenger List' – a man killed on shipboard and buried at sea, whose ghost keeps returning and requiring reburying because he had paid the fare for a whole transatlantic trip – begins in suspense and ends in banality. Allen and Hickman could both manage better the artful craft of literary silliness.

Hickman, for example – and perhaps this was the quality that Knister acknowledged in him: a sensitivity to social attitude that could express itself in literary nuance – wrote a story about an architect from Ontario who on a visit to a Quebec bar is disrespectful to Montreal, and is promptly taken up Mount Royal and made to apologize to all the city's institutions separately. In another story Hickman drily observes that

In North America there is a small but delicately perfumed army of young ladies who have made it their business to start an aristocracy. For certain obscure reasons, including the lack of aristocrats to fill it with, they have failed; but, instead, they have what is called a plutocracy, which is the same thing from the inside, though from the outside it is quite different.[60]

Although still other stories show that Hickman was capable of overwriting adventure, he was also adept at indirect satire; one forgives a lot of overwriting for a polished sentence like this one: 'Miss McNab ... braced both feet against the sloping footboard and labored with her expression.'[61] Hickman's stories are, in other words, like Haliburton's long before him, about politics and manners rather than about combat in nature. They are no less real for that. And they are no less unaffected by fashion – as Hickman himself was aware. He opens his story 'Oriented,' for example, this way:

This is a poor story, for it has no plot, and all stories written in America are supposed to have a plot. Nothing else matters. This story has a girl and a man and a chief event.[62]

The language of the time tells us about the social relations of the time; it also helps to distinguish between the plotted American tale and the fragmentary Canadian sketch form, which Hickman (like Scott, and like Leacock and Callaghan and Hugh Hood much later) was making his own.

By contrast, Grant Allen's work owes more to the witty mystery tale, a form that in Canada John Charles Dent had reached some skill with in *The Gerrard Street Mystery and Other Weird Tales* (1888). Full of pungent asides (a definition of 'bigamy' as 'occasional marriage,' or an observation that 'two things go to produce success – the first is change; the second is cheating')[63] Allen's *An African Millionaire* is subtitled 'Episodes in the Life of the Illustrious Colonel Clay.' It tells of the escapades and final capture of a Robin Hood-like character with an indiarubber face, an elusive name and nationality, the profession of wax-figure-maker, and the skills of a con man – whom the crowd loves and the narrator deplores. Over the series of linked adventures, what emerges is a revelation of the 'honest' narrator's shady morality, which it is tempting to read as parable; using the familiar convention of the honest conman, Allen reports on the connection between South African economics and European politics, and more particularly on the inability (or the failure) of ordinary public power to contend with multinational enterprises. Allen writes to entertain rather than to preach, but he pens a clear message anyway, a message of some literary facility and some political sophistication. If he is not a great writer, he is at least as good as many from the same period who are now known better. And his skill with narrative point of view – with indirect revelation of the narrator's personality – takes the methodology of story-telling in Canada ahead another step. But he was an expatriate, and his mannered message was one which post-Victorian Canada would either dismiss as formal contrivance, or find irrelevant to the new century and the growing nation, or ignore.

It was precisely such mannered comedy that Stephen Leacock would parody in *Nonsense Novels* (1911), *Winsome Winnie* (1920), and other books, and that the religious and nature book writers would counter through their implicit and explicit claims to documentary credibility. But when we look at those writers – Seton, Grenfell, Parker, Roberts, Grey Owl – we run again into disparities between form and tacit purpose, of which the authors themselves seem somehow unaware. Grenfell's case is the most obvious. The declared purpose is to assert the viability of a code of ethics in difficult circumstances – a code made up out of duty, love of Woman, justice, Christian faith, and an attitude to death that enshrined pathos and the rewards that would follow suffering. As Henry Van Dyke avers, introducing Grenfell's *Off the Rocks* (1906): 'you who feel that religion is just as real as Nature, just as real as humanity, and that brave adventures may be achieved in the name of Christ, – this book is for you. This is the real thing.'[64] But as with *Down North on the Labrador* (1911) and *Labrador Days: Tales of the Sea Toilers* (1919), the tales Grenfell tells attempt to elevate suffering so much that the effect is grotesque rather than eloquent.

These tales may well be stories drawn from life, as Grenfell declares; certainly the photographs of his own Labrador travels, which he includes in his books, reiterate his veracity (and confirm how often publishers by this time were using the camera to reinforce by eye the documentary marvels they were marketing in words). But the tales' cumulative effect does not heighten a reader's sympathy towards human misfortune so much as it emphasizes Grenfell's presence at the disasters he describes. The narrator intrudes into these tales just as much as a narrator occupied nineteenth-century anecdotes, but with a twist: for it is less the declared selflessness of this narrator than his undeclared ego that commands a contemporary reader's attention. The difference between intention and effect only stresses further the flaws in Grenfell's artistry, and by contrast stresses again the achievement of Scott, who as much as Grenfell accepted a personal set of moral standards but made his readers come to understand them through art – using his art to reveal life's values in the context of daily uncertainties.

While the religious writers were attempting to prove the natural reality of the spirit, the nature writers gave themselves a related purpose: to demonstrate the spiritual reality of Nature. Through this effort Sir Charles G.D. Roberts, Ernest Thompson Seton, Theodore Goodridge Roberts, and to a lesser degree Grey Owl (George Stansfeld Belaney, in his children's book, *The Adventures of Sajo and Her Beaver People*, 1935) won a faithful readership; altogether the four authors produced almost 150 books of fiction – mixtures of natural observation, sentiment, and historical romance. Seton was the best naturalist, Charles G.D. Roberts the best stylist of the four, and both held strong views on the validity of their enterprise. As Patricia Morley has observed,[65] Julia Seton comments on her husband's attachment to the truth that an animal story could reveal; and Roberts himself – who came to animal story writing after reading Seton's first publications in the 1880s – went on in his introduction to *The Kindred of the Wild* (1902), a set of stories integrated by their New Brunswick setting, to specify the value he located in the form:

The animal story, as we now have it, is a potent emancipator. It frees us for a little from the world of shop-worn utilities, and from the mean tenement of self of which we do well to grow weary. It helps us to return to nature, without requiring that we at the same time return to barbarism. It leads us back to the old kinship of earth, without asking us to relinquish by way of toll any part of the wisdom of the ages, any fine essential of the 'large result of time.' The clear and candid life to which it reinitiates us, far behind though it lies in the long upward march of being, holds for us this quality. It has ever the more significance, it has ever the richer gift of refreshment and renewal, the more humane the heart and spiritual the understanding which we bring to the intimacy of it.[66]

In some degree escapist, such stories thus give Roberts an opportunity to make a greater claim – for the 'natural' (rather than simply post-Edenic, hence cursed and 'barbarous') character of the wilderness, and therefore for the morality of the human response to it.

Coupled with these part-Protestant, part-pantheistic expectations of trial and transcendence by nature are Roberts' Darwinian analyses of Natural Law and both Roberts' and Seton's commitment to the psychology of animal behaviour. Yet for all their naturalist's care, the stories about crows, bears, mountain sheep, and all the other animals are fundamentally anthropomorphic: ultimately extensions of observations of human behaviour – for which they have been variously praised and attacked.[67] Therein lies a difficulty, for while the authors gained a reputation as documentary recorders of the physical world, they asked for readers' sympathy to remain with the animals, not because they saw the animals as class victims of external forces and the intransigent laws of a survival-of-the-fittest world, but because they wished to command readers' spiritual identification with nature. For Roberts and Seton – as in the Boy Scout sentiments that Sir Robert Baden-Powell was at this time promulgating[68] – the physical world was not an end in itself but a guide to truths of another order entirely. Hence, despite their topical subject of animal behaviour, their focus remained on humankind. Their 'documentaries' took on the character they did because their expections and public judgments of human behaviour remained rooted in contemporary conventions: conventions that were political and literary as much as they were behavioural and moral.

The literary conventions are most apparent in Roberts' work when he fastens directly on human figures, as he does recurrently in the stories of animal life, memory, and dream that, for example, make up *Earth's Enigmas* (1895). Like Parker in this respect, Roberts lays reality on his characters externally, by adjectival statement. One of Roberts' stories opens: 'He was a mean-looking specimen, this Simon Gillsay, and the Gornish Camp was not proud of him'[69] – establishing immediately a connection between appearance (that which is documentarily observable and recordable by adjective) and moral judgment. Less artistically effective still are those occasions when the adjectives are intended to raise the moral tone but instead prove reductive because the diction is hackneyed or the comparison forced. Hence Roberts:

Her hair, in color not far from that of the red ox, was rich and abundant, and lay in a coil so gracious that not even the tawdry millinery of her cheap 'store' hat could make her head look quite commonplace.[70]

And Gilbert Parker, in *Pierre and His People* (1894):

He was busy with the grim ledger of his life.[71]

And Parker again, in *A Romany of the Snows* (1896):

'For heaven or hell, my girl!' he cried, and they drove their horses on – on.
  Far behind upon a divide the flying hunters ... saw with hushed wonder and awe a man and a woman, dark and weird against the red light, ride madly into the flicking surf of fire.[72]

In order to demonstrate their human nobility, Roberts' characters repeatedly have to discover their 'slumbering manhood' (adjective noun). And Pierre's frontier compatriots have to express their 'keen discernment.'[73] What the nature stories did was give a kind of topical documentary validity to the romantic tale. But by not fundamentally challenging the inherent romanticism of the form – of the techniques of tale-telling itself – the nature stories were ultimately as imbued with romance as they were with documentary, and thwarted by their own method. The paradox was that the stories of urban fashion (by Barr, Allen, Thomson) were moving towards a shrewder assessment of political change and literary technique at precisely the time they were falling topically out of favour; it was a time when the so-called stories of real life – which emphasized Pathos more than Style, sentiment more than wit, nature more than society – were coming to *redefine* 'reality' for a generation of readers. Roberts' stories legitimized Canadian nature in literature, but in doing so they perpetuated a rural illusion of Canada that – subsequently reinforced by the wilderness landscape mythologies of Emily Carr and the Group of Seven – would take several more decades to shed.

The work of Norman Duncan, Stephen Leacock, and Edward William Thomson illustrates some of the contradictory facets of this paradox. Duncan, for example, became known and celebrated for the pathos of his Newfoundland stories, collected as *The Way of the Sea* (1905), while his stories of immigrant New York went unnoticed. *The Soul of the Street: Correlated Stories of the New York Syrian Quarter* (1900) – though it is marred by the degree to which it perpetuates the verbal conventions of the Romantic Oriental Tale – is a sensitive account of a newspaper editor's passion for 'The Language Beautiful' (his commitment to articulate Arabic tradition) and of his culturally based sense of responsibility to children, all the while he notices the forces of illiteracy, ego, and ambition taking over the life of the streets on which he lives.

But the life of the street apparently held less marketable attraction than the tales of the sea. Indeed, the word 'tale' seemed to carry enough of a cachet that when Thomson revised and reissued his 1895 book *Old Man Savarin and Other Stories* in 1917, he used it in a new title that would emphasize the book's romance of 'real life' characters and locale: *Old Man Savarin Stories: Tales of Canada and Canadians*. Standard critical commentary has tended to single out as significant among Thomson's work primarily those French dialect tales which amiably reflect the convention of the 1890s: those glimpses of Imperial sentiment, habitant life, and clever villagers that constitute the Savarin stories themselves. ('Dey's fight like dat for more as four hours,' says one character; '"God be praised, I die in British waters!"' breathes another.)[74] But the revised volume, shedding some of the weakest of the early works, also added new stories which stemmed from Thomson's journalistic career in Boston – 'Boss of the World,' for example, and 'Miss Minnely's Management.' In these Thomson appeared to give up the genial ironies of his earlier work and let loose a cynicism that amply satirized the urban political manoeuvres and business ethics of the new age. From a 1980s vantage point – though for Thomson himself the cynicism may have been an expression of disappointment in public behaviour – it is these later stories which seem the most satisfying, the most shrewd and accurate of his revelations of 'real' life. And they are so in part because of their language. They openly draw attention to the fact of artifice in tale-telling and the effect and effectiveness of using artifice to broadly political ends. 'Miss Minnely's Management,' for example (a story about a redoubtable woman's management of a newspaper, and of her ability to outwit the men who would take her over), opens with one of her writers 'sardonically' applying to each of the lines he is editing 'a set of touchstones — "Will it please Mothers?" "Lady schoolteachers?" "Ministers of the Gospel?" "Miss Minnely's taste?" None of which he particularly respects:

George Renwick substituted "limb" for "leg," "intoxicated" for "drunk," and "undergarment" for "shirt," in 'The Converted Ringmaster,' a short-story-of-commerce, which he was editing for "The Family Blessing." When he should have eliminated all indecorum it would go to Miss Minnely, who would "elevate the emotional interest." She was sole owner of "The Blessing" ... Few starry names rivalled hers in the galaxy of American character-builders.[75]

In writing this way, Thomson is doing more than simply satirizing publishing practice; he is also attacking the platitudes of sentiment and style that he felt were currently subverting public taste and literary practice, though whether taste preceded practice or vice versa he leaves unclear. But a satire directed at a reader's tolerance for pap was unlikely to carry widespread appeal; indeed, satire seemed tolerable only if it kept the reader on side, so to speak — attacked a conventional target (Americans or government or the pretensions of professionals), or were disguised in banks of nostalgia. Such was the literary climate within which Stephen Leacock made his mark.

Leacock's social and political writings amply display his conservatism.[76] He was an enthusiast for the Empire, but not for colonial status, hence like Sara Jeannette Duncan championed the cause of Imperial Federation; he was economically doctrinaire, which in later years alienated his younger (socialist) students like David Lewis; and he used his humour at least until the 1920s as an agent of social weaponry. Alan Bowker observes, following H.A. Innis, that *Sunshine Sketches of a Little Town* (1912) and *Arcadian Adventures with the Idle Rich* (1914), his two finest and most unified single books of humorous sketches, are not psychologically wrought embryo novels — nor even satisfactorily integrated collections of short fiction — so much as they are exercises in the analysis of social institutions. 'The real main characters ... are Mariposa and the City'[77] — that is, the political attitudes of mind that take shape in political region and economic structure. But the structures which Leacock championed were not by this time stable ones — after World War I, a national pluralism began to replace Protestant imperialism as the dominant attitude in Canadian society — and to a post-war audience eager to loosen imperial connections and to find relief from social pressures, Leacock was out of phase; increasingly he became a kind of captive funny man, whose works were entertainments of the moment only, their occasional wistfulness interpreted more as genial nostalgia or an amusing stance than as a disconsolate personal revelation.

Clearly Leacock had his literary side; his many burlesques of literary form showed him to have an acute eye for stylistic as well as political foible, his theories of humour have their point as well as their wit, and his later efforts to assert the 'reality' of Dickens's characters (in the face of the then fashionable preference for Thackeray and social realism) show him reiterating his belief in the animating power of language. In some sense his defence of language against poetasters and publicists is not dissimilar to Thomson's satire; the aims are related — a determination to free language from convention, and so free a people from the restraints that unthinking convention imposes upon them — yet their forms and the function they hope to serve by them differ. Leacock's attacks upon Mariposa's provincialism, in *Sunshine Sketches*, and his attacks upon the 'arcadian adventures' of the urban bourgeoisie (as typified by the would-be theosophist Mrs Rasselyer-Brown), constitute ironic critiques of the shallow imitativeness of colonial forms of behaviour, and implicit defences of traditional codes of manners and mores. Leacock's eye was on Imperial Federation and its theory of equality. But smalltown Mariposa can look only as far as the city for its models, and the local city to Leacock proves almost as limited as the small town in its imaginative reach. Hence irony rules. The harder edge to Thomson's tone declares not so much a desire to reaffirm one's part in a cultural tradition as it does a disenchantment with contemporary life, as though there were no hope of altering current behaviour despite its unsatisfactoriness.

It would be a mistake, I think, to presume from this distinction that Leacock was therefore necessarily the more genial man; he was not kindly disposed towards provincialism, or the sufferance of provincialism (the latter seems to have offended him most), and in *Sunshine Sketches* he does not simply toy with human weaknesses: he savages the pretension, the graft, the pettifoggery, and the naïveté which allow provincialism to thrive — all the while himself affecting a naïve narrative air which gives the book the illusory sunshine of its title. In fact the town's language is riddled with ostentation — the Continental Hotel, the Pharmaceutical Hall, the 'houses with verandahs, which are here and there being replaced by residences with piazzas.'[78] Such language gives the town its character: it values ostentation, because it doesn't know enough not to. It is a town in which Josh Smith, the swaggering outsider with his facsimile urbanity in taste, clothes, and politics, can rise to economic and political power and faithfully 'represent' the town's aspirations. And the concluding 'L'Envoi' then suggests that the town evokes a way of life which urban-dwellers look back to with hazy fondness, remembering it as the good reality that remains near to their heart.

It is perhaps the book's fate to continue to be read as genial memoir – the scenes and exaggerated characters have charm and the comic events appear untroubled by reality – yet such an oversimplification distorts its argument. Given the fact that the reader is asked first to recognize the town's pretentiousness and then invited to claim such a town as a shaping force in his own development, it is hard not to see Leacock's double blade: the society that mistakes sentiment for culture is doomed to perpetuate its own provinciality. Why 'sunshine' then? Because the form of the sentimental regional sketch sequence – of Le Rossignol, Fréchette, Henry Cecil Walsh, George Moore Fairchild – was a popular current medium of ostensible portraiture which Leacock knew was conveying nothing but political romance; he wanted to argue another view of society, and used literary form to do so. *Sunshine Sketches*, like much of the rest of the work Leacock wrote, was a literary burlesque with a political message, taking its form from literary convention and using the power of voice to turn convention on its ear. It is that apparently naïve narrator's voice – which ably scores political points for the author – which was Leacock's signal contribution to the growth of short fiction in Canada. He did not invent new forms, but he mastered the art of tone, which had the effect of making the old form into a new one at least in function. Leacock's controlled irony required the reader to listen past the literary surface, to understand by voice as well as by vocabulary, to appreciate the fact that there might be a disparity between the two and that the fact of disparity might be more politically instructive than any surface glibness or superficial veneer of tale-teller. After Leacock, it is hard to trust a Canadian narrator again. But in the immediate future, irony was to take another guise, and literature and politics seek different ends.

As with Roberts, 'reality' for Leacock lay as much in an attitude of mind – in a code of values that declares itself in human behaviour and human institutions – as in the physical world; yet the fashion for the nature story that Roberts had done so much to develop ultimately led in a different direction. Sentiment aside, it encouraged definition by documentation, empirically verifiable art. Merit came to lie in recording the world that was, not the world that might have been. But such 'reality' was governed by its own mythologies. During World War I there was a hiatus of sorts, while popular essayists and short story writers – Isabel Ecclestone Mackay and others – turned public attention to formula tales of heroes, spies, patriotism, enemies, and Canada's Historical Greats. A different order or exception is represented by Jessie Georgina Sime's striking feminist collection *Sister Woman* (1919). Cast as a frame story, Sime's book begins when a man asks a woman what issues women want to talk about; the subsequent vignettes portray by example their sense of a different experience: they tell of a mistress whose lover dies, of English immigrants who offend by their air of superiority, of a seamstress who rejects marriage because of her mother's slavery to it, of a divorcee, a drinking woman, a woman who chooses single parenthood, and a woman whose child is stillborn. But post-war writers for the most part soon fastened back on the Northern World of Nature's Trials that was presumed to distinguish Canadian landscape and national character. For the new writers of the 1920s, therefore, the challenge of making an art out of reality had two fronts, verbal and political; if they wanted to counter the imperial sentiments of writers such as Leacock and declare what they saw as the political truths of post-war nationhood, they had also to combat the sentimentalism with which Roberts and Parker had endowed people's connections with – and understanding of – the natural environment.

By its choice of contemporary writers in 1928, Raymond Knister's anthology *Canadian Short Stories* gives some indication both of who the new writers were and how they set about shaping subject and language. Knister included Morley Callaghan, Thomas Murtha, Will Ingersoll, Merrill Denison (who became better known as a satiric playwright), and might well have included his own work in this company. (Indeed 'The First Day of Spring,' which was left unpublished when Knister drowned in 1932 at the age of thirty-three, is the finest single Canadian story to emerge from this period: a farm story with a lyrical opening, it turns into an account of irresponsibility and violence – of a runaway marriage and a baby left to die in a pigpen – and closes in a quietness that belies its subject; but the true subject lies in the rupture of innocence that the story causes, and in the vain flight from recognition that the modulations of tone, rather than the turns of plot, more accurately and admirably convey.) Like many earlier short story writers, the new writers were teachers and journalists, an experience which reinforced both their editorial skills and their observers' view of empirical reality. Murtha taught, Knister worked briefly with *The Midland*, and Callaghan, who had met and been influenced by Ernest Hemingway while working on the *Toronto Daily Star*, later was a columnist with *New World*.[80] Severally, Knister, Callaghan, Murtha, and Graeme Taylor sought an international readership by publishing stories in journals as various as the *Star Weekly*, *Saturday Night*, *Scribner's*, *Esquire*, *The Midland*, and the new experimental European magazines like *transition* and *This Quarter*. And Callaghan in particular, after 1928, appeared regularly in the annual American collections of 'best' stories edited by Edward O'Brien and Martha Foley.

One challenge that faced them in this context was to balance their sense of rootedness in Canadian experience with their desire not to limit their art to a regional audience alone; one danger in trying to avoid imposing a narrowness of access on their work, however, was that the formal internationalism they sought could turn into a stylistic neutrality in practice – a danger which the best of their work fortunately avoids. A concern about regional limitation, of course, could and did work in two directions; as early as 1887, a writer for *The Week*, commenting on Australian literature and praising Henry Kendall, Adam Lindsay Gordon, and Marcus Clarke, asserted, somewhat phlegmatically and certainly ambiguously: 'Brunton Stephens has published a volume of minor productions in the style of Bret Harte, but the greatest portion of them are suitable only to Australia.'[81] Canadian writers of the 1920s were concerned not to invite comparable dismissal, and part of their literary lives was governed by this need to avoid the charge of parochialism. Morley Callaghan observed, of his compatriots Knister and Murtha, that they were

attempting to find a beginning on their own soil, and are on absolutely solid ground. The older generation, regarded so seriously now, never found a beginning, were not interested in technique and had no identity. That is why they have always been regarded in the United States, where they attained some popularity, and where their books sold, as popular writers purely and simply.[82]

Callaghan was responding here to a review of Knister's anthology earlier that year by B.K. Sandwell, which had praised the book, but located its strengths in Scott, Roberts, Thomson, and Parker ('those four princes of the last days of the century') rather than in the moderns. Ambivalently, Sandwell had seen Knister 'filling up' the book with the newer 'accomplished and earnest youngsters':

Whether the material upon which these youngsters are working will prove in the long run to be as durable as that which fell to the hand of Roberts and Thomson and Parker remains to be determined; but nobody can deny the interest and value of the experiments which they are making with it. They are concerned in the main with types very different from those which attracted their predecessors – with life's failures and misfits and oddities, and the way the world rolls over them and squashes them flat. Sometimes we are given to understand that these misfits really have just as fine qualities as the kind of chaps who made the heroes of the old stories ... At other times there is no suggestion that they would ever have amounted to anything anywhere ...

The characteristic of the age is undoubtedly a lively interest in futility, but it is not certain that that interest will be permanent, or that any human being is actually quite so futile, if you could see right into him, as the futilitarians make him out to be. But they do it very cleverly, and the hero business was so terribly overdone in the early years of the century (the Rooseveltian years) that we welcome their efforts as a desirable change.

There is also a striking change in the literary style of the recent stories, a change about which it is equally difficult to be sure whether it is for permanent good. The old stories were written with great dignity and formality in a language based on Addison and tempered by Scott. They were the work of men who regarded themselves first and foremost as 'literary men,' with a tradition to uphold and a law to follow ... But in the last period there is a definite revolt against style, or against everything that passed for style in the good old days.[83]

But earlier still that year, in conversation with Margaret Lawrence, Callaghan had attempted to make clear how style and politics were one:

'I have a literary faith about Canada. It is a great and awful country. Like the whole of the continent. [Its] literature and its art should be like the country. Tempestuous and dark. Think of the rocks and the pines. But we try to be like the English. We should do as the Dublin group did. Get back to our native sources.'

'But is there no drama in a people trying to be like the people they came from? We are English in tradition. Isn't blood a source?'

'Certainly. But we change in a new country, and we won't admit the change. We look backward, and it makes everything we do lifeless. We compare everything to English literature.'

'But how can we help it. Language?'

'Yes, it is the same tongue. The Dublin people wrote in English, but they went back to their Celtic beginning. We should go back to the Indian. We will. Everything is tending that way. The continent was his, or rather he was of this continent. To reach our fullness we must let America get us.'

'Ah, you are Irish. That is a mystical point of view.'

'He laughed. 'The Irish are realists. They know that we do not get away from the soil. They stuck to their soil and made a great literature. We could do the same in Canada, if we would pull away from our colonial traditions.'

'Don't you think that must be done unconsciously?'

'No. It looks unconscious to the historian afterwards, but it begins with the conscious efforts of a few individuals to be true to their own life. I am writing what I see with my own eyes and hear with my own ears in my own country. I am writing after the manner of the modern because it seems to me to create union between the writer and the reader. The story must touch the imagination, and it must go on touching it. It does not finish neatly because life itself does not. It is not decorated because human lives have, in the main, no ornament.'[84]

To the historian, such a conversation bristles with ironies, not the least involving the Canadian literary connection with 'America'; Callaghan in 1928 was thinking more continentally than governmentally, yet the shift from allegiance to a European empire did not overnight give Canadians their literary independence, and the adoption of American models even blurred for some the kinds of political distinction which had previously been clear to them. Consciously courting an American market – as Callaghan and Knister did, for example – could also be interpreted as a quest for external ratification as much as any comparison with English literature ever had been. And the (perhaps off-the-cuff) conversational assertion of the Indian heritage of Canada – though it anticipates, by forty-five years, later statements by Rudy Wiebe, John Newlove, and others – appears in this context to endorse Grey Owl and the Nature School. Indeed, only the year before, Michel Poirier had penned these absolutes in *Queen's Quarterly*: 'The best Canadian painters specialize in landscapes; the best Canadian poetry describes nature; the most original contribution of Canada to literature is the animal story.'[85] Yet basically it was this attitude that Callaghan was combatting, seeking the reality of language and expression rather than seeking distinctiveness by subject. And in this way, both Callaghan and Sandwell lead us back to the central issue of the decade: style.

By 'style' writers did not mean simply using a contemporary idiom. Martha Eugenie Perry tried to do that in 'Suzanne and Susanna,' one of the works in her 1931 book *The Girl in the Silk Dress and Other Stories*, only to produce sentences like this one: '"I say, Sis, Buster's bringing over his old man's limousine to take Dot and me to the movies; just you hold on a sec', and we'll spin you over to Fifi's in style".'[86] A writer had to use idiom to a purpose, and derive meaning from the arrangement of words as well as from the words on their own. William Murtha's quotations from his father's private notebook sharply illuminate the conscious efforts the 'experimental' writers were making to combat what they saw as fulsomeness and indulgence; for example, the entry for 28 September 1927 reads (at least in part):

Character is the interesting factor in a story; not adventure. A character may be any age. Descriptions of them should be as terse as tabletalk in this hotel. People may say that Henry James was great. I think he did violence to his art by losing himself in a maze of uninteresting details.[87]

For Murtha, characterization by terseness was still an exercise in description, however; he watched behaviour closely, and attempted to use externally recordable actions and speech sounds to evoke character — most typically by reducing sentence length and complexity, by making minimal statement convey minimal action, and making minimal action carry the weight of the shifts in relationship that interested him. For Murtha, that is, narrative lies not in 'adventure' or plot, but in nuance, as in the concluding paragraph to his best-known story — that which Knister collected — 'Susie and Perce':

Mrs Heenan's son opened the door for Percy and Bill to carry out the box of dishes. He didn't say anything. Susie knew he was sore over Perce talking to his mother, and was afraid he would say something nasty. She didn't see Mrs Heenan at all, and she was glad, for she felt that if she had, she would have been obliged to leave their new address. And that would have made Perce sore. But there was nobody around except the son. She knew his name was Jack. He was good-looking. He had a good job, somewhere. She didn't speak to him though. She walked ahead of Perce and Bill out to the old Ford, thinking how cold it would be with no top on the car.[88]

Faced with the loss of a job, the disruption of a life, the need to move, Susie is alive with mixed emotions at this point but only distantly alert to each of them; it is not that she drifts, but that she pieces her way to her decisions moment by moment, a process less methodical than it is simply sequential, a case of mind reacting to necessity, as the deliberately short flat sentences strive to say.

Murtha's method thus takes us into character, which constitutes the centre of his interest, but as with so many other writers of this period the characters were interesting to the authors because they were caught at moments of change — most particularly at moments of loss, of deprivation, or of a realization that might amount to the same thing. There may have been some social context for such an interest; clearly, reconciling oneself with loss and separation was a recurrent post-war attitude, for which gaiety was sometimes a mask, and from which cynicism was often a barrier. The chief literary effect was that tone and topic were thus integrally related.

Farm life provided a recurrent setting for such stories of change — Knister's 'Mist Green Oats' records a boy's determination to get away from the limitations which his father and his father's farm impose upon him; Denison's 'The Weather Breeder' is a mordant account of a harvest that was almost reaped, and a storm that makes effort and hope seem futile; Ingersoll's stories recurrently tell in dialect of English immigrants' efforts to contend with Canadian farm life; Frederick Philip Grove's farm stories[89] — whether the interconnected personal narrative sketches of *Over Prairie Trails* (1922) or individual later works like 'Snow' — tell of the need to know the subtleties of the land in order to survive nature's unpredictability, and of the moments of choice, the dangers of ignorance, and the psychological pressures of isolation. But the farm was a social and political setting as well as a rural and regional natural backdrop. Whereas Ingersoll's characters continue a line of stories of English connection (which extends back to Moodie and Traill), Knister and Grove, with their German background, are part of a wave of writers that in and out of itself brought another kind of change to the Canadian literary and national character.

Though the 'new ethnicity,' if it can be called that, was not particularly marked – Knister's father, too, was Ontario-born – it showed up in the Teutonic structures of much of Grove's prose, in wooden formal dialogues, and in the self-aggrandizing romanticism which saturates the style and perspective of a story like 'The Boat.' It shows up more indirectly in the way Knister's central character in 'Mist Green Oats' feels the need to flee his father's farm in order to find articulateness as much as to find freedom – indeed, the two might well be one: on the farm the boy can communicate better by gesture and symbol than by word, and he feels constrained by that. An effective language always seems to lie elsewhere. But what Knister's, Denison's, and Murtha's stories do is acknowledge the limitations of the local language, whether it is rural or urban, and at the same time express through the vocabulary and cadences of the local vernacular the characters' sense of experiencing the realities of a marginal existence. On the margin of poverty, of success, of love, of failure, of culture, of understanding, they think of themselves as on the margin of speech as well. Hence, broken and non-standard English became for the writers a mark of authenticity. Mild oaths did not so much record an immorality of speech or attitude as they served to establish a largely inarticulate people's moments of emotional intensity. (Though it is sometimes difficult to gauge the accuracy of the slang and the swearing of another culture or another day, there seems a qualitatively functional as well as a merely temporal difference between, for example, Denison's tight-lipped '"By gawd, she's goin' to be a hell-bender. But I knowed she'd come. I knowed it".' and Le Rossignol's less artful, more mannerly, but also more artificial '"Holy smoke! Sacred little virgin"!')[90] The controlled simplicity of style was thus not a sign that authors had abandoned moral aspirations or noble hopes, but an indication that they refused to sentimentalize them – that, in the environments that were real to their authorial eye, such hopes and aspirations were usually locked in silence and halted by speech, and, if they could be released in prose at all, had somehow to occupy the rhythms of narrative through which the reader came to recognize them.

It was the nature of this stylistic transition that B.K. Sandwell could not follow, when he complained that newer writers are writing dialect, not merely when their characters are talking but when they are thinking, and not merely when the characters are thinking but when the author is thinking to himself. It is as if it were necessary for the author to impersonate an individual of the class with which he is dealing.[91]

Sandwell's enthusiasm for the articulate but imitative tales of Leslie Gordon Barnard, as specified in his introduction to Barnard's *One Generation Removed* (1931). indicates in yet another way his uneasiness with the newer style. Not with topic: Barnard's topics include 'American' gangsters, father-son tensions, urban jealousies, priest's efforts to deliver last rites, the morality of friendship – all the topics that Callaghan made his own – but Barnard tells of them at length and from a tender authorial distance, which allows the reader as well to sympathize from afar. Sandwell even went so far as to claim Barnard's cultural representativeness, basing his view on what he clearly saw as an appropriate ethnic precedence:

These stories ... could not have been written by a British author nor by an American author. They have a sense of the continuity of racial tradition among Anglo-Saxon peoples which has been lacking in American literature since the time of Hawthorne; but they have also the characteristic cheerfulness of a new people in a new land with a good deal of power to control the direction of their own development. Mr Barnard does not feel, and I suspect few Canadians do feel, that despairing helplessness of the individual oppressed by an exceedingly rigid and unwieldy social and political structure, which is so characteristic of the serious literature of the United States at the present time.[92]

Dialect was not the issue – that had existed before – but class was. In Sandwell's mind class appears, moreover, to be affected by ethnic background, an attitude which seemed to affect his and other critics' assessment of the legitimacy of topic. Nor was impersonation the issue; point of view was. For the newer writers were attempting not to construct rolling sentences and anecdotal plots but to shape sentences that would emulate the shifting cadences of speech rhythm, so that – even when the narrator / author was omniscient, or observing from the outside – the movement of the prose itself would carry the tensions and mark the changes in understanding or response that had had before to be enacted in 'story.' The techniques of tale were abandoned, in other words, in favour once again of the techniques of sketch, with this difference: that the apparently objective sketch now lost its narrative objectivity, and style rather than event became the means of revealing drama.

It would be convenient to claim that such a development grew directly out of a nascent national tradition, but to do so would in no small way falsify literary history. It is true that Knister was influenced by D.C. Scott and that the long history of the sketch in Canada is related to the story developments of the 1920s and 1930s. But the most direct influence on Morley Callaghan, who of all the new Canadian writers of this time established the most formidable reputation, was the same one that affected Hemingway in the United States and Frank Sargeson in New Zealand: the American Midwestern writer Sherwood Anderson. In his autobiographical *A Story Teller's Story* (1924), Anderson tells of his discovery of the abstract techniques of new American painting, and his admiration for Gertrude Stein, and he impressionistically records his growing commitment to the speech-based form of story-telling that was so to influence Callaghan, Knister, and Murtha:

In telling tales of themselves people constantly spoiled the tale in telling. They had some notion of how a story should be told got from reading. Little lies crept in ...

There was a notion that ran through all storytelling in America, that stories must be built about a plot and that absurd Anglo-Saxon notion that they must point a moral, uplift the people, make better citizens, etc. The magazines were filled with these plot stories ... 'The Poison Plot,' I called it in conversation ... What was wanted I thought was form, not plot, an altogether more elusive and difficult thing to come at ...

It was a peculiarity of the writer's craft that one must of necessity give oneself to the people about whom one wrote, must in a quite special way believe in the existence of these people ...

Very well then, the words used by the tale-teller were as the colors used by the painter. Form was another matter. It grew out of the materials of the tale and the teller's reaction to them. It was the tale trying to take form that kicked about inside the tale-teller at night when he wanted to sleep.

And words were something else. Words were the surfaces ...

Would the common words of our daily speech in shops and offices do the trick?[93]

Fastening on urban experience – as much of a 'wilderness' as the natural environment ever was – Callaghan, too, sought the resonances of such plain words. (Knister was always at his best when rendering farm life or the character of small town events as in his fragmented and often comic glimpses of a place he called Corncob Corners; for Callaghan, place was urban, and as Robert Weaver said to him in 1958, 'Your region happened to be downtown Toronto.')[94] When Callaghan came to collect fourteen of his separate stories in *A Native Argosy* (1929) as a broken sequence under the single title 'American Made,' it was the plain words of a continental America that give them their unity of effect: not theme, not plot, not setting, not character, not metaphor, and not moral message. But however plain the words were, they were still arranged; technique was still a matter of artifice, not of unedited tape-recording. Plain speech was an illusion to an end.

Callaghan's effort was to 'place' his words in such a way that the reader would 'hear' or appreciate more than surface statement would appear to declare. Victor Hoar, for example, points to the effect of this passage from 'A Girl with Ambition' (a story which appeared in *This Quarter* in 1926 before being collected as one of the 'American Made' group):

Mary hurried to the man that had been nice to her and demonstrated the dance she had practised all winter. He said she was a good kid and should do well, offering her a try-out at thirty dollars a week. Even her stepmother was pleased because it was a respectable company that a girl didn't need to be ashamed of. Mary celebrated by going to a party with Wilfred and playing strip poker until four a.m. She was getting to like being with Wilfred.[95]

The flatness of the statements perhaps conveys something of the girl's steely calculation, but Callaghan's eye is on the greater irony of her seemingly easy adaptation to the realities of her daily experience. It is not that she leads an immoral life; the fact is that moral appearance is a deliberate mask in her society, and the apparently conversational sequence of words in this passage – *nice, good, well, pleased, respectable,* and *strip poker* – conveys without making a point of it the dimensions of the ironic disparity she lives with and accepts.

Similar ironic turns and dualities govern the shape of many of the best of Callaghan's other stories as well – 'The Red Hat,' for example, or 'Two Fishermen,' 'The Shining Red Apple,' or 'A Wedding Dress,' all of them except the last collected in Callaghan's second short story volume, *Now that April's Here, and Other Stories* (1936). Typically, the words uttered or the deeds done at moments of tension or temptation carry more than a single meaning, and between overt and covert meanings, it is always the covert which is the most disturbing and the least clear to the characters themselves. In one of Callaghan's finest works, 'A Sick Call,' for example, which first appeared in *Atlantic Monthly* in 1932, the overt story concerns an old priest's efforts to give absolution to a sick woman, against the wishes of her husband. Mentally dismissing their non-Catholic marriage as pagan, the priest uses his deafness, his tiredness, and his age as ruses to get the man out of the room to fetch him a glass of water, so that he can then go through the motions of confession and absolution, and leave – leaving the woman asleep or dying and the man (reminiscent of the effect achieved in Katherine Mansfield's 'The Stranger') bitter that some other presence has now come between person and illusion, between love and memory. But the covert story concerns the priest, who in the name of good has stooped to fraud; who casts himself in Pilate's role, not Christ's, washing his hands of person in order to follow procedures; but who is made only dimly uncomfortable by his own actions because he rationalizes behaviour into morality rather than translates morality into behaviour.

But while 'A Sick Call' works by structural ironies, two other stories illustrate more clearly how Callaghan could use shifts in sentence pattern to convey the attitudinal change that constitutes his centre of narrative interest. 'A Cap for Steve,' for example, a somewhat laboured and overlong story about class conflict, class presumptions, and the gradual reconciliation between a father and his son, opens with this paragraph:

Dave Diamond, a poor man, a carpenter's assistant, was a small, wiry, quick-tempered individual who had learned how to make every dollar count in his home. His wife, Anna, had been sick a lot, and his twelve-year-old son, Steve, had to be kept in school. Steve, a big-eyed, shy kid, ought to have known the value of money as well as Dave did. It had been ground into him.

and closes with this one:

Steve, who had never heard his father talk like this, was shy and wondering. All he knew was that his father, for the first time, wanted to be with him in his hopes and adventures. He said, 'I guess you do know how important that cap was.' His hand went out to his father's arm. 'With that man the cap was — well it was just something he could buy, eh Dad?' Dave gripped his son's hand hard. The wonderful generosity of childhood — the price a boy was willing to pay to be able to count on his father's admiration and approval — made him feel humble, then strangely exalted.[96]

What the two paragraphs establish is not just the initial abruptness of the father and his implicit surrender to the status quo, but more importantly the change that takes place in the boy's position in the family. Initially the boy is cast in a subordinate role by all the passive sentence structures: he exists in relation to his father's authority and carries no authority himself — yet by the end of the story Callaghan uses active voice, in order to express what the boy does do and to show what impact this change of manner has upon the father. The boy — not the cap or the father or the possession of money — becomes an agent of change in the family's life, and the syntactical expression of agency constitutes the writer's means for revealing the magnitude of what this change implies about social authority and moral responsibility.

Similarly, in 'Ancient Lineage,' from *A Native Argosy*, the effect of change in perspective is again dependent on a sensitivity to a shift in sentence form, in this case involving length and rhythm. The story opens with Callaghan's typical illusion of empirical reality, with an uninvolved young man named Flaherty arriving at his destination to gather facts:

> The young man from the Historical Club with a green magazine under his arm got off the train at Clintonville. It was getting dark but the station lights were not lit. He hurried along the platform and jumped down on the sloping cinder path to the sidewalk.
> Trees were on the lawns alongside the walk, branches drooping low, leaves scraping occasionally against the young man's straw hat. He saw a cluster of lights, bluish-white in the dusk across a river, many lights for a small town. He crossed the lift-lock bridge and turned on to the main street. A hotel was at the corner.

Truth appears incontrovertible (the repetition of 'was,' 'were,') and the young man seems not given to fantasy ('He hurried,' 'He saw,' 'He crossed': statements of directional purpose). Yet his path is a 'sloping' one, and the paragraph ends at a 'corner' after he has 'turned.' Subsequently, rather than finding simple facts, he discovers a person instead. Miss Rower, the daughter of the woman he has come to interview, initially antagonistic and unwilling to share what she knows, slowly opens up into a reverie. That the reverie also expresses her sublimated sexuality is something the reader recognizes from the altered sentence rhythm:

> She said vaguely, 'I daresay, I daresay,' conscious only of an interruption to the flow of her thoughts. She went on talking with hurried eagerness, all the fine talk about her ancestors bringing her peculiar satisfaction. A soft light came into her eyes and her lips were moist.
> Mr Flaherty started to rub his cheek, and looked at her big legs, and felt restive, and then embarrassed, watching her closely, her firm lower lip hanging loosely. She was talking slowly, lazily, relaxing in her chair, a warm fluid oozing through her veins, exhausting but satisfying her. He was uncomfortable. She was liking it too much. He did not know what to do.

But in the final analysis whose sublimation is it? As much the young man's as Miss Rower's, and when the story ends it does so inside Flaherty's consciousness, with the slowly ebbing rhythms that take him from excitation to sleep:

> In the hotel he asked to be called early so he could get the first train to the city. For a long time he lay awake in the fresh, cool bed, the figure of the woman whose ancient lineage had taken the place of a lover in her life, drifting into his thoughts and becoming important while he watched on the wall the pale moonlight that had

softened the lines of her face, and wondered if it was still shining on her bed, and on her throat, and on her contented, lazily relaxed body.[97]

Neither his method nor his subjects won Callaghan an unalloyed critical reception at home, and even Callaghan's defenders were sometimes a little backhanded. Margaret Lawrence, for example, wrote: 'these stories are Canadian. It is not a matter of street names and cities ... Nor is it a business of being what they call nationally conscious ... At the moment it is unimportant whether Morley Callaghan's stories are good or bad. Doubtless, they are bad from the critical standpoint of the academician, and also of the newspaperman. The style is bare and there is no clinch. He uses speech, not language. [But] The story ... [goes] on in your imagination ... '[98] Such a statement reveals the degree to which the popular magazine definition of the short story had become embedded in readers' minds. But so, too, had conventions about topic. Sexuality motivated behaviour in much of Callaghan's work. But then Bertram Brooker, attacking Toronto critics in 'Nudes and Prudes' for complaining about sexuality in Callaghan's writings, said that they imputed 'motives without evidence in order to have a full-course orgy of offensiveness with which to regale their readers.'[99] Sir Charles G.D. Roberts, for his part, discussing the 'modernism' that he felt had come 'more slowly and less violently' to Canada than elsewhere, found Callaghan acceptable because he was not violent; and yet the violence of human contact and psychological pressure permeates almost every page Callaghan wrote. Roberts was seeking moderation:

What I have said of Canadian poetry applies also to Canadian prose fiction. The Canadian temperament is set against extremes. It will go far along new lines, but it balks at making itself ridiculous ... Mr Morley Callaghan is reputed as having declared himself a humble disciple of Mr Hemingway ... If this be so, the disciple has on many counts excelled the master. Compare ... *Strange Fugitive* and *The Sun Also Rises*. The latter is marred by eccentricities in the vogue of the moment. You find yourself skipping whole pages of conversation whose only purpose is to display the reiterant vacuities of the drunken mind ... [But in Callaghan the] style is clear, bare, efficient ... – 'modern.' But it has sanely avoided the modern fault of striving after effect.[100]

Yet 'effect' – for a moral purpose, understood from a Catholic perspective – was in a strictly literary sense precisely what Callaghan *was* after. As with Knister and Murtha, Callaghan came to perceive reality as psychological revelation (fulfilment or loss, stasis or change). which had to be enacted by the movements – the 'effects' – of words alone.

What this meant was that the nature of the short story itself had to change;

Callaghan and Knister, like Mansfield and Sargeson in New Zealand, or like Anderson and Hemingway in the United States, were redefining what the form could do. It is not surprising, then, to find among Knister's unpublished papers an appreciative essay on Katherine Mansfield. He found in her work a justification for the short form, a justification for a view of experience as a set of fragments rather than as a whole world complete in itself and separable from life. Even about Callaghan, Knister could write that 'The method is objective, and as for style, he contrives clever ellipses. Every statement is plain, concrete, but it leaves a great deal between itself and the next for the discerning reader. Of course the danger in this method and attitude is that the whole work may fail to move the beholder, or give him any of the exaltation of life itself.'[101]

For Knister, this relation between life and art mattered; he found that, after Chekhov, the task of using the short story form to render Goethe's principle – '"All that happens is a symbol and, by representing itself perfectly, it reveals the significance of all else"' – became 'immeasurably simplified. Without transilient experiment in the arts, as in the sciences, advance is not possible; and this is the contribution of our age to the short story.'[102] Mansfield did not attempt the novel form, Knister writes (a mistaken assumption, though his point is of interest still), because of the way she saw life happening around her. It was not because she repeatedly sought a kind of 'symbolic imagism' that her art had genius (Knister found this less effective, in fact, than the straight object on the page, acting symbolically without being a symbol – a subtle distinction), nor because she was at heart (he claims) a lyric poet, but because of her 'knowledge that in being sincere every mood would necessarily play obbligato to her pervading weary questioning, the negative conviction that life had passed everybody by.'[103] What her form of the short story provided her with was a way of representing those sliding moods, the sequence of fragmented perceptions of experience which constitute the process of life when the sense of life's coherent wholeness – or one's ability to grasp it – has passed away.

Persistently lyric, Knister himself wanted none the less to root his observations in society. Writing in 1926 about his own poetry, he chides those who wish to veil life

in sonorous phrases and talk about birds and flowers and dreams.

Birds and flowers and dreams are real as sweating men and swilling pigs. But the feeling about them is not always so real, any more, when it gets into words. Because of that, it would be good just to place them before the reader, just let the reader picture them with the utmost economy and clearness, and let him be moved in the measure that he is moved by little things and great ...

It would be good for the flowers and birds and dreams, and good for us. We would love them better, and be more respectful. And we might feel differently about many other common things if we saw them clearly enough. In the end we in Canada here might have the courage of our experience and speak according to it only.[104]

But as the 1930s and 1940s progressed, weary questioning turned out to be a bitter fact, not a musical stance; and shared experience turned out to be that of drought, Depression, war, class division, poverty, and machines: there were people who tried to be lyric about such things (mainly in retrospect) but material social realism was for the most part to take lyricism's place. Sandwell and Barnard were to give way. Callaghan was to come into his own: urban, matter-of-fact, status-conscious, international; and writers like Dorothy Livesay and Dyson Carter joined him as recorders of the economic history of the current day.[105] Sinclair Ross, too, published in the 1930s his earliest stories of prairie deprivation; and A.M. Klein, in 1936 stories in *The Canadian Forum* and the socialist journal *New Frontier*, addressed the facts of joblessness and beggary in fierce ironic parable. There was a new vocabulary of machines and politics to use. But what happened then to the art form? How did it contend with the pressures of the present and the judgments of the past?

Writing for *First Statement* in 1944, John Sutherland (whose editorial voice was the most important one of the next decade) was to make clear the conflicting tensions of creativity and criticism. Claiming that, during a social upheaval, people's thinking must necessarily absorb political ideas and literature deal with them, not flee in escapist fashion into sheer style, he wrote: 'Against a background of social chaos, of which the war is only the violent and morbid symptom ... social pressure is reflected in the cry for social function in art ... But the final criterion of judgment is still the standard of the art itself – good taste, which derives its authority from a long tradition, and from a sense of what is significant and close to human nature. This, and nothing else, decides whether "social significance" will be artistically valid or not.'[106] Such a statement raises supplemental questions even while it attempts to answer the initial ones: what tradition, for example? And whose taste, when it is clear that standards are not universal? And what kind of 'function' will be deemed meritorious? Such questions brooded behind the new journals of the time, challenging the writers of the 1930s and the two decades that followed to choose their subjects 'responsibly' and defend the validity of their literary technique. Their several answers did not produce the single national identity many people had long sought from their literature; instead they revealed a greater diversity still in the social fabric and the further adaptation of literary form to its demands.

The Tensions between Story and Word, 1930–1980

Clearly, 'realism' had become the modern watchword, but what it meant is less easy to pin down. 'Realism' was a way of representing 'Reality' – but 'Reality' lay in empirical solidity and empirical motion, political system and political attitude, spiritual rule and spiritual aspiration, flesh, food, metaphysics, and metaphor. The Depression and World War II made it evident that disparities between life and language continued to exist even after the Jazz Age had revolutionized literature and society; in many cases new stereotypes had simply replaced old ones, and a lot of attitudinal housecleaning was still in order. Figuring largely in the shaping of a different set of attitudes, the Holocaust led to the mass movement of people beyond their accustomed national borders, and also to the reassessment of foreign policy and domestic custom. The idea of 'Europe' could no longer be adequately represented by images of a romantic and traditional crenellated past: Europe was now the violent present in which Canadians were morally involved. Moreover, as details about the Holocaust began to filter out of Germany in the 1940s, Canadians had not only to recognize the horror of Auschwitz over there but also, if slowly, to admit to the endemic anti-Semitism at home.

Old structures of power persisted in Canadian society (though new ones grew up in tandem); but by the 1950s the language was already bending to accommodate unestablished voices, as the short story showed. In Canada the genre made room for English-born Malcolm Lowry's flights of psycholiterary association, for New Zealand-born Desmond Pacey's reportorially laconic memoirs,[107] for South Africa-born Ethel Wilson's stylistic evocations of the rhythms of women's lives and west coast life, for Mordecai Richler's Montreal Jewish humour, Patricia Page's symbolic sketches, Thomas Raddall's tales,[108] Will Bird's and Ernest Buckler's Maritime sentiment, Joyce Marshall's blunt feminism, and A.M. Klein's fables. Years of formal experiment were still under way.

Merely to list the names of a dozen writers of the time is to indicate the new quarters to be heard from: W.O. Mitchell, Sinclair Ross, Desmond Pacey, Malcolm Lowry, Henry Kreisel, A.M. Klein, Mordecai Richler, Norman Levine, Irving Layton, Miriam Waddington, P.K. Page, Joyce Marshall, Ethel Wilson, Mavis Gallant. We can categorize them bluntly by place, politics, gender, and religion: the new speakers of stories were Westerners, émigrés, women, and Jews – and though such categories overlap and interlock, any one of them immediately defined the writers as coming from outside the tradition as the tradition had so far established itself. Hence the writers found themselves struggling with 'alien' expectations as well as with alien forms.

They faced a challenge in their subject and in their audience, in the language they had to speak with and in the form that was there to use, in the distance they were from home or reader and in the very opportunities they had to publish. There were changes imminent on all fronts.

The format of 'publication' typifies the extent of such change. While many journals continued to accept 'serious' short fiction – *Queen's Quarterly*, *Dalhousie Review*, *The Canadian Forum*, *Chatelaine* – in fact the Canadian print market was limited: *Maclean's* published popular works; *The Canadian Magazine* had died in 1939, reduced to publishing articles on 'Meat and Imagination'; the new journals, like John Sutherland's *Northern Review*, were small; and the regionally-rooted journals (*Fiddlehead*, *Atlantic Advocate*, Harold Horwood's *Protocol* in St John's) did not at least initially reach much beyond their own locale. Naturally such journals, together, drew the major writers. Most of Sinclair Ross's stories appeared in *Queen's Quarterly*, for example; so did several by Ralph Gustafson, Henry Kreisel, Desmond Pacey, and others, though more of Pacey's appeared in Maritime journals, more of Gustafson's in American journals like *Atlantic Monthly*, *New Mexico Quarterly*, *Story*, and the *Virginia Quarterly Review*, and almost all of Mavis Gallant's (after she left the Montreal *Standard* and moved to Paris) in *The New Yorker*. But it is a mistake to think of *story* and *print* as inseparable terms during this time, for the growth of radio in Canada, particularly after the Canadian Broadcasting Corporation was established in 1932, meant that stories could be spoken and listened to as well as (or instead of) printed and read.

One man was almost single-handedly responsible for opening radio up to Canadian fiction writers: Robert Weaver, who joined the CBC in 1948. It was Weaver who edited the stories that were to be read on the air on programs like *Canadian Short Stories*. The series *Anthology* continued this tradition – Weaver began it on 19 October 1954. with a story by Mordecai Richler. Later still, stories were purchased for another program, called *Wednesday Night*, and the CBC prize story competitions in the 1970s and 1980s brought greater annual publicity to the process of selection. It was Weaver, too, who because of his enterprise became for years the chief Canadian arbiter of the short story form. He was long the only local public enthusiast for Mavis Gallant's work, for example. His radio efforts led directly to four anthologies: *Canadian Short Stories* (which he assembled with the radio producer Helen James in 1952; a collection from the period 1946–51); *Ten for Wednesday Night* (1960; a collection of ten stories broadcast in 1960); *Small Wonders* (1983); and *The 'Anthology' Anthology* (1984). His concern about artists' opportunities led him to help found *Tamarack Review* in 1956, to continue as one of the editors until it ceased publication in 1982, and to turn it into the major Canadian literary magazine of its time. And the four volumes of his Oxford anthology *Canadian Short Stories* (1960, 1968, 1978, 1985), reiterating and extending the outline of the Canadian canon that Raymond Knister had mapped in 1928 and Desmond Pacey updated in 1947 with his anthology *A Book of Canadian Stories* (even though Weaver, as part of his anti-nationalist critical stance, claimed there was no tradition to update), were for two decades to shape critical judgments of national practice in the genre.

It was not, however, simply the opening up of radio to writers that effected a formal change; it was what happened when the story became an oral medium. Commenting in the Montreal *Standard Review* on a broadcast of Canadian short stories, Mavis Gallant wrote in 1948 about the 'valuable lesson' that listening to a story could be for a writer: 'There is something relentless about a story being read aloud. Lack of rhythm, vagueness and faulty characterization are glaringly obvious because you can't skip and you can't reread.'[109] Writers like Knister and Callaghan had been sensitive to the written force of rhythm – and Leacock, the lecturer, had in practice been able to use the cadences of Canadian ironic utterance to literary effect. But in the 1940s actors like Bernie Braden and John Drainie came into their own as oral performers of stories like Leacock's or W.O. Mitchell's (Mitchell's 'Jake and the Kid' stories, Mary Grannan's 'Just Mary' children's tales, and the *Cuckoo Clock House* readings engaged an entire generation of radio listeners); the effect, although there persisted for years on the CBC a kind of midatlantic norm for actors' 'serious drama' accents, was to validate the actual sounds of Canadian speech as a medium for fiction. 'Dialect' no longer immediately conveyed inferiority; 'language' now included whatever speech was used locally: because speech was 'real.' Hence Mitchell's laconic 'Crocus, Saskatchewan' idiom was to achieve literary respectability, and all across the country – in Bob Edwards' prairie jokes, Ray Guy's Newfoundland anecdotes, Paul St. Pierre's episodic *Cariboo Country* tales – what had been a somewhat subterranean vernacular literature was to surface as public art.

That it was a *comic* public art also says something about the intricate relation between speaker and listener in a spoken story. In some forms of humour the 'joke' is based on a simple put-down, on the condescending dismissal of the quaint or curious actions of lesser beings; it is the sort that relies frequently on dialect as a means of distancing the teller from his topic, or relies on racial stereotype, or creates another form of hierarchical distinction as when Leacock appears casually to dismiss the talents and aspirations of women. But in other forms of humour – as in Mitchell or St Pierre, or later in the Silas Ermineskin stories of W.P. Kinsella (eg, *Dance Me Outside*, 1977, or *Scars*, 1978) – the comedy is ironic; the teller appears to be self-critical, but the story tonally invites the reader to identify with the teller, and to recognize the criticism not as some masochistic form of rueful cultural abasement but as a celebration of the power to persist under pressure. Chagrin does not necessarily require a surrender of personality. The indirect narrative mode, relying on pacing and tone more than on plot or a distinctive lexicon, presumes readers' ability to listen: ie, to respond to the nuance of speech and to infer their way past surface statement.

Such comedy can, as a result, have a political function. St Pierre's stories of Smith and Ol' Antoine, Basil Johnston's tall tales of the Moose Point Reserve, and Kinsella's stories of Silas at their best champion Indian rights causes; but they do so more attitudinally than polemically, from within the structure of the story rather than from without. The comedy does not diminish the stature of the characters, but nor does it falsify their actual power in the real life to which the fiction connects: it celebrates, but it protests. In comparable fashion, stories that fasten on a regional, female, or Jewish perspective repeatedly articulate an indirect criticism of mainstream Canadian presumptions, often simply by enacting the alternative attitudes which constitute the reality of their author's experience. How, for example, does one respond to the stories of Ross, Wilson, Marshall, Kreisel, and Klein? Ross's tonally bleak separate stories – collected as *The Lamp at Noon and Other Stories* (1969) and *The Race and Other Stories* (1982) – date almost entirely from the period 1934–52; they twin a sensitivity to the 1930s prairie landscape (both physical and social) with a skill at using literary symbol, and they have appealed to readers beyond the region in which they are set because of their honesty about personal relationships. There is no comedy here; all is tense with oppression, which in turn derives from the apparent powerlessness of an entire community to affect the weather, the economy, or their own future.[109] Man and woman alike, as in 'The Lamp at Noon' (1938) or 'The Painted Door' (1939), are trapped by their own limitations and their dependence on others, knowing at the same time that such dependence and such limitations are what makes them human and gives them hope. But Ross's expression of this dependence in regional as well as psychological terms makes the stories function as a kind of sociopolitical *cri du coeur* as well. The prairie communities Ross evoked in prose suffered enormously from the Depression droughts, found themselves dependent on governments and churches, on social programs and ritual, which they needed and objected to simultaneously. Such tension – need and blame, inextricably mixed – showed in the narrative conflicts Ross repeatedly established; it manifested itself, too, in the elliptical phrasing Ross honed in 'One's a Heifer,' a story first published in Ralph Gustafson's 1944 anthology *Canadian Accent*. The phrasing constitutes a variant form of those laconic cadences which Mitchell in the 1940s and Robert Kroetsch in the 1970s identified as characteristic prairie speech. In the social context, that is, communication is an indirect act; hence the elliptical medium of the story comes to embody the ambiance which it has been the intent of the writer to convey. The characters in 'One's a Heifer' may all, to one degree or another, recognize their own motivations, but they all repress them; the literary effect is that, controlling what they admit, they suppress plot: the central figure, a boy, thinks he has solved one mystery, only to intuit another[111] – but the community around him, perhaps knowing the truth already, knows also that it does not want to know what it knows, so hushes the boy up, preserving what surfaces there are even while reality lurks melodramatically beneath them. It is neither the resolution to conflict nor the initiation of conflict that lies at the heart of Ross's world; it is the tension of living with uncertainties one finds so dislocating and yet so wants, and the tension of living with the certainties one cannot prove and cannot abide.

In Mitchell's world, the characters live with laughter because the next best thing is despair; in Ross's, they live with grim determination because they suppress the violence of open confrontation. (Ross's later *Journal of Canadian Fiction* story,'The Flowers that Killed Him,' 1972, is more openly violent, though it so telegraphs its 'surprise' ending that it dissipates the dramatic energy it should be building.) But in the work of Ethel Wilson and Joyce Marshall, violence breaks out everywhere: in rape, murder, mindless damage, war, weather, and psychological pressure.[112] Always the body is vulnerable, but that is not what is most worrisome. In Wilson's stories (which began with 'Hurry, hurry' in *The New Statesman and Nation* in 1937 but were not collected until *Mrs Golightly and Other Stories* appeared in 1961) the body's weakness is a reminder of natural mortality, the flow of nature. What is worrisome is the mind's susceptibility to threat, whether (as recurrently in Wilson) it shows when people become aware of their own destructive creativity, their power to invent violence, or (as most directly in Marshall) it shows when women give up their right to live and think independently. Hence for these two writers the social pressures of the thirties and the world wars provided both an historical frame of reference and a literary metaphor: invasion. Invasion was intrusive, confrontative, imperial, arbitrary; it established power by force; its proponents expected capitulation and counselled surrender to the way things are or the ways things have always been; it did not describe love, but it did describe the sexual battleground. And it was Wilson's and Marshall's subject because they were determined that a female perspective should not be simply dismissed as fanciful romance or domestic hobby.

'"I don't object to truth being stranger than fiction",' says one of Wilson's characters; '"what I object to is that Truth is so hard to tell ... [and] that truth is often very uncomfortable".'[113] Through her, the author speaks both of subject and of method. How, the author by implication asks, is it possible to tell of such discomfort through the intrinsically comforting techniques of fiction? Wilson relies on the associative powers of natural metaphor (the invading fog in 'Fog,' the abrupt storm in 'From Flores,' the delusive snow in 'Hurry, hurry,' which gives an illusion of innocence to a landscape that hides a murdered body) and upon the suggestive powers of rhythm, the potential ironies of form. 'We have to sit opposite,' for example, is a quietly brilliant comic allegory about the onset of World War II; comic on the surface, full of verbal oneupmanship as two doughty Canadian ladies contend with a collective German family on a European train, the story is far from comic in implication, as even the ladies begin to realize. By responding to what they have seen as provocation, they become involved in an illogicality that masquerades as logic: 'The whole absurd encounter had begun to hold an element of terror. They had been tempted ... they were implicated in fear and folly.'[114] The resulting danger is that they then surrender to the terror in themselves.

In a powerful scene in another story, 'The Window,' the central character Mr Willy looks out a plate glass window to see an intruder immediately outside and his own image superimposed on the other's in the mirroring night-time windowpane; danger approaches from without, in other words, but the greater potential danger is within himself, in the human susceptibility to folly and fear. Repeatedly in a Wilson story, the style unmasks the characters; it sails along with a kind of placid equanimity that is easily mistaken for society chat – but which is designed to entice the reader into just such a passive frame of mind so that the inevitable abrupt shock to the character will require a self-critical assessment on the reader's part as well. There is no thought, it seems, without discomfort, and no real discomfort without the shattering of illusion.

Like Wilson, Joyce Marshall not only writes fiction that will break through the ease of comfortable assumptions but also claims the right to optimism even in the face of the violence and terror she expresses. Such optimism isn't always possible; it's often qualified. But what this means is that when it can't be a naïve faith for her characters it can't be an easy option either. At the end of one of her best stories, 'The Enemy,' for example (a CBC *Anthology* story later collected in *A Private Place*, 1975), the central character reflects on her recent and continuing fright and on the man who has been mindlessly ransacking her rooms:

she would have liked to see for once and close at hand the face of what is the real enemy, whether within or without. She might have known something then – not why she was marked out since that seems to have been sheer savage randomness but why, chosen, she was so open, her life so ready to come apart ...

And where are the other threats? She knows there will be others, that they only wait. Perhaps that is why she goes on talking about it, living one day and one day. And almost trusting.[115]

'Would have,' 'almost,' 'perhaps' — these are words of regret for an order gone, but also a woman's positive claims on the future's independence and the future's uncertainties. From her earliest published short stories 'Come Ye Apart' (*Fiction*, 1936) and 'And the Hilltop Was Elizabeth' (*Queen's Quarterly*, 1938), Marshall has claimed such independence; though in the ultimately sentimental story about Elizabeth, the title character's statement comes close to soap opera cliché ('"David, I want to be left alone to think for a while",')[116] that does not diminish the seriousness of the claim. Marshall's subsequent work, in fact, reads like an extended gloss upon it, investigating the effect on women of work, war, family, and education, the way in which women prey on other women and are not just victims of men, and the need for an honest record of women's experience and language.

Sometimes her record is direct, as when the nonagenarian physician Aunt George in 'So Many Have Died'[117] muses on World War I: 'What a society, she thought with an old, undiminished rage — it had to murder its men before it could value its women.'[118] Sometimes it is embodied in the nature of symbolic actions and in the implications of idiomatic speech, as in 'The Old Woman' (1952), a story about a man's love for the machine he works on, written some twenty years earlier than Jack Hodgins' stories of Spit Delaney's infatuation with a railroad engine. While there is pathos behind the comedy of Hodgins' characters, however, there is in Marshall's story a sharper delineation of role — between the man's inability to distinguish life from mechanical action (hence his failure to relate adequately to others: the 'old woman' is the machine that wins him) and his wife's commitment to creative life (she discovers a useful and personally satisfying role as a midwife in a French-Canadian community, even though she begins as an immigrant, not knowing the language).

Always the question of language is important. Miranda, for example, determined to tell her ransacked story in 'The Enemy,' does not tell it in orderly sequence: 'No-one points out that she doesn't tell the story as it happened but breaks right into the climax as if she's forgotten how slowly and intermittently it began.'[119] But Marshall constructs this sentence deliberately, not only to correspond to the randomness of the break-ins, but also to remind the reader, through the vocabulary itself, of the implicit (however sublimated) sexuality of the violent attacks. The serial triptych that comprises 'So Many Have Died,' 'Windows' (1977). and 'Paul and Phyllis' (1977) makes the point about language even more directly. The first story tells of Aunt George's accomplished career, her enfranchisement from male structures and female conventions, and of her murder; the second recounts her granddaughter Phyllis's continuing quest for liberation, particularly in light of the conventionality of the generation between them, and of her encounter with the murderer: the third tells of Phyllis's later growth towards love, with the man of her parents' generation who has helped to release her and thereby to carry himself as well towards some measure of freedom.

Spelled out this way, the actions seem contrivedly allegorical, yet however dramatic here, the sequential plot is of less consequence than the way the style shifts from story to story. Crankily unconventional for the old doctor, deliberately blunt, frank, even obscene in the mouth of the young woman who strikes out uncertainly in her rebellion, the shifting speech patterns reveal differences in motivation that at once link and separate the generations. Phyllis has to claim, in effect, the inheritance her grandmother has fought for; but she can only do so by recognizing her grandmother's independence and then, losing her grandmother, by reanimating that spirit in her own terms. Yet such understanding comes indirectly. She claims freedom first in the vocabulary of liberation rhetoric, as is spelled out near the beginning of 'Windows':

How did you do it, Aunt George? I know *what*, after all you're famous and a living family legend. But how? The little things, day after day? Did you have a mother who was always trying to squeeze herself into your head so she could run around in it? (Well, I fooled you, Mummy. You thought I was Gerda, the saintly girl who talked to flowers, and Thumbelina and the Hazel-nut Child, all those cute things, but I was really little Kai and I just kept getting colder.) And a father whose love was all outside, baby-names and kissing. So that there was no part of you anywhere that wasn't yanked and pulled.

Sandy had wanted to make a list of questions – what do you think about (1) abortion (2) group sex (3) the lesbian option – but Phyllis had thought she'd just like to improvise. It didn't seem so simple now. Because how was she going to look at Aunt George – skin cracked all over like very old leather, lizard eyes – and ask her, as she must somehow, what she used to do about being horny. Always use real words, Sandy and the others said, and Phyllis did, even with her parents now. But the group teased her still, called her the Westmount girl, though they were most of them Westmount too. Because she was a year younger. Small. All her life was she going to be the little one? Always stretching ... But what *did* you do about men, Aunt George? You couldn't have been two things – your own self free and firm inside and on the outside playing sexist games. Did you masturbate? Or turn to sister women? And why did you fail us? Because between you and me there's Mummy. I've had to go back to the beginning. Why didn't you give her something to give me?[120]

87 Canada: Story and History

Though such contemporary terms run the risk of enclosing identity as sharply as the fairy-tale models ever did, the fact remains that they do constitute the reality of – the verbal medium for – the current experience under analysis; and Marshall's concern as a writer is to match her mode of expression with this perceived reality. If one cannot imagine such words from Sara Jeannette Duncan or Susanna Moodie, that is part of the point; and to recognize that Ethel Wilson's post-war milieu allowed her an occasional phrase that was genteelly risqué – as when a naïve young male waiter in 'A drink with Adolphus' refer embarrassedly to hors d'oeuvres as 'hot ovaries'[121] – that is part of the point, too. Women writing in Canada from the 1940s on were rebelling against ignorance, against limitations on the structures of language as well as against those on women's options in life – but so were the women writing before the 1940s: given, therefore, their common concerns and their differences of expression, the challenge to the newer writers became one of finding a language that would adequately articulate the matriarchal connection they wanted to claim and that would build its perspectives and values into the received social and cultural tradition. Indeed, in some respects, it is through writers like Marshall that later writers, overtly concerned with women's roles (Margaret Atwood, Anne Cameron), could connect with earlier ones like Jessie Georgina Sime and Nellie McClung.

Henry Kreisel's work demonstrates yet another side to this question of reinventing the national tradition through language; parallel to the efforts of women in the 1940s to articulate their enfranchisement were the efforts of the many people who as immigrants and 'displaced persons' brought to Canada languages and faiths that up to this point had been culturally unfamiliar in the Canadian landscape. Born an Austrian Jew, Kreisel learned his English as a teenager in a Canadian refugee camp, later took an Honours English degree at the University of Toronto, was presented with the work of Marjorie Pickthall when he sought the traditions and accomplishments of Canadian writers,[122] went on to teach at the University of Alberta, and wrote. Wrote of Canada. Yet wrote of Canada in such a way as to make clear that his perspective would alter how Canada could be conceived.

It would be easy to invent a category, 'immigrant writing' and let it contain all such writers: Kreisel, Lowry, Pacey; British-born John Metcalf; U.S.-born Audrey Thomas, Clark Blaise, Kent Thompson, Leon Rooke, Ann Copeland, Susan Kerslake, Elizabeth Spencer, Jane Rule; Kenya-born Bill Schermbrucker; Australia-born Daphne Marlatt: Malta-born Sean Virgo; Barbados-born Austin Clarke; Trinidad-born Sam Selvon; and others with backgrounds in Italy, Germany, India, Chile, Guyana, China, and Japan. Yet to do so would be implicitly to find a way of excluding them from the mainstream, of defining them as a group called 'other' to be consequently held apart.[123] And while it would be blind to deny that some Canadians would regard this as a proper attitude to take, it has in fact been more characteristic of Canadian experience to make the otherness its own. What this distinction means literally is that somehow the subjects and language of these writers came to express the experience not just of the special immigrant group but of the larger community. The fragmentation implicit in the upheavals of immigration found resonance in the seemingly chaotic social changes of post-Holocaust history. But in language, fragmentation became an art.

Austin Clarke, for example, at the beginning of 'The Motor Car' in *When he was free and young and he used to wear silks* (1971). uses Caribbean dialect ebulliently, in order to play with words, but also to remind the reader of the relevance of the black slave past in a modern worker economy, where racism is not unknown and dreams and ambitions run wild; the tone is consequently mixed, of the sort that critics call 'bittersweet' or 'tragicomic,' catching comedy at the edge of isolation.

Audrey Thomas's stories of miscarriage, the disintegration of a marriage, pressing sexuality, and foreign travel – as in *Ten Green Bottles* (1967), *Ladies & Escorts* (1977), *Real Mothers* (1981), and *Goodbye Harold, Good Luck* (1986) – are also simultaneously stories of social upheaval, personal distress, and linguistic fragmentation: a fragmentation based on verbal play, on the tricks of speech that beguile and bedevil the mind's eye. Mordecai Richler, in *The Street* (1969), made the Montreal Jewish street accent into a commentary on modern mores. And Henry Kreisel's stories, collected as *The Almost Meeting and Other Stories* (1981), repeatedly focus not on the conflict between a commitment to change and a resistance to change but on the paradoxical simultaneity of the two.[124] Whether in didactic terms, as in 'Chassidic Song,' which tells of a modern young man being reminded of his ritual verbal roots in a rabbinical past, or in comic terms, as in 'The Travelling Nude,' about an Alberta community's division over morality and art, Kreisel does not seek to replace one code with another. He fastens instead on the indirect modes of communication – the symbols of fixity and movement, like the title image of 'The Broken Globe,' or the go-betweens who link generations and communities – by which a multiple culture can be seen whole, its chaos perhaps unresolved, but accepted with a modicum of dignity.

What is most clear by the 1960s is that the 'plain speech' of earlier decades was no longer sufficiently shared to characterize contemporary society or embody its concerns. Poets – Ralph Gustafson, P.K. Page, Colleen Thibaudeau, Irving Layton, and Miriam Waddington, for example – had endeavoured in prose in the 1940s to reinvest plain speech with lyrical intensity and symbolic dimension. But the plain urban Callaghan mode more generally became sentimentalized. Just as the Harlequin formula conventionalized lyricism, the 'tough romance' took over the devices of 'realism.' Kenneth Millar, for example, began publishing with a story in *Saturday Night* in 1939, but went on to greater fame in the United States as the mystery writer Ross Macdonald. And in the string of books that Hugh Garner published from the late 1940s on, such subjects as urban poverty, working class labour, and street behaviour – far from being made literarily 'real' – became more obviously the conventional trappings of a solemn and determinedly unironic bluff literary stance. The new serious vogue was for irony, complexity, density of allusive utterance, and the reality of artifice itself.

It was A.M. Klein, a man totally familiar with urban life and openly committed, until his self-imposed silence, to political causes which advocated economic and social equity, who most clearly broke with the real life / plain speech equation. Reviewing Ariel Bension's *The Zohar* for *The Canadian Jewish Chronicle* in 1932 (fifty years before the 'Tao of Physics' was to turn the disparity about), Klein dismissed those 'rationalists' who 'with a supercilious lift of an all-too-logical eyebrow' themselves dismiss

'the poets of the esoteric': 'Creator of natural laws and inventor of scientific hypotheses, [the rationalist] knows no exceptions; all mysticisms are mystifying; they do not sit on syllogisms and are therefore foundationless all. Immune to parable and impervious to metaphor, he condemns every philosophy which he can not understand as being either the forgery of a fakir or the document of a lunatic. Attributing insanity to works mystical, he ... commits the unpardonable offense of mistaking the Veil of the Shechina for the Mask of Mephistopheles ... ')[125]

At once championing the instructive power of metaphoric utterance and attacking the moral exclusivity of rationalist 'science,' Klein reveals here as well the characterizing features of his own style: alliteration, arcane allusion, balanced parallel phrasing. Seen simply as a resistance to the plain speech movement, such technical devices might easily be put aside as signs of an intellect that is wilfully resistant to reality. Yet it is important to remember that even for Callaghan, plain speech was as often a way to parable as to empirical documentation, and parable a way to a humane sympathy that transcended the moment. The understanding that a story generates may take place in a momentary 'flash,' yet the controlling author so constitutes this movement that it conveys the shape if not the substance of the interlocking events of an implied narrative. There is always a story behind the story: the newsreporter's dream. For Klein that was precisely the point: reality for him lay not just in people's daily political experience but also in the relevance to that experience of the political and religious traditions in which they were rooted. Parable and metaphor, transcending the present moment, became technical devices by which to encompass present experience in a larger context, to give cultural resonance to the here and now. And the 'culture' he envisioned had to be broadly enough conceived to accept the presence of Jewish and Catholic mysticism as easily as it could rest on literalist, rationalist, pragmatic, or Protestant fundamentals.

Most of the early stories Klein wrote, those he published in *The Judaean* and *The Canadian Jewish Chronicle* in the 1930s, furnish ready examples of the parable form. Theological by impulse, allusive by nature, anecdotal by structure, they expound points of moral doctrine in a contemporary political context and against a literary background that includes both Sholom Aleichem and James Joyce.[126] A story like 'Friends, Romans, Hungrymen' (printed in *New Frontier* in 1936) most clearly shows how Klein could adapt parable, with a bitter ironic indignation, to attack Canadian social policy in the 1930s. The opening, for example, undercuts the potential romance of the language of legend by mixing a contemporary idiom with the traditional form:

So one day, way back in the time of the fairytales, the boss he called me into his cave and said that he was sorry but he was going to lay me off. He said it nicely, like an ogre elocuting fee-fi-fo-fum. He grabbed me, wrapped me up in a little package, and laid me down upon a dusty shelf. Then he stuck out a long tongue, licked the gluey side of a strip of paper, pasted it on me and read it over: Unemployed.[127].

The story goes on to indict God (who recommends a 'swell flophouse'),[128] employers (who offer only impractical solutions and empty advice), and all other middle class authorities (who eat too well to understand deprivation) before it comes to the moral paradox that lies at its sociocultural heart; when the unemployed narrator contemplates suicide, he is chastized for his *sinfulness* and not allowed to act *because he belongs to the state* – yet all along it has been possession of person that has proved so problematic. The question is: who owns the Self? And who owns the State? And where does the real immorality lie? For the artist the question goes further: what freedom does the artist have in his own medium, what freedom to shape language to his own purposes, and what freedom from the external imposition of critical and cultural norms?

Klein's finest story takes up this latter question at length. Written probably in 1955 (the manuscript is dated January 1956), 'The Bells of Sobor Spasitula' was not published until M.W. Steinberg edited the collected *Short Stories* in 1983; the story concerns a Russian émigré's memory of a world rich in tradition and creativity, a world rich in people, rich in friends, yet a world from which he is banished both in place and by time and to which he now has access only in the rhythms of recollection. Technically, it is this question of rhythm which is important; the prose moves in pulses, accommodating a memory that responds to the mnemonics of sound, then in repeated peals reclaims the past and the central story of the narrator's friend Terpetoff, a musician who composes for love of music rather than for service to a political creed, whose musical rebellion leads to his death, to his politically controlled eclipse, and to this story. Terpetoff's creative impulse is rooted in Russian Orthodox ritual, his theory of composition clear from a passage that describes one performance:

Though Terpetoff had designated his work by a mere number (again his predilection for the abstract), the melodies of which it was composed were so identifiable, so pregnant with association, that their sequence alone did in fact seem to tell a story ...

The music, in other words, evokes association just as the method of Klein's own story does: 'scoreless and unplayed,' the narrator asks, 'how may its essence be communicated?' Only through words, themselves dependent on the reader's sensitivity to sound, to voice:

Whether the same verbal associations had run also through the composer's mind, Terpetoff would not say. Since Terpetoff did not compose in language but in rhythms, alternations, patterns, it did not matter, for they were either these very associations, or others akin to them that whispered behind his ear-drums. Whatever they were specifically, they were in general pattern an amalgam of the earthy and the heavenly and opened for me yet another window onto my friend's temperament.

Yet it is neither personal temperament nor a question of soul which the revolutionary state requires his art to address, and Terpetoff rebels: '"Is this ... your idea of cultural freedom? ... Do you think it compatible with civilized notions concerning the dignity of art that the composer should be compelled to recant his staff-notation ... simply because a politician wants to listen to music politically?"'[129] In outline a plea for the integrity of art, Klein's story is more besides: not without its own political point in the narrow, McCarthy-minded context of 1950s attitudes, but also an illustrative inquiry into the process of fiction itself. Like several other writers of the time, Klein was torn between his recognition of political fact and his realization that the very language that mind and soul responded to was a territory apart. Fabricating language was therefore to be comprehended as a dangerous act for the creator; entering artifice, he sought illumination, but at the risk of permanent exile in the world of words.

In the work of Mavis Gallant and Malcolm Lowry, we see the two impulses of Klein's world, the political and the linguistic, joining and dividing in other ways again. Gallant's hundred or so stories, only some of which have been editorially arranged into her five collections: *The Other Paris* (1956), *My Heart is Broken* (1964: called *An Unmarried Man's Summer* in the British edition), *The Pegnitz Junction* (1973), *From the Fifteenth District* (1979). and *Home Truths* (1981) — attach themselves firmly to both the world of history and the world of the imagination. Rooted in observed behaviour, they take shape as stories, as structures of words on the page. The stories Lowry designed as *Hear Us O Lord from Heaven Thy Dwelling-Place* (posthumously published in 1961) are by contrast rooted in literary allusion and personal experience, and take shape on the page as histories of the imagination, as documentary journals of the mind's peregrinations into self.

The effects of each narrative choice carry the reader in the reverse direction: through Gallant's careful artifice, we approach her inquiry into political modality, and through Lowry's use of documentary, we approach the personal psychology that led him to see the world by imposing the single person, the multiple self, upon it. Gallant stretches the illusion of realism not in order to mirror the empirical world but in order to probe the attitudinal fluctuations which result in political choices, or, broadly speaking, political action. Each of her stories is a separate phenomenon, even though — in the six Linnet Muir stories in *Home Truths* or in the German stories of *The Pegnitz Junction*, for example — there is occasionally a deliberate overlap of character, setting, or theme; and within each story, the text asks us to fasten on the sequence of modal changes that directs a moment of decision. In Lowry, by contrast, the interest is not in the separate stories, but in the links between them and in the enlarging effects of simultaneity. While the stories of *Hear Us O Lord* connect with each other in a sequence, it is a sequence of artifice rather than of time; each subsequent story echoes the *form* of what has gone before, ramifying its implications, until the whole book coalesces in the final story,'The Forest Path to the Spring,' about the harmonious cycles of existence in which all things — including the unnamed narrator of this story, the multiple and separate narrators of the other stories, many of whom possess the same name (Sigbjørn Wilderness), and the author himself — can find place and meaning.

While it is possible in this way to say that Lowry's stories are 'about' such subjects as natural harmony, psychological wilderness, exile, separation, and love — and equally possible to say that they are 'about' the language that enacts such themes, about the literary forms in which the themes become art — it is less productive to fasten on theme as the central core of Gallant's stories. Many of her stories do begin and end by probing the nature of exile, but the exile itself is not the key issue; the probing is. Lowry's interest is in pattern, Gallant's in manner, and the difference in focus affects the stylistic structure each writer devises. Lowry writes in names, in the patterns of nominal signs and the adjectives that colour them; Gallant writes through verbal aspect. Consider, for example, sections from the openings of six of Lowry's stories:

93 Canada: Story and History

It was a day of spindrift and blowing sea-foam, with black clouds presaging rain driven over the mountains from the sea by a wild March wind. ('The Bravest Boat')

This is the engine of the *Diderot*: the canon repeated endlessly ... ('Through the Panama')

Sigbjørn Wilderness, an American writer in Rome on a Guggenheim Fellowship, paused on the steps above the flower stall and wrote ... in a black notebook ... ('Strange Comfort Afforded by the Profession')

It was the early afternoon of a brilliantly sunny day in Rome, a young blue midsummer moon tilted down over the Borghese Gardens ... ('Elephant and Colosseum')

In thunder, at noon, in a leaden twilight ... ('Present Estate of Pompeii')

It was a warm, still, sunless day in mid-August. ('Gin and Goldenrod')[130]

The stories begin in symbolic names, colours, landscapes, weather conditions – each moment caught suspended before it continues in the cyclical round that the stories, by repetition, build into a paradigm of human life. But compare these openings with the beginning of one of Gallant's finest stories, 'The Moslem Wife':

In the south of France, in the business room of a hotel quite near to the house where Katherine Mansfield (whom no one in this hotel had ever heard of) was writing 'The Daughters of the Late Colonel,' Netta Asher's father announced that there would never be a man-made catastrophe in Europe again. The dead of that recent war, the doomed nonsense of the Russian Bolsheviks had finally knocked sense into European heads. What people wanted now was to get on with life. When he said 'life,' he meant its commercial business.[130]

Part of the effectiveness of this paragraph derives from its irony, an irony which derives at once from the reader's knowledge of history (the fact that World War I did not end all wars) and from the implied disparity between the 'life' of business and the 'life' of art (here unheard-of, and in any case 'about' the death of the late colonel and the inability of his two daughters to break free of his influence). These are ironies of perspective, reinforced by the two verbal sequences that the paragraph contains:

The first verbal movement declares the paradoxical simultaneity between the unheard but active process of art and the overheard but ineffectual prediction of stasis; the second movement reveals that Netta's father's dream of the present is couched in verbs of the past. It is this subtlety of modal relationship at which Gallant excels; moreover, the forms of English verbal aspect she uses here reinforce the way in which we come to see Netta's predicament in the story that follows. Netta enters marriage passively, more as a business arrangement than anything else, but discovers life most tellingly during the time she is trapped by World War II in what is now her (and was once her father's) hotel; ultimately, however, she cannot articulate this independent sense of her life, and failing to find words for her understanding, she surrenders her future to what she recognizes is her husband's invalid but articulate memory of wartime and pre-war events. The reinvented past thus becomes the model for the post-war present, limiting life and so enclosing the imagination; not just coincidentally it also leaves art to spell out the actual sequence of relationships and wait to be heard.

With Gallant we once again see a writer declaring that the words in which stories are told are suspect, and yet writing stories, devising a technique to connect the careful reader with the actual experiences that generate history. The reader works with a Gallant text, deliberately and intellectually rearranging perceptions to stay with those of the characters, whereas the reader receives a Lowry text, for all its careful intellectual contrivance, more as a passionate revelation of faith in an order larger than that which perception alone allows us to see. It is as though the two writers stand on two sides of a temporal and technical argument, like the Mennonite historian and the documentary film-maker who talk at one point to the narrator of Robert Kroetsch's 1983 novel *Alibi*; the one 'knew what history is,' while the other was 'forever interrupting with her theories of how to make a realistic film, a documentary that is at the same time art. "Distort," she said. Selection is distortion, and distortion breaks the truth into visibility. The historian and I disputed, agreed, talked about the design that is not created but, rather, creates us ... '[132] Lowry, in particular, sought to reveal the design that he felt himself to be written by, yet clearly both he and Gallant are selective arrangers of detail and hence creators of 'visibility.' And while Gallant more successfully mastered the artful craft of shaping the individual short story, it was Lowry, pressured by his sense of fragmentation and his need for a greater design, who theorized about a way to reconcile the two impulses – seeking a book-length form, or even a multi-book form, which would unite the passion of the fragment with the composure that order promises.

As early as 1940, he wrote to the Irish writer James Stern that he thought it possible to compose a satisfactory work of art by the simple process of writing a series of good short stories, complete in themselves, with the same characters, interrelated, correlated, good if held up to the light, watertight if held upside down, but full of effects and dissonances that are impossible in a short story, but nevertheless having its purity of form ...

He did not, he added, mean the sort of book written by Fearing or Prokosch,

in which the preoccupation with form vitiates the substance, that is by a writer whose inability to find a satisfactory form for his poems drives him to find an outlet for it in a novel. No. The thing that I mean can only be done by a good short-story writer, who is generally the better kind of poet, the one who only does not write poetry because life does not frame itself kindly for him in iambic pentametres and to whom disjunct experimental forms are abhorrent ...

He wanted to write 'something that is bald and winnowed, like Sibelius, and that makes an odd but splendid din, like Bix Beiderbecke.'[133] One can see him here arguing both sides to the middle somewhat, claiming to be truly poetic but not merely poetic, claiming to write free from restricting form yet to write in form free of experimental disjunction. But as he came to write the stories for *Hear Us O Lord*, and to arrange them, his theory began to take shape. When he could sell none of the separate stories either in Canada, where in 1950 he felt there was no story market at all, or in New York, he complained; but by deliberately arranging the stories, he discovered (as he wrote in 1952 to Albert Erskine, his editor at Reynal and Hitchcock), that '*Hear Us* ... seems to be shaping up less like an ordinary book of tales than a sort of novel of an odd aeolian kind ...i.e., it is more interrelated than it looks.'[134] Such a form was not as new with him as he perhaps liked to think, and certainly it was not new within Canada, making his view of the history of Canadian literature in some ways as European as his claim on Canadian wilderness; but what he did with the form in Canada altered the integrated story sequence from a pattern that based its unity on recurring characters (as in Haliburton and Leacock, and to some degree, Scott) or on a consistent setting and tone (as in Scott, Duncan, Leacock, and Knister), into one which used the structures and rhythms of language itself as its unifying device, with an eye on conveying a faith in the further unity that was possible in the worlds of society and spirit. Such a form was to have its counterparts in poem sequences as well; and even in the arena of literary commentary, Northrop Frye's *Anatomy of Criticism* (1957) was to resurrect the *anatomy* form from the eighteenth century in order to claim the intellectual unity of a series of related inquiries into the variant shapes of a literary theme. But in the 1960s and 1970s there also emerged a score of talented story writers who adapted the interrupted sequential form to their own ends, largely political or moral; among these were Margaret Laurence, Jack Hodgins, George Elliott, Alice Munro, Hugh Hood, Dave Godfrey, and Clark Blaise.

The new wave of cultural nationalism that surged through the 1960s was partly responsible for the increased visibility of Canadian writers in the community; the *Massey Report* had recommended greater support for the arts, the Canada Council (established in 1958) began to furnish such support, new journals came into existence to pay attention to Canadian writers (*Canadian Literature, Prism, Liberté, Canadian Fiction Magazine, Journal of Canadian Fiction, Capilano Review, Room of One's Own, Exile*, and many others), school and university courses in Canadian writing became more widespread, bookstores began to stock Canadian books, new legislation assisted the distribution of Canadian books, and Canadian writers and writing began to blossom on some sort of national scale. The country teemed with anthologies, for almost any subject and every market (in 1972 Alec Lucas claimed that the anthology itself almost constituted the national genre);[135] there were anthologies of region and theme, of West Coast and Arctic stories, Maritime and Toronto stories, of stories in translation and stories from Quebec, of Mounted Police stories, Alberta stories, ghost stories, and Wendigo stories, anthologies of comedy and adventure, of folk-tale and fantasy, of surrealists and magic realists, myths of place that governed the national consciousness, collages, national treasures, and experiments in language and abstract form.

These events, political and literary, did not mean that a national literature had somehow been born; but for a generation of writers whose stories began to be noticed in the 1960s and 1970s, political viability and linguistic vitality became related ideas: loss of the one invoked constraints on the other, exhaustion of the one meant exhaustion of the other – and the possibility of an imaginative regeneration of the one suggested at least the possibility of innovation in the other. If there was no agreement on the nature of either a definitive nationality or a viable form of verbal experimentation, this fact, too, was characteristic of the cultural flux. There were some who denied the existence of Canadian culture; there were others who claimed it existed only to so narrowly define it as to leave out most Canadians or so widely define it as to include everyone else. But the multiplicity was the common denominator: multiculturalism, bilingualism, regionalism – all such isms (even separatism) were asserting the need to accept variation. The society was polymorphic, yet growing a recognizable tradition. And the fiction that took the culture as at least one level of its subject – that is to say, some fiction, not all fiction – sought a generic method for expressing the shifting multiple set. The art of fragmentation came into its own.

97   Canada: Story and History

A key phrase remains 'a recognizable tradition.' Clearly for many people such recognition was difficult. What with a further increase in immigration during the 1950s and 1960s (hence the arrival – often of English speakers – with none the less foreign expectations of art and social order), as well as the perpetuation among the native-born of attitudes schooled in a lingering colonialism, it was inevitable that there would be impediments to appreciation. The impulse to overclaim stature and quality ran headlong into the failure to see anything at all – or at least to see the value in much of what was happening, and to appreciate that value can derive in some degree from social insight just as it can derive from moral function or psychological credibility or verbal dexterity. Social insight was not to be taken as equivalent to descriptive empirical realism. To share the insight, however, required some sensitivity to the society; and to be sensitive to the society meant having some feeling for its current variety, for the slow growth of its traditions, and for its cumulative adaptation of language to the stories it had to tell.

It is paradoxical that just at the time so many able writers were embracing the form, the short story should constitute a critical problem, but that appears to have been what happened. Some anthologists made of the short story a kind of tour guide of Canadian regions, emphasizing its ability to record empirical scene; some writers declared it was a territory to be claimed by voice, its reality inhering in the associations of sound and rhythm; most critics tended to ignore or underestimate it. Hugo McPherson, for example, wrote in Carl Klinck's *Literary History of Canada* in 1965 that

> the record of the short story is good, but its importance in Canadian expression is declining ... [Despite the fifty volumes published since 1940] the short story has lost much of its prestige; a generation ago it was the recognized proving-ground for aspiring novelists ... in 1960 it still flourishes in small reviews and student literary magazines, but the majority of writers abandon it after their apprentice years.[136]

(The passage was expunged from the 1976 revision, and reference made instead to the short story's resurgence.) The notion that the short story was an apprentice form – that mature prose writers wrote only novels – was a common misapprehension, born of the short story's length, its seeming simplicity, its comparatively recent generic development, and the fact that the novel tradition was so much stronger than the short story tradition in England. In some sense, Canadian writers, by claiming the different form, were claiming their own separateness (lacking a tradition for the form, they had to grow one); but lacking a received context within which to weigh authors' cumulative effort and accomplishment, critics tended to weigh instead their failure to do something else – to shape the language of their literature to other people's expectations, for example, under the impression that foreign traditions were somehow universal.

This uncertainty about standards is one of the reasons the history of the anthology is so important a part of the history of short story criticism in Canada; the anthology was one context that an editor-critic could individually establish, a kind of open ground within which a tradition could be arranged or a set of critical principles grow. It would not be definitive; each would in turn contribute to the cumulative understanding of the form. Yet saying this, we have also to balance the sense of internal cultural growth with an acknowledgment that neither story-writing nor anthology-making takes place in isolation from foreign models. Influence abounds, and the stimuli to growth can come from anywhere. The distinctiveness of what Canadians do – as Richard Bailey points out about Canadian English itself[137] – lies not in a set of unique features (though there may be some) but in a combination of tendencies: it is a distinctiveness of mix, and therefore less easy to categorize and identify. But 'real.' There are those who will refuse to acknowledge the tangible effects of an externally influenced cultural history upon the present or who will be insufficiently sensitive to Canada's culture to recognize its individuality; repeatedly they will mistake the constantly shifting balance of the mix for a set of random borrowings without cultural resonance or antecedent or substance. They will be wrong.

Yet it has almost become a custom to pretend that the past does not exist or that, if it does, it bears no relation with the present. When John Metcalf, in the midst of 'Editing the Best,' which is one of the sharpest and most insightful commentaries on recent short fiction, musters a rhetorical attack on the 'revisionist attempt to create an indigenous literary tradition'[138] because, he says, such efforts distort the reality of the past and damage the way we read the present, his statement does not radically depart from Canadian habit; indeed, he reiterates both Raymond Knister ('There has been no national Burbank to create a Canadian subspecies of the short story ... It emerged ... in a spirited emulation ... or a shallow imitativeness ... of foreign models') and Robert Weaver ('There have been so few collections of Canadian short stories that there is no tradition which an editor is required either to follow or to explain away').[139]

The differences derive from contemporaneity and from what contemporaneity says about stylistic quality: Knister finds it in Scott and Callaghan, Weaver in Garner and Gallant, Metcalf in Hood and Munro. Among other things, literary practice does reflect shifts in taste and judgment. But if influences come from outside – Callaghan being affected by Anderson, Margaret Laurence by Chinua Achebe, Metcalf by Anthony Powell, not to mention the impact on others of Sir Walter Scott, Charles Dickens, Gabriel

García Márquez, Germaine Greer, and Richard Brautigan – they also come from within. Laurence has acknowledged her debt to the female pioneer journal writers like Catharine Parr Traill; Kreisel has acknowledged the impact of Klein; and Hugh Hood, commenting on his own frame of reference, epitomizes what is important about this question; asked which Canadian writers have influenced him, he replies: 'there are two Canadian writers who have had some degree of influence on me ... Stephen Leacock, in relation to *Around the Mountain*; and ... Morley Callaghan ... [for talks] about realism ... Grace, and ... the novel form ... But I wouldn't say that I was influenced by Leacock or Callaghan as an artist. I don't think they're good enough arists.'[140] He means as a conscious intellectual designer of form. Then later in the same interview he specifies further his connection with Leacock (and through him to Turgenev's *A Sportsman's Sketches*):

I was asked to speak about *Around the Mountain* at McGill and I was asked by one of the students why these stories had this tentative and unfinished quality so that your imagination could wander off along the lines into an undefined space. I said, 'It's a sketch book,' and then talked for a while about this form we're talking about. It has a good deal in common with what used to be called travel sketches. Leacock explicitly calls his book *Sunshine Sketches of a Little Town*, and he's thinking of that water-colour or pencil portfolio that an amateur artist might have collected – perhaps a woman artist – in the 80s. The characteristics of these are an agreeable tenuousness, an endearing tentative quality. They don't have the whomp, whomp, whomp, full close, of a novel. For example, I think of Delius, or Vaughan Williams, or writers for the orchestra of that kind, who would produce a work in an open form like this, a pastoral idyll perhaps, that doesn't have the rounded and formal finality of a symphony. Or, again, of water-colour or sketch works where the lines are done deliberately with haste and with a hit-or-miss accuracy because accuracy is not what is aimed at. Evocation is what is aimed at – evocation in the breast of a reader, of agreeable feelings.[141]

To acknowledge the past is not necessarily to be bound by it or to wish to repeat it; it is to recognize the continuing shaping of the set of tendencies which supplies a context for composition in the present. In this way traditions exist *for* the present, *in* the present – not as a form of enclosing ritual to be forever re-enacted, but as the active winnowing of the accumulating heritage. In this sense traditions also exist only in retrospect; they are the mind's acknowledgment of connection and continuity all the while the pen is spelling out disparities and differences in the present and celebrating the possibility of literary distinction.

Continuity / discontinuity: connection / fragmentation. Once again we return to the simultaneity of these impulses and to the way in which they bear upon both social attitude and literary form. One of the characteristic features of the critical stances that Metcalf, Weaver, and Knister take in attempting to come to terms with the short story in Canada is the practice of defining by negative exclusion: 'there has been no X and therefore Y' (one might compare this structure with a recurrent short story opening: 'It was *not until after* he arrived home' [Knister], 'There was a house *on the outskirts*' [Scott], 'It was a day of spin*drift*' [Lowry], 'His mother was *warmth and coolness*' [Laurence] – all of which convey only the illusion of permanence and solidity, and imply a moment of change at hand). Assertion appears to come with negation, not necessarily as a reaction against it but somehow in accompaniment, as though recognition required the presence of an alternative possibility. It is the sort of notion Stephen Scobie refers to as 'alterity' – otherness – in his comments on the nature of documentary form.[142] And it is a recurrent cultural motif, surfacing everywhere, as in Ken Dryden's comments on hockey in his 1983 book *The Game*:

Yesterday, I did an interview with a Philadelphia journalist. After some minutes, he shook his head and told me I was different from other athletes ... 'How do you relate to these guys?' he whispered ... I think it took me so long to want to be part of the team because I was afraid of a team. Afraid of always having to do what a team does; afraid of losing my own right to be different. Then I realized I wasn't very different at all. The Philadelphia journalist didn't understand.[143]

Haliburton brings the 'Other' figure in from outside, in the form of the Yankee pedlar; Moodie is herself the outsider, recognizing the foreignness of wilderness; D.C. Scott investigates the 'otherness' of French-speaking Quebec; Margaret Atwood's fabular 'true stories' – her term rife with ambivalence – find unfamiliarity in the femaleness her characters want to claim and familiarity in the (male?) violence they want to spurn; Rudy Wiebe's stories (particularly in his splendid meditation on art and history, 'Where Is the Voice Coming From?') probe simultaneously the distance of the Mennonite artist from his Cree subjects, and the difference between any artist's ability to evoke the truth of what seems to be reality and a coldly objective evaluation of what seem to be empirical facts. In the stories of Margaret Laurence, set variously in Canada and West Africa, the 'other's' presence becomes a shaping guide to the self in formal as well as thematic ways. In her early stories the author delineates an Africa to which she comes to realize she does not belong; but the observations and discoveries are not without function: they lead her back to her homeland, with a heightened appreciation for its own stories, and also with an ear more finely tuned to the cultural force of the voices of story-telling.

Laurence's autobiography *The Prophet's Camel Bell* (1963; called *New Wind in a Dry Land* in its American edition, 1964) spells out the contrast between her expectations on going to Africa and her discoveries while there. In the beginning all seemed exotic, herself the norm travelling through a world she found colourful and strange; but the longer she stayed, the more she found herself to be the strangest discovery, a feeling to which her subsequent readings in O. Mannoni's *Prospero and Caliban* gave intellectual substance.[144] She learned to distinguish between an implicitly imperial attitude (presuming a fixed hierarchy as a normative distinction between cultures) and an egalitarian one (recognizing self as other and allowing contact with the other to modify the self). Where the autobiography examines the series of experiences that leads to this change in her own attitudes, the stories of *The Tomorrow-Tamer and Other Stories* (1963) project such discovery into the alienated lives of Africans and Europeans in Africa: the English teacher in 'The Rain Child,' the new generation trickster in 'The Pure Diamond Man,' the English architect, the American missionary, and the African artist in 'The Merchant of Heaven.'[145] Repeatedly Laurence draws a contrast between those who possess the language of the place and those who must rely on translation, and repeatedly this distinction operates not simply as a thematic metaphor (language as an indicator of alienation) but as a way through the actual literary technique of exemplifying a people's control – or loss of control – over its own mode of cultural expression.

A key distinction is that between story and speech. Within traditional African culture, it was speech that carried power; a story told would enact what it said, whereas a story in print was powerless. But the culture over time surrendered some of those beliefs in favour of others, and transferred power in different ways to systems initially foreign. Laurence's stories frequently waver between *documenting* such change (using a written mode) and *enacting* the changes through the shifts of oral (if recorded) speech – ambivalence of form itself conveying her cultural perspective and her distance from Africa. Within the stories characters often find themselves on the point of effective speech; but opting for silence or withdrawal instead, they render themselves politically impotent, or they adopt forms of speech which have lost their effectiveness and so reveal their culture's susceptibility to manipulation. It was this appreciation of the old power of voice to evoke the ancestors – the source of authority and authenticity within the culture – that Laurence came to understand in Africa, and took with her back to Canada. But within Canada, her own experience – contemporary, female, prairie – had still to declare its voice and place its heritage. To do so it had to find an appropriate form.

The stories of *The Tomorrow-Tamer* are individually separate, despite their thematic overlap, and individually experimental in that they try out separate tale-telling strategies (trickster tale, internal tale, parable, memoir). By contrast, the eight stories in *A Bird in the House* (1970) are all part of Laurence's 'Manawaka' series, which sees western Canadian history anew through the eyes of its women, and tells its cumulative story through their voices. But only one, 'Horses of the Night,' can stand satisfactorily alone; the rest require their surrounding stories, so that the real narrative 'unit' in this case is the fragmented whole. And the fragmentation, as much as the arranged sequence and cumulative unity, is an integral route to the effect desired. The heritage the author is trying to articulate, the narrator to claim, is not the product of a constant development; it was broken, erratic, silenced, and is retrieved now only in waves of narrative memory. The book's form thus serves as a modal process by which the local 'ancestors' – characters and history – acquire effective voices: effective in that the act of reading establishes a living connection between present and past, giving access to heritage through narrative without falsifying experience through an orderly rhetoric.

A dozen or more other substantial works of fiction follow in Laurence's wake, marked by similar concerns for region, person, and story if not directly influenced by her particular place or narrative style. Though Audrey Thomas, for example, made stylistic use of fragmentation and the rhythmic cycles of nature – as in 'The More Little Mummy in the World' or 'Natural History' – her several story collections from *Ten Green Bottles* (1967) to *Real Mothers* (1981) display much more concern for the rhetorical independence of each story; the fragmentation takes place internally rather than as part of a book-length strategy. But with Gertrude Story's *The Way to Always Dance* (1983) and Elizabeth Brewster's *A House Full of Women* (1983), the narrative unit is again the book, shaped in glimpses, and the basic subject is again the interrupted lives of women. For Dave Godfrey, it was Laurence's inherently political account of the connection between region, nation, and language which proved attractive, and which affected the writing of *Death Goes Better with Coca-Cola* (1967; revised 1973) and *The New Ancestors* (1970).[146] Other writers made the interrupted sequence a means of articulating the multiple voice of a region, as David Adams Richards does sombrely with the Miramichi in *Dancers at Night* (1978) or as Jack Hodgins does comically with northern Vancouver Island, first with the loose anatomy of a society in the 'Selected Stories' of *Spit Delaney's Island* (1976) and then with the more structured, more preceptive, and less dramatized account of family and authorship, *The Barclay Family Theatre* (1981).

Still other writers – Alden Nowlan with *Various Persons Named Kevin O'Brien* (1973), Alice Munro with *Lives of Girls and Women* (1971), and Rudy Wiebe with *The Blue Mountains of China* (1970) – transformed the broken fragments into a recognizable novel, a unit in which the segments are not separable at all. In Nowlan's hands, the form became a *Bildungsroman*; in Wiebe's it became a means by which to explore the differences between oral and written history and the different processes by which values are handed from generation to generation, to be preserved, refashioned, discarded, or resurrected; in Munro's it became an anatomy of the faithfulness of memory, hence an imaginative record of growing up and a documentary history of the growth of the artistic imagination. For all of these writers narrative is important; even with the fragment, each is determined to tell a good story. But with a writer like Munro, or like George Elliott in *The Kissing Man* (1963), something else is happening too; the narrative of events is coloured by the perceptual imagination with which it is twinned, with the result that the more important narrative is implied, happening less at the level of plot than at that of emotional change. With Elliott's characters – the adolescent Froody most of all – the change takes place in a kind of Joycean epiphany, a dimly understood illumination of a moment's duration and a lifetime's grace; but with Munro, change occurs at a more evolutionary pace, to be absorbed in meditation.

Perhaps for this reason, it is the endings of Munro's stories which exert such a fascination. The beginnings are always deeply engrained with ambiguous possibility – the reader is induced to think one way, then to realize another; and critics have repeatedly shown how Munro uses the oxymoron to structure the sometimes enfranchising, sometimes debilitating simultaneities in her characters' lives[147] – but the endings brood over the contradictions that the narrator and reader realize. Given Clark Blaise's distinction between endings that lead the reader back into the story and those that lead away, Munro's work belongs to the former group; the latter – either by way of rhetorical flourish (as characteristically in Laurence's endings) or a metafictional code (as in Leon Rooke's endings) – remind the reader of the story's artifice, hence of the reader's separateness from the characters. But, says Blaise, in stories of the former kind, the ending is 'sunk deep in the story's texture,' forcing 'the reader to dig up the whole story in order to resolve its tensions ...' Such endings

hit a glancing blow at the reader, but generally ignore him. By approximating the most casual of voices, they manage ... to sound most urgent. By ignoring us, they speak to us directly. What remains unresolved and undisclosed becomes inviting and forbidding. They offer us no way out of their bland circularity; thus, they linger with us.[148]

Itself full of paradox and oxymorons, this passage is a good guide to Blaise's own stories as well, like the terrifying 'Eyes' or the brutally ironic 'A Class of New Canadians,' two works from his tri-sectioned *A North American Education* (1973). But to look at representative endings from Munro's several collections is to realize how her stories, in addition, reiterate the practice of locating direction by negative pattern; for example:

It was not Adelaide calling; it was Lois. 'Thanks for the Ride,' from *Dance of The Happy Shades*, 1968)

He might have meant to talk to me, to ask me to have coffee, or a drink, with him, but he respected my unhappiness as he always does; he respected the pretense that I was not unhappy but preoccupied, burdened with these test papers; he left me alone to get over it. ('Material,' from *Something I've Been Meaning to Tell You*, 1974)

She had removed herself, and spent most of her time sitting in a corner of her crib, looking crafty and disagreeable, not answering anybody, though she occasionally showed her feelings by biting a nurse. ('Royal Beatings,' from *Who Do You Think You Are?*, 1978; the book is called *The Beggar Maid* in the U.S. and British editions)

Life is. Wait. But a. Now, wait. Dream. ('Chaddeleys and Flemings. 1. Connection,' from *The Moons of Jupiter*, 1983)

What the most recent of these excerpts epitomizes is the degree to which all of Munro's work depends on the rhythm of glimpsing significance as much as on the details observed; the details are always accurate – precisely caught in metaphor or precisely chosen to distil the topical quality of a time, a place, a character – but it is the rhythm of expression (the rhythm of observation) that carries them, in the process transforming Munro's world from one of simple mimetic realism into one that might more accurately be called mimetic impressionism. It is not just that the interruptions to strict sequence (producing verbal rhythm) have their analogue in a fractured history and fragmented memory, but that the persistent rhythms induce a visceral sense of the simultaneity of disruption and connection. The interrupted close of 'Connection' is a case in point: the effect of the interruptions here is to sustain ('Now, wait') both a song and a lingering hold on memory, and through memory to allow the narrator to claim a connection with her family even while she wants her freedom from it. As readers we are fascinated by the separate characters of Munro's other stories. But we come to appreciate the Munro world by submitting to the effect of its rhetorical method. The unity of Munro's collections comes less from recurrent characters and the repeated rural Ontario setting (the stories of Flo and Rose in *Who Do You Think You Are?* notwithstanding), but from their structure. The rhythms of discourse allow the reader to make connections among the stories that the stories would not seem thematically always to sustain. In this way the author invites the reader inside the artifice of story-making, inside the emotional artifice of the imagination – not to be divorced from the world (the empirical details retain the connection with it) but to recognize at once the substantive nature of language and the purely approximate relation between words and experience upon which literature must rely.

In this context, Kent Thompson's comments on his own fiction are apropos:

the starting point is essentially negative. I know only what I do *not* want, I do not want the reader of my stories to clap his hands and say, 'I see the point.' I do not want the intellectual progress toward an epiphany.

What do I want then? I think I want to control an emotional experience. That is, I want to send the reader through a set of circumstances which will alter the reader's emotional awareness. I not want to 'change the reader's mind.' I want to 'change his emotions.' (I am well aware that this might be a Romantic – and false – dichotomy.) In other words, I want to induce an emotional attitude, and to do this I try to take the reader through a number of attitudes and circumstances. The total accumulation of these experiences is to be the effect of the short story. Inevitably, I think, my way of writing a short story throws the emphasis of the short story away from the dramatic point or the intellectual insight and onto the immediate *experiencing* of the character.[149]

He goes on to talk of pacing, syntax, diction, rhythm (a substitute, he says, for dramatic structure) – and of the impulse to write, which transcends all of these by translating conversation, fragments of phrasing, memories, and overheard encounters into imagined attitudes. Often for the writer this process has little to do with theory ('the thinking about the short story') and much to do with practice ('the doing of it').[150] But for critical readers of a story of this kind, the 'doing of it' is of necessity a collaborative venture. Induced to appreciate some emotional nuance, such readers also become creators, or co-creators – with this difference: that they seek not only to enjoy the aesthetic experience but also to understand what allowed it to happen. Hence criticism becomes pedagogical, fastening on the empirical elements in the structure (diction, rhythm), on the more nebulous question of response (the reasons that rhythms of different kinds can induce, in a given language and culture, incantatory or soothing or disrupting effects), and on systems of interpretation which appear to give the reader an articulate way of expressing this response.

But as John Metcalf points out in his 1980 anthology *New Worlds*, the desire to '*feel and see more*' which leads to analytic techniques of reading too often turns in practice into a scramble for a 'hidden meaning,' as though a story were a fortune cookie with a secret message inside, waiting for some initiate to announce it.[150] There is a difference, in other words, between *hidden meaning* (implicitly bad, the gimmick of gamesmanship) and *held meaning* (implicitly good, the quality that gives substance to verbal arrangements). But on the question of how a story's words can best be made to hold meaning – and indeed, on the question of what kind of 'meaning' a story can under any conditions convey – there is less agreement among contemporary critics and writers. And the fact of their disagreement in theory has led to some of the sharpest disparities in short story practice that the history of the genre in Canada has seen.

Essentially the distinction is that between writers who take their stories from the world of empirical experience and by some means ultimately redirect their readers' attention back to that world (ie, 'modernists,' in some sense of that loose word) and writers who direct their readers' attention to the sheer artifice of their own arrangements of verbal and visual signs (ie, 'fantasists' or 'postmodernists,' to various degrees). Among 'world-directed' writers of the 1970s and 1980s one might place Edna Alford, David Arnason, Nancy Bauer, Neil Bissoondath, Jean-Guy Carrier, Ann Copeland, Barry Dempster, Marian Engel, Margaret Gibson Gilboord, Kristjana Gunnars, Basil Johnston, Philip Kreiner, Oonah McFee, Alistair MacLeod, Ken Mitchell, Bill Schermbrucker, W.D. Valgardson, Guy Vanderhaeghe, and David Watmough. 'Sign-directed' writers would include Sandra Birdsell, Michael Bullock, Virgil Burnett, David Donnell, Brian Fawcett, Keath Fraser, Raymond Fraser, Lawrence Garber, Stephen Guppy, Terrence Heath, Ann Rosenberg, Andreas Schroeder, Ray Smith, Martin Vaughn-James, Sean Virgo, Sheila Watson, J. Michael Yates, and David Young. But of course such a simple dualism is misleading. The narrative words of world and time do not divide so easily from the constitutive words of space and sign. Three members of the Montreal Story-Teller Group of the 1970s (Blaise, Hood, Metcalf) find themselves on one side of the imaginary line and two others (Raymond Fraser, Ray Smith) on the other, and this despite the fact that Hood and Blaise have recurrently written in emulation of Smith and Fraser. An individual work like Dave Godfrey's *Dark Must Yield* (1978). moreover, with its internal tripartite division into 'Tales,' 'Realities,' and 'Fables and Inputs,' deliberately mediates between such formal extremes, and constitutes (in an age as deliberate in its desire to see what form will do as was the nineteenth century) a new kind of *Rahmenerzählung*, serving aesthetic as well as psychological and political ends.

One might even conceive of some in-between category to contain such disparate figures as Godfrey, George McWhirter, Atwood, Blaise, Hodgins, Hood, Michael Ondaatje, and Thomas, all of whom are writers as conscious of the shape of words as of the shape of the world outside themselves. At times the divisions blur. For Gwendolyn MacEwen in *Noman* (1972) and Sheila Watson in *Four Stories* (1979), meaning inheres in the structures of myth and the possibility of perceiving the ironic re-enactment of old myths in modern dress – ie, in perceiving the (perhaps ironic) relevance of myth to current behaviour, through language. Thomas draws on fairy-tale, Ken Mitchell on tall tale anecdote, Andreas Schroeder on allegory, Basil Johnston on Trickster narrative tradition. And for both Atwood and Gunnars, it is parable and folk-tale that supply a directive structure, though the basic problems of story-telling lead them each into a separate balance between the reality of society and the reality of form.

Keeping in mind that this balance (however various authors achieve it) continues to exist, one discovers that the controversial theoretical positions which lie behind authorial practice emerged into print during the 1970s and 1980s as the Wars of the Anthologies. An indication not only of the vitality of the publishing scene during the 1970s, before the economic crises of the 1980s slowed things down, the sheer number of available anthologies suggests the growing size of the market, the increase of interest in the short story form (Oberon Press in Ottawa especially fastened on it). and the pedagogical intent of much commentary (about half of the fifty writers just listed hold or have held academic positions). There were annual samplers, like Oberon's volumes of the best stories of the year; there were samplers of formal and coterie practice, like Coach House Press's *The Story So Far* series; there were collections of contemporary stories (like those edited by Donald Stephens, Clark Blaise, John Metcalf, Michael Ondaatje, and Geoff Hancock) and historical collections (like those edited by Wayne Grady, John Stevens, Alec Lucas, Ivon Owen and Morris Wolfe). John Metcalf's various collections – among them *Sixteen by Twelve*, 1970; *The Narrative Voice*, 1972; *Stories Plus*, 1979; *New Worlds*, 1980; *Making It New*, 1982 – are particularly important, for they gathered authorial 'position papers' along with stories themselves, and always showed a fine discriminating eye for artistic quality. But taken together, the diverse editorial positions in these anthologies constitute more than just a collection of introductory comments; they become, implicitly or explicitly, part of a debate.

Consider, for example, the opposition inherent in the statements of John Stevens on the one hand and George Bowering, Ray Smith, and Leon Rooke on the other:

Stevens: Most short story writers of note in English Canada today work from the assumption that to achieve a symbolic 'everywhere' they must start with a recog-	*Bowering*: Most anthologies of Canadian stories seek to present ... a range of confederation in terms of space or time. [In this book] ... The act is not description,

nizable 'somewhere' and that no character can be 'everyman' without first being given the physical and psychological particularities of a distinctive human being.

Since the mid 1960s some writers have departed from those principles and from the associated traditional view that a short story should move a protagonist through a series of related incidents to a climax of victory or defeat ... In exuberant word hashes and melanges of discontinuous incident they explore alienation, fragmented identities, rootlessness, generational conflicts, and the new sexual freedom. The results tend to be absurd in the common understanding of the term rather than in the technical sense intended by the authors. The worst among them remind you of those chlorinated cake and pudding ready-mixes that food companies try out on volunteer housewives ... The best, like the stories by Cohen and Smith, have the merit of artfully concocted Singapore slings and Vienna sachertortes; they provide an amusing fillip to the palate before and after dinner, but make weak substitutes for the main course.[152]

or at least that is not the first impulse. Characteristically, the writers here seem to be trying to find something rather than trying to pretend they understand something ...

Certainly the idea of a story-teller having control over language is the more specific barbarity. Language is the property of no man. We who share its use & its using of us would serve & be served if we listen for the words of a story-teller who continuously discovers his own speech as phenomenon ...

The artist excels as he enters, not as he controls. He arranges himself among the particles.[153]

Smith: ['A Cynical Tale'] is about italics, capital letters, parentheses, the semicolon, a floating point of view, *non sequitors* [sic]. over-plotting, flat characters, spy thrillers, high rise apartments, lingerie, short stories, overstatement, understatement, dropped endings, and plum cordial. It is not I swear, about homosexuality.[154]

Rooke: Leading towards that future hour when the children churned up within this neighborhood ... will inherit what is theirs by unresolved law of blood and lair – pointing towards that time when they will find themselves living out of their own variations on and extensions of ... *the story*.

Maze, as in the Sunday comics, it being each generation's labour to trace down the undiscovered exits.

This being not so much what the story is about as what it comes to.[155]

'About' vs 'come to' — the distinction between story as referential object and story as artifice-in-process here takes on another guise. But again there is a danger in accepting the division as a dualistic choice, for to do so would be to underestimate the degree to which the referential stories rely on stylistic rhythm and lexical arrangement and the degree to which the 'process' stories are at some level documentary in impulse.

Comments by Hugh Hood, Matt Cohen, and George Bowering touch on these interconnections. Hugh Hood makes clear the inseparability within his own work of a strict formalism and a cultural moral interest in people's behaviour as a recognizable subject. Writing in the *Kenyon Review* in 1968, for example, he specifies:

Much poetry seems to me to lie to one side of this strictly social function of literature: the lyric, the poem of linguistic experiment, the poem treated as physical object (found poetry, concrete poetry), determinedly symbolic poetry. But the historical motive, the creation of the conscience of the race, seems to me to lie at the sources of the great prose forms: legal codes, liturgies, religious histories, sacred scriptures, records of myth, some epic narratives, and finally the novel and the story. I think that the chief *telos* of fiction in all its forms, whether in verse or prose, the long fiction or the short, epic romance, myth, novel, tale, story, is located in the storyteller's function, which is that of giving assurance to his readers or hearers of the persistence of the inner values of their culture. Story is by nature 'realist,' and the great story forms are realistic and historical, about the behaviour of men and women ... in real observable human societies ... Fiction may exhibit a high degree of formal organization ... But I will never concede that language is about language, that a linguistic system is purely self-reflexive, that the universe of language closes on itself ... The language of fiction is arranged so as to elicit in the audience's imagination the representation of human societies and the modes of conduct there deployed.[156]

Almost any work in Hood's substantial canon gives ample evidence of such a fervent commitment: the stories of *Around the Mountain* (1967), a behavioural sketchbook woven into an annual cycle; the stories of *Flying a Red Kite* (1962) and *The Fruit Man, the Meat Man & the Manager* (1971), with their meditation on people's double personalities; the stories of *Dark Glasses* (1976) and *None Genuine Without This Signature* (1980), with their explorations of the rituals people enjoy (Hallowe'en, baseball), the reasons they enjoy them (for safety, for pleasure), and the subtle way they double humour with worry at their openness to fear. The fascination with simultaneity leads Hood in 1972 to add to his earlier theorizing a statement about form and belief that is deeply coloured by his Catholicism and that deeply marks his affirmation of meaningful pattern; speaking of the Christian number symbols that structure his novel *You Can't Get There from Here*, he asserts that 'It makes a kind of scaffolding for the imagination,' and proceeds:

I had ... and still have, an acute sense of the possibilities of close formal organization of the sentence, syntactically and grammatically, and in its phonemic sequences. I paid much attention to the difficulties of writing long sentences because I knew that simple-minded naturalists wrote short sentences, using lots of 'ands.' I did not want to be a simple-minded naturalist ...

My interest in the sound of sentences, in the use of color words and of the names of places, in practical stylistics, showed me that prose fiction might have an abstract element, a purely formal element, even though it continued to be strictly, morally, realistic.[157]

Just as clearly, we can see that Cohen and Bowering acknowledge the kind of connection Hood extols at the same time as they resist its attractions – resisting them because they reject their documentary applicability. In other words, it is a documentary, historical reason that leads them into their own versions of broken form. But in doing so they are also performing an historical act, an act in history and with antecedents. Perhaps unconsciously, they are reiterating D.C. Scott's 1922 insight into the nature of a literature appropriate to a turbulent age, and so updating the cultural paradigm; and by performing a literary act that now has analogues in their cultural past, they are re-enacting his revolution for a 'postmodern' age.

Cohen made his position clear in 1973, in his introduction to *The Story So Far / 2*:

The short story form originated during a period when people believed in science and rational order; it developed rules and flows of logical structure. But the rational order corresponded to a moral order and when the moral order foundered people stopped pretending to believe that everything was tied up neat and happy or tragic. The residual need for that form has been met with great success by TV soap operas; now the short story is sprung loose to be more approximate to whatever realities the writers perceive.[158]

With society foundering and fragmenting on its own decadence, Cohen adds, the recognized chronological or 'factual' order of written narrative could no longer credibly function as a 'background' to characters' actions, leaving the spoken language – still functional, despite its inexactness, because of its continuous energy – to rescue literature 'from its own sterile conventions.'

Bowering makes a comparable point in the introductory notes to his *Fiction of Contemporary Canada* (1980):

When photography became an art, the artist produced pictures characterized by a feeling of rest, because that is what nineteenth-century painting prized ... The modernist writers, though abjuring the referential order of the nineteenth-century realists ... still maintained one aim inherited from their forebears. This was the sense of completion, or rest, if you like, of continuity. That is, the modernists look for non-individual patterns, but with a desire to see them sewn up ... The reader was invited to observe & decipher the structure, but he still had to keep his hands off, as clearly as the cause-&-effect reporter had pretended to do. The post-modernist invites his readers, & sometimes his characters, to take a hold somewhere & help him move the damned thing into position.[159]

Whatever resistance one might have to the generalizations here, the way in which the spoken idiom permeates the argument serves implicitly to support what Cohen had to say: there is an energy that carries the reader past discontinuity. Tangentially, however, in a subsequent note on David Young, Bowering points to what he considers an irony, the social base for Young's prose:

while Young's departure from the usual Canadian realism is necessarily at variance with the accepted notions about issues of national consciousness, he, like any good social satirist, deploys his attack out of a deeply-felt identification with the country's mental life & social behavior.

J.M. Yates's fiction, too, for Bowering, 'is proof that one does not need to revert to sociological realism to probe the great subconscious themes of Canadian life.'[160] 'Ironies' only if one requires fiction to have *no* connection with society, such observations serve more readily to demonstrate the degree to which the short story genre, while still open to individual shaping, has become adapted to the particularities of Canadian experience at each stage of cultural demand. No longer needing to document external geography, as the early sketches had done, the new stories can turn to sketching the state of mind. But if not so directly *about* a national culture as before, such stories are inevitably still *of* the culture, marked *by* the culture; and those documentary details which at one time served as a delimiting subject, claiming the separateness of national territory, can appear to disappear into the assumptions of genre and mode.

Conversely, too, the formal attributes of genre can prove instructive about a writer and a society, even when they may be avoiding overt social commentary. Hugh Hood observes about the art of characterization (and about his own philosophy of life) that

What we are united to in this world is not the physical insides of persons or things, but the knowable principle in them ... What I know, love, and desire in another person isn't inside him like a nut in its shell, but it is everywhere that he is, forming him. My identity isn't inside me — it is *how I am*. It is hard to express the way we know the forms of things, but this is the knowing that art exercises.[161]

In parallel fashion, it is the knowing that criticism exercises as well, seeking not to fasten on a kernel and claim it to be nationally distinctive, but to recognize the character of the literature through its forms: by seeking its past, tracing its changes, and observing in the present *how it is*.

3 New Zealand: Story and History

The problem, in writing a history of New Zealand short fiction, is Katherine Mansfield. She not only produced a substantial body of high quality work, she also produced much of it while living abroad in England and France, was claimed by English criticism and so given honorary English literary citizenship, died young and became a cultural icon, and managed all this so early in New Zealand's social history that her very existence cancels all easy generalizations about cultural and historical 'progress.' Yet to acknowledge these facts about Mansfield's career is to risk mistaking the particular facts for other kinds of general principle. Transforming Mansfield into an 'English' writer is as misleading as claiming her to be a quintessential New Zealander – indeed, her very difference from prevailing English models is what led her contemporaries in England to modify the way they characterized her work. Finding it not quite English, they leaped to claim that it was 'therefore' shaped by Chekhov and the French, a narrow conclusion which reveals their ignorance of colonial literary practice as much as their knowledge of continental literature.

For while Mansfield appeared 'early' in New Zealand's social history, and had some impact on those who followed, she did not appear right at the beginning; there were years of social development before her arrival on the Wellington scene – years of literary expression and of the shaping of convention, against both of which she responded directly. Simply by writing as she did, she challenged these conventions, but she did not quite remake them; and while she inspired imitators (and has attracted almost as much critical commentary as the rest of her literary compatriots combined), she did not thereby direct the way her culture subsequently grew. There were future generations of artists to be heard from, writers who would challenge conventions again or even challenge the pre-eminent position Mansfield came to hold in the minds of critics and readers; there were writers who helped to shape and perpetuate an image of New Zealand as a country preserve of athletic males, and writers who fastened on the exceptions to such a stereotype. There came to be a way of identifying New Zealand literature *with* Mansfield, and of excluding her *from* it; and a way of coming to understand how her writing contributed to the growth of New Zealand literature without thereby limiting its definition of quality or its power to change. Tracing the course of New Zealand short fiction begins, then, in the 1860s, gathers momentum in the 1880s, and follows a set of developments that I shall discuss under the following headings: (1) The Transformations of Kathleen Beauchamp; (2) Frank Sargeson & Sons; and (3) The Match with Homogeneity. Such a discussion also traces the recurrence of particular patterns of prose fiction, and the manipulation of these patterns to locally-rooted purpose.

The Transformations of Kathleen Beauchamp, 1860–1920

Kathleen Mansfield Beauchamp was born in October 1888 in Wellington; she grew up there with the nickname of 'Kass,' married twice, transformed some of her memories and observations of childhood into stories of a girl named 'Kezia,' and herself began to write using the names 'Kathleen Beauchamp,' 'Julian Mark,' 'Katherina Mansfield,' and 'K. Mansfield' before finally settling on the nom de plume by which she established her international reputation. A 'multiplication in search of an identity,' John Carswell called her.[1] The reasons for her changing her name stem from a variety of complex biographical rivalries; the reason for (even briefly) using a male name is less complex: it reflects her determination to be accepted as a serious writer at a time when most critics and reviewers equated 'serious' with 'male.' It was the same reason Olive Schreiner in South Africa published as 'Ralph Iron,' the same reason Sara Jeannette Duncan published as 'Garth Grafton' all the while her newspaper reports were appearing from New Orleans (though in Duncan's case, as in Mansfield's, the newspapers were in on the disguise). But it is less the specifics of such changes of public identity that concern me for the moment than the fact of change itself. What Mansfield typified at the end of the nineteenth century in New Zealand was a local variation of a widespread colonial impulse: the need to rebel against the biases of gender, race, place, and romantic speech which during the previous half-century had coloured cultural aspiration and literary expression. But this was also to be part of the ongoing tension which fragmented Mansfield's own life: by rejecting colonial culture, she was in some sense repressing some aspect of herself, yet to accept colonial values was for her unthinkable. The problem was that the choices appeared so acutely to present themselves as mutually exclusive options, when the reality of her experience required some acknowledgment of both colonial and metropolitan influences on her development.

When Sir Robert Stout, attorney-general in Sir George Grey's government, and later premier with Julius Vogel, surveyed in 1890 'The Rise and Progress of New Zealand,' he gave voice to the most enthusiastic of current perceptions of colonial culture, and to the sort of failure of discrimination which so irritated Katherine Mansfield. Stout records the progress of publication:

Little by little, stray poems appeared, racy of the soil; and then came tales for weekly papers, written by New Zealand natives and by those whose life had been almost wholly spent in the Colony. The first poems and the first tales, like the beginnings of American literature, were English. There was little distinctively of New Zealand in them. Local colouring was rare, and though tales have been multiplied, and our weekly papers once a year at least give prominent space to locally written novellettes [sic], there is still little New Zealand in them. The United States is now getting a distinctive literature – Cooper, Bret Harte, Clements [sic], Whitman, are thoroughly American. We have not yet had a novel of high excellence that is wholly of New Zealand.

Then after going on to describe the abundance of libraries and booksellers, he asks if New Zealand's island nature will make its literature 'idiosyncratic':

Its high mountain ranges, its peculiar evergreen forests, its volcanic belt with its geysers, the fiords with their walls of green ... the Native people ... and the Pacific laving the shores, will surely beget a literature and a poesy – New Zealand's own. Nor do we think it will be open to the charge of Philistinism or narrowness – for we are not like England – two islands near a continent where many foreign languages are spoken and where intercourse in literature has been nigh impossible. We are linked with Australia, and our Mail Service to San Francisco is like a shuttle, sent monthly, weaving as with a silken thread to sixty millions of English speaking people, having a literature yearly rising in importance and complexity.[2]

Such comments step swiftly from history into boosterism, and in so doing typify their own colonial perspective; inadvertently they reveal ingrained expectations of literature and race – the Maori are part of a list of distinguishing landscape items, the rhetoric of expression relies on an inflated poetic diction, the novel is seen as the acme of literary expression – and yet at the same time they declare the inexact familiarity with North America which is another recurrent element in New Zealand culture. The American connection functioned in part to allow the colony to claim its literary independence, its separateness from the metropolitan British centres it relied on, yet despite this claim London long continued to be the effective arbiter of taste, and London recognition – witness Mansfield, Alan Mulgan, Dan Davin, and others – the arbiter of value.

The 'papers' Stout refers to included the *New Zealand Gazette* (from Port Nicholson, 1840, though a pre-emigration issue had appeared in London dated 1839), the *Nelson Examiner and New Zealand Chronicle* (begun in 1842, and edited for a time by Alfred Domett), *Chapman's New Zealand Monthly Magazine* (which lasted from August to December in 1862), the *Monthly Review* (which flourished from 1888 to 1890 (attracting contributions from writers like Edith Searle), *Zealandia* (which William Freeman began in Dunedin in 1889, in hopes of establishing a national critical magazine), and some forty or so others before the nineteenth century came to a close.[3] The *Gazette* was established by Samuel Revans, who with H.S. Chapman had previously brought out the *Montreal Daily Advertiser* until Revans was forced to flee Canada following the 1837 Rebellion; concerned mostly with the political events of the day, the paper served more as a guide to political actions and expectations than as a vehicle for literary invention, though there are plentiful examples of literary rhetoric (and, one suspects, fictional mask and imagination) among the letters to the editor. *Chapman's Monthly* was deliberately narrower in scope, far less successful, apparently aspiring before its time to be an agent of national expression. The editorial in its initial issue spells out its high-minded goal, but perhaps also indicates one of the reasons for the journal's failure: its presumption that 'literature' was somehow identifiable by subject, and that a literary subject was more locatable in Europe than in the colony:

The raw material of literature is not so plentiful in new [sic] Zealand as in London ... But there is, doubtless, a very great amount of literary talent among us, which only requires a little judicious training to make it perennial. The aim of the Editor will be to develope [sic] a taste for writing among the colonists; and when the modesty natural to true genius shall have worn off, there is no reason to doubt that the NEW ZEALAND MAGAZINE will be supported by a numerous and intelligent staff of contributors.[4]

The contents of the journal's five issues spell out further the editorial distinction between high literary endeavour and everyday experience. Beside excerpts from Macaulay and translations of Horace, for example, the journal printed articles on plant cultivation, Christian liberty, and New Zealand trees and geology; when it came to fiction, it sought to collect 'tales' from surviving missionaries and pioneer settlers, and published romantic accounts of Maori behaviour and anecdotes about camping. Judith Wild quotes an Auckland review which quite rightly finds these stories 'fustian' and 'twaddle'[5] – yet in the midst of the effortful attempts at literary tale-telling, there appear a number of lively sketches of landscape, manners, and Maori, by F.E. Maning (whose work was later published as *Old New Zealand*) and Charles Heaphy.

In the sketches lie the roots of New Zealand short fiction, not in the tales; what was important was the fragmentary nature of their attempts at literary documentation (their length due more to the exigencies of newspaper publication than to any gestating National Oversoul) and their ability to use local experience and local speech to literary effect. Yet the critical impulse to locate value elsewhere – in Europe particularly – persisted, implicitly carrying a different message: that the colony must be incomplete outside Great Britain (or beyond the extended imperial limits of the notion of Greater Britain), and that *literary* reality was somehow distinguishable from *empirical* reality, meaning that local experience was deemed a fit subject for high art only if it was glossed over by the (British, foreign) conventions of romance. In practice, such a dichotomy between form and subject was not fixed, but its effects were to last well into the twentieth century, imposing covert restrictions on writers' techniques and directly affecting the vocabulary of critical judgment.

The fragmentary formal structure of the longest of the early fictions in New Zealand gives some evidence of the multiple purposes they were trying to serve. The impulse to tell of muscular adventure won critical praise – the *Melbourne Argus*, for example, congratulated Dugald Ferguson ('An Old Colonist') for 'telling a capital story which is brimful of adventures, and of a wholesome, manly, open-air tone which is very refreshing.'[6] And romance conventionally added charm to manly trials: W.M. Baines, in the preface to his *The Narrative of Edward Crewe: or, Life in New Zealand* (1874), likens his tales of 'half-savage life' to those of Sindbad.[7] More striking still is the presumption within Baines's narrative itself of European superiority to the Maori, and the *documentary form* – the air of factual reportage – which his commentary on race differences takes on. Variously quoting from Tasman's journal, discoursing on the qualities of the kauri tree, and attacking narrow-minded pietism, Baines conveys the illusion of being a discriminating observer even after he has announced he is telling Sindbad's tales of marvels – despite Sindbad, the illusion of reality is one founded in form, not in substance, though the work would have been accepted at the time as substantially true. He observes at one point that the Maori will be glad to be given tobacco but not grateful, because gratefulness requires the presence of civilization.[8] At another he observes: 'A *Redskin* will bear torture better than a white one, as also will a Maori, whose nerves are not so *alive* as our own, and are wanting, perhaps, in "encephalon," or the refining process developed through a civilized ancestry.'[9]

What I am concerned with here is the fact that the romance form makes the 'savage' adventure acceptable, while at the same time the illusion of documentary record gives credence to the most self-justifying fables of superiority. At the height of Empire, such beliefs seemed axiomatic to Europeans. Sir George Grey comes back as governor, in Mrs J.E. Aylmer's *Distant Homes; or The Graham Family in New Zealand* (1862), 'to administer justice to the mistaken natives';[10] and Captain H. Butler Stoney begins *Taranaki: A Tale of the War* (1861) with the observation 'We shall freely use the liberty of a British subject and write of all as we found them,'[11] as though citizenship guaranteed objectivity. The point is that, while the reportorial mode supported the romance of Imperial adventure as far as the nineteenth-century reader was concerned, for the twentieth-century reader it is the romantic style which disrupts the narrative's documentary authenticity. And repeatedly the fiction of the time adopts romantic and reportorial stances together, if not quite indiscriminately then at least without any apparent sense of the disparities of message that derive from the artistic inconsistency.

Consider, for example, the parallel patterns in Mrs Aylmer's and Captain Stoney's books. Mrs Aylmer is at once matter-of-fact about the absolute virtues of English hierarchical order —

The settlement of Canterbury having, as you know, been first proposed and founded by a company of gentlemen who knew the blessings of education and order, you may believe that the first thing they looked to was to start their new country upon the foundation of Church and schools.[12]

— and fulsomely dependent on adjectives when she comes to her descriptive record of the immediate locale:

The western portion of Nelson, stretching far along the sea-shore, is very wild and barren. Rugged mountains, covered with gloomy forests; a rock-bound coast, against which the waves dash with terrific force, and, dreaded by European and native seamen, is only inhabited by a few wretched and half starved natives, who live upon the roots of the fern.
It is in this part of the country, that the strange bird called the Kisvi [sic] is found ...[13]

Reality is English, in other words, and the substance of New Zealand a fabulous romance. Comparably, Stoney's *Taranaki: A Tale of the War* — his extended title continues: 'with a description of the province previous to and during the war; also an account (chiefly taken from the despatches) on the principal contests with the natives during the eventful period — purports simultaneously to be historical record and 'tale.' Essay thus blends (altogether

119 New Zealand: Story and History

perceptibly) into adventure and love story, the purpose being more didactic than escapist, but sufficiently escapist to give narrative colour to the sketches – in this case sketches of the fertility of the Taranaki Plain. Yet despite its determination to record factual details, the work closes in a set of conventional tropes:

> Our tale is now over. Tried in the harsh furnace of affliction, our friends have gained fresh hope and courage, and will again return to their lands with cheerfulness and hope; with grateful hearts to the all-wise Dispenser of all things; with renewed courage to begin the world anew; and by their example, courage, and assistance to those worse off than themselves, once more convert the desolated waste to the flowering glade, and the ruined and devastated sites of their former homes to new and still more happy abodes, – contented with their lot, and ever blessing the Heavenly Ruler for all the favours still in store for them.[14]

It is a rhetoric which is implicitly declaring the absolute virtue of European civilization, embodying such virtue more or less equally in Christian hierarchy, male courageousness, female passivity, Caucasian race, and the closed forms of romantic expression. Yet the society was not static – in particular, the Maori and female elements in the population refused to be contained by a closed design – and a documentary form that would declare the reality of the local world rather than its romance was constantly battering the limits of rhetorical convention, trying to find a congenial home.

Alexander Bathgate's preface to *Waitaruna: A Story of New Zealand Life* (1881) spells out this literary dilemma. Bathgate sees it as a problem of subject, though more properly it might be seen as a problem of form:

> In writing the story of Waitaruna, it has been the aim and endeavour of the author to present to the reader some true pictures of life in the southern portion of the colony of New Zealand, as it was a short time ago, and to some extent still is; but already the rapid advance which the country has made within the past few years has wrought many changes. Although the pictures are drawn from life, they are not pre-Raphaelite in detail; for the depicting of the ordinary humdrum routine of station life, or work on the diggings, would have proved neither an agreeable task to the writer, nor interesting to many readers. Yet sufficient glimpses of such details have been given to enable the reader to complete the pictures which have been strung together, as it were, by a story, not very interesting in itself, perhaps, to the ordinary run of novel readers, but one which it is hoped will help to a better knowledge of life in the colony.[15]

Bathgate tries, in other words, to devise a story that will string together a set of separate, didactic, incomplete, reader-involving sketches. He might well have said he was trying to devise a formal string by which to tell a story — but his sense of his accomplishment was less of a serial accumulation (which would modify an initial view through a process of extension) than of a set of individually incomplete pictures that were the internal fragments of a coherent (perhaps 'homogeneous' is implied) social unit.

As New Zealand short fiction developed during the nineteenth century, these two impulses — to transform the land through romance and to transform the reader through information — were in constant quarrel, even sometimes within a single author, suggesting some uncertainty about who the readership was as well as uncertainty about the dimensions of the form. For B.L. Farjeon the intention was clear enough: to publish a book that would serve 'as a link in the chain that binds the hearts of residents in the Colonies to their home-lands,[16] an inspiration that runs through the writings of Lady Barker (Mary Anne Stewart, later Lady Broome), William Davidson, and subsequently Blanche Baughan as well. But for Davidson and Baughan, the first commitment was to the need to chronicle New Zealand; for Farjeon, the first commitment was to English recognition — he dedicated *Shadows on the Snow* to Dickens, and was ready to fling up his job and head to London the moment Dickens acknowledged his work. In cold print, as Farjeon's daughter Eleanor later revealed, the letter from Dickens (dated May 1866) was studiously neutral, reading in part:

I am concerned to find that I have by an accident left your letter of last January's date unanswered.

Your dedication, as an interesting and acceptable mark of remembrance from the other side of the world, gave me great pleasure ...

But I am bound to lay before you the consideration that I cannot on such evidence (especially when you describe yourself as having written 'hurriedly'), form any reasonably reliable opinion of your power of writing an acceptable colonial story for All the Year Round.[17]

Farjeon's stories in practice were an odd combination of the blunt commonplace ('Very commonplace reading this; but life is made up of lights and shades, and ordinary events require but ordinary language to express them')[18] and the pre-Freudian romance of characters with two faces and mortals with radically unresolved outer and inner lives. For Lady Barker, too, collecting stories into book-length units meant working out a balance between the matter-of-fact and the sentimental. And recurrently, with these and other writers, the formal result was the development of the *Rahmenerzählung*, whereby a series of story forms (sometimes, and sometimes not, involving separate narrators) was brought together within the thinnest of frames, to allow documentary sketch and sentimental tale more or less equivalent space, if not simultaneous play.

Lady Barker's various collections of anecdotes and pathetic tales, whether for children (as in *Ribbon Stories*, 1872, or *Stories About*, 1887) or for adults (as in *A Christmas Cake in Four Quarters*, 1872, or her sketches of backblock experience, *Station Life in New Zealand*, 1870, and *Station Amusements in New Zealand*, 1873), alike demonstrate the author's deliberate story-telling structures. *Ribbon Stories* acquires its title from the notion of a little girl sifting a silk ribbon through her fingers and telling the sequence of stories she finds in it (corduroy tells horrid stories, we are told, and satin ones go too fast). The results are mostly English dreams of sylphs and dolls' adventures, whereas those in *Stories About* balance imperial adventures (snakes, cruel negresses, madmen, and monkeys) with equally conventional pathetic tales of death and Christian conversion; *A Christmas Cake in Four Quarters*, like the station life sketches, more readily reveals the author's ability to be amused at herself, but once again the ostensibly real-life framing anecdotes (of sheep mustering, for example) balance the internal tales, which are ghost stories and other adventures of what is portrayed as a whimsical imagination. It is the balance which seems important, as it is for Henry Lapham. Lapham's *We Four, and the Stories We Told* (1880) however, more intricately manipulates the *conventions* of tale-telling, perhaps drawing on the pattern Dickens adopted in the 1852 Christmas number of *Household Words*. Assembling four characters one winter night in a hotel parlour, he has each in turn tell a story of fright. Though the four voices do not much vary, the tale forms do: one is all incident, colloquial and informal; one announces it will be a strange adventure and turns out to be simply a sentimental character sketch; a third is a yarn, with a rudimentary plot; and the fourth is a horror story. But the overall narrator interrupts, before the fourth story is told, to say:

the art of story telling is one of the Pater's special accomplishments, and many a pleasant hour have I passed in listening to his gruesome Highland legends, his tales of 'suffering, want, and wee' in the Crimea; his reminiscences sounding like pages from 'The Arabian Nights' — of the ruined palaces or desolated shrines at Delhi and Lucknow, and his vivid descriptions of the life and scenery of that wondrous Oriental land.[19]

We are duly warned. When the narrative proceeds, the fourth character tells what purports to be 'real experience' — of sleeping with a corpse — which so frightens everybody else that they find immediate reasons to go home. And the book abruptly stops. Lapham brings convention to earth, in other words, refusing to romanticize reality and wittily calling attention to the techniques by which people do romanticize reality and then accept the faulty inferences of their own delusion. Lapham, that is, uses literary convention against itself, in order to free both himself and the form from current restraints. But the process of transformation would be slow.

Many of the individual stories of late-nineteenth-century writers first appeared in newspaper format: Lady Barker, for example, published in *Good Words for the Young*; Susan Nugent Wood in the *Australian Journal* and the *Otago Witness*; Blanche Baughan in the *Christchurch Press, Current Thought, The Citizen*, and the London *Spectator*; Alfred Grace in *The Free Lance, The New Zealand Times, The Auckland Star, The Sydney Bulletin*, the Christchurch *Weekly Press*, and *The Triad*; and William Baucke in the *New Zealand Herald* and the *Auckland Weekly News*. Devising books from such material did not always result in formal coherence. When Susan Nugent Wood collaborated with her (then less well-known) brother Henry Lapham to bring out *Waiting for the Mail and Other Sketches and Poems* (1875), she noted that the book had been assembled 'at odd moments, chiefly those generally so tediously spent in wondering when the letters would come,'[20] and the result is more a miscellany than a shaped structure, as is William Davidson's collection *Stories of New Zealand Life* (1889).

Yet Davidson's ten stories none the less assemble a range of reports, tales, anecdotes, and episodes that ultimately balance such subjects as drunkenness and gambling, treated with the broad strokes of man-of-the-world irony, with those of British citizenship and manly camaraderie (the 'Moral' of 'Nineteen Hours on a Common Jury' declares: 'Tobacco, good liquor, and good company, are wonderful softeners of the rigid virtues, but when they are combined to lively yarns, and good songs, old Harry himself, "would tak a thocht and mend"').[21] When Wood and Lapham combine talents, moreover, her impulse to tell pathetic stories of death, babes, and godliness balances his impulse to write dialogues of drunks, policemen, blacksmiths, and flash women. Between them they illustrate not just differences in literary convention, but also differences in social convention, both on the point of giving way. And the key points at issue involved the public and literary image of women (something related to, but different from, the role a particular woman might perform in society) and the public respectability of speech (which differentiated an idea of *literary* practice from the fact of the society's vernacular).

Susan Nugent Wood, for example, in 'The Weaker Vessel' (more of an essay than a story, in *Waiting for the Mail*), asserts that women should cluck, not crow, be firm but gentle; her brother's stories in *We Four* record a parallel attitude, using the spoken word. "'It's hard to reason with a woman, you know, boys",' says one character; "'Women can't keep a secret ... It's their nature, poor things, so you can't blame 'em",' says another.[22] As late as 1889, reviewing Julius Vogel's novel *Anno Domini 2000* (a book celebrating female suffrage and probing the possibility of war with the United States, and portraying a female president and prime minister), *The Monthly Review* observed: 'If this book proves anything, it is that government by women is absolutely hopeless.'[23] And H.B. Marriott Watson's tale, 'The Hand of God: A Story of the Waitiri Gorge,' contains this sequence, recording the moment when the man Miss Marion Lister loves, reaching into the gorge for a rata flower for her, falls in:

'Marion. Marion!' said Alice's voice, 'what was that noise? what have you left the horses for?'
'She's admiring the gorge there,' said Crawford. 'Good gracious! isn't that a dangerous place, my dear?'
... 'Marion, my dear, where's Mr Craven?'
'Good heavens!' said Drummond suddenly; 'why, I believe she's fainted.'[24]

The failure here is of language as well as of social insight, but it is the sort of convention that explains the sharpness of Edith Searle Grossman's subsequent feminism. Grossman's novels tell of battered wives, of women deprived of an education their fathers do not think they need, of women who become their husbands' possessions, of repressed sexuality in the claustrophobic bush, the pressures of a Jewish inheritance, and the virtues of the Salvation Army; yet for all her seriousness, there runs through her work a self-sustaining irony. A character in *The Heart of the Bush*, for example, 'wished that she were Early Victorian. and could let herself faint, it would have been such a rest,'[25] but such a statement is at the same time a charge of infidelity against earlier writers' literary version of women.

By Grossman's time there were some signs of change; the popular and influential *New Zealand Illustrated Magazine*, to which Grossman occasionally contributed, was in 1902 directing articles to a female readership, but they were not substantially more honest than the form of fiction that the magazine in February 1904 referred to as 'storiettes.'[26] In the August 1902 issue, for example, women are told to be brave because they have a cross to bear, but that mattress-cleaning is a 'new employment for women';[27] the same issue prints Johannes C. Andersen's saccharine romance of a Maori girl, called 'The Wooing of Hine-Ao,' and Edith G. Woolcott's story 'Judy: An Old Fashioned Girl,' appears at first to be recording the title character's liberation, only to close by fencing the liberation inside a possessive male boundary. The narrator turns to the reader, at least challenging the formal convention of doing so, and asks:

Are you disappointed because Cyril Courtney did not turn out to be the rich prince (or merchant, it is all the same nowadays) of the story, and Judy had nothing to do all day but read and play with a bit of fancy-work?

This is not a romance, in the story-book acceptation of the term, but a chapter from a very real life. True, the drudgery of Judy's work was forever a thing of the past, but her talents would have been wasted upon a very rich man. Moreover, the doctor was very wise, and he knew that his Judy would not be happy unless might work. She was, and always will be ... one of those convenient folks who are very ready to aid others ... It was just her nature to be so, and the ways of Nature must be fulfilled whatever path in Life we take.[28]

Socially, it is an ambivalent conclusion — if radical in some respects, then 'safe' in others, challenging convention from inside rather than dispensing with convention altogether. The literary call for literature to be a chapter from life, however, picks up what throughout the nineteenth century had been the documentary strain in New Zealand fiction, which by the 1890s was also increasingly evident in critical attitudes to speech and literary form.

The issue of speech — which I mean both lexicon and sound system — has in New Zealand been a source of long-standing debate, surfacing as recently as 1979 in the local *Reader's Digest*, among other places, in a quarrel between the Fendalton mystery writer Dame Ngaio Marsh, who throughout her career championed British standard norms as the mark of the educated New Zealander, and the Scots-born educator (and author of the weekly *New Zealand Listener* articles on language standards and practice), Ian Gordon, who championed a blend between grammatical accuracy and local usage. The astounding thing is that Gordon still found it necessary to write: 'It is silly to write off as inferior a speech so uniformly used by three million people ... I find New Zealand English vivid and effective, its speakers articulate, its writers worth reading ... You need never be scared to open your Kiwi mouth. You have nothing to lose but your inhibitions.'[29]

But an ordinary Kiwi accent had only within that decade been heard on New Zealand radio programs other than sports broadcasts; an approximately British norm had characterized other programming. Parenthetically this distinction had the effect, for the preceding decades of radio communication, of asking listeners to identify athletics with reality and to identify literature-on-the-air (drama, short story readings, critical comment) with something external, with England, with a world of words of which New Zealand was only a distant fragment. The nineteenth-century equation between *literary reality* and British standards and expectations proved durable. But even within the nineteenth century there were writers pushing at the formal restrictions inherent in the assumption. Lady Barker would use local speech, but apologize for it afterwards, however indirectly:

'The trews were hard to manage, but 'Phairson wears 'em with gaiters, and I rolls 'em up; so though they're a deal too short for him and too lang for me, we manage first class,' said M'nab, relapsing into colonial phraseology.[30]

Local speech was a signal to the reader. Repeatedly, it was the subject, or the very mode, of comedy. Writers laughed. Other writers simply found exact renderings of local speech and behaviour to be shocking and ungentlemanly,[31] though they used this observation to call for greater *true romance* and *realism of story*, terms which in such circumstances began to lose meaning. But Louisa Baker, writing as 'Alien,' in the prefatory 'Note' to *The Untold Half*, defended such usage:

Several of my critics have observed that the speech of my characters of humble life differs from that to which one is accustomed in England. That is entirely true. The speech of the average New Zealander of to-day is quite without provincialism, is spontaneous, free, and often picturesque.[32]

One might wonder whether the words 'humble' and 'picturesque' none the less still constitute an apology of sorts, but the main thing is that New Zealand writers were beginning to marshal a defence of the subjects and speech around them – even to the point of erecting geographical barriers to define the national cultural enterprise.

When William Freeman established *Zealandia* in 1889, for example, he set out in his opening editorial the principles that would govern the shape and substance of his journal:

in spite of the many well-meaning periodicals which have been established in New Zealand with varying success, no thoroughly popular – and therefore not thoroughly successful – effort has yet been made to systematically bring forward the very large amount of literary talent which is known to exist here ... ZEALANDIA is the outcome of this conviction ... Colony though it may be, New Zealand is a nation – not yet beyond its embryonic form, but still a nation; and to the realisation of this truth is due the fact that ZEALANDIA has been established as a distinctively national literary magazine. Its contributors will be all New Zealanders, and no subject will be dwelt upon in its pages that is not of interest, secondarily, to all the world beside. But, whilst it is intended to assist New Zealand authors, and, in fact, *in order* to assist them effectually, rigid care will be exercised as to the quality of the literary pabulum provided in ZEALANDIA's pages ... It is, moreover, clearly recognised that ... to be permanent it must be popular. Therefore the most strenuous efforts have been made to accommodate ourselves to the prevailing taste ... Fiction will be ... represented by a complete tale in each number. Every number will also contain an article ... descriptive of some part of New Zealand

... A corner has been found for our poets. Natural History, always an interesting subject in a new country, has its allotted place. Specialists have been engaged to meet the requirements of our ladies, our girls, boys, and our chess and draughts players.[33]

The hierarchy of such subjects is self-explanatory. In subsequent public advice to correspondents, Freeman added:

TO Mrs H.E.W., Newmarket. If your tale is 'essentially English' it would clearly be out of place as the main attraction of a *national New Zealand magazine*. Why cannot New Zealand have a literature of its own?
TO Paul BLACK, Auckland ...why do you needlessly shift scene out of New Zealand? ... How are we to infuse a national spirit into New Zealand literature if our writers persist in seeking inspiration from countries which many of them have never seen?[34]

The important connection between national literary practice and popular public taste underlies the success of *The New Zealand Illustrated Magazine* as well, though the *Illustrated* did not limit its subjects by national border. Where the *Illustrated* had its effect was in the realm of qualitative judgment — both in the choice of stories to publish and in the critical reviews, many of them by the editorial writer who published as 'The Sage.' The stance was enthusiastic for local speech and experience, but socially conservative — espousing literary tidiness (as in Woolcott's 'Judy') and the continuing virtues of Empire (as in notes on Australia, the Cape Colony, and British Columbia) — finding order in the nation, and transforming order into a national virtue. The Sage's approval of the works of Sabine Baring-Gould demonstrates what was thought to be literary achievement:

Chris displays admirable skill in managing her club of unruly factory girls, and equal ability in setting things straight all round, and bringing about the happy ending so necessary to make one put down book with the proper amount of satisfaction.[35]

And his tempered enthusiasm for G.B. Lancaster's *Sons o' Men* (1904) reinforces this assessment; about 'the storm and stress of life in the back-locks of Southland,' it is, he avers,

one of the best collections of Southern New Zealand stories yet written, and bears promise of even better work in the future. A little toning down of the style would perhaps be an improvement.[36]

Edward Kempe's comments on Edgar Allan Poe further stress how far literary taste in New Zealand had shifted, from its early enthusiasm for florid romance to its determination in the 1900s to root literature in real life:

In all that Poe wrote there is a malarial taint, the delusive realism of fever, the lurid colouring, the half-belief, half-fear that it is true and the wish that it were not so. Other writers one associates with the moorland or the ocean, the breezy country or the cheerful haunts of man. But Poe has no place with healthy nature. In imagination one sees his lonely figure moving as in a nightmare, hag-ridden and melancholy, among the streets of cities, where the light flickers on blank walls, barred windows and endless pavements.[37]

Yet we must ask if the *Illustrated*'s picture of life and letters is fundamentally any more realistic than that which went before, or simply a claim upon another form of romance. The latter seems the likelier answer. The picture was based upon a male view of order and of healthy nature (both of which the work of Grossman, for example, repudiated). It was rural. And it was based upon a continuing condescension towards and romanticizing of Maori culture – as in the short stories of Johannes Andersen (August 1902), the comic anecdotes of 'Tangata Ke' (October 1904), or the portrait of a 'Maori Pocahontas' (November 1904). To give Andersen his due, he was attempting to be precise in his deliberate use of Maori vocabulary, but he stereotyped character as well as plot. And such romantic stereotypes of culture underlay the prevalent assumptions about the relation between society and fiction.

In separately published books, the sketches of the most successful of turn-of-the-century story writers, Alfred A. Grace, were to reinforce the comic stereotypes of the wily Maori and the public assumption that the Maori were, as Grace put it, a 'dying race,' but in Grace's case there was a difference both in degree of familiarity with Maori culture and in degree of literary craftsmanship. For Grace, the Maori were 'dying' because they were being assimilated. Just as William Baucke drew upon his substantial knowledge of Maori custom, history, and legend to write the series of articles that turned into *Where the White Man Treads* (1905), Grace drew upon his acquaintance with individual Maori to write anecdotes, tales, and sketches of *Maoriland Stories* (1895), *Tales of a Dying Race* (1901), *Folk Tales of the Maori* (1907), and *Hone Tiki Dialogues* (1910). Yet just as Baucke was hampered by his predilection to use extended metaphors and archaic diction, Grace was hindered by his inclination to use elevated phrasing for noble sentiments, and dialect for Maori and children. Baucke's Kiplingesque concern for the depredations of the European in New Zealand occasionally results in a resonant phrase – as when he comments on the early American whalers who, being of Puritan stock, 'sinned in moderation'[38] but more often it leads to an implicitly patronising one, as when he hopes that his books will 'deepen the recognition that we owe duties to our brown companion.'[38] This attitude, too, has its parallel in Grace, in throwaway phrases like 'They made love much after the fashion of the Red Indians, without exchanging many words,'[40] or the concluding phrase in a passage in 'The Chief's Daughter,' which has more to say about Grace's notion of artistic composition than about the 'dying' civilization he wishes authentically to record:

He then went before ... and placed the girl and her father, who willingly complied with his unspoken request, together with some half-dozen more of the tribe, in a picturesque group under the foot of the cliff. And some more he grouped about the canoe, and then went back to his easel and, without delay, produced, in a 'study,' the animation that was needed to make his picture Art – whilst the rest of the Maoris stood round him and criticised his work, asking him questions and indulging in banter, as Maoris love to do.[41]

Yet in some of his sketches, Grace rises sufficiently above his usual method to warrant reading still – especially in 'Rawiri and the Four Evangelists,' 'Pirihira,' and 'Putangitangi and the Maere' (all from *Dying Race*), and 'A Delicate Subject' (from *Hone Tiki Dialogues*). For all their suspect anthropology, they manipulate the familiar forms of folk-tale, fable, and trickster narrative to expose the naïveté of the European in Maori contexts more than to dismiss customs conventionally considered primitive, and thereby acquire a degree of literary subtlety that neither the inflated tales nor the simple records of fact possess. With Grace, in other words, the sketch is reinvented.

It is important to bear in mind that Grace's popular appeal was based less on his covert reappraisal of Maori culture than on his apparent service to the reigning public image: the Maori were wily – but comic, figures of pathos and entertainment – and they were arrangeable in picturesque groupings, however critical of the result they themselves might prove to be. Yet for Grace and his publisher – Charles Nalder Baeyertz, the outspoken editor of the journal *Triad*, which flourished first in New Zealand, then in Sydney, between 1893 and 1913 – the central concern appears to have been as much aesthetic as social. Grace's observation that the 'study' was a way of animating a picture into Art tacitly declares his commitment to the documentary sketch but to the necessity of a shaping artifice. The question was: what criteria would govern the shaping? If 'pure' documentary was not to be considered art, did that mean that the alternative was yet again to be another form of imported techniques and standards? or was it possible to be rooted locally and aesthetically pleasing at the same time? *Triad* was inconsistent on this point. It published Grace, and (although it seemed to think 'sourdough' meant 'remittance man') praised the Canadian poet Robert Service because of the Spirit of the Wild that had him in its thrall.[41] But Baeyertz was adamant that literature was an art, that art possessed quality, and that 'quality' by definition implied superiority over the norm. 'TRIAD,' he wrote, has insisted for many years that the public is always wrong in regard to any question of taste, until it is by slow process converted to the right way of thinking by the educated and thinking minority.[43] No greater contrast with *Zealandia*'s enthusiasm for public taste could be imagined.

In retrospect, it is hard to think of *Triad* as a particularly avant-garde journal, though (as with E.J. Brady's Melbourne periodical *The Native Companion*) that was its contemporary reputation. But there is sufficient difference between these two and the general run of New Zealand publications at the time to see why the image would develop. *The Native Companion*, Tom Mills (of the New Zealand *Evening Post*) told Kathleen Beauchamp, published vignettes '"of the sex-problem type".'[44] And it was to *Triad* (in 1908) and *The Native Companion* (between 1907 and 1909) that Kathleen Beauchamp / Julian Mark / Katherine Mansfield turned to publish her first six works.

The choice seems inevitable. It was not just a question of choosing to publish in a context that found Rossetti, Wilde, Maeterlinck, and Elgar congenial, but the fact that by doing so she was deliberately rejecting the social and literary popular norms that were embodied in *Zealandia* and the *Illustrated*. Returning to New Zealand from her English schooling in October 1907, complete with an acquired Queen's College accent, she rejected her father's control over her, rejected the male networks that controlled power in his society, and sought out the Maori on a 1907 camping trip through the heart of the North Island (which her father had arranged).[45] And she celebrated an intensity of feeling rather than the mode of anecdotal record. Yet a key feature of even these earliest of her works is the degree to which they coupled an impressionistic method with a sharp eye for perceived detail and a skill at using such observations to document the transitory character of a given feeling. Like Alfred Grace, but in a different way, she was modifying the sketch form, turning it inwards into psychological drama whereas he effectively turned it outwards into public theatre. Both of them probed character more than history and landscape, but she relied on image and rhythm, he on dialect and dialogue. And he, arranging his verbal effects, found acceptance within his society because his works simply modified the established norms; she, in full rebellion against them, found repeated forms of alienation, and in July 1908, as Katherine Mansfield, she set sail once again for England, this time alone, in search of a country of Art — only to find out how distant she remained from England's norms and how emotionally close, if artistically closed, New Zealand at a distance came to feel.

In some sense Katherine Mansfield at this juncture drops temporarily out of

New Zealand literary history. Though there were occasional New Zealand notices of her publications in England,[46] her career there went ahead without reference to writers who were her contemporaries in New Zealand (Grace, Blanche Baughan). And though the English-born Baughan's several attempts to chronicle New Zealand life from the outside (in *Brown Bread from a Colonial Oven*, 1912, for example) serve almost as a reverse mirror to Mansfield's expatriate attempts to document New Zealand character from the inside, Baughan also appears to have written without reference to her better-known contemporary. Mansfield was meanwhile entangling her private life in further complications and gradually establishing a remarkable literary reputation in London, writing satirical sketches for A.R. Orage's *The New Age*, beginning in 1910, then two years later shifting her primary affiliation to John Middleton Murry's *Rhythm* (which she jointly edited with him), its successor *The Blue Review*, and *The Athenaeum* (which Murry briefly edited in 1919 and 1920 while Mansfield attempted to recuperate from tuberculosis in France and Switzerland).

Later stories appeared in journals like *Signature*, *Sphere*, the *London Mercury*, and *The Dial*. In *The New Age* appeared the sketches that were to be collected as *In a German Pension* in 1911, a volume which (after its initial run) Mansfield resisted having reprinted during her lifetime; the major stories of her later volumes — *Bliss and Other Stories* (1920), *The Garden Party and Other Stories* (1922), and the posthumous *The Doves' Nest and Other Stories* (1923) — are more impressionistic and less overtly caustic than these. While they do not radically differ in theme, they differ markedly in formal technique, an advance which is further emphasized by the posthumous publication of her early stories — *Something Childish and Other Stories* (1924; the American title is *The Little Girl*), and 'Juliet' (1970, in *The Turnbull Library Record*) — and the various narrative fragments on which she was still working at the time of her death or which she had previously discarded.

Mansfield's career has lent itself to a number of critical approaches: biographical, political, thematic, formal. Critics have asked who was the *real* Mansfield? was she an English *or* a New Zealand writer? why was she attracted to movements like Major Douglas's Social Credit or Gurdjieff's Institute for the Harmonious Development of Man? what did she write *about*? is she a cynical or a sentimental writer, accurate or effusive? and what is the quintessential *centre* to her art? Each of these questions carries its own limitations, as do most of the critical answers. There are almost as many Mansfields as there are critics: the rebel, the middle class child, the healthy adolescent, the closet lesbian, the wit, the shrew, the loving wife, the gentle sister, the strong female, the vulnerable woman, the tart friend.[47] Dealing in either-or questions distorts both the kind of person she was and the nature of her literary accomplishment, and narrowing her literary creations into autobiographical portraits (turning 'the man without a temperament' into Middleton Murry, or 'Kezia Burnell' restrictively into young Kathleen Beauchamp, for example) mistakes the source of a literary impulse for its textual result. My concern here is to fasten more upon literary form than upon the personality of the creator, but to see her modifications of form in the context of her attempt to reconcile her growing understanding of her cultural sympathies with the demands of her intellectual milieu.

That she repeatedly saw her home culture and her acquired culture in tension with each other is evident from her own decisions about residence and career, from the many reflections on the subject that appear in her letters and journals, and from the thematic and formal tensions that structure so many of her stories. The thematic contrast makes the tension between present and past (or between fashion and nostalgia) obvious, and perhaps the obviousness of the contrast is what makes some of the stories now seem somewhat slight. In 'Marriage à la Mode,' for example, the brittle rhetoric of 'high fashion' is shown to be empty and cruel, yet seductive – mostly because the opposing rhetoric of sentiment (and there appear to be only the two options), however well-meaning it might be, is demonstrably ineffectual. 'Feuille d'Album' closes with a comparable contrast, when the narrator steps into what has become a banal and sentimental story, about an inarticulate infatuation, to round it off with a smart joke: sweeping to perform the gallant formal courtesy of picking up his young lady's dropped handkerchief, the central figure hands her what she has in fact dropped – an egg. But even more than it functions as a narrative conclusion, this device appears to be a means to allow the author / narrator to escape the mesh of wishful thinking – the story may be 'about' romance, but it works only as an exercise in the limits of story-*telling*.

For all their weakness, then, these stories remind us of Mansfield's repeated concern to address fact through fiction, and to reject those fictional techniques which proved to lead her into falsifications of what she saw to be true. But we must be wary of this generalization. For 'truth' did not lie simply in empirical fact; it lay in emotional identification as well, and in social injustice (the war that killed her brother), attitudinal corruption, and literary practice.[48] If the forms of sketch and documentary were never far from her command – stories as late as 'Spring Pictures,' 'Miss Brill,' 'The Wind Blows,' and 'Bank Holiday' can formally be read as late versions of the mood-sketches she wrote in 1907 for the *Native Companion* – she was constantly trying her hand at other forms with which to couple the sketch: forms such as allegory

('How Pearl Button Was Kidnapped'), plotted tale ('The Woman at the Store'), drama ('The Black Cap'), satire (*In a German Pension*), discarding what she found end-closed[49] until she moved into the open forms of 'Prelude,' 'Daughters of the Late Colonel,' and 'At the Bay.' Far from writing to appeal to English fashion, she was towards the end of her life writing in conscious combat with it: 'won't the "Intellectuals" just hate ["Prelude"],' she wrote to Dorothy Brett in 1918. 'They'll think it's a New Primer for Infant Readers. Let 'em.'[50] Such a statement carries both a casual air of confidence and the bluster of bravado. Yet what Mansfield did know for certain was that she was shaping story form to her own purpose, and that her own purpose was in turn shaped by the multiple dimensions of her experience.

The plotted story was not something she was much taken by – 'The Woman at the Store' is far more interesting for its New Zealand vernacular and its cluster of motifs (women, madness, violence) than for its linear narrative – which may be the chief reason she never pursued to completion her notion of writing a novel (tentatively titled 'Karori'). Certainly by 1921 she was writing disparagingly of a story form she had grown beyond. To her cousin 'Elizabeth,' the Countess Russell (author of *Elizabeth and Her German Garden*, 1898), she wrote of Clement Shorter's request for a serial:

But he stipulates for 13 'curtains' and an adventure note! Thirteen curtains! And my stories haven't even a wisp of blind cord as a rule. I have never been able to manage curtains. I don't think I shall be able to see such a wholesale *hanging* through.[51]

And a month later to Dorothy Brett she complained of a 'stupid' anthologist she suffered through at tea:

He is bringing out an anthology of short stories and he said the more 'plotty' a story I could give him the better. What about that for a word! It made my hair stand up in prongs. A nice 'plotty' story, please.[52]

Her complaints were thus both about language and about conventional narrative structure. The method she currently favoured was that which she described to Murry's brother Richard:

It's a very queer thing how *craft* comes into writing. I mean down to details ... In *Miss Brill* I choose not only the length of every sentence, but even the sound of every sentence. I choose the rise and fall of every paragraph to fit her, fit her on that day at that very moment.[53]

She was conscious not just of the musicality of rhythm but also of its power to induce sensation; and with her deliberateness of word choice and arrangement she could convey meaning modally as well as lexically. For instance, 'Miss Brill' (a story somewhat undervalued by contemporary readers) opens with a series of copula verbs, underscoring the static nature of the title character's life, a stasis of imaginative reach as much as of ambition or activity. What activity does take place is distanced out of the first person (Miss Brill avoiding responsibility) and coupled with a sense of change that Miss Brill would rather not acknowledge. The story requires her to acknowledge it, though this admission subsequently isolates her even further from herself and from the rest of the world. 'The air was motionless,' Mansfield writes, encapsulating the potential story in both structure and image; then shifts into second person for the ramifications: 'but when you opened your mouth there was just a faint chill ... '[54]

'Miss Brill' is not without its problems, most notably its difficulty in reconciling the character's sentimentality with the story's desire to avoid sentiment; what Mansfield wrote somewhat caustically to Ida Baker –

Do you mind cutting out the descriptions as much as you can? That kind of yearning sentimental writing about a virginia creeper and the small haigh voices of tainy children is more than I can stick – [55]

might occasionally be heard as self-criticism, an attack on false Englishness as well as on emotive hyperventilation. Indeed, the satiric mode through which she began her career in England seems a deliberate stage in her attempt to purge her writing of false sentiment – false sentiment which she then identified with naïveté, dependence, powerlessness, and colonial imitation. While the satires thus mark a stage in her progress away from the Wildean sketch, they also represent a mode she subsequently found shallow. In 1920 she wrote to Murry,'I am sure O.W. was negligible but he *is* an astonishing figure. His letters, his mockeries and thefts – he's a Judas who betrays himself.'[56]

Satiric barbs did not disappear from her writing, though her later stories were more inclined than the early ones to accept people's foibles and weaknesses as integral elements in life's pathetic comedy. Yet *In a German Pension* contains greater strengths than her restrictions on it might suggest. It is full of sharply evocative phrases, as in the *non sequiturs* of 'Luft Bad' or the gossip in 'The Sister of the Baroness': 'we gorged on scandals of High Birth generously buttered.'[57] And Mansfield mordantly controls the ambivalence of the language that defines gender biases, as when she evokes the self-pity of Andreas Binzer in 'A Birthday' or the scarcely suppressed anger of the title character in 'Frau Brechenmacher Attends a Wedding,' both stories which anticipate the gender tensions of 'Mr Reginald Peacock's Day' and 'At the Bay.' When the man in 'The Swing of the Pendulum' drags a woman to bed (saying '"Don't be silly – come and be good!"'),[58] Mansfield's deliberate emphasis on 'good,' when the man so clearly means 'usable,' angrily stresses the irony of his manipulation of the language of morality. And at the end of 'At Lehmann's,' there emerges directly a contrast which informs much of Mansfield's subsequent commentary on the politics of gender: *babies* for the women in her stories are a constant reminder of the *consequences* of their sexuality, whereas for the men they constitute a proof *product* of their own virility. Repeatedly the women seek freedom and are constrained, whereas the men seek ratification and are suffered to continue in their own insensitivity.

What Mansfield establishes in *In a German Pension* is the link between politics, gender, and language. 'Being A Truthful Adventure,' written at the same time but not collected until 'Something Childish,'reiterates the connection in a yet more documentary form: what emerges from the story is Mansfield's distinction between the sentimentalizing language of guidebooks, the falsifying language of fashionable causes, and the truthful language of experience – and it is to the last that she strives to dedicate her subsequent work. Naïveté, it appears, is as much as anything in her work a function of language. As 'The Little Governess' specifies, the failure to *interpret* accurately will prove self-destructive. But 'interpret' has itself to be understood as a word with multiple levels of signification. It means not just 'decode a verbal meaning' but also 'translate the significance of nuance and gesture' – respond to the *absence*, that which is unsaid, as much as to the *presence*, that for which there are words.

The development of story form is thus related to Mansfield's attitude to the political implications of being female. But we must keep in mind here that for Mansfield there existed a close connection between her attitude to culture and her attitude to gender politics. The New Zealand she left in 1908 was defining itself literarily by means of male norms, and her cries for literary, social, and attitudinal reform all sprang from the same deep recognition of the interconnection between words and power. It is not surprising, therefore, to find that the record of her attitude to New Zealand follows the same course as the record of her attitude to herself and to literary form – first embracing satire, which asserts her distances; then affecting intellectual independence; then acknowledging the complexity of the cultural connection, from which she draws emotional sustenance even while alienated from its source, and to which she brings her mature skill with words.

In 1914 she artfully records in her journal: 'Dreamed about N.Z. again – one of the painful dreams when I'm there and hazy about my return ticket.[59] In

1920, quoting Coleridge to the effect that 'language, religion, laws, government, blood – identity in these makes men of one country,' she adds ascerbically: 'The sod under my feet makes *mine*.'[60] Yet writing to her father the year before she died (one hears reconciliation in her words, based on her mature independence, rather than a pose contrived for the letter's recipient), she observes: 'the longer I live the more I turn to New Zealand. I thank God I was born in New Zealand. A young country is a real heritage, though it takes one time to recognize it.'[61] Paradoxically what she turned to was a New Zealand of her memory rather than the New Zealand of the present, but the inevitable fragmentation of memory – reinforced by distance and her continuing alienation from the country's social norms – became part of her mature literary technique, as in 'Prelude,' 'At the Bay,' or the best sections of 'The Garden-Party.' She contained by fragmentation, in effect – a statement which applies to her personal identity as well as her literary method – allowing the moments of sketch to suggest the nuance of what remained unsaid as well as to shape the moment itself.

Clearly her method is oblique. But an oblique method was something she needed if she was to make any headway combatting the New Zealand literary / social conventions. The point is not that she denied these conventions existed; she admitted them, rejected their applicability to herself, used them, and then proceeded to allude to the presence of alternative conventions (those of women, children, Maori, lower classes), all with a life of their own, co-existent with, yet largely unseen by, the world that held power and so defined the myths of identity. Imagery plays a part in articulating this multiplicity. When Kezia, in 'Prelude,' goes exploring the gardens of the new family home, she discovers it has two sides – one 'a tangle of tall dark trees and strange bushes ... the frightening side, and no garden at all,' the other with 'a high box border [where] ... the paths had box edges ... '[62] One might fairly see this comment as a description of the New Zealand landscape, part native bush and part English import. Mansfield is ambivalent about the choice between them; she allows Kezia to be attracted by the English flower garden, but that is the one with the 'box' enclosures. At least she acknowledges the duality, and her 1907 journal entry – 'When New Zealand is more artificial, she will give birth to an artist who can treat her natural beauties adequately'[63] – can perhaps be taken as an admission of the limitations of her own education in English standards.

Certainly there are constraints to her effectiveness when she does try to portray Maori, maids, seamstresses, and others not in the Beauchamp circle. But partly her narrative method is structural as well, both on the level of vocabulary and on the level of story design. The opening of 'Prelude,' with its attention to verbs, rapidly establishes the narrative role of the several characters and by implication the social role allotted them: Pat, the handyman, in the active; Grandmother Fairfield by a copula; Linda by a negative; Isabel in the passive. In the larger scheme, the story is in fragments: we see by glimpses, inferring the connections between character, events, and the cultural mores, observing that (despite the pressures to conform to rule) there persist independent impulses to life. It is these impulses with which the author identifies – expressing self indirectly, and often suppressing self in order more acutely to identify with her created characters.

Yet one of the paradoxes of Mansfield's career derives from her duality about the implications of her mature method. She wanted at once to declare self and to hide self, to embrace the *dégagé* and to find a tidy orderliness that would explain all. She once advised Murry not to lower his mask until he had another prepared beneath; she praised Emily Brontë's writing because it revealed Emily, 'not Emily disguised'; and she argued with herself:

I should always be trying to tell the truth. As matter of fact I dare not tell the truth ... The only way to exist is to go on and try and lose oneself – to get as far away as possible from *this* moment.

Then she added: 'Once I can do that all will be well.'[64] Repeatedly she seeks this security of wholeness, a unity that will structure experience for her – even her final sojourn in the Gurdjieff Institute for Harmonious Development might be seen in this context – and her fondness for stories like 'The Garden-Party' and 'Bliss,' with their neat closures, over looser stories like 'At the Bay,' offers tangible literary evidence for this aspect of her aspiration.[65] Yet she wearied, too, of neatness. Her last letter to her cousin Elizabeth asserts: 'I am tired of my little stories like birds bred in cages' – 'it seems to me we live in new impressions.'[66] 'I used to fancy,' she wrote to Richard Murry,

one knew all but some kind of mysterious core (or one could). But now I believe just the opposite. The unknown is far, far greater than the known. The known is only a mere shadow. This is a fearful thing and terribly hard to face.[67]

And to William Gerhardi she wrote:

that is what I tried to convey in *The Garden Party*. The diversity of life and how we try to fit in everything, Death included. That is bewildering for a person of Laura's age. She feels things ought to happen differently. First one and then another. But life isn't like that. We haven't the ordering of it.[68]

But the failure of 'The Garden-Party' is tied up with the failure of the story's ending and the inadequacy of the characterization of Laura's brother Laurie, to whom the ending is given. For all her commitment to uncertainty and the unknown, Mansfield still with this story tries to find a final phrase that would encapsulate all. It may be that the characterization of Laurie is more apt than I suggest, and that Mansfield is intentionally using the language of male 'finality' to silence the female before she actually speaks. If such is the case, then Laurie's 'finality' is both illusory and false, and the focus remains on Laura, inferentially. Certainly Mansfield's more lasting gift to the short story form (both in New Zealand and in the world at large) derived from her skill with fragmentation more than from her skill with revelatory phrase. She coupled what she had learned of the documentary and impressionistic sketch with what she made of Chekhov: he 'just touched one point with his pen (.———.) and then another point: *enclosed* something which had, as it were, been there for ever.'[69] Out of the combination she produced an art of inferential narrative: a way of documenting incidents so that the reader would be able to animate what lay unstated in between. By so doing – by making absence an integral creative element in her stories – she fastened attention on the inarticulate (or at least unarticulated) sources of people's motivation.

For her own culture she also in the process gave voice to a dimension of the society for whom the literary norms did not adequately or quite accurately speak.

Frank Sargeson & Sons, 1900–1970

It would be naïve to have expected that Mansfield's accomplishment would immediately modify either short story method or social mores in New Zealand; and neither eventuality occurred. Where she was imitated, the results were largely sentimental portraits of childhood, perpetuating the inaccurate notion that Mansfield's own portraits of the Burnell children were somehow idyllic. And where she was criticized, the reasons stemmed largely from the fact that she did not reinforce the myths of farm and manly wilderness that were coming to be accepted as national truths. We are dealing here with attitudes and language as well as with simple subject. M.H. Holcroft, editor of the influential *New Zealand Listener* between 1949 and 1967, could as late as 1969 aver that there was a preoccupation with childhood in the stories that were submitted to him because it was housewives who wrote stories.[70] He adds that, because of the 'practical bias of the New Zealand mind,' factual stories rather than imaginative ones reached a readier market: 'Facts are the framework or background within which the story develops; if facts are wrong, the reader's attention is deflected, and imagination, which should bring an enlargement of the real, is seen to be illusion.'[71] In other words, probability is all. When one contrasts the documentary work of W.H. Guthrie-Smith with the sentimental excesses of writers like Mona Tracy and Mary Gurney, one sees his point. But inevitably there was some quarrel in the society over what constituted reality, a dispute as to whether reality was to be identified by local reference, Britishness, language, accent, home, 'Home,' or self-image.[72]

Two of the most popular journals of the early twentieth century were industrial magazines which published some fiction, *The New Zealand Railways Magazine* (1926-40) and *Red Funnel* (1905–9). In them are to be found the kind of manly adventures which won general approval; 'J.G.'s' 'The Fijian Girl and the Octopus,' for example, is advertised as a 'true story,' but while the reader of the time may have accepted the credibility of its language – because committed to the values it conveyed – the modern reader responds more to its story-book paradigms (and perhaps to its Freudian implications): monster of the deep, fair maiden captured, heroic rescue necessitated (based on unequal odds: 'Unfortunately I had forgotten my sheath knife'). The language offers a combination of the exact and the conventional: 'The little lassie was only wearing a *liku* ... For a moment I hardly knew what to do; but, lifting struggling girl and fish on my shoulders, made for the shore. Ugh! the great gnawing beak, the slimy, flabby thing against my neck and on my head, made my flesh creep ... '[73] Characteristic of such writing is its reliance on adjectives and the light dusting of native terms that awkwardly adorns it, as though such practice authenticated the literary observation. Some three decades later, the techniques were still common, as in one of the earliest of modern New Zealand story anthologies, John Kington's *Pataka*. One of the stories Kington collected opens this way:

Jan stood beneath the giant kauri tree and sighed. She always sighed when she stood thus, looking out at the vast monotony of rolling plains.

Born to the backblocks, she knew not the significance of the word 'city,' yet pondered deeply when the South bound express whistled beyond the purple-blue hills that surrounded Pat McKyne's prosperous dairy farm.[74]

Pataka (or 'Treasure House') was dismissed by *Art in New Zealand*: 'The semi-literary treasure will be cherished ... chiefly by the individual contributors and their friends and relatives.'[75] Yet what the book underscored was the persistence of the descriptive school of New Zealand fiction. Portraits of the Maori, as in Pat Lawlor's *Maori Tales* (1926) simply perpetuated outsiders' views of the native as comic figure. External judgment constituted a pervasive mode of perception. Authors portrayed landscape as the characterizing feature of New Zealand, using local and native terms to establish what it looked like, from the outside, equating visual perception with credibility and authority. It was Mansfield's talent to evoke not what things looked like but what things felt like, but such sensibility was in New Zealand at this time largely dismissed as female.[76]

This was a time when Hector Bolitho could seriously declare:

In neither Canada nor Australia have the people developed the same love of the earth as you will find in a New Zealand farmer ... The earth belongs to this white man because his grandfather fought for it and made it what it is. He would hate the idea of selling it. He has traditions to respect, and his farm has a reputation for producing good cattle and exceptional butter.[77]

Or when D'Arcy Cresswell, though in a more suspect tone, could declaim:

women love men, men love heroes and poets, and these love the gods; and this upward current is the cause of all glorious periods of faith and power on earth ... [Yet it is a process that can be upset, for it poets and heroes love women before men as though that were natural, then men should love] not women who love them, but animals, to whom women are next of kin.[78]

Inevitably, such attitudes touched the language of criticism. 'Virility' became a vogue word to describe language, subject, and attitude, as when W.S. Dale (despite the incongruity of his observation) asserts that 'Rosemary Rees ... has not the virility of Jane Mander or the scintillation of Katherine Mansfield..'[79] One of the most forthright commentators at the time, A.R.D. Fairburn, challenged current biases by claiming Mansfield's greatness in these terms:

You must not expect power and virility from Katherine Mansfield's poems, though she is capable of sturdy realism ... [B]ut let us thank the gods for giving us at least one writer of genius, even if she was a woman.[80]

The point in quoting such comments today lies in the revelation they offer of the difficulties Mansfield presented to New Zealand critics. In the terms of the day, she received international recognition, and therefore must be good, but she was a woman, and therefore could not adequately represent New Zealand: critics were stymied by their allegiance to criteria that seemed mutually exclusive, and as a result they invented sometimes irrational ways out of their dilemma.

One response was to deny that Mansfield had any international reputation at all, a point of view that as late as 1955 was still appearing in the columns of the *New Zealand Listener*. Another was to deny her her nationality. The contemporary historian Tony Simpson is one of the latest of disclaimer writers:

Culture was something they had at Home. If one wished to be cultivated one went to England or one did one's best by aping the cultural conventions one had left behind ... And above all, one felt terribly inferior and awfully colonial. It is for this reason that it is a grave error to claim Katherine Mansfield as a New Zealand writer. She was not, and to try to lay claim on her as such is to reveal how callow we still remain, what a dependent frame of mind we still retain.[81]

A third response disputes her quality, either on linguistic or sociological grounds. Noel Hilliard, for example, writing in the *New Zealand Listener* in 1968, complained that Mansfield was getting an unwarranted reputation as a social rebel, but that it never crossed her mind to have Kezia, in 'The Doll's House,' take Lil and Our Else 'out to the kitchen and [give] them a good feed':

No poignant moments in bread and butter though. No art to be created out of Aunt Beryl suddenly materialising and whisking the plate away, and Our Else lamenting at the roadside, 'I saw the little cold potatoes.'[82]

Earlier still, in 1951, there was a series of readers' letters to the *Listener* complaining that none of Mansfield's stories was memorable, well-written, true-to-life, or anything more than 'the apotheosis of the trivial, dabbling and dithering in minutiae of excruciating dullness.'[83] Each of these commentators wanted something different – the letter-writers often wanted an escapist plot with an O. Henry ending; Hilliard rejected anything that wasn't Maori or working class or Depression, though in his own writing he managed to sentimentalize these subjects till they seem trivial; and Simpson, despite his nationalist concerns, seems implicitly to accept the adjective 'New Zealand' as a limitation of quality rather than a neutral description of origin.

All Commonwealth nations have experienced the excessive border-defining of a national literary movement, and perhaps that is what is at the back of Hilliard's rejection of Mansfield; yet it is now clear that the notions of urban propriety, squattocratic class, 'proper' schooling, 'proper' accent, and European connections – which to some degree she epitomized – are as much a part of the New Zealand social structure and the New Zealand cultural heritage as are the notions of the egalitarian, plain-speaking, country Kiwi. The kind of co-existence they have managed is what characterizes the place. But the first fifty or so years of the twentieth century were in large part spent quarrelling over which separate image portrayed Representative New Zealand accurately. It is a context which makes Frank Sargeson's appearance in the 1930s important for what it says about critical expectation as well as for the intrinsic quality of Sargeson's prose.

By the 1930s the National Image which had won fairly standard acceptance involved British homogeneity and the orderliness of fair play. Game metaphors were commonplace. The *New Zealand Railways Magazine* published stories in 1926 on 'playing the game,' and as late as 1966, Monte Holcroft would editorialize in the *New Zealand Listener* on 'Rugby as a Way of Life':

> The game as we play it reveals our national characteristics – an impulse to act together in a crisis, a bias towards scientific method and a distrust of imagination, a seriousness of mind, a sense of humour which favours banter but is reserved for proper occasions, a dislike of levity, and a fondness for the firm and tidy result. These qualities or habits belong to life in New Zealand, and will not disappear simply because some people are unable to like them. On the football field, when the pressure grows, they become a little larger than life.[84]

While a number of writers demurred, their general effect was to challenge the notion of Englishness more than the impulse behind the image of the masculine game. Hence A.R.D. Fairburn's striking claim that the history of New Zealand 'has been a progress from teat-jerk to quidnunc' served to challenge New Zealand writers to emulate American literary models rather than what he considered outmoded British ones; he even claims D'Arcy Cresswell as Thoreau.[85] But in practice at this time, American models led more often to popular anecdote (as in the 'Me and Gus' stories of Frank S. Anthony which began to appear in weekly newspapers in the 1920s) than they did to Thoreau, and resulted in reviews which overlaid an American allusion on the familiar conventions, as in 'A.M.'s' comment on *Me and Gus Again*:

> The situations are well conceived, and the telling is direct and masculine, a complement to the feminine element in our rural annals, but not without subtlety ... There is a lot of fun here ... and also social history. In one of the funniest stories, reminiscent of American folk literature, Gus's eloquent negative in a debate – on 'Should Women Milk?' – ends in his being chased round the hall by an infuriated husband. Otherwise culture hardly enters these bachelors' lives, and I can't say I miss it.[86]

In addition to the reach for an American connection, there was in the *New Zealand Listener* a whole series of allusions to Canadian culture as a potential model for New Zealand; but unlike the images of the United States these appear to have had no effect on literary practice whatsoever.[87] Australia was closer. And while New Zealanders often abruptly rejected Australian cultural models (as Canadians imitate and reject U.S. ones), these none the less had the usual impact of proximity. New Zealand political and economic life ran generally parallel to that in Australia, and the smaller society was not unaffected by the larger one.

All of these attempts at modelling were closely literary as well as broadly social — recurrent attempts to find a culturally acceptable literary form. As Elizabeth Smith phrased it in 1939, there was a paradox involved in hoping to expect realistic subtlety from an unintrospective people: 'Imagination of a kind, yes. Heroes and villains in sharp juxtaposition, involved plots and fantastic theories abound, but of real characters in whom we can believe there are none.'[88] Yet for most critics the phrase 'real characters in whom we can believe' referred precisely to that group of 'unintrospective people.' They wanted those characters, they wanted a *male* writer to portray them, and they found the combination they wanted — with the American influence thrown in — when Frank Sargeson began to publish his sketches in *Tomorrow* in 1935.

In retrospect one can see how determinedly some readers laid claim to Sargeson's prose. His early stories, written under the mantle of Sherwood Anderson, relied on rhythm rather than plot, pared language of ornament, recorded the often banal utterances of unextraordinary people, and generally combatted readers' preconceived notions of story. Despite his subject, moreover — ostensibly the laconic, down-to-earth males of an egalitarian rural society — his stories dealt with violence, monetary rivalry, inequalities, and homosexuality. And they dealt with language. Some readers balked. W.F.R. Anderson wrote to the *New Zealand Listener* with remarkable candour: 'It amazes me that Frank Sargeson should be presented ... as New Zealand's foremost short-story writer. In fact, most of our modern New Zealand writers amaze me. Frankly I cannot understand them ... '[89] Others needed time to react. Oliver Duff spent most of his 1940 *Listener* review of *A Man and His Wife* working his way into enthusiasm: Sargeson is Mansfield's successor, his words are deliberate and under control, if he wants to exploit 'toughness' that is his affair, and though he'll make his mark the fact is that it

is a curious mark. In itself it would suggest to posterity that New Zealand during the last twenty years has been a kind of rural slum; a few disgusting exploiters and a large number of brutish victims. Most of us don't see it like that. We don't see our neighbours as morons, our young people as sensual louts, our teachers and preachers as liars and hypocrites, our patriots as profiteers. We know, however, that such people exist, and their place in the picture need not worry us if Sargeson sees them, can't take his eyes off them, and can't help presenting them as they are. It is his affair and not ours if he chooses to be a laureate of hoboes.[90]

Warring in Duff's mind are his anglophilia (something closely allied to his enthusiasm for Mansfield) and his determination to read New Zealand vernacular writing as in some measure documentary history. In another context A.R.D. Fairburn countered:

I should like to make a point about Sargeson's prose. His use of an idiom based on common speech is not to be taken as a concession to illiteracy. It is a literary device, used to express character and to define an attitude. As such it fully justifies itself, whether or not it exactly reflects New Zealand speech. The canons of realism should be applied with caution. Realism, as a complete theory of artistic expression, is indefensible.[91]

In other words, Sargeson was no more representative of all New Zealand than Mansfield was, but that is beside the point. Sargeson chose not to make his art subservient to the popular stereotypes of society, but to use those stereotypes in his art — in the process subverting the stereotypes and teasing nuance from the vernacular.

This is not to say that he gave up connections between art and society — far from it. The connections that he actually perceived between art and society were what stimulated him into writing. *More than Enough*, the second volume of his autobiography, records that, in the early 1930s, after reading all the New Zealand fiction he could find, he was distressed to conclude that 'virtually always the more or less formal language of the English novelists had been used to deal with the material of New Zealand life (and in my view that was to say colonial life).' As he himself had been aiming first at a Galsworthian style, his observation became a self-directed challenge to technique: 'the question became inevitable: whether there might not be an appropriate language to deal with the material of New Zealand life?'[92] The result was his connection with the left-wing Christchurch magazine *Tomorrow* and the series of mini-sketches he wrote for it, beginning with 'Conversation with My Uncle.' *Tomorrow* led subsequently to most of the stories that were collected in *Conversation with My Uncle and Other Sketches* (1936), *A Man and His Wife* (1940; revised 1944), and *That Summer and Other Stories* (1946). ('That Summer' first appeared in the *Penguin New Writing* series, and was anthologized again in 1984, in Anthony Stones' selection from the series, *Celebration*.)

Like Callaghan in Canada, he was fascinated with the artistry of speech rhythm that Sherwood Anderson had mastered. 'I had moved (or been moved),' Sargeson wrote, 'in the direction of composing short clear sentences which, in a vivid and unexpected way, would transmit a good deal of what writers might fairly grant to be common human experience ... What especially delighted me was that despite the simplicity of my sentences, they could in a page-long sketch achieve an unexpected totality not to be compared with the meagre sum of parts.'[93] Two covert messages underlie this statement of intent. The emphasis on unexpectedness[94] draws oblique attention to the function of indirect narrative; and the concern for the totality into which fragments cohere reveals Sargeson's continuing interest in tidy units of social and literary order. Repeatedly he tried his hand at the novel (among them *I Saw In My Dream*, 1949; *Memoirs of a Peon*, 1965; *Joy or the Worm*, 1969), but his greater talent lay in his eye for episode[95] and his greatest success was the long story 'That Summer,' with its interrupted sequence of events and its interrupted line of narrative communication. (The repeated transitional phrase in the story is 'but instead.') It is the surface interruptions which give the illusion of the characters' laconic inarticulateness — hence these which convey to socially minded critics the authenticity of Sargeson's portraiture. But it is the fact of interruption itself — interruption, or contrived silence, as a literary device — on which Sargeson was largely focusing.

In other words, though it is thematically possible to say that 'A Great Day' and 'Sale Day,' for example, are about violence among men, either irrational or vengeful, or that 'The Hole that Jack Dug' and 'Boy' are about males' vulnerability in a world of rigid rules and severe women, or that 'A Pair of Socks' and 'That Summer' are about discoveries of covert homosexuality, such descriptions still fasten on narrative subject rather than narrative method as the identifying feature of the art of story-telling. For Sargeson the interruptions were not just a means by which to represent rural New Zealand male speech but a verbally bounded way to enact an 'unhistoric story.' Most clearly Sargeson was asserting that New Zealand's history / story did not unfold smoothly from England's: one either followed the model, retold the tale, and remained a colony, or somehow interrupted those patterns and sketched the nation into speech. Behind this process was a second one, implicitly undermining that other linear pattern, the patriarchal line of power. But while many readers fastened on Sargeson's ordinary working bloke as a national image, and some observed the puritan vehemence of his anti-puritanism, few followed the subversive implications of Sargeson's linguistic forms.

Helen Shaw's 1954 anthology of comments on Sargeson, *The Puritan and the Waif*, gives some hint of the contrast in responses: Erik Schwimmer seeks his social conscience, Winston Rhodes his moral presence. D'Arcy Cresswell locates his nationalism, and James K. Baxter his spareness. Cresswell, finding New Zealand national goals to be different from those of other nations — different from the English deference to order and rank, the American deference to materialism, the Australian ideal of physical vitality, and 'that nearly speechless Canadian awe at mere space and size' — finds Sargeson's method full of 'masculine clarity,' 'objectiveness,' and 'transparent thinness,' which is 'right, if it's a native art we are after.'[96] Sargeson, that is, eavesdrops on people's values. Baxter writes that Sargeson's problem is 'to impose aesthetic order on that world of flux in which he lives,' and that at best his prose has 'considerable liturgical power. Its value lies far less in an accurate reproduction of common speech than in the creation of a new art form.'[97]

Yet how new is it? It takes a new advantage of the sketch's brevity, but for all the Andersonian influence, there is more Mansfield in Sargeson than at first seems apparent; both writers framed silence so that it became articulate, Mansfield using it to assert that women's experience could not be described by current structures and Sargeson to say that men's experience was curtailed by those same structures. Men in Mansfield's stories recurrently seem bumptious, predatory, or ineffectual; for Sargeson it is women who as a group come off badly. Repeatedly they serve on his pages as shadowy agents of temptation, punishment, and revenge – and men's vulnerability in their company reveals the flimsiness of the patriarchal structure that on the surface they seem to be representing.

Sargeson takes those national images of mates, loners, and rough-hewn land and turns them on their end, using the laconic rhythms of speech (those rhythms prized as 'masculine' because they are not florid) to enact the emotional violence of stillborn relationships. As even his first sketch makes clear, talking and communication are not synonymous, and most of his early characters, tight-lipped and elliptical, withdraw from others because their speech disconnects them. They are limited by their own fragmentation. – by the closed dimensions of what they have to say: 'Gosh,' 'oh gee,' 'Somehow,' 'Maybe,' 'Who could say,' 'If only,' 'It didn't seem as if,' 'I'm trying to explain,' 'I didn't know what to say.' Such are the catchwords by which they stutter their uncertainties. Yet to leave Sargeson characterized by his early work would be to fail to acknowledge the extent of his impact on New Zealand letters, and the dimensions of his own shaping talent. The narrators of his later stories are articulate, ironic, even garrulous, and sometimes judgmental or droll; by the 1960s speech rather than silence had become the norm, for other writers as well as for Sargeson. (The mock pompousness of *Joy of the Worm* begs for comparison with Maurice Gee's *Plumb,* and while the bitterness of 'Making Father Pay' [1975] is reminiscent of the enclosed world of 'Boy' or 'A Good Boy,' the solemn ironies of 'Beau' [1965] and 'En Route' [1979] tell of a more sophisticated mastery of speech than the early characters are capable of.)

The point is not, however, that the later characters are suddenly sophisticated, or that New Zealand literature has in the meantime Grown Up, but rather that Sargeson's later characters are less dislocated by their own idiosyncrasies, more comfortable with the masks that their own language allows them to wear. They grow, as it were, into their own fragmentation; the speech they possess gives them a kind of possession of speech – out of which the articulate irony grows. 'Listen,' say the early characters, robbed of all but their intensity and their need to connect; 'I'll say,' they nod colloquially, claiming speech for themselves only by reflecting what others can do. Yet the later characters can actively *say, whisper, exclaim,* and even aspire to music and poetry, as in 'Just Trespassing, Thanks'; their colloquiality has given them roots, given them a security in place and speech. If not always fulfilling, these distinguishing masks no longer automatically deny them fulfilment because they are local. Sargeson freed the forms of local discourse from their self-imposed closure, freed them to become (in the hands of a subsequent writer, Maurice Duggan, for example) a medium of introspection and open play. It was not his ultimate accomplishment to nationalize language in New Zealand, but rather to demonstrate its flexibility, and it was that potential for suppleness which he offered as a bequest to those who followed him.

Yet in the thirty-year period that began about the time of World War II, New Zealand short fiction went into the doldrums. Lawrence Jones sharply refers to the work of the time as 'The Persistence of Realism.' His comments are instructive; appearing in 1977, they were also mildly revisionist.[98] For most New Zealand critics the period was regarded as one of high accomplishment: there was an increased number of writers with moderate talent about, they published both at home and abroad, most of them were male, they wrote about ordinary New Zealand workers rather than about the upper middle class, they recorded local speech – they were the first entire *generation* of writers in New Zealand who could be read as narrative documenters of the New Zealand condition, and they became the staple core of modern anthologies. Yet they were basically as much imitators as those earlier writers who had contrived to affect a BBC accent or who modelled their work on European romance. Although they were imitating the home-grown Sargeson, they were for the most part missing his underlying point about language. Instead of running with his innovations with *form*, they echoed his particular *subjects*: rural childhood, homosexual uncles, Dalmatian immigrants and their difficult adaptation to New Zealand norms, absent fathers, oppressive mothers, loners, and the sublimated violence of puritan mores. They took Sargeson as 'realist' – by which they meant: 'representer' – rather than as stylist and innovator, and their satisfaction with such realism meant that Sargeson's points of difference with the conventional image of his society were not immediately apparent in the work of these 'Sons of Frank.'

Clearly these are generalizations, which touch to different degrees the dozen or so writers involved: Roderick Finlayson (*Brown Man's Burden*, 1938; *Tidal Creek*, 1948; *Other Lovers*, 1976; *Brown Man's Burden and Later Stories*, 1972), Dan Davin (*The Gorse Blooms Pale*, 1947; *Breathing Spaces*, 1975; *Selected Stories*, 1981), A.P. Gaskell (ie, Alexander Gaskell Pickard: *The Big Game and Other Stories*, 1947; *All Part of the Game*, 1978),

John Reece Cole (*It Was So Late and Other Stories*, 1949), Noel Hilliard (*A Piece of Land: Stories and Sketches*, 1963; *Send Somebody Nice*, 1976; *Selected Stories*, 1977), O.E. Middleton (*Short Stories*, 1953; *The Stone and Other Stories*, 1959; *A Walk on the Beach*, 1964; *The Loners*, 1972; *Selected Stories*, 1976). James Courage (*Such Separate Creatures: Stories*, 1973, chosen by Charles Brasch), David Ballantyne (*And the Glory*, 1963). Phillip Wilson (*Some Are Lucky*, 1960), all of them in some sense culminating in Maurice Shadbolt (*The New Zealanders: A Sequence of Stories*, 1959; *Summer Fires and Winter Country*, 1963; *The Presence of Music: Three Novellas*, 1967; *Figures in Light: Selected Stories*, 1978).

It is not surprising that so many of these writers were reporters and editors — Davin, Hilliard, Shadbolt, Wilson, Ballantyne. Essayists manqué, they sought through their characters, images, settings, and stance to be both representational and representative. Typically they report their characters from the inside (first person vernacular) but see them from the outside (third person removed). With them, Sargeson's laconic mode turned into a national art form, deliberately contrived to portray the distinctive types that were held to constitute the society. In Gaskell, for example, the 'big game' is both social metaphor and particular fact, a test of the main character's resilient masculine readiness as much as a dramatized event. In Middleton and Finlayson the test of resourcefulness is the economic upset of the Depression; in Cole and Davin it is the war. The Church immobilizes them — Davin's Catholicism separates him here from other writers. And for most of the characters in these stories, sexuality is burdensome and barren, companionship their greatest hope, and family their desire and concurrently the source of their debilitation.

In Wilson's 'Some Are Lucky,' Courage's 'An Evening for a Fish,' and Cole's 'The Sixty Nine Club' to name only three instances, a mother intervenes in the perception of a son, or a mothering wife in the perception of a husband, reducing man to boy by reducing what has been held to be an heroic (or at least adult) exploit into a mere boyish escapade; Davin's 'Milk Round,' probably his single best story, runs a close parallel, showing how a class-conscious girl, using her mother's language, can shatter a farmboy's heroic daydreams. The sheer recurrence of such paradigms suggests several possible interpretations: the limit of imagination, the existence of a single source of influence, the prevalence of an imitative mode, or the prevalence of a particular image of the society. Perception is the key issue — whether it is that of the writer, recording what he sees or thinks he sees, or more subtly (and ironically) that of the characters, of the whole society, portrayed as thinking they see more than their limitations permit them.

Shadbolt's *The New Zealanders* takes eleven of these standard images of New Zealand — among them the couple with the latent homosexual attraction, the boy and father who are strangers to each other, the young man with an overprotective mother, the woman who finds New Zealand 'alien,' the newspaperman who writes about rugby, and the left-wing Depression protester – and constructs stories around each of them, assembling the collection into a sequence that represents and ostensibly evokes the social collectivity. The book doesn't work – the stories are too deliberate, functionally overstated – and the problem holds with Shadbolt's *Summer Fires and Winter Country* as well, another book full of set scenes rather than revealed dramas. Instead of gaining from its unity, the book surrenders the individual stories to the overall structural plan, in such a way as to draw attention from the author's artistic sympathies to his intellectual (and political) interest. Shadbolt complains in his 1973 comments on *The Presence of Music* that New Zealand critics (he sees the flaw as endemic to small countries) insist on reading their writers as sociologists and historians or as oracular prophets, overlooking their plain human talent for story-telling. In large part he brings the judgment on himself, not only by direct statement – in the same article he asserts: 'A national sensibility is something largely received through the creation of the artist'[99] – but also by the very way he manipulates form (by sequence in *The New Zealanders*, by triptych in *The Presence of Music*) to record a vision of social unity.

He claims, indeed, that 'If you care to see New Zealanders as a new tribe of men and women in the South Pacific, then these [his stories] ... are tales of that tribe.'[100] Yet in direct comments on short story form he reveals an uneasiness about the genre that suggests why in practice his stories always seem to be striving for a large, clear, ordered (aesthetic, social) pattern. On the one hand, he wrote with studied ornament for the *Kenyon Review* survey of short fiction in 1969:

the real challenge ... of the short story ... is to produce ... that hallucinatory point in which time past and time future seem to co-exist with the present, that hallucinatory point which to me defines the good or great short story; a point which, like a stone tossed in a pool, sends ripples widening across all that we see and know, and all that we have never really seen and known, at the instant that it sinks out of sight itself.[101]

But when he quoted this passage again in 1973, he prefaced his comments with the observation:

The hazard of the short story ... is the temptation towards pure performance, clever craftsmanship, decoration rather than revelation. And performing seals, doing the same tricks over and over, are more evident in the short story than in any other literary form.[102]

Paradoxically, dismissing the idea of decoration, he is none the less drawn to the practice of decoration, which results in his stories appearing artificial despite their obvious rootedness in his feeling for his culture. The problem lies not with subject — if anything, Shadbolt's themes are more varied than those of other writers of the period — but with self-consciousness, the artifice of neatness; his formal pattern less emerges from the stories than it appears imposed upon them, action and image always turning portentously into symbol. The overall form thus becomes an act of authorial closure rather than an act of authorial accommodation, implying a greater determination to declare a unity of effect than an ability to perceive a homogeneity of behaviour.

Such a discrepancy has a rough parallel in the way many of A.P. Gaskell's tense stories close with a neat, gnomic, capsule statement about the meaning of the world — 'I had seen some of the strange and terrible things in life,' 'it has all made a great difference to Maude,' 'it seemed so awfully sad to think that someone always had to be the loser'[103] — yet with Gaskell (Sargeson's closest rival as an accomplished realist story-teller) this formal discrepancy between absolute and uncertainty appears to have more to do with the function of language in the society being portrayed. Always, in Gaskell's world, characters struggle to make sense of uncertainty — an uncertainty made more problematic because the only language they have to deal with it is articulating absolutes which have lost their relevance or their meaning. And as they rattle around inside their own language, so they rattle around inside the social frame that encloses them. It is a recurrent theme and motif. Hence, more characteristic in New Zealand short fiction than the Shadbolt sequential pattern is some form of internal fragmentation, a kind of discontinuous set of understandings contained within a formal boundary. In this respect the work of David Ballantyne and J.R. Cole offers a link between Mansfield and Sargeson before them and Duggan, O'Sullivan, and Russell Haley after. Most New Zealand story collections, in fact, emphasize their own disparity by including a phrase like 'and other stories' or 'stories and sketches' in their title — a generalization to which Davin's *The Gorse Blooms Pale* and Shadbolt's *The New Zealanders* are notable exceptions.

In 1949, moreover, writing about Roderick Finlayson, the Brazilian critic Paulo Ronai observed:

There is here, as in other stories, such as those by Frank Sargeson, a conscious seeking for half-tones, the joining of strands which are slack and loosely sewn; and a systematic use of 'points,' all of which seems to be characteristic of recent New Zealand writing, and which show the predominant influence of Katherine Mansfield, Chekhov, Virginia Woolf among others on New Zealand writers.[104]

Despite the hazy cultural history of the last phrase, the sense of a 'system of points' is well taken. The recurrent method suggests a striving for one form of expression within the context of another; while the specifics of person beset by inarticulateness may vary (man, woman, immigrant, Maori, society at large), repeatedly the framing structure (language, nationality, system of social values), *to which the characters continue to hold allegiance*, proves inadequate by itself to convey the dimensions of their sense of the lives they actually lead. Within the frame (the boundary of points) lie the ragged fragments of reality, articulate by inference rather than by expression, articulate in their volatile fragmentation rather than in the false illusion of pacific unity.

One must be careful, against this practice, of misconstruing the apparent story sequences through which a number of writers have told large segments of family history. Mansfield, for example, wrote a number of stories about the Burnell family which in some respects link with each other, and another group of stories about the Sheridans. Dan Davin, over two volumes, wrote a dozen stories specifically about members of the Connolly family, and a number of others that a reader could read as Connolly stories. James Courage wrote several about the Blakistons; Maurice Duggan wrote several about the Lenihans. And in each case there appears to have been in the author's mind a glimmer of a novel based on the family's life; there has certainly been a determination on the part of some critics (Middleton Murry among them) to read the resulting stories as though they were latent novels. But one must distinguish between the artistic accomplishment in each case and the critical desire for something longer, something coherent in a different way. It is not the putative unity of the stories we should fasten on but their separateness, not the structure of sequence but the structure of fragmentation.

The impulse to find connection, to read for novel-sized gestures, is strong in modern critics; in some sense it betrays a presumption rooted in an arbitrary aesthetic hierarchy, in a nineteenth-century system that celebrated the extended tale over the narrative sketch. Yet in every critical attempt to link New Zealand stories into 'full' novels there has been an attempt to explain the New Zealandness of the leaner form. James K. Baxter, in his 1954 tribute to Frank Sargeson, for example, parenthetically put down Davin's *The Gorse Blooms Pale* because as he saw it, it was trying to be a novel: its stories were long-winded and introspective, Baxter said, mere 'draughts for chapters,' not *spare* like the stories of Sargeson.[105] While there is something to be said for this judgment – the restrained 'Milk Round' is an exception, but many of Davin's stories, particularly the later ones, proved to be florid games with imitation English attitudes,[106] or narrative jokes that make him a transition figure between Frank Anthony's *Me and Gus* and Barry Crump's *Warm Beer*

151 New Zealand: Story and History

and Other Stories (1969) — there are also problems with its implicit national definition of art. When, in his story 'On the Bus,' Noel Hilliard has a cow-cocky and a woman named Miss Prisk sit side by side, resenting each other for the trip's duration, he is producing a telling metaphor for this kind of social bifurcation: the cow-cocky looks out at the landscape and sees it as *mine*, Miss Prisk (desperate for European culture) sees it as *there*. Proximity, time, and nationality link them, but attitude and expectation divide them, and it is the division as well as the connection which art tries to voice. Though there were a number of attempts to deal with this duality, it was not until 1978, in C.K. Stead's seventy-fifth birthday tribute to Frank Sargeson, that a critic recognized form itself as metaphor. 'Your fictions,' Stead wrote, in 'A Letter to Frank Sargeson,'

are composed of anecdotes, just as poems are composed of images. The skill is to make them seem to flower from one centre, not to look like washing strung out on a line. The anecdote is the image.[107]

Without themselves becoming anecdotal, that is, the stories made use of that Grace-Anthony-Davin-Crump line of narrative form and combined it with the subtleties of psychological sketch. Rather than make anecdote an encompassing structure, Sargeson turned it into an internal form of comment and revelation, punctuated by silence and interruption which were formally not silent, but told more vocally than words could do of dreams of speech and violence.

Yet it was not violence but order that remained the prevailing cultural myth, an order still founded in notions of Europeanness and homogeneity, rejecting any interruption (social or verbal) which would appear to challenge such authority or stir the surface illusion of calm control. As late as 1969, J.C. Reid would assert that violence was rare in New Zealand literature, and kept to a minimum (this in a society that had simultaneously applauded and reeled at the authoritarian severity that set down the 1951 wharfies' strike); it is, he claims, 'through *imported* popular fiction and mass media material that New Zealanders are brought into contact with violence on a large scale'[108] — a view that was immediately attacked as naïve. But in a context that deemed local inarticulateness natural, fluency was inevitably suspect; hence speech itself became a modest form of revolution. Dan Davin, who declared himself consciously committed to 'copiousness' (and to exile),[109] recognized in Sargeson the authenticity of articulateness deliberately disguised. As with the colloquial Kiwi soldiers on the Egyptian desert in 1942, he said, emotion was a danger, humour a release, imagination a greater danger, and 'skepticism a more invaluable protection.'[110] The protective disguise was there not to deny the force or the existence or the irrationality of violence but to cover over men's vulnerability to it.

If the surface order was taken as the entirety of substance, that, too, invited danger. It was Sargeson's gift to be able to catch this duality; he could present the laconic surfaces of his society and at the same time tap its recesses of articulate disruption. He makes us aware, Charles Brasch wrote (both of Sargeson and of the painter Colin McCahon), of 'a rawness and harshness in New Zealand life which are too easily passed by or glossed over ... '[111] By contrast, several other writers of the time — the periodical story-tellers Elsie Locke, Marie Bullock, John Graham, Catherine Styles, Isobel Andrews, and Marie Insley, for example — simply sentimentalized appearances. And while for the most part Sargeson's direct followers imitated the surface tempo of his prose, their stories came most alive on those rarer occasions when their language admitted of subterranean complexities.

James Courage, for example, is most adept at portraying a kind of displaced animosity towards mothers: 'Uncle Adam Shot a Stag' is an effective Freudian case study, which offers an indirect gloss on Sargeson's own stories of boys and their uncles; and when Courage restrains his urge to draw an overt moral, as in 'No Man Is an Island' (a story of mental illness and the irrational logic of affection and allegiance), his stories fasten on the power of the teller rather than depend on any intrinsic fascination presumed in his subject. O.E. Middleton is best at evoking the political essence of attitude, as in 'The Crows.' John Reece Cole can effectively dramatize the violent underside of war — not the heroics of battle but the anti-heroic wars of accommodation through which returned soldiers ironically reconcile themselves with civilian pretensions and civilian ignorance. 'Up at the Mammoth,' one of Cole's most striking works, sketches the reactions of a set of separate characters, dramatizing their interrupted lives with an ironic logic (portraying the Maori who have lost their language, to be taught it again by the pakeha who do not securely possess a language of their own) and an interrupted prose. And in A.P. Gaskell's best works — 'School Picnic' and 'Fight the Good Fight,' for example — irony transforms the conventional subjects (the happy Maori, the heroic manly war) so that the stories become formal challenges to the blind acceptance of tradition, formal declarations of the dishonesty of appearances. On the surface of Gaskell's stories are the conventional dichotomies that the society he depicts lives with as though they were absolutes: pakeha vs maori, male vs female, authority vs privacy, winners vs losers.

But if Gaskell's characters repeatedly fail to achieve the 'sophistication' that their absolute system promises them (in 'School Picnic' neither the biased white school-teacher 'Miss Brown' nor the presumptuous Maori community separately possess virtue or illiberality) Gaskell himself keeps an authorial eye on private possibility. The sympathetic characters live in hope, but like the others they are transfixed in the present by the codifications that are built into the institutionalized language they use: the restrictive platitudes of a certain kind of church language, the restrictive regimentation of army speech. Such language requires those who reject it to feel guilty, a role and result which Gaskell as story-teller refuses to accept. Yet this refusal, symptomatic of so many of the writers of the post-war period, leads not to a resolution of the society's dualities but to greater fragmentation still, at least on the surface. There were more communities than two to be heard from, to be given voice. But surfaces remain untrustworthy. As the myth of New Zealand's homogeneity was challenged, New Zealand short fiction writers began more frequently to experiment with open and non-linear prose forms. Partly this development reflects a simple international change in fashion; but with New Zealand it represents a further attempt to articulate the silent — or silenced — understanding. Once again the indirect mode, for all its narrative aspirations, serves below the surface as an oblique documentary, a verbally self-aware report on plain experience.

The Match with Homogeneity, 1940–1980

Just as the notion of cultural homogeneity manifested itself in several ways — in the appeals to Englishness (into which the enveloping term 'pakeha' absorbed all Europeans), to virility, and to egalitarianism, for example — so did the challenges to homogeneity take several forms. The urban areas grew (though only Auckland grew to large city size; and Vincent O'Sullivan referred to it as a 'toy California').[112] Urbanization emphasized the attitudinal and political gulf between town and country, between the pastoral image of New Zealand (the 'external' or Utopian view, its mythic orderliness paradoxically validated by its being reportorially claimed, by its formal illusion of objectivity) and the muddy realities of raising sheep. Persistently, moreover, women challenged prevailing attitudes, though they sometimes faced censorship or felt the need to emigrate (as did Jean Devanny and Rosemary Rees). The Maori were clearly no longer a dying race — or one that would integrate unvocally into the pakeha mainstream; declaring themselves both linguistically and literarily, they found ways of asserting to European society the set of cultural attitudes built into the Maori language, parenthetically making Europeans' identification with 'the local' more complex, requiring them to identify with another people and cultural attitude as well as with landscape and distance from England.

New immigrants also refused to be absorbed simply into the dual (pakeha-Maori) ethnic system; Cook Islanders, Samoans, Yugoslavs, Danes, and others all began to declare their separately identifiable status within New Zealand. And regional differences became apparent in speech variations and in literary portraits of community: in Dan Davin's Southland, Bill Pearson's West Coast, Amelia Batistich's Northland, R.H. Morrieson's Taranaki, and Yvonne du Fresne's Manawatu. Yet it is important to add that region functions differently in New Zealand than it does, say, in Canada. While in both these societies regionalism is a cultural notion rooted in place, associated with differing degrees of political power, New Zealand's regions operate within a norm of synchronic time, whereas Canada's polychronic zones imply a constantly shifting norm as an adjunct to variation in place. Region in Canada, in other words, implies cumulative change; in New Zealand it reconfirms equivalence and simultaneity as much as it recognizes the particularities of settlement and adaptation.

Such variations in cultural development had their counterpart in changes in literary format as well. New journals emerged, starting in the 1940s, with an astonishing incidence, celebrating the new nationalism urged on by the war years and the spirited literary aspirations of coteries. Among such enterprises from the 1940s through to the 1970s were *New Zealand New Writing*; Charles Brasch's still-continuing *Landfall* (begun in 1947); *Arena* (1943–75); *Islands* (begun in 1972), *Book* (1941–7), an irregular miscellany from Caxton Press; a host of short-lived and sometimes born-again journals such as *Hilltop* (1949; becoming *Arachne* in 1950), *Argot* (1969–72), *Here and Now*, (1949–54), *Edge*, (1971–3), *Frontiers* (1968–70), and *Numbers* (1954–9); *Mate* (1957), which became *Climate* in 1978; *Cave* (1972–4; with its supplement *Outrigger*, 1974–6), which became *New Quarterly Cave* in 1975 and *Pacific Moana Quarterly* in 1978. *Te Ao Hou* (begun in 1952) provided a political and literary forum for Maori writers, encouraging J.C. Sturm as a story-writer, for one, though her 1960s collection *The House of the Talking Cat* did not appear in print until 1984.

If *Tomorrow* and the *New Zealand Listener* had simply by their format encouraged literary innovation within the page-long sketch, the new journals provided opportunities to publish works of greater length as well and those that more markedly departed from received form. The process of modification was slow, and only partly served by the various yearbooks and anthologies which also emerged; it was stimulated most by another group of writers whose work began to appear in the 1940s and 1950s: G.R. Gilbert, Erik de Mauny, Amelia Batistich, Greville Texidor, Yvonne du Fresne, Philip Mincher, J.K. Baxter, Renato Amato, Maurice Duggan, Barry Mitcalfe, J.C. Sturm, Helen Shaw, Marilyn Duckworth, Janet Frame.

Through them the forms of story-telling began to change, and the voices of Maori, Woman, and Immigrant began to be sounded more directly, with effects upon style, transforming the outsider's portrait of experience sharply into the insider's revelation. Although Jacqueline Sturm's various accounts of domestic disharmony less present a picture of a specifically Maori frame of life than they describe the more general constraints of class, using the family as a metaphoric structure, they none the less indicate the beginning of a change in image. Lawlor's comic Maoris disappeared, and in Sturm's work and that of Arapera Blank, literary Maori turned into real people; it remained for Maori perspective to shape English style – for Finlayson's poetic-English observer's evocations of speech and attitude to turn in the 1960s (in the work of Rowley Habib, Patricia Grace, Hone Tuwhare, and Witi Ihimaera) into an insider's language. At that point the Maori literary consciousness would acquire a certain militancy as well, their stories asserting the dignity of person, heritage and language as well as the ironic consciousness of minority status within the egalitarian state.[113]

In parallel fashion, the stories of Shaw, Texidor, and other female writers of the 1940s frequently examined the pressures in women's lives, but it remained for writers like Grace, Fiona Kidman, Joy Cowley, and Sylvia Ashton-Warner to attempt to address these issues in contemporary feminist terms. And with Batistich's *An Olive Tree in Dalmatia* (1963). Amato's *The Full Circle of the Travelling Cuckoo* (1957), and du Fresne's *Farvel and Other Stories* (1980), the immigrant experience was told from the inside. The plight of the foreigner, attempting to become invisible in the new world, continued to be a fascinating theme for the outsider – Sargeson's 'The Making of a New Zealander,' Shaw's 'The Samovar' (in which an orphan finds life and love through recognizing her Russian past), Chris Else's 'Ivars' (*Arts Festival Yearbook*, 1966; about a Latvian worker who understands a loneliness that the 'matey' workers cannot fathom and possibly fear), John Montieth's 'November Fifty-six' (*Arena*, December 1964; about a Hungarian refugee), and many others – but with Amato, Batistich, and du Fresne, the achievement is to control the language by which immigration turns from a record of a physical move into an act of relocating the imagination.

Yvonne du Fresne, portraying the Danes of the Manawatu, manages the motif most relaxedly and comically, as when in 'The Looters' she describes the competitive nature of her family's dinner table conversation:

But this night, the night when my Reading Problem reached its crisis, into the room burst my Onkel Henning.
'Great Scott!' cried Onkel Henning, 'dash my wig! By Jove! Food!' Then he paused. His military bearing lost its crispness. He did not know what to say next. Henning's favourite subject for looting expressions from was Major Gore. Miss Gore's broder.

But Henning had not listened carefully enough to what Major Gore said in the privacy of his home when he clapped eyes on his dinner.
 'Great Scott,' said Henning feebly. He gave up. He struck his hands together like a pistol shot. 'Now for our good dinner!' cried Onkel Henning in Danish.
 My Fader's eyes sparkled. He bore down on the table. He stooped like a dwarf. He made his mouth as thin as a twist of string.
 'We-ll, Sonny,' he drawled, 'yer goin' ter have yer tucker now, eh?'[114]

Batistich is more content with evoking the atmosphere of pathos, the sadness of the dislocated memory, as when a girl catches sight of her mother dancing for her in 'The Mazurka Afternoon.' But in Amato's stories, the experience becomes more dislocating still, and for all its occasional brush with wit, a ratiocinative exercise in formal misdirection. Describing the end of the war in Italy, Amato's narrator detachedly observes that to be German or partisan – *they* or *we* – is 'only a matter of grammar.' Then he goes on:

We listened to each other but I don't know that we were interested in what we had to say. More than anything, we merely heard those sounds, as some sort of unnecessary background noise, and when they stopped we took the interruption in turn as a cue to our own little line, our own little speech.[115]

Repeatedly his characters 'walk into the shadow,' as one of his titles puts it, shadows out of the past or on the edge of their understanding. Asking for acceptance, they are repeatedly misunderstood. For them, *translation* turns into *lying*.[116] And in a sketch called 'Nothings,' an elaborate game of mental solitaire (through which the mind moves associatively from observation to observation) leads noplace: which is either the immigrant's Utopian goal or its denial – or both, the fragmentation of understanding (as enacted by the prose form) constituting at once the breakdown of a coherent system and an as yet unfulfilled promise and process of enrichment.
 Dan Davin's first series of Oxford's *New Zealand Short Stories* (1953) was to collect stories by several of these writers, along with works from Lady Barker and Henry Lapham through to Ballantyne and Middleton; but Davin's interest was in representing New Zealand – the stories were chosen for the realism of their settings, and by the editor's decision that the settings had to be New Zealand ones. It is interesting therefore to compare his choices with those of Frank Sargeson, whose anthology of fifteen stories, *Speaking for Ourselves*, had appeared in 1945, and to contrast both their books with O.N. Gillespie's *New Zealand Short Stories* (1930). Gillespie's book had emphasized Maori anecdote and Anglo-Saxon sentiment ('delightful' Maori, 'Nordic' stock, lack of national consciousness, and manliness in games were

the watchwords of his preface) and it had drawn the bulk of its examples from Australian publications.[117] Sargeson, by contrast, as his title implies, emphasized the language in action.

H.W. Rhodes, reviewing Sargeson's book in the *New Zealand Listener*, observed: 'it is refreshing to read sketches which, whatever their limitations may be, are firmly rooted in people, places, and things.'[118] Characteristically for the time, Rhodes (perhaps inferentially comparing Sargeson's choices with Gillespie's) responded to the book's elements of social realism, but in comparison with Davin's later volume, Sargeson's work seems the more experimental.[119] It is as though the critical approval of realism informed the later anthologist's selections, whereas Sargeson responded more to a writer's independent creative control of artifice. Hence Davin selects Duggan's 'Race Day' (one of the family chronicle Lenihan group), Gilbert's 'A Girl with Ambition' and Texidor's 'An Annual Affair' (both sombre accounts of emotional restraint), Helen Shaw's descriptive 'The Blind,' and A.P. Gaskell's paradigmatic 'The Big Game'; Sargeson selected Duggan's 'Notes on an Abstract Arachnid' (an abstract composition in present participles, deliberately evoking through its fragmented style a sense of the actual passing of moments of time), Gilbert's 'Mrs Pornog's Afternoon' (a sardonic fable about violence, establishing a stylistic contrast between the fixity of geometry and the fluidity of nature), Texidor's 'Anyone Home?' (an ironic commentary on the force of the word 'Home' to a returned soldier), Shaw's 'Noah' (one of her most elliptical stories), and Gaskell's 'Purity Squad' (one of his indirect attacks on the rigidity of moral exclusiveness).

From these and most of the other stories in his anthology – his own 'The Hole that Jack Dug' and stories by less well-known writers such as Audrey B. King, Lyndall Chapple Gee, E.M. Lyders, E.P. Dawson, and D.M. Anderson – we are made aware of Sargeson's attack on fixity and his celebration of process: Anderson's main character, a student, cannot explain why he does not act 'sensibly,' Gee and King fasten on the changes that the war causes in the lives and attitudes of women and children. Yet finally it is Sargeson's choice more than the authors' visions that the book records, for even among many of these writers it was the fixity of representational writing rather than the fluidity of process writing which constituted their most typical manner of expression.

Shaw, for example, in her uncollected stories in *Book* and other journals, and in *The Orange Tree* (1957; six of these stories re-collected with four subsequent ones in *The Gypsies and Other Stories*, 1978), struggles to dramatize memory and dream but usually ends up with a (sometimes overstated) observation, a process that is reinforced by the way (at the time) she thought of short story writing. Seeking a correspondence between words and an 'unwritten original,' she claimed that 'The drive to summarize, give pictures, in the form of a short story, started with a sketch, 'She Wore Red Gloves,' little more than bones, hardly holding together ... '[120]

Yet for other writers – primarily Gilbert, Frame, and Duggan – the conclusiveness of 'summary' was precisely what they were trying to avoid. G.R. Gilbert's experiments with participial constructions took his sketches away from fixed conclusion and into the shifting mood effected by image and cadence, as in 'Wellington 1940,' in his 1942 book *Free to Laugh & Dance: Stories:*

Just now the tiredness of the land ... the dreadful expectancy of quiet everlasting calm and weariness, the tired cities and the lagging streets, the leaden-footed search in all the streets for lost things, dancing in the afternoon, feeding the dull hungry night with things seen vaguely, hardly done, lightly listlessly fingered.[121]

Here the form clearly indicates the persistence into the later twentieth century of Katherine Mansfield's early tonal sketch style – other effective examples include Patricia Excell's 'From the Testament of Eurydice' (*Numbers*, November 1954) and Jules Riding's 'Sea-Gull's Cry (A Sketch)' (*Arena*, December 1968 – but Gilbert's range is wider. Though his stories are more experiment than accomplishment, he remains an interesting and pivotal figure, able to integrate American vernacular neatly into the tonally comic conversational interchanges in 'A Warning to New Zealand Fathers.' or to satirize the clichés of New Zealand history and literature in 'Kosciusko' and 'Story for a Xmas Annual,' or to respond stylistically as well as laconically to cultural rivalry and advertising practice ('My heart, he said, it is not broken. He had picked up the foreign accent in Sydney for business purposes').[122] And it is through his truncated experiments with fable and the stylistic shifts of consciousness that the world of Sargeson links with the idiosyncratic worlds of Maurice Duggan and Janet Frame.

In his introduction to *New Zealand Short Stories*, Dan Davin had disputed the existence of a 'special New Zealand quality in the form,' but added that

we may still find it in things less obvious than the settings. Editorial bias is surely not the only reason why almost all the stories here are about people at work or never very far from work. There are none which depend on wit and only one ... which approaches fantasy.[123]

This was the received post-Depression judgment of literature and society. Yet there has been a persistent strain of wit and irony in New Zealand fiction from Lapham through to the present, and fantasy lies just under the surface of ostensible report.[124] In the 1950s and 1960s satiric asides and solemn burlesques even became a standard way of dealing with the perceived inadequacies of a notion of a Received Culture. James K. Baxter, for example, wrote for *Numbers* in July 1954 'Apple Mash: A Moral Fable,' about pigs, double standards, and hypocrisy – pale Orwellian, but none the less pungent in this context. Marilyn Duckworth, in a 1959 story in *Numbers*, wrote even more critically about 'Insania – a little no man's land between Auckland and London – where we are educated'[125] (a phrase echoed three years later by Janet Frame: 'an affliction of dream called Overseas').[126] Duckworth's feminist twist emphasizes the dislocating effect that the conventional definitions of society have upon women; the result is madness (as in the works of Grossman, Devanny, and Frame as well), tempered here only by the irony, which functions as a defence against dissolution.

Recognizing that the national image of the working man was one devised by others, Barry Mitcalfe's stories attack what is seen as pretension or a false intellectualism, often deliberately using the conversational idiom that the 1930s had celebrated as the national voice. Young journal editors (Erik Schwimmer of *Te Ao Hou*, followed by Norman Simms with *Cave*) disputed the very notion of nationalism in literature and attached the prevailing assumptions about monoculturalism.[127] Writers like Philip Mincher and Richard Packer attacked puritan restrictiveness on subject and language. Packer's 'Nothing But the Best' (direct in its account of the violence that follows an adolescent's guilt concerning sexual discovery) caused a stir about salaciousness and blasphemy after it appeared in *Numbers* in February 1959. Mincher's 'Notebook(4)' (in *Arena* 1954) combines the idiomatic with the allusively literary in its reflections on the fit language of literature and the need not to fear critical bias. And in the linked stories of his later collection *The Ride Home: A Story Sequence* (1977) Mincher contrives to convey by means of prose rhythm rather than explicit vocabulary the intense sexuality that (along with the sublimated violence of the land, the activities of biking, fishing, hunting, and an ambivalent attitude towards the rules of a life-style) binds his two central characters. That many younger writers in the 1970s should continue to address the sexual mores of language demonstrates the persistent impact that the Calvinism in the culture had upon individuals, shaping an attitude of mind that perceived sexuality, articulateness, and violence all in some degree as acts of rebellion – the result of which was presumed to be a measure of independence from the social norm, though the nature of the rebellion was itself shaped by the very norm being rejected.

Several of the satires addressed these issues – image, language, nationalism, sexuality, and literary form – all together, in critical burlesques. These range from essays like A.R.D. Fairburn's 'Sketch-Plan for the Great New

Zealand Novel' (*Parsons Packet*, 1950) and Edmund Lee's 'On Writing the Great N.Z. Novel' (*Arena*, 1953) to Vincent O'Sullivan's marvellously outrageous full-length narrative, *Miracle: A Romance* (1976). Most relevant here is A.K. Grant's spoof both of critical somemnity and creative repetitiveness, 'An Inquiry into the Construction and Classification of the New Zealand Short Story' (1973), which divides New Zealand fictional practice into a finite five forms:

(1) The sensitive Maori kid who doesn't quite know what is going on short story ...
(2) The Ordinary Kiwi working bloke short story ...
(3) The if you think you're depressed already just wait till you read this but it may help me to make some sense of my breakdown short story ...
(4) The loveable housewife and mother coping with adolescent kids in the suburbs short story ...
(5) The zonked out of one's skull in Ponsonby short story ...
(6) The sub-Katherine Mansfield 'At the Bay' short story ...

for all of which Grant provides his own exemplary stylistic excerpts. These range from 'I knew there was going to be trouble as soon as Fred, our foreman, brought Mortimer over' to 'The first rays of the sun slid over the peak of Mt Winterslow and stabbed downward to a dew-drop trembling on the tip of a toitoi plume,'[128] and they demonstrate Grant's own skill at manipulating the language he attributes to others. They also reveal his recognition of the continuing appeal within his society both of stories that claim to document reality and those that claim to document nuance, and the continuing division this represents in national self-image. Most particularly, however, he is attacking the recurrent failure of artistic language and exposing the failure of current writers (the 'zonked out of one's skull in Ponsonby' story) to build on the linguistic independence for which Janet Frame and Maurice Duggan had been striving a decade earlier. It was not 'New Zealandness' that either of these writers was after in fiction; though they both wrote of and out of their experience of New Zealand, they sought most of all to animate the independent life of language on the page.

For Frame, this effort meant walking from 'that' world (of social roles and conventions) to 'this' (of the words and lives at 'the edge of the alphabet');[129] repeatedly her characters struggle to communicate with others, to have their story told and understood, and repeatedly, just as the reader absorbs the story each character tells, Frame adds another filter to it; each new filter alters the reader's perception and requires that the putting together of story (of reality, of understanding) take place in the reader's mind. But as with Amato's 'Nothings,' understanding turns out to be always multiple and never whole –

the process of reading words (like the process of living life) being a process of (constant, irregular) tesselation rather than a system of unlocking a finite code.

Frame's first story collection *The Lagoon* (1951; expanded as *The Lagoon and other stories* in 1961) records stories of death, school, factory life, childhood, Depression, treasure, and life in a mental hospital – but such themes are always metaphors, processes of transformation, never fixed subjects. Technically the stories emphasize the possibilities of alternative vision – things that seem obvious are always qualified, and one of the most striking stylistic characteristics of the book is the recurrence of the word 'if.' In 'Swans,' for example, the sea becomes a medium that transforms two children's expectations:

It was dark black water, secret, and the air was filled with murmurings and rustlings, it was as if they were walking into another world that had been kept secret from everyone and now they had found it. The darkness lay massed across the water and over to the east, thick as if you could touch it, soon it would swell and fill the earth.[130]

Initially Frame conceives these worlds of vision and restriction as strict alternatives to each other; 'do we ever know, do we ever live where we live,' she asks in 'The day of the sheep': 'we're always in other places, lost like sheep, and I cannot understand the leafless cloudy secret and the sun of any day.'[131] Under such circumstances, the world casts the visionary into the factory or the mental hospital, and the visionary rejects the world. But Frame's actual texts increasingly argue the interpenetration between the visionary and the everyday. Her stories blend enigmatic metaphor with vernacular utterance; they contrive deliberate run-on sentences to convey the flow of association that takes a character from one dimension of perception to another; they rely on the reader's ability to hear verbal echoes and convert half-rhymes into logical associations – even if, in the process, the cold rules of formal logic are overturned. In 'Jan Godfrey,' for example, a girl in a mental hospital wants to write a short story:

This story came last night. Everything is always a story, but the loveliest ones are those that get written and are not torn up and are taken to a friend as a payment for listening, for putting a wise ear to the keyhole of my mind.
    hell
    me
    me
    me

I am writing a story about a girl who is not me. I cannot prove she is not me. I can only tell you that her name is Alison Hendry.[132]

When the story ends with the girl claiming she *is* Alison Hendry, such a conclusion may appear to disobey the 'rules' of realism – but the story is asking readers to follow not the sequential systems of empirical 'proof' but the incremental filters of associational narrative. The world Frame rejects is the one that is limited by its belief in 'facts'; the world she embraces is the one that comprehends the power of fairy-tale. Children thus figure repeatedly in her stories not because of some cultural notion of romantic innocence but because of their capacity to enter dreams and embrace monsters while at the same time they retain the powers of speech of their concrete identity. Beyond such childhood is the world of the lost: of those who stifle possibility in themselves and live safely but emptily in the language of cliché and of those whose power of vision gives them access to a language of such intensity and privacy that they lose the ability to communicate beyond themselves. In the shapes and layers of language, then, lie Janet Frame's readings of the world; syntax, vocabulary, and narrative form come to be not just the simple vehicles of documentary expression but correlatives of the imagination.

Frame's subsequent stories seek further ways to tap these resources of the word. The subtitles of her two 1963 books tell a great deal about her experiments in methodology: *The Reservoir: Stories and Sketches* and *Snowman Snowman: Fables and Fantasies*. (Margaret Dalziel helped Frame choose a selection from these two works to appear as *The Reservoir and Other Stories* in 1966; additional stories, like 'The Bath,' 'Winter Garden,' 'Insulation,' and 'Two Widowers' appeared in journals like *Landfall*, *Cornhill*, and *The New Zealand Listener* from 1965 through to the late 1970s; and *You Are Now Entering the Human Heart*, the author's selection of twenty-five stories from all her work to this point, appeared in 1984.) But while these experiments produced some of Frame's finest work – 'The Reservoir,' for instance – the fables proved largely end-closed and mechanical, serving a preconceived and rigid scheme of judgments rather than serving as the medium of narrative discovery that the earlier stories had promised. In 'Solutions,' for example, a man severs his head from his body, gets some mice to get rid of the body he no longer thinks he needs, and teaches his head to fly; then he gets rid of all but his brain – which promptly shrivels: so then the mice eat it, too, thinking it's a prune. Such a story is an exercise, all message, its own language incidental to its intent.

Repeatedly in these stories the author's need to tell overcomes her need to speak. While there are moments of dramatized language – as when the DANGER sign in 'Obstacles' loses its initial letter, or when the girl in 'A Sense of

Proportion' reveals she can't draw *appearances*, or when the passive 'It was said to be' in 'The Reservoir' enacts the way a conventional language both impedes and feeds children's imaginations — Frame for the most part here overinstructs and overexplains, as when a photograph doesn't expose 'properly' in 'Snowman Snowman,' and she writes:

Solid brick, wood and stone were rendered insubstantial, became part of a landscape of nothingness, while everything covered with snow ... all that is fragile became strong and bold, as certain as stone and steel, capable of withstanding ordeal by season and sun.[133]

As though recognizing the limitations of such rhetoric, Frame turns in her subsequent stories — most eloquently in 'Winter Garden' — to dramatize imaginative limitation less as a failure of speech than as a failure of perception. In doing so, she reclaims realism for herself, writes of illusion and memory — of characters who see past appearances into symbolic action and emotional connection, and of others who define in advance what they will allow themselves to see — implicitly asking her readers by means of the story to measure their own capacity for sight.

Influenced like Frame by the presence and encouragement of Frank Sargeson, Maurice Duggan, in a quite separate way, rejected the realm of tight-lipped functional language. She sought the private shapes of experience and word; he was an advertising man, aware of the word's public dimensions and impact. As a story-writer Duggan even began in experiment, with stories like 'Notes on an Abstract Arachnid.' Three books followed: *Immanuel's Land* (1956). *Summer in the Gravel Pit* (1965), and *O'Leary's Orchard and Other Stories* (1970). A fragment called 'The Magsman Miscellany' was posthumously printed in *Islands*, 1975, and C.K. Stead edited his *Collected Stories* in 1981. Over the course of his career his stories experimented with verbal play as well as with styptic memory, and if he often runs close to the maudlin, he also pursues in his fiction an emotional range that escapes the reach of most of his predecessors. He turns from his frequently bitter acknowledgment of Bunyan's land — the emotionally barren if visually beautiful New Zealand of his first book, to what Terry Sturm calls 'Riley's Handbook': 'a kind of *Pilgrim's Progress* in reverse,' charting the temptations of love and sensuality in a world where only the self (and that decaying) is considered reliable.[134]

He moves from fragmentary sketches of a Roman Catholic boyhood and the emotional severances that characterize the life of the Lenihan family (stories not unlike Davin's sketches of the Connollys, though much more clearly influenced by Joyce's *Dubliners*) to ebullient monologues, dancing-drunken streams of consciousness, and associative adventures in style that constitute by their very form a rejection of local literary conventions. But the burden that the later stories intone involves the force of cultural convention even on the lives of those who would be free of it; hence these stories have to be seen as reactions to the status quo and recognitions of psychological reality, not simply accepted as self-contained verbal designs. The point is not to make an either-or distinction between language-as-functional-(factual)-statement and language-as-sheer-ornament, but to accent the possibility that language-in-action can comment obliquely on society even while it seems most adamantly engaged with artifice itself.

Karl Stead notes a specific instance, quoting from one of Duggan's finest stories 'Along Rideout Road that Summer,' at a point where the narrator, with sumptuous Coleridgean embroidery, recalls the bare facts of his first conversation with a rural Maori girl on whom he has designs:

Gooday. How are yuh?
All right.
I'm Buster O'Leary.
I'm Fanny Hohepa.
Yair, I know.
It's hot.
It's hot right enough.
– and so on. 'A genuine crumpy conversation' Buster observes; and in that gibe at a fellow-author (Barry Crump) Duggan dissociates himself from the line of New Zealand fiction which has gone in for the realism of inarticulacy.[135]

But it was a dissociation which did not remove him from his culture; rather, it was a stance that endeavoured to reveal the degree of articulateness that was present in the culture, to make clear that the 'inarticulate hero' of New Zealand fiction was not descriptive of the New Zealand character but only of the character that New Zealand critics and readers had accustomed themselves to accept as real.

Such a distinction required Duggan to write his way out of the set attitudes of the Lenihan documents – hence in some degree out of the pain of a particular childhood – into the intelligent engagement with irony and scepticism that marked his mature work. But this change did not win easy acceptance. H.W. Rhodes found his world fragmented and unattractive; Lawrence Jones found the style of even some of the middle stories to hinder communication; Dan Davin, in a review of the *Collected Stories*, approved more visibly of the 'consequent narratives' than of the associational ones, even though he called 'Riley's Handbook' an 'agonizing masterpiece.' It

165 New Zealand: Story and History

remained for Terry Sturm to reject what at one level was an equation between simple sequence and a notion of organic short story unity, and to discover in Duggan the paradigms of indeterminacy that resulted from the author's control over the nuances of fragmentation.

> The exploitation of perspective ... is crucial to the effect of a Duggan story; there is always some kind of ironic distance between Duggan's total perspective on the world he creates in his stories and the partial or limited perspective of individual characters. The actual linear movement of the narrative in the stories is often distorted or attenuated ... He is particularly fond of a structure which breaks the story into a series of sections, each one establishing a new perspective on the central event or character. In this kind of patterning, actions and objects are perhaps less important in establishing some objective, external world or contribution to plot, than in presenting states of mind and feeling ...[136]

But this is a structure which New Zealand fiction had made use of since the nineteenth century; it was Duggan's accomplishment to take the miscellany and reclaim it — in 'Chapter,' 'Voyage,' 'Six Place Names and a Girl,' 'Along Rideout Road that Summer,' and the later stories — as the territory of the subjective mind. When the magistrate's question in his early story 'Towards the Mountains' ('What's the Atkinson woman got against the others?') elicits an equivocal answer, it is the equivocation that is instructive, culturally as well as psychologically: ' — Nothing; or everything ... Religion; money. I don't know; it's a small place.'[137] It was not clarity Duggan attacked, but the ease with which people accepted a false clarity: false because it limited reality to an empirical system and by extension identified acceptable prose as a medium of descriptive classification rather than of invention and uncertainty.

'I conceive it a presumption to think of one's marginalia as being possessed of any special interest,' begins 'The Magsman Miscellany,' and continues:

> they exist. A greater presumption might be to embark upon a central text ... There are so many arguments in favour of silence; and not a few of the arguments are both noisy and abrupt.[138]

But the word 'magsman' invites the reader to suspect the disingenuous, and Duggan's deleted preface to the story explains his character directly:

> A miscellany is, one supposes, a random book carefully planned. A preface hardly seems in order. 'Magsman' is a piece of nineteenth-century slang used by Ben McGoldrick at once to confess himself to himself and also to conceal himself, by

self-confession, from others; it may be thought of as a euphemism, a code or evasion.[139]

Such reversals are everywhere in Duggan, from the humour, which is the flip side of solemnity and pain, to the May-December relationship in 'O'Leary's Orchard,' which in New Zealand terms is autumn-spring. Faced with the unhelpfulness of 'careful phrases' (like those of the Brother Superior in 'Guardian'), or 'false looks' (like those of Terry and Mrs Lenihan in 'Now is the hour'),[140] his characters strive repeatedly for mask and parody in order to win a brief reprieve from recognition. 'Something of myself, we must come to it obliquely,' says Riley, in 'Riley's Handbook':

Patience. I will find the tone for it when the pain for it fades. The labour of casting off that skin, that nymphal early form, has rubbed me raw. Have patience; we'll make space in time. There's a story in it somewhere. What's the sense you are knowing? Well you may ask. Hoaxed by dates and dazed by days, hour by hour; for what seeming cause would that be? I'm serious, writing as I would paint, have painted, spontaneously, without formal preconceptions and prejudices, out of one corset into another straightjacket, doubtless. To fail again? Surely. How can I know what I think until I think it and how can I avoid the expression of that with all its dubieties and fixations? I know what I'm attempting: it would be another jape altogether to attempt what I know.[141]

But they live with their compromises, Buster in 'Rideout Road' with his ambitions and his prejudices, hitching a ride on a hearse; May Laverty in 'Blues for Miss Laverty,' having the light go out on her but laughing querulously; Hilda in 'An Appetite for Flowers,' humming softly on the staircase because she is *not* being followed. O'Leary, in 'O'Leary's Orchard,' closest of all of them to joy — recapturing romance from age, admitting the repetitive boredom of fantasy and the incredible variety of real life, rediscovering his delight in sensuality, embracing the theatre of life and the theatre of language — even O'Leary cannot fix happiness; when Isobel goes from him, crying and smiling at once, he realizes he holds everything and nothing — the circle and the zero — simultaneously:

His life had been a preparation for a sense of loss. He had missed her often enough already, over the years. It would continue, an indulgence of himself, O'Leary's O of regret, unvoiced. It was what his life was fashioned to contain, this gentle fabrication, this bright figment.[142]

Himself an artful fabrication as well as a fabricator, himself he accepts.

Through artifice he discovers life, and claims it. And though constantly haunted by ethical dualities, Duggan's fiction lays claim also to life, through artifice, accepting the invalidity of resolution but confronting by its own appreciable measures the charge of idle disarray.

Duggan sums up, then, the first wave of reaction to the Sargesonian style, but he did not overturn it, and one looks, in the 1970s, for Duggan's bequest to the next generation of writers. Such connections are less specific than they are attitudinal; they lie in expectations of language and artifice, of fantasy and sexuality, and of the social frame that writing accepts or disputes. The most obvious social claim of contemporary New Zealand writers is to a freedom from nationality. A *Landfall* symposium in 1977, asking writers if there was a distinctive New Zealand literature and if writers should (or did) choose topics specifically relevant to New Zealand, elicited almost unanimously a refusal to be limited by a nationality they took for granted, a suspicion of any effort to restrict topics by nationality, and an attack upon critics who sought to 'define' New Zealand Literature rather than to consider the individuality and integrity of each work of art. At the same time, the writers admitted to writing from within a social context, and admitted, too, that each individual's separate literary expression in some sense grows out of and contributes to an evolving cultural traditon in place. Hence in looking at the stories of the 1970s and early 1980s, one finds a complex knot of attitudes about art and society affecting the shape and tenor of what writers actually wrote. Everywhere there is evidence of a plurality with a common core, within a common frame. The core lies in the stories' sense of silence, in the shape and substance of (hi)stories authentic and unsaid; the boundary is the set that articulate speech imposes from abroad, breaking silence by claiming fictional record as its own, hence reiterating empire against the silences of resistance.

For all their apparent variety, the new forms of story read as permutations of the old, and the new heterogeneity as a complication, rather than a rejection of the social pattern that had gone before. There were writers like Anne Spivey and Murray Edmond writing impressionistic sketches, and Keri Hulme (*The Windeater Te Kaihau*, 1985), and Joy Cowley, and Owen Leeming adapting impressionistic techniques to stories of greater length. At the same time, Barry Crump was continuing to pen anecdotes of the inarticulate male, and C.K. Stead – in 'A Fitting Tribute,' for example (first published in The *Kenyon Review* in 1965, collected in *Five for the Symbol*, 1981) – was writing an articulate fantasy that was at the same time a mock-solemn spoof of the anecdotal form. John Bentley, in a story like 'Beginnings' (*Landfall*, 38, June 1984), reveals his debt to Duggan (and through him to Laurence Sterne); by contrast Owen Marshall's work lays claim both to Sargeson's dualism, to the world of emotional fantasy that underlies the problematic life of New Zealand males, and to the continuing homogeneity of New Zealand society and character.[143] Barry Mitcalfe and Maurice Gee appeared to be continuing the realistic fictional patterns that had become the country's 'established' mode, yet the most effective of their stories are the compact ironic or comic inversions of those patterns — Mitcalfe in 'Happily Unmarried,' for example, in *'I Say, Wait for Me': A Collection of Short Stories* (1976), or Gee in 'The Champion' (1966), revised with ten other stories from the period 1955–75 in Gee's *A Glorious Morning, Comrade* (1976). In 'The Champion,' we find again the familiar Game metaphor, this time used not to evoke the nation directly but to describe the competition between a particular husband and wife — he a former boxing champion, she a current croquet champion, he utterly unwilling to admit her precedence in any way or to alter his conception of his own role. Despite the story's claim to narrative independence, clearly the notions of role (and the writer's use of metaphor) are not without sociocultural reverberations. The point is that the form carries its own message.

Comparably, writers like Fiona Kidman, in *Mrs Dixon & Friend* (1982), openly championed changes in the kind of role-modelling that were prevalent in her society — and in moralistic stories aimed primarily at youth, J. Edward Brown (in *New Neighbours*, 1981) and Bernard Gadd (in *Where to Go?*, 1981) championed the cause of race relations, acknowledging the existence of racism in New Zealand and urging greater understanding between Maori, pakeha, and Cook Islander — yet all three of these cases for reform are cast in conventional realistic guise, confirming by technique a kind of order their overt message in large measure disputes. Malcolm Fraser and F.P. Wilkins, in 'The Legend of the Lost Mythology' (one of an 'anthology' of representative new directions in contemporary story writing in a 1974 issue of *Islands*) satirized the faith that New Zealanders placed in their cultural myths (the Edenic fortress, the solitary hero, the practical builder); but then when Yvonne du Fresne, drawing on the Danish myths of her family's roots, challenged what seemed an impassive hegemony of Britishness in pakeha culture, she none the less wrote in *Farvel* a set of variations on the characteristic narrative paradigms that pakeha writers from Mansfield to Middleton had produced, laying claim at once to her family language and the social structures that her society had converted into narrative.

Such deliberate duality (or, sometimes, contradictoriness) is further illustrated by the way so many contemporary stories expose the unstable substructure of notions of reality, sometimes through metaphor, sometimes by allowing moments of fantasy to blast the illusion of order. In Michael Morrissey's 'This Is New Zealand,' for example, a character drives quickly along the beach to avoid being caught in quicksand: the 100-Mile Beach allusion is at once a documentary setting and an effective symbolic image. In Karl Stead's novel *Smith's Dream*, a character racing through the volcanic centre of the North Island puts his foot through the crust of the earth. Again, the real and the symbolic interpenetrate, overlap. The old order may reassert itself, these writers say, but change is at work in the society, and then fantasy becomes a means of recording – through ruptures in the surface of realistic prose – ruptures in the mindset of the people whose prose this has been taken to be.

The decade of the 1970s was particularly important in stimulating such awareness of change. Norman Kirk, of Maori lineage, became prime minister, and what with that and the society's increasing urbanization, the blithe passive conventions about race futures and race relations could not persist. There was substantial immigration – from Britain, the Mediterranean, the Cook Islands, and South Africa – and substantial emigration: Sydney, Australia coming to house the world's largest Maori community. Moreover, after New Zealand's active involvement in Vietnam, the nation found itself less 'distant' from the rest of the world, an attitude given the stimulus of economic necessity when Britain's entry into the European Common Market required New Zealand to readjust its patterns of trade. Yet in opening itself to its Polynesian connections and its transpacific neighbours, the country also opened itself to a taste for American television violence, and to the reach of American slang and postmodernist fictional forms. But such speech, such television formulae, and such fictional techniques, for all their rootedness in New Zealand, carried in the context of the still prevalent norms of 'realist' order something of the sense of fantasy, of being from 'outside' and therefore not real. Hence when writers like Vincent O'Sullivan (in *Miracle*) or Karl Stead (in *Smith's Dream*) write romances of an American invasion of New Zealand, the mode of apparent fantasy carries a political message all the sharper for its *seeming* to be bizarre. And when Russell Haley (*The Sauna Bath Mysteries*, 1978) and Ian Wedde (*The Shirt Factory and Other Stories*, 1981) employ American slang to tell of New Zealand violence, they appear to be concocting verbal illusions and fantastic entertainments that could exist only on the page, whereas in fact they are critically exaggerating the local realities of contemporary speech and attitude. As with Duggan, that which appears to be fantastic proves to be closely affiliated with what people customarily accept as real and true.

John Barnett's 1981 anthology, *All the Dangerous Animals Are in Zoos*, takes this premise as its covert principle of organization. A collection of new stories by twelve writers, including Stead, Mincher, Grace, du Fresne, Haley, Wedde, Bruce Stewart, Michael Morrissey, Graeme Lay, and Bill Baer, the book announces even by its title the oblique presence of inverse meaning.

Not only does the phrase invoke one of the most durable of New Zealand catchwords – 'there are no snakes in New Zealand': a truth which distinguishes the place from other former British colonies, but which also sidesteps the instability (quicksand, earthquake) of the land itself – it also invites the reader to infer that people (animals outside zoos) are safe. Unless, of course, as the stories then go on variously to suggest, the catchword is a myth, or the whole place is a (metaphoric) zoo, and people are the most dangerous animals of all.

At the end of Ian Wedde's 'Snake,' for instance, his character Flag knew 'in his heart, where his unfinished songs seemed to absorb the venom and grow cold ... that the snakes were here, they had come at last, and nothing was ever going to be the same again.'[144] Comparably, at the end of C.K. Stead's 'A New Zealand Elegy,' the (Utopian?) paradise in the heart of Auckland refuses to live up to its name; the narrator stopped 'By the clump of native trees at the far side of the ground ... and stared up at the hulking darkness of Mt Eden brooding over the suburb. Everything was dark and ugly and there was nothing to be done and nowhere to go.'[145] Negation is everywhere. In Russell Haley's 'The Palace of Kandahar,' the narrator seeks a naked perfection, but finds instead both the clothing of illusion ('Things ... erode, change, become clothed. A volcanic island sprang up in the harbour seven hundred years ago and now is covered in green')[146] and the nakedness of a sexuality he is unprepared to accept. Once again (as repeatedly in Sargeson) the old repressive puritanism bursts forth in violence, generally against animals, or against women, perceived as the agents of fall. Even women attack women, as in Graeme Lay's 'The Suburbanisation of Esmerelda,' a story of a 'Latin' woman's flouting of suburban convention – swearing at the grocer, walking around naked, renting rooms to Maori women – only to break out in racist slurs and her most vitriolic Anglo-Saxon when she discovers that her boarder enjoys casual sex with a man, without her.

Most of all, however, the disenchantment of these writers is with the language they have inherited, a language in which they claim they do not feel at home: every time their characters use words, they are aware of deceit – not of deceiving themselves, but of doing disservice to what they know. Wedde's character in 'The River' flinches at the thought of animals: 'It was almost like admitting his misanthropy, which, as a last resort, he was in the habit of calling "realism," without however deceiving himself.'[147] And Russell Haley's narrator Wildeman in 'Here Comes Your Canadian Father' (in *The Sauna Bath Mysteries*) is desperate for the language that comes sound-by-sound from within, and confounded by the fact that in order to write he finds himself putting fragmentary notes on English stationery ('bond' paper at that) or winding blank pages into a foreign-made machine. Yet even these disclaimers are suspect — they are worried about audience as much as about creation, invitations to appreciate the contextual validity of indirect narrative. The opening of Vincent O'Sullivan's 'The Professional' makes clear this desire, with a story about story-telling:

> I decided pretty early on that if the only way you can survive this tangle we call 'life' is by telling lies, then you can't be too careful about the lies you're going to tell. Before I was ten it occurred to me that the kids who were great liars, who were caught and thrashed and stood in corners were the lesser brotherhood, they were *bad* liars. They were fabulists, fantasists, they in fact wanted a lie to be like a cowboy film that they suddenly lived in ... They are the ones who never knew what the true point of lying was — that its gift is balance. It is carrying across a room a glass with the water not only to the brim, but a little above the brim, while everyone expects it to spill. A lie is that miniscus. It's the arc where you control the appearance of things.
> Let me start with a story.[148]

Such a story invites the reader to become an agent of transformation, like the central character of 'Letter from Orpheus,' who 'crosses' into imaginative prose as he takes the details and realities of the lives of his fellow workers in a shoe store and turns them into fiction. Repeatedly, in O'Sullivan's prose — most notably in *The Boy The Bridge The River* (1978), though the stories in *Survivals* (1985) also probe estrangement — characters find themselves on bridges, poised between choices, suspended between the ordinary and the extraordinary, associatively linked with the pull of 'overseas.' While this fiction draws its 'realism,' its documentary specificity, from its overt accuracy with things and times, it invites readers actively to associate rather than simply passively to receive. For all its documentary illusion, in other words, it reminds us that it is illusion, and that its greater reality lies in its inventive balance, its capacity to articulate the powers of association by which an author envisions his social context and connects with his readers.

It is possible to read this active engagement with the language of art as one of Duggan's bequests to O'Sullivan's generation, but it is important, too, to appreciate the social context of such a bequest. Like Duggan, Davin, and M.K. Joseph, O'Sullivan was educated at the same Marist school (Sacred Heart College) and by the same teachers. And it is not hard to step from this observation to the conclusion that the Catholic writers constitute an alternative tradition in New Zealand, seeking the reality of fiction and the truth of symbol while the documentary Protestants settle for the reality of appearances and the immorality of graven lies. But to do so would be at once to overstate the likeness among these four writers, to distort the cultural differences within the culture, and to narrow both the role O'Sullivan has individually embraced and the nature of the alternatives within contemporary New Zealand society. O'Sullivan, besides being story-writer, is poet, playwright, radio writer (like Gee and du Fresne, among others), and along with Margaret Scott the scholarly editor of Katherine Mansfield's manuscripts; he was for two years literary editor of the *New Zealand Listener*, and he is editor of a contemporary poetry anthology and the third volume of the Oxford anthology of New Zealand short stories. He inherits *all* his society, in some sense, and his writing asks not for the definition of a tradition within it but for the understanding of how a multiple set of experiences coalesce in language and await the transforming eye and ear and mind of writer and reader together.

But this process of transforming inheritance, so that it no longer seems alien, emerges most clearly in contemporary New Zealand fiction in the stories of the Maori writers, Witi Ihimaera and Patricia Grace. Like Katherine Mansfield before her, sounding speech for the silent women, and like Frank Sargeson, finding a voice for the inarticulate males, and like Janet Frame and Maurice Duggan, seeking a language of art and feeling beyond the critical embrace of *either / or*, Patricia Grace has used words to break past a cultural silence. She has tried to find in English a way of writing out her awareness of being Maori: which means writing for a Maori readership, writing out of a knowledge of and feeling for Maori heritage and experience in the context of contemporary society, and writing about Maori experience for those who know nothing of it – it means, as one of her titles put it, of responding insightfully to 'A Way of Talking' and discovering in oneself the proud capacity for connection that sometimes – in *aroha*, for example – evades English equivalence, and sometimes does not require words. In order to establish this conscious presence, however, Grace has to first face an absence. Hence like Noel Hilliard dismissing Mansfield for what he sees as her class blindness – to fasten on the undeclared biases of his own time as much as to chastise the past – Grace attacks the flippant (ie, culturally disembodied) use of Maori words in pakeha stories (like those of Roderick Finlayson) and the social limitations of pakeha portraits of Maori women. They are sexual, she says, without being relational:

Earliest works depict Maori girls as passionate hip swingers with flashing eyes ... In later writing the Maori woman seems to exist in fiction for one reason only. In Mulgan's *Man Alone* the main character has a sexual relationship with someone else's wife (illicit), she's the boss's wife (doubly illicit), she's a Maori (triple banger?) ...

In Maurice Gee's *The Big Season* we are told that one of the major character's 'first woman' was a Maori – the woman is never mentioned again, but we've been able to note what an unconventional character the man is ...

But that does not mean that I am trying to say that these writers have been wrong. Writers do use minor characters in order to show the development of a major one. And the writers whose work I have mentioned are of course serious and able ... I am worried only about the heaped up effect, so that in the meantime it is more important for me to write about other relationships with the hope that better balance is obtained. After all, sex is important in all societies — cousins are not, elders are not.[149]

Her point about elders and cousins — the significance of family, and the traditional reciprocity between people and the land — is taken up by Witi Ihimaera as well. In 'Cousins,' for example, in *The New Net Goes Fishing* (1977), Ihimaera tells of a young Maori university student regretting his cousin's death — regretting it because he realizes only at the point of loss that he has never known him, and that (by committing the 'heresy' of having 'willingly embraced the pakeha world')[150] they have separately transformed the *connection* 'cousin' into an ordinary *word* meaning 'stranger.' Yet Ihimaera structures his story as a traditional lament, with ritual repetitions, requiring the reader to react to the language of form as well as to the distorting form of the acquired language. Ihimaera rejects neither the past or the present; conscious in his own generation of a dual heritage, he seeks a balance that will allow both laughter and dignity. Seeking language, that is, is a matter of seeking power, a power that derives from the authenticity of understanding and the accuracy of expression.

The formal structure of *The New Net Goes Fishing* emphasizes the stresses and temptations to which such dualities give rise, but of all the techniques Imahaera has used, it also most clearly reveals his talent for oblique instruction. A book of eighteen stories, the collection separates the first and last — 'Yellow Brick Road' and 'Return from Oz' — as a frame; two of the enclosed stories are called 'The Greenstone Patu' and 'I, Ozymandias,' and a story in Ihimaera's 1972 collection *Pounamu Pounamu* — or 'greenstone greenstone' — is called 'In Search of the Emerald City.' The deliberate allusions to the perfectible fantasy world of the American writer L. Frank Baum[151] are clear on the surface: they invite the reader to perceive the American fantasy in New Zealand — with all that that implies: imported norm, embrace of the irrational, acceptance of Utopia, surrender to political reality. At the beginning of *The New Net Goes Fishing*, a child is excited at moving to Wellington, moving to the city, moving to a fantasy country of pakeha possibilities. But the success of wish-fulfilment depends on the adequacy of the wishes, and on the power of self-possession, as the characters in *The Wizard of Oz* found out. Ihimaera's contained stories and sketches tell not of wicked witches killed but of lost family, lost relationships, lost meanings for rituals and words; they tell of drifting, pollution, money, and violence, and of a new (American) language of confrontation (black vs white) and separation. While the final story asserts the possibility of returning home, it also acknowledges the inevitability of change. Oz was a fantasy, Ihimaera says, but so, he implies, is any denial of reality, the pakeha impact on Maori culture included.

His concern as a writer is to ensure that cultural impact is not a force that moves only one way, and he adapts his literary form to expose the reasons for loss and to reaffirm the continuing presence of values that ask for recognition. Given a language that appears at once to part him from his past and deny him his own angle on experience, he adopts a method that is indirect, in a way that characterizes much of the form that New Zealand short fiction has acquired. Behind the simple surface pattern of alien but spoken allusions lies a different net of local but unspoken allusions which the alien ones *almost articulate* and so set inferentially in relief. 'Oz,' for example, identified in the story as Wellington, none the less carries some of its colloquial reference to 'Australia'; hence while the book tells openly of the urbanization of the modern Maori, within New Zealand, it tells covertly of mass emigration, cultural difference, and cultural dispersal. The verbal echo in 'Ozymandias' tells conventionally of the doom awaiting blind pride, but it also links English literary traditions with the American ones sounded by 'Oz' — establishing that both are foreign transplants to New Zealand, related by time and distance, but born anew, if they are to stay alive, in local speech. The emerald in 'Emerald City' associatively echoes the 'greenstone,' the native jade which in Maori tradition was preserved for — and symbolic of — that which was most prized by the culture, but which commerce has turned into ornament, product, and souvenir.

Yet to leave the contrast at that would be to turn the author into a conventional romantic elegist, which is neither his purpose nor his accomplishment, nor the characteristic stance of contemporary New Zealand prose. Much contemporary writing asks acerbically if there were ever any values to be possessed, and answers no. But if 'Oz' is a fantasy to Ihimaera, 'home' is not. Through his double levels of allusion, he reclaims the force of the word 'souvenir' itself: he asks his culture (not Maori alone) *to remember*, and through the act of a faithful memory to claim the full range of values which — even, or perhaps especially, in the face of upheaval — remains the heritage of New Zealand's divided story, still within realistic reach.

PART THREE
STORY AND STRUCTURE

4 Altering Cycles:
Duncan Campbell Scott's
In the Village of Viger

In retrospect it seems fair to say that Scott's *In the Village of Viger* has had to train its own readership. When first published by Copeland and Day of Boston in 1896, the book was welcomed by those who saw it as a collection of conventional pastoral sketches – a glimpse of a way of life that was simple, rural, French, and distant: of consequence only as a reminder of the beauty of nostalgia. For example, in a survey of Canadian short story writers, Allan Douglas Brodie wrote of Scott's '10 capital sketches of French-Canadian life, possessing both dramatic interest, and a certain poetic beauty all their own' – a judgment to which he added:

As a prose writer, Mr Scott is a rare acquisition to the ranks of that clever little band, who, by the fanciful charm of their pens, amuse, instruct, and generally delight the thoughtful reading public. I understand he intends in future to devote more time to prose work than he has hitherto done, and, though he will always live in the hearts of the Canadian people as one of their first poets, as a short-story writer he will be thrice welcome.[1]

Writing in 1914, Bernard Muddiman penned what amounts to an enthusiast's footnote to Brodie's view, equating beauty with a world of past perfection, poetry with florid image, and spiritual aspiration with total fleshlessness:

Possibly there is a vein of limited prettiness in much of [Scott's work] that will destroy his ever attaining the glory of anything but a side-scheduled niche. But, at any rate, it will be all his own. It will be stamped with a certain refinement that never swerved to popular idols in an age of half-silk-hosed chorus girls, of fiction purveyors with 'best seller' climaxes, and of poets who celebrate their vespers in brothels ... He comes to us not arrayed in the divine flame, but with the smell of it about his garments ... As a short story writer he is the most artistic Canada has produced, and, some day, his work will come as a revelation to those who love all beautiful things ... [T]hese works, like broken rose petals about a garden doorway, tell us of a world of perfect colour and perfume within.[2]

While Scott was in some sense happy with *all* the attention his book got – he later complained when B.K. Sandwell reviewed the reprint of *Viger* in two brief sentences ('has long been cherished by friends of the poet and deserves wide circulation')[3] – there was a certain practicality about Scott which Muddiman missed. He was concerned with the beauty of book design, the colour of printing ink, and the quality of paper as well as with Mutability and Eternal Verities. He was also irritated when readers missed *Viger*'s realism and its coherence;[4] it was not simply a random assemblage of 'capital sketches' but a book, asking for recognition of its textual integrity and formal arrangement.

Scott provided some indication of his sense of the book's indivisibility by refusing during his lifetime to allow any of the *Viger* stories to be separately reprinted or anthologized.[5] He did try to get a Canadian reprint of the entire book to appear as early as 1926, but after McClelland & Stewart refused the offer[6] the project remained in copyright limbo until Lorne Pierce of Ryerson Press took it up in the early 1940s. The history of this publication also illuminates Scott's intentions. Again Scott insisted on its totality, refusing to cut the ten 1896 stories down to six.

Pierce's idea was to bring out an edition illustrated by Thoreau MacDonald, but Scott refused to place blind faith in the artist and asserted his own sense of design whenever he could. He retained the right of approval over the illustrations; referring to MacDonald, in all his letters to E.K. Brown, consistently and sardonically as 'the Impeccable One,' he kept suggesting changes to him. On 14 July 1944, he wrote to Brown: 'It is a pity that the Viger book is held up ... I trust that it will be out well before the Christmas season; for it would, among many other values, make a very attractive gift book. I hope the impeccable artist is correcting his peccata.'

Two weeks later he added: 'The Viger book has made some progress; the Impeccable One submitted ten drawings which I have approved, as being fairly suitable; he is now trying for a Jacket Cover.'[7] In between (17 July 1944), he had written in more conciliatory tones to MacDonald himself:

I return the drawings at the earlie[s]t moment for they are so good that there would be no point in my considering them further. I am very pleased with them and must congratulate you on getting so well the *feel* of the stories. I will even let you keep the original design for The *Little Milliner* as you like it, and so do I; but wanted to omit the Church from all these designs ...

I am in doubt about the Jacket Cover; I return the small pencil sketch. I do not like the author's name at the head of the page. You will remember that I wanted the words, Stories of French Canada left out, and you have done that, but the pencil sketch is too small for me to hazard an opinion.[8]

Scott's intent was clear: minimize the pastoral conventions and social stereotypes, and stress the particularity and reality. Despite his efforts, the Church crept into the designs anyway, asserting a presence that the stories quite pointedly downplay; and despite the fact that the stories are set on the edge of an expanding city, a wilderness isolation persists in the illustrations: as Brown remarked to Scott, after the book appeared, 'The impeccable one could not quite rid himself of the sense that all this was somewhere north of Chicoutimi; but some of his effects are pleasing ... '[9]

In some ways more damaging to the book's fate was Pierce's attempt to capitalize on an image of Scott (and an image of Canada) that the market already possessed and apparently wished to see confirmed. The dust jacket quoted from E.K. Brown's comments on Scott in *On Canadian Poetry* ('he has best succeeded in making great literature out of such distinctively Canadian material as our aborigines supply ... The perfection of his best Indian pieces is matched in his best nature-verse'), and Scott wrote to Brown: 'I did not know he was going to do this and as it refers to verse it does not seem very appropriate.'[10] In fact such comments invited distortion. Early in 1947, Scott wrote again, this time about the *Times Literary Supplement* review:

I remark that you never get anything from English authors by way of literary criticism ... Even in their publications they deal but scantly and in some cases misunderstandingly, about American and COLONIAL books. As a case in point you no doubt saw the Lit. Sup. notice of Pratt's *Collected Poems*; it was headed. 'Stories in Verse'; my own modest *Viger* was listed under the head of 'Country Life.' Well we must bear up, and carry on our own show.[11]

Hence *Viger*'s reputation as a sketchbook of bucolic French-Canadian Arcadia was reborn, and managed to persist for three decades more. Closer attention to the text itself, however, rather than to preconceived notions about French-Canadian themes and settings, reveals the cumulative argument that is embodied in the fictional form Scott chose to use.

When Stan Dragland in 1973 wrote the introduction to the New Canadian Library edition of *In the Village of Viger and Other Stories* (the extended title indicates the inclusion of seven of Scott's later stories in a section appended to this reprint of *Viger*), he confirmed what occasional anthologists like Raymond Knister, Roberto Ruberto, and Giose Rimanelli had earlier declared: that the force of Scott's stories derived from their realism. And he drew attention to some of the ways the text challenges the very notions of pastoral perfection which other critics had presumed it to represent. By image, Dragland reveals, Scott invites readers to respond to the realities that underlie the illusions of orderly permanence:

Viger is a village in transition: 'New houses had already commenced to spring up in all directions, and there was a large influx of the labouring population which overflows from large cities.' This sentence comes from the opening paragraphs of 'The Little Milliner' which not only set the scene for that story but introduce an urban undercurrent which surfaces several times in the volume ...

Swamp and city motifs are part of the ironic underside of pastoral Viger, and would tip the reader off to the presence in Viger of something more than the pleasant relief from our cares that Scott promises in his opening poem, even if there were no other irony in the book.

In fact, some of the settings are ironic, like the situation of the Arbique Inn in 'Sedan': 'There was something idyllic about this contented spot; it seemed to be removed from the rest of the village, to be on the boundaries of Arcadia, the first inlet to its pleasant dreamy field.' The key word is 'seemed'[12] ...

Two of Dragland's key words are 'undercurrent' and 'underside.' Elsewhere in his introduction, 'understatement' is a third. Dragland uses these terms to describe Scott's realism but they suggest something more as well: that Scott was aware of hidden faces and submerged motivations, and that he used language with deliberate subversive indirectness in order to reveal the truth behind linguistic and social conventions. In Viger, neither temporal nor social order is permanent; all that lasts are time and change, both of which require the characters to respond to the alternatives their lives present them with. They can embrace them, live with them, or explain them away in myth and mystery. But they must contend. And both thematically and structurally, their ways of contending shape a pattern of fictional discourse through which Scott's insights into social behaviour amount to more than mere glosses on the surface charms of an imagined country life.

At a simple thematic level, these alternatives are both political and psychological. The stories tell of the political enmities of the Franco-Prussian War in 'Sedan,' and of private battles for power: Eloise Ruelle's callous manipulations in 'No. 68 Rue Alfred de Musset' and Mme Laroque's wars with her rivals in fashion and love, Mlle Viau in 'The Little Milliner' and Césarine Angers in 'The Wooing of Monsieur Cuerrier.' They tell also of the villagers' psychological fear of outsiders, as in 'The Pedler'; of their failure to recognize the stranger as their own as in 'The Tragedy of the Seigniory'; of the madness they suppress, as in 'The Desjardins,' and the madness that others must contain, as in 'Paul Farlotte.' And they tell of blindness and dream, the companions of insight and practicality, as in 'The Bobolink' and 'Josephine Labrosse.' Always the characters live with this companion otherness, this extra dimension of themselves which they scarcely recognize, yet which affects them variously with conflict or with grace. And from his observations of their behaviour under stress, Scott teases his cumulative portrait of a whole way of life facing change, finding eloquence in the moment of passing and challenge in the moment at hand.

Internally, the particular themes overlap – 'Sedan,' for example, concerns love, family, jealousy, prejudice, and the motivations for love and enmity in general, not the Franco-Prussian war alone – and such themes, like the recurrent images of birds encaged and in flight, tie the stories together by motif. More broadly, the thematic pattern invites the reader to perceive the social and moral ramifications of the notion of a synchronic alternative self. *In the Village of Viger* is set in Quebec, and follows a string of nineteenth-century English-Canadian fictions (by William Kirby, Gilbert Parker, and others) who used Quebec as a symbolic landscape, at once familiar and foreign, in which to explore the enticements of corruption. By and large these were Protestant versions of Catholicism, celebrating British restraint but covertly fascinated by that which they found most alien. By minimizing the presence of the Church, and by rejecting the label 'French-Canadian stories,' Scott signalled that he was doing something different – not portraying *then and over there* so much as he was finding an external design for the world *now and right here*, the otherness being part of 'here' and demanding to be recognized as self, not an exotic worthy only to be watched and excluded.

The repeated determination to classify the book as a set of local colour vignettes says something about the readership and the persistence of certain social stereotypes and their verbal associations, but Scott's individual stories make clear some of the difficulties of identifying with that which seems foreign (the key word is still 'seems). What the characters – and through them the readers – are asked to identify with (or admit to) is jealousy, vindictiveness, sibling rivalry, enmity, prejudice, blindness, madness, fear, dream, ignorance, imagination, love, loyalty, laughter, fidelity, and song. It is a daunting list. But it is also a list in which the clearly 'alien' experiences (madness and prejudice, for example, identified as 'other') and the clearly familiar (loyalty and love, claimed as one's own) overlap in ignorance and are linked by the (alienating or familiarizing, depending on perspective) processes of dream and imagination. Fear can transform dream into nightmare and distort the intent of language, as when, just before sleep, Monsieur Cuerrier resolves to woo Césarine (he sees it as a 'campaign') and is haunted by the vindictive Widow Laroque instead:

in the dream that followed he found himself successfully wooing the widow, wooing her with sneers and gibes, and rehearsals of the old quarrels that seemed to draw her smilingly towards him, as if there was some malign influence at work translating his words into irresistible phrases of endearment.[13]

But the artist can also make language the tangible medium of imagination, hence a means of revelation. The artist can shape it to show the nuances of aspiration and despair, to justify the process of image-making, and to combat the ignorance that underlies prejudice and enmity.

'The Tragedy of the Seigniory,' for example, is a tale of the once-and-still-noble but now impoverished Rioux family, whose faithful servant Louis kills the returning young master because he mistakes him for a stranger, an interloper, a villain. His ignorance thus causes him to act, but in the process it also transforms him into the villain, identifying him with his secret fear, while in the face of the 'tragedy' the master's dog (named Fidèle) disappears. The allegorical reverberations of this structure are magnified further by Scott's use of setting. In the past time of the events of the tale itself, while the young master is away trying to make his fortune to redeem the estate, surveyors with theodolites close in around the property, allowing the roadways of Viger to circumscribe and diminish it; so, in the present time of the telling of the tale, is the city closing in on Viger.

On the surface, Scott seems to be writing an elegy for the passing of an old and stately way of life; but to pursue the terms of allegory – the implications of indirect mode – is to realize that he is probing a different question entirely, involving the blind preservation of the past, the susceptibility of the ignorant to outside manipulation, and the challenges that accompany any familiarity with knowledge. In the political and moral terms of the stories, those who fight knowledge surrender to the dictates of their own ignorance. But those who wield knowledge run the equivalent danger of susceptibility to ambition. They can destroy each other. But they are related to each other, even part of each other. And this capacity for self-destruction, the underside of the potential for joy, marks the world that in actuality is theirs to inherit, its realities made clear less by any inherent wickedness than by the imperfections of its pastoral face.

The forms of story thus themselves constitute social messages; they are both the vehicles of narrative and the embodiments of perspective upon experience. Like many other nineteenth-century story collections, *In the Village of Viger* assembles a variety of conventional patterns into a kind of miscellany. There is a sentimental fable in 'The Bobolink,' a comic anecdote in 'The Wooing of Monsieur Cuerrier,' a romantic tale in 'The Tragedy of the Seigniory,' a folk-tale in 'The Pedler,' a melodrama in 'The Desjardins,' a sketch in 'Josephine Labrosse,' and elements of allegory in 'Sedan.' When Arbique's adopted daughter Latulipe accepts the implicit (tactile, non-verbal) proposal of Hans Blumenthal, Scott writes that 'She was giving herself to the enemy,' and the reader is made aware that Arbique's Franco-Prussian quarrel with Hans over the Motherland masks a deeper quarrel – over the 'possession' of Latulipe – that is sexual in origin, if political in expression, something which he sublimates past the point of recognizing. Again, the failure to recognize leads to death, this time Arbique's; when Latulipe catches his last word it is 'Sedan,' his birthplace, not the landscape of her name: the knowledge he admits to is circumscribed, and he consequently surrenders authority to another.

But it is not the fact of miscellany alone – the variety of tale types in this collection – which proves instructive about the book's formal effect. Arrangement and sequence also constitute tacit shapes of communication. At the heart of the book, for example, the two adjoining central stories – 'No. 68 Rue Alfred de Musset' (named for the ironic and romantic French poet) and 'The Bobolink' – are respectively the most ironic and contemporary and the most sentimental and old-fashioned in the entire collection, the effects of each achieved partly by contrast with the verbal world of the other. When Eloise Ruelle, in 'No. 68,' realizes she has no future in an old house with a sick brother, she resolves to trap a rich lover and dispose of the brother who loves her most of all – all of which she manages, dissembling with language, feigning innocence and helplessness, getting her brother to don a guise of madness so that she can have him incarcerated, and running off with the shallow suitor who thinks her innocent. She recognizes (at 'the beginning of her career,' Scott writes, twisting that last word so that it is no longer respectable) that she is 'leaving everything' but that with 'her sweet smile' she has 'also gained all – everything.'[15] But her actions are a parody of the Christian virtues such an exchange structurally represents. 'The Bobolink' immediately follows, in which a blind girl demonstrates a selflessness that throws Eloise's actions into pointed relief. Even the vocabulary reiterates the connection. Thinking that a caged bird doesn't sing 'because he only saw you and me, and the road, and our trees, when he used to have everything,'[16] the little girl – Blanche – frees the bird to the air. In so doing, she gives herself to some loneliness, gaining little, not even altruistic warmth of feeling. She has insight perhaps, but she had that before, and she still has not sight; and what the reader is told to see is not fulfilment but regret. As fable, the story suggest's that Blanche possesses some freedom in her real innocence – it is not a mask, feigned, like Eloise's – but at the same time the fable does not pretend that such innocence (any more than naïveté) is much of a guarantee against the manipulations of the Eloises of the new age. The very fact of contrast thus shapes our response to Blanche's story as much as to Eloise's; the stories interconnect.

The recurrence of particular motifs invites the reader, moreover, to seek meaning in the patterns that contrast creates. In some sense, for example, the whole book can be read as a set of permutations on the character of flight, with the bobolink as central symbol. There is flight from the city and back to it again in 'The Little Milliner,' flight to get married in 'Monsieur Cuerrier,' the calculated and cautious flight of Eloise Ruelle, the refusal to flee in 'Sedan' and 'Paul Farlotte,' flight into and away from sexuality and wealth and mechanism, and so on. Expanded to a general theme, such flight could be read as a commentary on the nature of moral responsibility or on the stresses of responding to guilt, power, shame, or modern times. All of which would be true. Yet it would not take account of Scott's basic structural technique, which is that of the sequence of story-telling; through this device he achieves one of the most instructive of his indirect and cumulative effects.

The stories appear in the following order:

1 The Little Milliner
2 The Desjardins
3 The Wooing of Monsieur Cuerrier
4 Sedan
5 No. 68 Rue Alfred de Musset
6 The Bobolink
7 The Tragedy of the Seigniory
8 Josephine Labrosse
9 The Pedler
10 Paul Farlotte

This simple linear sequence contains a more complex one, made up of two internal cycles, their structural parallels marked by significant shifts in emphasis. We can tabulate these forms as follows, noting the (vertical) sequential repetition and the (horizontal) structural variation:

Nos. 1 & 6   two stories of innocents in flight, the first hounded into departing, the second released into freedom and regret;
2 & 7   two stories of man's estate as an internal hell, the first closing in self-contained madness, the second in self-imposed guilt;
3 & 8   two stories of courtship and love, the first telling of the man's choice, the second of the woman's, both ending in song;
4 & 9   two stories involving the rejection of strangers, the first telling of the passive survival of persecution, the second of the mythologizing of the irreligious renegade;

5 & 10 two stories involving an engagement with the outside world, the first abandoning a system of values in order to manipulate it, the second learning to rely on the values that accompany the knowledge it possesses.

Clearly there are adjacent contrasts to be appreciated in the book – contrasts between innocence and guilt, between love and rejection – and also contrasts to be appreciated from cycle to cycle. The story sequences are not mirror reversals of each other, but alternate variations. They constitute a *set* within which alternatives have value and variation has meaning.

The first cycle (Nos. 1–5) begins in ignorance (the widow Laroque 'suffered greatly from unsatisfied curiosity,' and even at the close of 'The Little Milliner' we are told that 'No one knows what will become of the house'),[17] then traces the weakness of innocence, and ends with the kind of knowledge Eloise possesses: the kind that uses innocence for self-interest and that sacrifices values in order to acquire power. The second cycle (Nos. 6–10) begins in innocence, traces the weakness of ignorance, and closes with an exploration of the mixed blessing that knowledge can be: at times a goal so enticing it provokes irrational pursuit, at other times the power that sustains a sensitive man through times of crisis. In 'Paul Farlotte,' the closing story of the entire collection, Guy St Denis gradually gives up moderation and gives himself over to the 'labyrinths'[18] of his mechanical invention; Paul Farlotte, meanwhile, the sensitive outsider who recognizes the dangers of such absorption, keeps postponing his return to his mother in France in order to look after the family he has adopted. Inverting some of the premises of 'Sedan,' the echoes here suggest a kind of psychosexual freedom it is beyond Arbique's power ever to achieve. More importantly, 'Paul Farlotte' closes with Paul giving up entirely his intent to return, the apparent sadness of the decision countered by the covert implications of his no longer needing to do so; and the book closes with these words: 'Later in the day he told Marie that his mother had died that morning, and she wondered how he knew.'[19] As with the end of 'The Bobolink,' there is a temptation to read this phrase as maudlin sentiment, but to do so would be to ignore the resonances it derives from the book as a cumulative whole. The emphasis here is not on feeling, but on knowledge, with implications for how we are to understand Scott's fictional accomplishment.

The twin cycles chart options for Viger – Eloise and Paul providing opposing models of self-possession – yet at the end Viger is left still without all the knowledge it appears to desire. Extrapolated to metaphor, we can see Scott commenting in this way on his society's vulnerability in its lack of sophistication (a vulnerability even to its own sense of image). 'We must bear up, and carry on our own show,' he had written to E.K. Brown, but to do so meant suffering through a variety of misconstructions. Scott's Canada may have been relatively unsophisticated, but it was pastoral and quaint only to the uninformed outsider who could not read its complexities. His book rejects the idea that social naïveté is equivalent to moral strength, and also that change is equivalent to moral degradation; at the same time its conclusion is intensely moral in nature, claiming the need for sensitivity and knowledge to engage with each other if the *sense* of community (as opposed to the *boundary* of community) is to persist or enlarge. Most obviously, by shaping and resolving his book in terms involving knowledge, he is explicitly declaring Viger to be a post-Edenic world – with all the implications this admission has for the imperfect lives of its inhabitants, but without surrendering to blame or guilt in the process. The 'underside' of pastoral is really its main face. The challenge is to deal with it. Moreover, knowledge as the agent of resolution is also paradoxically the agent of further change. 'Paul Farlotte' and the book close at the end of a second cycle, but the form of the whole book reminds us that cycles neither repeat themselves perfectly, nor stop. Scott's engagement with memory thus turns into a subversion of an escapist belief in stasis. And one of the continuing appeals of *In the Village of Viger* derives from its adaptation of a cumulative formal structure to precisely this end.

5 No Longer Living There:
Margaret Laurence's
A Bird in the House

The eight separate stories in *A Bird in the House* (1970) have in common the character of Vanessa MacLeod, whose childhood and adolescence constitute the overt subject of the book. They have in common also the basic setting (that of the invented Manitoba town of Manawaka in the 1930s) and the narrative perspective (that of Vanessa some twenty years later, selectively remembering and rearranging the events of her past into personal and public mythology.[1] But while these elements go far to unifying the book thematically, they leave the formal arrangement still to account for. The book is not linear: hence it does not simply tell 'Vanessa's history.' And it does not close in a single illuminating resolution: hence it does not lend itself to summary by apophthegm or moral closure. It is cumulative, but it is not sequential: hence accounting for the unified structure of the whole means it is necessary to account for the unifying effect of broken or interrupted sequence and open form.

On the surface the book appears to adopt a frame structure. The first four stories ('The Sound of the Singing,' 'To Set Our House in Order,' 'Mask of the Bear,' 'A Bird in the House') and the last ('Jericho's Brick Battlements') concern Vanessa's connections with her parents, her Aunt Edna, her Connor and MacLeod grandparents, and the Connor house ('part dwelling-place and part massive monument')[2] she carries with her in ambivalent memory; and these enclose three stories ('The Loons,' 'Horses of the Night,' and 'The Half-Husky') telling of her connections with more distant relations (the Métis, her dreamer-soldier-madman cousin, and the less respectable townspeople), all of them leading to violence before each narrative is over.

Yet a true frame enclosure would thus imply that the violence is contained by the order of the family house. Here, while it is true that the family in its way persists, the emphasis must be on *in its way* as much as on *persistence*. The time-frame of the 'contained' stories precedes and overlaps that of the initial stories. Moreover, one thing Vanessa has learned is that 'whatever God might love in this world, it was certainly not order';[3] the house itself passes to strangers who do not maintain the shrubbery; and the family members to a person die or disperse. It is the breaking, the violence that accompanies the persistence, that matters to the persistence. The generations do not come alive in imitation, but in refashioning their inheritance into themselves. Hence the frame is illusory, not fixed; and the rupture represented by the breaks in the cumulative story form comes to be an integral part of Laurence's narrative argument.

These breaks occur not just in the physical disjuncture between individual stories (Kent Thompson, on reviewing the book when it first appeared, wrote of the *series* that escapes the 'imposed sequence that is the psychological failing of the novel form')[4] but also in the temporal contraction represented in Laurence's handling of historical sequence, narrative process, and narrative memory. The temporal perspective is multiple, but cumulatively simultaneous, as remembered historical events come to be re-enacted for both Vanessa and the reader in the narrative present, each event overlaid vertically on the others, the final result being more like that of stacked transparencies than that of horizontally arranged murals. Once again, the effect is to draw attention to the pattern that derives from formal overlap (a patterning both of congruency and of difference) rather than to one of narrative sequence.

Laurence herself drew attention to these matters when in 1972 she wrote an essay called 'Time and the Narrative Voice' for John Metcalf's short story anthology, *The Narrative Voice*. Attempting to explain the paradox of authorship and first person narrative – over the fictional Vanessa, and Vanessa's control over the temporal structure, the choice of a past to be remembered and revealed – Laurence writes that her eight stories were initially published separately,

> but conceived from the beginning as a related group. Each story is self-contained ... but the net effect is not unlike that of a novel. Structurally, however, these stories as a group are totally unlike a novel ... In a novel, one might ... imagine the various themes and experiences ... as a series of wavy lines, converging, separating, touching, drawing apart, but moving in a *horizontal* direction. The short stories have flow-lines which are different. They move very close together but parallel and in a *vertical* direction.[5]

Further, speaking specifically of 'To Set Our House in Order,' she explains that

> The narrative voice is ... that of ... an older Vanessa [who, like any character, 'bears the responsibility for the treatment of time within the work'] ... What I tried to do was

definitely *not* to tell the story as though it were being narrated by a child. This ... would have meant denying the story of one of its dimensions, a time-dimension ... The narrative voice had [to convey both the older Vanessa and the ten-year-old she was and now remembers] ... had to speak as though from two points in time, simultaneously.[6]

Laurence's immediate conclusion is thematic, and directed at the reader:

Given this double sense of time-present, Vanessa ...reveals ... what the story is really about. It is actually a story about the generations, about the pain and bewilderment of one's knowledge of other people, about the reality of other people which is one way of realizing one's own reality, about the fluctuating and accidental quality of life ... and ... about the strangeness and mystery of the very concepts of *past, present* and *future*.[7]

Through the fact of separateness, in other words − her own and others', seen in space and over time, overheard and held in speech and story − Vanessa comes to recognize her own reality: her ancestry, family society, womanhood, artistry − such themes accumulate and interlink. But a further examination of the forms of language Laurence uses to reach this end − and of language itself as one of the book's motifs − reveals how the formal structure she uses sustains her argument, and gives artistic shape to her faith in an evolutionary individuality.

The formal challenge Laurence faces is to represent change without either becoming linear or implying total severance between story elements or generations. Her resolution to the problem involves her in various techniques of overlap: metaphor, allusion, doubling, tense shift − all of them requiring the reader to perceive an implied as well as a declared presence. The opening paragraph of the first story thus serves both as a technical instruction in how to read the book and as a simple setting of scene and theme:

That house in Manawaka is the one which, more than any other, I carry with me. Known to the rest of the town as 'the old Connor place' and to the family as the Brick House, it was plain as the winter turnips in its root cellar, sparsely windowed as some crusader's embattled fortress in a heathen wilderness, its rooms in a perpetual gloom except in the brief height of summer. Many other brick structures had existed in Manawaka for as much as half a century, but at the time when my grandfather built his house, part dwelling place and part massive monument, it had been the first of its kind.[8]

The practice of doubling ('part dwelling place, part monument') is a device

Laurence characteristically uses to join apparently disparate attitudes together. Here the tension between family and ego is caught up in the twinned images of the Connor house; later on, Vanessa is declared to be 'shivering and listening' for news of her mother in hospital, 'fascinated and horrified' at Chris's stories of dinosaurs, as though the act of hearing invited discomposure.[9] Which of course in Vanessa's case it does: language is at once her escape and comfort and the means of violent awakening to upsetting truths.

The metaphors of this opening passage further emphasize the ambivalence of Vanessa's physical and verbal landscape and the illusory absolutes with which she must learn to contend. The house is 'plain as turnips' (domestic, idiomatic) and at the same time 'sparse as a crusader's fortress' (romantic, formal); the gloom is 'perpetual' (absolute), 'except' for a moment (the absolute denied). She has the 'family' to deal with and also 'the rest of the town,' whose processes of knowing give an unfamiliar name to the alien territory (her grandfather's house) which she comes for part of her life to call home. But she no longer lives there: the tense shifts tell us that. They take us from the present (the narrator beginning her story *now*: 'that house *is* the one I carry') back into the past she recalls (*Known*, it *was, windowed*') and the past she has been told ('*had existed, built, had been*') and must now outgrow. The shift represented by Grandfather Connor's revolutionary 'built,' altering the seeming permanence of what 'had existed' before, thus serves as a model Vanessa must re-enact rather than imitate; others may imitate him (his house '*had been the first of its kind*') but she cannot live either in the past he once refashioned or the past he shaped for *his* family in the illusory permanence of brick and seclusion.

Yet it is not easy for Vanessa to break from the past or (speaking modally as well as about her character) to break into the present. Still a child at the end of 'The Sound of the Singing,' Vanessa runs after her ebullient great-uncle Dan when her grandmother, as sensitive to private person as her grandfather is to public form, says '"Go with him ... keep him company".' It is a phrase that invites structural as well as simple narrative reading: Agnes Connor is not telling her granddaughter to live in a stage Irish past or be a drunken failure, but to hang on to the will to sing. Dan sings; Grandfather Connor only bellows, for all his moral uprightness and strength of personality. 'And I ran, ran towards the sound of the singing,' Vanessa writes; 'But he seemed a long way off now, and I wondered if I would ever catch up to him.'[10] The past still embraces 'now,' holding Vanessa, too, in speechless wonder, racing her off towards her grandfather's generation and yet still holding away from her the control over utterance that it must be hers to gain: it is the sound of the singing rather than the singing itself that at this point leads her on.

Subsequent stories in the collection do not advance Vanessa's life-history so much as they record resonant moments in this same process of working out the connection between *now* and *then*. Each time a moment of change approaches, something happens to reinstall Vanessa in the past. At the beginning of 'To Set Our House in Order,' her mother is pregnant with her brother Roddie, but the story opens with a reversal of normal order: 'When the baby *was almost ready to be born*, something *went wrong* and mother *had to go* into hospital *before the expected time*.'[11] The story recounts, among other things, stories of others thwarted before their time: a stillborn child; Vanessa's eighteen-year-old Uncle Roderick, killed in World War I; and her dead grandfather MacLeod, whose intellectual life in Manawaka was limited by his inability to find anyone who shared his knowledge of Greek. But the main line of narrative involves Vanessa's preliminary glimpses of her father's life and family.

Given over, during her mother's hospital stay, to her Presbyterian, aristocratic, and formal grandmother Eleanor MacLeod, Vanessa is surrendered to the orderly authority of the past just as she nears an understanding of the disorder of life being lived. She intuits something of the romantic, heroic models her father had to live by from the adventurous titles of the books on his shelves, and he in time gives way again to his mother's will to name his life for him. But Vanessa also catches a glimpse of something else: reality – an adventure of a different kind, an adventure in chaos, for which she does not yet have a name:

On a shelf by themselves were copies of the *National Geographic* magazine, which I looked at often enough, but never before with the puzzling compulsion which I felt now, as though I were on the verge of some discovery, something which I had to find out and yet did not want to know.

Nor does she find out. An imposed order intervenes; her grandmother controls such realities by denying their relevance to her:

'What on earth are you doing?' Grandmother McLeod enquired waspishly, from the doorway. 'You've got everything scattered all over the place. Pick it all up this minute ... '
   So I picked up the books and magazines, and put them all neatly away, as I had been told to do.[12]

But by now this passivity is assumed. In glimpsing 'strangeness' and 'disarray,'[13] Vanessa has felt some of the adrenalin rush of the will to shape things for herself, and she is then brought into sympathy with her smart-talking, mask-wearing Aunt Edna and into open confrontation with her grandfather, Timothy Connor.

When 'A Bird in the House' opens, Vanessa is choosing to resist her family, though in doing so she demonstrates her immaturity as often as her independent-mindedness: 'The parade would be almost over now, and I had not gone.'[14] The rhetorical structure repeats the now familiar control of past patterns over imminent changes. But in subsequent stories the rhetoric reverses itself. 'Horses of the Night' opens with a declaration of an event that challenges the absolute of the past: 'I *never knew* I had distant cousins who lived up north, *until* Chris came down to Manawaka *to go* to high school.'[15] The 'Half-Husky' records a parallel revelation in embryo: 'When Peter Chorniuk's wagon clanked slowly into our backyard that September, it *never occurred* to me that this visit *would be different* from any other.'[16]

When 'Jericho's Brick Battlements' begins, then, it inherits the indirect rhetoric of the preceding stories as well as their overt narrative lines. This final story records Vanessa's move to the Brick House after her father's death, her adolescent growth and rebellion, her move away from it, and the visit to Manawaka twenty years later that leads to the book's entire series of narrative reminiscences. It opens with an apparently simple account of setting and motivation:

Before we moved into it, the Brick House had always been a Sunday place for me. It was a fine place for visiting. To live there, however, was unthinkable. This would probably never have been necessary, if my father had not died suddenly that winter. That spring, with the wind only beginning to thaw and the roads flowing muddily with melted snow, my mother had told me that she and my brother and myself would be going to the Brick House to live.[17]

Even at the level of symbolic setting the passage seems to be indicating that the Brick House will enclose her. But enclosure is not the substance of the indirect message at all. Examining the rhetoric of the verb sequence in the paragraph, particularly in light of the book's cumulative rhetoric, suggests another level of meaning embodied in the discourse. Throughout the book, Vanessa has pursued change and been limited by age and the past, or accepted a pattern of events only to have it alter. Here the verb sequence suggests the nature of the attitudinal change that will allow Vanessa access to the present and her own life, full of reversals and constraints, but closing in the promise of process: 'Before we moved ... had always been ... was ... To live ... was ... would never have been ... had not died suddenly ... only beginning to thaw ... flowing muddily ... had told ... would be going ... to live.' Going to the Brick House *to live* – that is, in order to live, in order to break past it at last – does not imply constant forward movement. As the entire book signifies, the past has its attractions as well as its burdens, and Vanessa is

193 No Longer Living There

repeatedly absorbed into past time before she can reach the present and all that the present implies about perennial change. But it is to this result – ending in the text but ongoing in the implied narrative – that the rhetorical structure of the series of stories finally leads.[18]

Reality is disarray, the book says, and Vanessa must discover reality. But the author must so arrange words that the narrative, direct or implied, however interrupted, does not lose itself in inconsequential disarray in the name of preserving reality. Hence while the verbal patterns Laurence devises must serve as functional formulations of Vanessa's personal growth, they must also credibly articulate Vanessa's cast of speech if the reader is to accept the stories as Vanessa's own record of memory and understanding. What happens is that there emerges in the book a kind of tripartite stance towards the connection between reality and language. There is a set of characters, for example, for whom reality is shaped by fancy, bias, preconception, or belief. In their own way, Timothy, Eleanor, and Agnes all accept as real only those aspects of life which accord with their scheme of it. And there are other characters who allow themselves to be shaped by the strength of those positions – Beth, Ewen, Aunt Edna to some degree, despite her irony and her deliberate slang, and even Piquette Tonnerre in 'The Loons' who, unwilling to perform as a story-book Indian for Vanessa, instead adopts an equally make-believe urban identity, English boyfriend and all, with his 'real classy name ... Al.'[19] Vanessa, however, has to shed herself of a passive acceptance of others' definitions and by learning reality through memory, learn also the strength to choose what applies to her and the strength to refuse what does not.

Emerging from this confrontation between defined order and disarray is a third element: a version of what constitutes an authentic artistry, applicable to Vanessa the character and to Laurence the writer as well.[20] For neither one can imagination artificially shape reality; the disarray always intrudes. For both, reality must give voice and shape to the imagination. While for Laurence this conclusion means that her experiment in broken form must authentically record the interrupted history of a culture in place, for Vanessa the recorded changes in understanding must lead naturally to her ability to tell the stories that constitute the book. Hence for Laurence the resulting portrait of Manawaka becomes a representative cultural landscape, in which the forces of inheritance (Scots, Irish, Métis – MacLeod, Connor, Tonnerre) and the forces of disturbance (the emergence of Ukrainian names in the community's immigration – Chorniuk, Lobodiak, Kamchuck; the Depression; urbanization; and war – Dieppe in particular) emerge in a coherent and fluent new structure. But for Vanessa, the quest for language and freedom is a personal, not a political one; the language she struggles to hear and then say is one that will draw on her connections with her family and cultural past and also carry her into the future. The book is consequently permeated by allusions to language itself — as word, sign, feeling, and gesture — until the silences of memory turn into stories of acquiring speech.

'The Sound of the Singing' introduces this motif, and once again does so in a variety of ways, from the opening contrast between down-to-earth turnips and romantic crusaders, to the biblical passages on which Agnes Connor relies, to the stage Irish pretence of Uncle Dan — no more 'Irish' than Eleanor MacLeod is Scots, both of them Ontario-born and bred to think of themselves as citizens of another culture altogether — to Edna's slang ('toujours gai, kid'[21]) and Pig Latin, to laughter, tears, evasions, similes, muttered protests, domestic idioms ('Step on a crack ... ,' 'lazy as a pet pig,' 'no use getting in a fantod about it'),[22] romance, misapprehension, and euphemism (even the doll's feet are 'called "aristocratic," which meant narrow').[23] Things have meaning beyond their appearances and their sounds; and most of all the story makes us aware of Vanessa's 'camouflage of silence'[24] as she struggles to make sense of it all.

Subsequent stories show Vanessa learning to understand the art of indirect utterance, and the odd human necessity for evasions and lies. When her mother says (of her mother-in-law), 'Don't worry — she'll keep everything in order, and then some,'[25] we know (though Vanessa does not, yet) that there is tension between the two women. When other characters add 'Don't worry,' 'You're not to worry,' the very repetition of the negative ensures the reverse effect: Vanessa starts to worry, and though she can unload her fear on Edna, with whom she has an affinity, Edna, with Beth away, has no one but the walls to talk to. At once communication is a comfort and a burden; knowledge — understanding — intensifies both security and insecurity, the unstated but understood being even more forceful than the stated and inexact. Of Agnes Connor, for example, Edna (in Vanessa's hearing) says:

'*Good*. What a word. I wish I didn't know what she means when she says that. Or else that she knew what I mean when I say it ... '

I understood then that she was not speaking to me, and that what she had to say could not be spoken to me. I felt chilled by my childhood, unable to touch her because of the freezing burden of my inexperience. I was about to say something, anything, however mistaken, when my aunt said *Sh*, and we both listened to the talk from the living room.[26]

But when, later, Edna's erstwhile beau marries another woman, Vanessa understands enough to comprehend her mother's deliberate silence: '"I know, Vanessa. She knows, too. So let's not bring it up, eh?"'[27] The silence allows an illusion of decorum to persist, as a degree of comfort in the face of what otherwise seems to be anarchy. Eleanor MacLeod has said *'The MacLeods never tell lies,'*[28] as though it were a clan motto. She believes it to be true, though Beth knows it is not. Even Vanessa's father has lied to his mother, suppressing the realities of war (and perhaps of love) in France. An older Vanessa knows something of why this is so, too, imagining what she and Ewen might have said had he lived to her adulthood; in the process Vanessa learns something also of the limits of evasion. Hence she is taken beyond the immediate family and into a more direct contact with rupture than an orderly life allows.

In 'The Loons' and 'The Half-Husky' (the two weakest separate stories of the book) and in 'Horses of the Night' (the single most accomplished one), Vanessa acquires an education in violence, but she has also to learn to control what she finds out; only then will she be free to begin to command a language of personal expression. In 'The Half-Husky,' for example, she suffers when Harvey Shinwell tortures her dog; she is upset that the dog should itself learn violence from violent treatment; but she also learns that violence can be lodged in silence as well as in action. Knowledge does not have to be articulated in order to be a weapon. Her grandfather's phrase, when Vanessa asks him if he has known Ada Shinwell before their confrontation over Harvey, is therefore instructive both for what it says and for what it hides:

'No,' my grandfather replied without interest. 'She was nobody a person *would know, to speak of*. She was just always around town, that's all.'[28]

Propriety encloses him, perhaps shapes what he chooses to remember, certainly shapes his current speech. When at the end of the story Harvey is put away in jail, and the dog is 'put away' in another sense of this phrase, Vanessa in the present rises to irony over Ada: 'She was considered safe to go free.' But Laurence places this double-edged statement beside Vanessa's memory of her own deliberately hurtful refusal to speak to Ada: 'Once she said hello to me. I did not reply, although I knew that this was probably not fair, either.'[30] Her tempered words in the present thus acquire a significance both from what they say and from the very fact of saying, particularly in their context of silenced communication. Repeatedly, the characters in this book are unable to speak, afraid to speak out loud, apparently lost without adequate words for the occasion, or hampered by not having a listener. Learning to wield silence, first as camouflage, then as weapon, Vanessa has to go on to wield words as well, freeing herself from the silence and the formalities that permeated her childhood, discovering the richness of meaning lodged in idiom and the richness of texture that can emerge in a prose that accepts idiom as well as formal usage as its heritage.

Grandmother MacLeod's formal clan mottos and Grandfather Connor's solecisms therefore come together for Vanessa: she inherits them both. Edna, in the last story, when she is perturbed at her suitor Wes's ungrammatical utterances, is objecting to her father more than to Wes, and has to be cajoled (by Beth) into realizing that her indirect rebellion (the Pig Latin, the slang, the popular songs – 'Bye, Bye Blackbird,' 'Tiger Rag' – are all part of her verbal rejection of her father's *power*) should not be allowed to get in the way of her happiness. Silence should not become a weapon; utterance can not become a substitute for independence. That Wes is in some ways a variant form of Edna's father is one of the ironies that Edna's generation had to live with. But for Vanessa it is the balance, the multiple heritage, that is important – culturally embodied, verbally expressed – and nowhere in the book does the reach for balance become clearer than in 'Horses of the Night.'

At the plain narrative level, this story tells of Vanessa's connection with her cousin Chris. Determined to dislike him, she finds herself enchanted by his speech – by his direct address to her, by his stories, by the indirect glimpses he gives her of his dreams. The dreams and stories constantly overlay reality with romance (his horses Floss and Trooper he calls Duchess and Firefly), and the romance is partly in the telling, partly in the understanding. He tells of a house made of trees by an inland sea, and of monsters' prints in stone; only later does Vanessa appreciate the accuracy of an elderly log house, fossils, and dinosaur tracks, and it is later still that she appreciates Chris's loneliness as well as her own dimly articulated dread – 'the dimensions of his need to talk'[31] that led him to speak to her, a thirteen-year-old, because there was no one else, beside what was for him a peopleless place, a place of monosyllable, an 'alien lake of home.'[32] Seeking speech, Chris is seeking to have his doubts and dreams understood; but most of his gestures towards connection meet rebuff instead. Grandfather Connor belittles him in his hearing, so Chris contrives to appear to be absent; Vanessa misinterprets him (when he speaks of being a traveller, she thinks of Richard Halliburton instead of vacuum cleaners), and Chris leaves; Ewen appreciates what he's suffering, but Ewen dies; the army coerces him into confrontation and turmoil, and Chris recoils into himself, writing Vanessa that 'He'd fooled them. He didn't live inside [his body] any more.'[33] He begins in hope and talent, and he ends in breakdown and violence (a word Vanessa cannot connect with him), in silence and retreat.

While one of Beth's statements in an earlier story anticipates the action here ('people shouldn't let themselves think like that, or they'd go crazy'),[34] the central issue in 'Horses of the Night' is neither as moral and judgmental as this statement might imply, nor primarily social and critical. The story certainly criticizes what Depression and War did to people, but as the multiple references to language declare, it concerns itself mainly with the emotional tension between reality dreamed and reality reached and released in speech. Chris is a model for Vanessa as much as a character in his own right: he dreams perfect designs — but always he ignores the fact of human fallibility, his own included. Vanessa cannot grow if her designs are perfect, or even if she pretends they are; accepting limits, she sheds her childhood (at the end of the story she puts a toy away 'gently and ruthlessly,'[35] with determination refusing the temptations of romance), but she acquires speech. Early on, she has listened to her parents, pretending to be otherwise occupied; already she knows that 'To speak would be to invite dismissal. But their words forced questions in my head.'[36] Over the course of time she listens to Chris and is eager to support his dream of sales success even when others know how little likely it is to come about. But when she speaks she becomes aware of the difference between unquestioned assumptions and questionable truth: '"I'll bet you'll sell a thousand, Chris ... Yet now, when I had spoken, I know that I did not believe it".'[37]

It is not an epiphany. There is no single moment of enlightenment in any of these stories — there is a process of constant revisionary change instead. Language moves back and forth over memory like rain over water, shaping and reshaping the patterns in its reach. Indeed, 'enlightenment' implies the very kind of absolute that the stories are, if not exactly attacking, at least challenging. Eleanor MacLeod's perfect order is unreal; Timothy Connor's absolute rule is tyrannical; the myth of Manawaka's cultural homogeneity is inaccurate; and Chris's dream invites madness. What model lies here for Vanessa? Laurence's resolution to the story — in the allusion that gives it its title — contains her response to absolute assertion. Apparently referring to one work, it embodies a second reference as well: meaning is covert and indirect, in other words, and multiple, never *simply* plain.

Thinking of Chris, Vanessa remembers

Some words ... from a poem I had once heard. I knew it referred to a lover who did not want the morning to come, but to me it had another meaning, a different relevance.
Slowly, slowly, horses of the night –
The night must move like this for him ... I could not know whether the land he journeyed through was inhabited by ... the old monster-kings, or whether he had discovered at last a way for himself to make the necessary dream perpetual.[38]

His perpetuity, whether terrible or wonderful, is a notion she has to reject, and does — for in the very act of remembering him, she tacitly acknowledges that she lives in a world of time. The dual allusion, moreover, allows both for Chris's anticipation and Chris's fear — it refers to Marlowe's Doctor Faustus ('*O lente, lente, currite noctis equi!*'), which in turn quotes from Ovid's *Amores*.[39] In the one work, Faustus tries to ward off hell, having foolishly courted youth and sacrificed his immortal soul; in the other a lover, having fled the side of an immortal who has not retained youth, seeks the continuing vigour of another mortal. Ironies abound. But lodged in the deliberate ambivalent use of the allusion is Laurence's celebration (and Vanessa's cumulative realization) of the ambivalent nature and needs of humankind. Chris's inability to shed his desire for permanence doomed him to disappointment; in *A Bird in the House*, Vanessa's disappointments are those with which she must be able to live.

She needs words both in order to live and in order to write: in some sense, as the book proceeds, these two goals become one. The series of records of Vanessa-as-writer thus joins with those of her as listener and speaker to give dimension to her character and — sustained over time — to the artifact of the book itself. The autobiographical mode suggests how life turns into fiction; moreover, within the life record there appear anecdotes about writing stories, which at once provide a counterpoint to Vanessa's experience and serve as instructions in literary validity.

Repeatedly, Vanessa-as-a-child writes ('makes up' is her own term) her fictions as escapes, though she pretends they are realities; their connection with life always proves disconcerting. She puts aside her first book, *The Pillars of The Nation* ('"It's about pioneers"')[40] when she discovers that her grandfather was a real pioneer — but it is important to emphasize that she does so not because her work doesn't measure up to his reality but because his reality, to which she objects, punctures her romance. The next, *The Silver Sphinx* (it's about 'love': '"Good Glory," Aunt Edna said, straightfaced. "That sounds fascinating".'),[41] burns with biblical elevation, while all around her the life-sized love stories of her parents, grandparents, Edna, and Piquette progress with ordinary fervour, ordinary hope, and ordinary distress. At the end, writing another historical tale, this time of Quebec and the fur trade, Vanessa plots escape strategies for her heroine Marie, only now to let probability intrude: 'I no longer wanted to finish the story. What was the use, if she couldn't get out except by ruses which clearly wouldn't happen in real life?'[42] It is a reversal of her resolution to *The Pillars of the Nation*, but (submissive as it is) it is also still inadequate as a guide to her own independence. That (and her book's stories) come not from historical *tale* and biblical *romance* but from life.[43]

But clearly Vanessa's literary and life models while she is a child also invite her to romanticize her ancestry, to surrender to authority, and to order disarray. She tries to do so – in 'The Loons,' she tries to turn Piquette into a storybook character, temporarily concluding that 'as an Indian, Piquette was a dead loss'[44] – but listening and language compel her instead into fracture, ambivalence, irony, reality. A 'dead loss' is precisely what Piquette becomes, but in terms that invert the stereotype and mordantly criticize the society that can only think in cliché: the real person dies, is lost, and the community renames Diamond Lake 'Lake Wapakata, for it was felt' (the adult Vanessa writes in an evasive, ironic passive) 'that an Indian name would have a greater appeal to tourists.'[45] As an adult, that is, Vanessa demonstrates her literacy by resisting closed stereotypes and inviting the reader to become an open listener, along with the child-Vanessa, to a language in the process of acquiring dimension.

As writer, Vanessa (given her models) could be imitator, madwoman, escapist, tyrant, vivisector, or recorder. She chooses to be creator – but such a role does not exist in a vacuum, however much it implies *ex nihilo* fabrication: she is not God, but human. Her heroes are local, her dragons domestic. And ultimately the book celebrates her particular humanity. She writes at the end that her grandfather Connor's gravestone is not his monument. But nor is his house. That is the past, and she no longer lives there. The monument is herself in the present tense, the present text, *the house she carries with her*, the flow of ancestry. Edna early on notes Vanessa's likeness to her grandfather, and then tries to retract what she sees as a terrible label:

'for all you're always saying Vanessa takes after Ewen, you know who she really takes after.'
  'That's not so!' my mother burst out.
  'Isn't it?' Aunt Edna cried. 'Isn't it?'
  'I was hardly aware of her meaning. I was going instead by the feel of the words ... Her voice was high and fearful, burdened with a terrible regret, as though she would have given anything not to have spoken.[46]

But it is true. Vanessa inherits from her father, mother, and all her grandparents; from Timothy Connor she acquires a power of self-reliance that potentially isolates her, certainly in some respects makes her extraordinary. Ultimately it allows her to confront his originality, accept it, then separate herself from it as she assembles her own. Language is her medium. She knows all the while that the language she uses is not unknown before her, but it is all her own in its particular person, in her particular choice of balance. And that is what matters.

Thus in fracture there is creation, whether in the modal form of the book or in the social, personal, and verbal life of its main character. Vanessa as an adult revisits her parents' graves, and remembers 'saying things to my children that my mother had said to me, the clichés of affection, perhaps inherited from her mother. *It's a poor family can't afford one lady. Many hands make light work. Let not the sun go down upon your wrath.*'[47] In combination, they are at once idiomatic and formal, the catch phrases of her family life and heritage, which persist through time not to enclose experience but to give it voice, not to repeat the past but to sound the overlap between past and future. Because for Vanessa the inheritance can never be a single-stranded one, the voice is plural. In these broken, integrated stories of the education of an artist, Laurence and her narrator claim form itself as a language of narrative, revealing the potent force of apparent disarray and the shaping power of generation.

6 Pronouns and Propositions:
Alice Munro's *Something I've Been Meaning to Tell You*

Here my subject is Alice Munro, or – more precisely – the thirteen stories collected in her 1974 volume *Something I've Been Meaning to Tell You*. The reflexive character and function of this sentence will shortly become apparent; it emulates Munro's formal strategy (proposition followed by qualification pointing to alternatives), a strategy which unites by means of rhetoric what otherwise might seem a disparate collection, and which leads the patient reader towards an implied, embedded, narrative of speech. One of the stories, called 'Material,' concerns the way in which a writer finds a subject; it begins this way:

I don't keep up with Hugo's writing. Sometimes I see his name, in the library, on the cover of some literary journal that I don't open – I haven't opened a literary journal in a dozen years, praise God. Or I read in the paper or see on a poster – this would be in the library, too, or in a bookstore – an announcement of a panel discussion at the University, with Hugo flown in to discuss the state of the novel today, or the contemporary short story, or the new nationalism in our literature. Then I think, will people really go, will people who could be swimming or drinking or going for a walk really take themselves out to the campus to find the room and sit in rows listening to those vain quarrelsome men? Bloated, opinionated, untidy men, that is how I see them, cosseted by the academic life, the literary life, by women. People will go to hear them say that such and such a writer is not worth reading any more, and that some writer must be read; to hear them dismiss and glorify and argue and chuckle and shock. People, I say, but I mean women, middle-aged women like me, alert and trembling, hoping to ask intelligent questions and not be ridiculous; soft-haired young girls awash in adoration, hoping to lock eyes with one of the men on the platform. Girls, and women too, fall in love with such men, they imagine there is power in them.[1]

A critic's immediate reaction to the passage might well be to feel bloated, opinionated, and untidy, and impelled to urge an audience, with an argumentative chuckle, to go swimming. Such is the force of the writing. A more reflective reaction would take us back into the story itself, asking what is going on, asking why the story sets up this particular proposition and why the character who proposes it expresses herself the way she does.

I am reminded of Clark Blaise's approving reference to Donald Barthelme:

Endings are elusive, middles
are nowhere to be found, but
worst of all is to begin, to begin, to begin.²

Barthelme and Blaise are both concerned with the writing of short stories; my concern here is with the writing of a critical response to short stories. They are concerned with the imaginative writer's ordering reaction to experience; my concern is with the imaginative reader's reaction to the literary experience which the story's order affords. We are all concerned with language. Hence we must all be concerned with the resonances that words set in motion, and fasten back upon 'beginnings' as the moments when entire stories are born.

In 'Material,' for example, we can note several features of that first paragraph: the careful balance between the short jabbing sentences and the sentences full of cumulative and incriminating details (as in 'the novel ... or the ... short story, or the new nationalism'; 'swimming or drinking or going for a walk'; 'bloated, opinionated, untidy'; 'dismiss and glorify and argue and chuckle and shock'). We notice also the indirect declaration of identity ('People, I say, but I mean women, middle-aged women like me'); we savour the opening alternation between positive and negative assertions ('I don't keep up ... Sometimes I see ... I don't open – I haven't opened ... I read'); and we are conscious of the pronouns. All of these technical devices reiterate the central tension between the narrator and Hugo, her first husband, and as we later find out, between her and her current husband, Gabe, as well. The tension is between women and men, and the fact that the opening paragraph starts with 'I' and ends with 'them' seems naturally crafted to articulate this connection. The story renders an 'I-them' relationship. It is full of isolation and opposition. The narrator feels herself cut off from others yet bound to observe them, making judgments of others that are bound up with her sense of herself. This is Hugo's way as well. The writer in whom she has no faith, he does manage to write a good story, to transform the less-than-beautiful events of life into the effective details of art. And just as their acquaintance Dotty becomes his subject, he becomes the narrator's. People become the artists' 'material,' are filtered through their subjective eyes, are transformed. Paradoxically, writers' very capacity to *see* seems to divide them from the world with which they so closely relate. In writing, they remake the world, and reinvent their acquaintances in it.

Not all the stories in this volume are as dour as 'Material,' but their recurrent concern with frustrated communications suggests more than a casual reason for bringing them together. Another proposition seems naturally then to present itself: if there is design in the individual stories, is there design in the book? To hazard an answer, we are thrown back once more to the beginning, and to the story which gives the book its colloquial title: 'Something I've Been Meaning to Tell You.' That the title focuses on the processes of communication is at once obvious. The communication it describes is both one-sided ('telling,' not 'talking with') and unfulfilled. There is an 'I-you' relationship adumbrated here, but it doesn't seem to come to anything. Even the tense is significant; 'have been meaning' is that curious English construction, the present perfect progressive, describing an ongoing process just completed. Munro's speaker has yet to clarify whether she will go ahead and tell or not. The ongoing intention has been completed; the telling may or may not then begin. There is a taut suspension established, out of which the characters and their separate situations grow.

The fact that there is a writer writing these tales adds the literary dimension that 'Material' takes as its overt subject. Obviously there is something being told here, by a teller – but the book contains internal tales and internal tale-tellers. What *they* choose to tell and not to tell lies within the power of the writer to control, and each decision is a revelation of another side of the book's essential message. The control is established by means of the style. And in the style lies meaning.

Consider the opening and ending of the title story, a narrative about lost love and present compromises, possible poisons (which somehow empurple the story unnecessarily) and certain death. It opens this way:

'Anyway he knows how to fascinate the women,' said Et to Char. She could not tell if Char went paler, hearing this, because Char was pale in the first place as anybody could get. She was like a ghost now, with her hair gone white. But still beautiful, she couldn't lose it.[3]

And here is the closing paragraph:

Sometimes Et had it on the tip of her tongue to say to Arthur, 'There's something I've been meaning to tell you.' She didn't believe she was going to let him die without knowing. He shouldn't be allowed. He kept a picture of Char on his bureau. It was the one taken of her in her costume for that play, where she played the statue-girl. But Et let it go, day to day. She and Arthur still played rummy and kept up a bit of garden, along with raspberry canes. If they had been married, people would have said they were very happy.[4]

Again the pronouns are significant; we hear of 'he' and 'she' twice. 'He' at the start refers to Blaikie Noble, Char's ambitious lover from youth, and 'he' at the end to Arthur, her sedate widower. 'She' refers to Char and to her sister Et, both of whom adapt to lives that do not include the declaration of their most private feelings. These are distant 'he-she' relationships; 'I' and 'you' are left essentially out of account, or at any rate, are framed within the *he-she* context. '*She could not tell if* Char went paler,' we are told from the first, and in light of what follows, the phrase reveals a deliberateness which belies its tonal flatness; Et's being unable 'to tell' is given new meaning by the end; even the use of two 'if' clauses binds the two sections of the story together, and (for all the changes that the story details) reiterates the failure to achieve satisfaction which is the story's overt motif.

Later stories in the volume contain phrases that directly echo the title – 'Tell Me Yes or No' most obviously, by its title as well as by the language in it, but also 'Forgiveness in Families,' which opens: 'I've often thought, suppose I had to go to a psychiatrist ... I would have to start telling him about my brother ... '[5] 'Marrakesh' moves towards its close, with the grandmother, Dorothy, thinking: 'If she had been able to call out to them ... it would have been a warning ... '[6] 'The Spanish Lady' ends up with the declaration: 'This is a message; I really believe it is; but I don't see how I can deliver it.'[7] And 'The Ottawa Valley' closes the book with a reiteration of a writer's predicament: the writer finding it impossible to reconcile the realities out of which she has written her sense of what constitutes 'a proper story.'[8]

These overt declarations all indicate some measure of difficulty in communicating. But what causes the impediment? The stories offer three main reasons: generation, death, and gender; and these three sources of tension run like contrapuntal themes through the entire book. Again the title story introduces, 'begins,' them. Char's youthful beauty, Char's death, and Char's relationship with Blaikie and Arthur all confront Et as she seeks to tell what she has to tell, and all seem to constrain her. 'Material,' 'How I Met My Husband,' 'Tell Me Yes or No,' 'The Found Boat,' 'Marrakesh,' 'The Spanish Lady,' 'Winter Wind,' and 'Memorial' take up quite centrally the halting relationships that occur between the sexes; 'Walking on Water,' 'Marrakesh,' 'The Spanish Lady,' 'Winter Wind,' and 'Memorial' concern themselves with generation differences; and 'Walking on Water,' 'Forgiveness in Families,' 'Executioners,' 'Marrakesh,' 'The Spanish Lady,' 'Winter Wind,' and 'Memorial' enroll their characters, and their readers also, in the contemplation of age, death, separation, and estrangement. Widows and widowers abound in these stories, but seldom thrive. Young people discover how to lie; some people, like Edie in 'How I Met My Husband,' discover how to let other people think they are telling the truth; still others, like the 'Spanish Lady,' ask why it is 'a surprise to find that people other than ourselves are able to tell lies.'[9] Their world is full of deceptions, which the old – like the grandmother in 'Winter Wind' – often know and sardonically accept; which the young use but do not always admit; and which the middle-aged apparently realize and beat against with advancing futility. The closing story, 'The Ottawa Valley,' reiterates the three main themes, bringing them together once again in a narrative involving two generations' worth of childhood recollections, and then modulates their message from one of despair to one of curious celebration.

This modulation now deserves some attention, for through it we come closer to understanding the impulse that was present in the book from the very beginning, and to which the story variations have been attempts to give voice. I have been emphasizing so far the central siatuations in these stories and techniques by which the story openings set them up: the way in which the pronouns, for example, establish the personal relationships to be explored and repeatedly focus on *point of view* as one of the writer's dominant concerns. To say that the stories provide us with *I-you, I-them, he-them*, and *she-them* studies is to offer a pretty mechanical observation; to see the care with which Munro fictionally estabishes these relationships and to follow the implications they carry with them into the stories is to begin to appreciate the function of the style and the subtlety of its argument. The point is that the apparent relationships at the beginning are frequently not the essential relationships that the stories unfold, and yet that the beginnings provide us with the clues to the twists of circumstance which are later made clear.

Even in the relatively weak story 'Walking on Water,' for example, which (like three or four others out of the total thirteen) fails to make its young adult characters convincing, the language of the opening section articulates a complex set of relationships. The story concerns an old man's friendship with a young man named Eugene, who claims to be able to put mind over matter, and who tries to test his 'control.' Eugene fails to walk on water, and disappears; a callous and callow couple named Rex and Calla continue their lives apparently unchanged; and yet for old Mr Lougheed, matter begins to pressure mind with increasing effect. He goes in search of Eugene and suggests to his pretty tormentor, Calla, that Eugene might have committed suicide.

'I think his mind was disturbed. I think he might have tried to – he might have gone into the water again.'

'You think so?' said Calla. He had expected her to be surprised, to exclaim against this, even to smile at him for such an idea, but instead she seemed to be letting the possibility blossom slowly, seductively, in her head. 'You think he might have?'

'I don't know. I think he was disturbed. I think so. I find it hard to tell when one of you is disturbed or not.'

'He wasn't one of us,' said Calla. 'He was fairly old.'

'He might have wanted to do that, though,' she said in a minute.

'It's just another thing he might have wanted to do. If that's what he was going to do, then nobody ought to stop him, should they? Or feel sad about him. I never feel sad about anybody.'

Mr Lougheed turned away. 'Good-night now,' said Calla persuasively. 'I'm sorry if you don't like your door.'

Mr Lougheed thought for the first time ever that he might not be able to get to the top of the stairs. He doubted his powers even for that. It was possible that he would have to go into an apartment building, like the rest of them, if he wanted to continue.[10]

Even Eugene is alienated from others by the language here; he is neither 'one of you' nor 'one of us.' All that remains is the 'rest of them,' to whom Mr Lougheed feels it increasingly necessary to surrender. This story of a friendship, then – of an 'I-you' relationship that seemed to be working – turns into a study of the dissolution of an identity. Yet this threat was present from the start.

Here is the story's first paragraph:

This was a part of town where a lot of old people still lived, though many had moved to high-rises across the park. Mr Lougheed had a number of friends, or perhaps it would be better to say acquaintances, whom he met every day or so on the way downtown, at the bus stop, or on the walks overlooking the sea. Occasionally he played cards with them in their rooms or apartments. He belonged to a lawn-bowling club and to a club which brought in travel films and showed them, in a downtown hall, during the winter. He had joined these clubs not out of a real desire to be sociable but as a precaution against his natural tendencies, which might lead him, he thought, into becoming a sort of hermit. During his years in the drugstore business he had learned how to get through all kinds of conversations with all sorts of people, to skate along affably and go on thinking his own thoughts. He practised the same thing with his wife. His aim was to give people what they thought they wanted, and continue, himself, solitary and unmolested. Except for his wife, few people had ever suspected what he was up to. But now that he was no longer obliged to give anybody anything, in the ordinary daily way, he put himself in a position where now and again he would have to, as he believed in some way it must be good for him. If he left it all to his own choice who would he talk to? Eugene, that was all. He would get to be a nuisance to Eugene.[11]

On the surface the paragraph builds towards telling us how Mr Lougheed enjoys Eugene's company, but the prospect of this relationship is immediately blocked. The rhetoric of the situation rests on the sequence of syntactic structures: 'This was ... or perhaps it would be better to say ... occasionally ... He had joined ... he had learned ... His aim was ... Except ... But ... If ... that was all ... ' And in any event, the paragraph's details do not offer a sense of Eugene alone; they focus instead on the contrast he provides in Mr Lougheed's world. Friends, acquaintances, club members, customers, and even Mrs Lougheed belong to that category we call 'them.' The collective group 'a lot of old people,' to which the paragraph refers when it opens, provides both the frame of reference within which Mr Lougheed is identified and an indication of the pressures upon his independence of body and mind. He does not identify himself as 'old,' yet others identify him this way. Control over his identity thus subtly shifts into the minds of others, a process which comments ironically on his desire 'to give people what they thought they wanted, and continue, himself, solitary and unmolested.'

This phrase not only ironically anticipates the story's resolution; in the context in which Munro has placed 'Walking on Water,' it also comments on the closing utterance of the immediately preceding story, 'How I Met My Husband.' There, the narrator, Edie, who has married the postman who didn't deliver her the love-letters she expected because the 'lover' she planned to hear from didn't send her any, observes that 'He always tells the children the story of how I went after him by sitting by the mailbox every day, and naturally, I laugh and let him, because I like for people to think what pleases them and makes them happy.'[12] There is a sort of nervous laughter about her statements, stemming from the disparity between the sentiment itself and the role in which the sentiment casts the speaker. Edie is a woman; her role is defined by other people, and her identity is accordingly limited. This is a motif which appears in Alice Munro's other books – *Dance of the Happy Shades* and *Lives of Girls and Women*, for example – and also in several other stories in this collection. 'Women should stick together,'[13] muses Edie, in 'How I Met My Husband,' 'Women deceive themselves and usually suffer, being exploitable ... ,'[14] reflects the narrator of 'Tell Me Yes or No.' And the fact that Aunt Madge, in 'Winter Wind,' 'had been happily married'[15] is cause both for comment and for contrast. Observing this motif, however, we are taken back once again to the realization that the artist's rendering of a failure to communicate is itself a communication, which, given over to particular narrators, allows them also their articulate moment. Somehow they are sprung from their bonds, in order to let the nature of the bonds be better understood. In the process, they manage also to reveal the degree to which their condition, being human, defies classification.

It seems designed that the stories should bear thematic relationships with each other, and that phrases in them should link them directly. Links between past and present figure as the subject as well as the method of the stories; the recurrent flashback techniques show the characters responding to such stimuli, and the connections between the stories in a way invite readers to reflect and recall in parallel fashion. These recollections go so far as to establish the reality of the past's immediate presence. When Mr Lougheed dreams of his childhood and his parents, he wonders

How to convey the solidity, complexity, reality, of those presences – even if he had anybody to convey this to? It almost seemed to him there must be a place where they moved with independence, undiminished authority, outside his own mind; it was hard to believe he had authored them himself ...

Another thing he was made to think about was the difference between that time and now. It was too much. Nobody could get from one such time to another, and how had he done it? How could one man know Mr Lougheed's father and mother, and not know Rex and Calla? ... It was sensible perhaps to stop noticing, to believe that this was still the same world they were living in, with some dreadful but curable aberrations, never to understand how the whole arrangement had altered.

The dream had brought him in touch with a world of which the world he lived in now seemed the most casual imitation – in texture, you might say, in sharpness, in authority. It was true, of course, that his senses had dimmed. Nevertheless. The weight of life, the importance of it, had some way disappeared. Events took place now in a diminished landscape, and were of equal, or no, importance.[16]

And after the narrator of 'Tell Me Yes or No' takes us on her mind's adventure – 'I persistently imagine you dead,'[17] says the story's first sentence, and we are reminded of Et's inventiveness about Blaikie Noble in 'Something I've Been Meaning to Tell You' – she repudiates the substance but asserts the essence of her characters. – 'How are we to understand you?' she asks, and answers: 'Never mind. I invented her. I invented you, as far as my purposes go. I invented loving you and I invented your death. I have my tricks and my trap doors, too. I don't understand their workings at the present moment, but I have to be careful. I won't speak against them.'[18] Imagination's own world has its validity, for it is enacted daily in the lives of girls and women, men and boys.

Are all things true, then, in human experience? 'The Found Boat,' 'Executioners,' and 'Marrakesh' – the three stories which immediately follow 'Tell Me Yes or No' – promptly take up this question and consider the degree to which we all live with lies. 'The Spanish Lady' contemplates anonymity, death, and Rosicrucian transubstantiation, probing further the reality of the past in the present. 'Winter Wind' and 'Memorial' contrast order with confusion, wilderness with plan, in their portrayals of domestic reversals and re-enacted roles. And these two stories serve as a transition into 'The Ottawa Valley,' which retrieves the past, reassembles into a new form the elements of the other stories in the book, and calls upon its readers once more to contemplate the connection between rhetoric and meaning.

'The Ottawa Valley,' though it is full of family rivalries, is also full of family loves, and though about death and separation, is also about relationship and life. Despite the pressures in it, its tone is remarkably tranquil, and once more the opening paragraph creates for us the paradoxes of the situation:

I think of my mother sometimes in department stores. I don't know why, I was never in one with her; their plenitude, their sober bustle, it seems to me, would have satisfied her. I think of her of course when I see somebody on the street who has Parkinson's disease; and more and more often lately when I look in the mirror. Also in Union Station, Toronto, because the first time I was there I was with her, and my little sister. It was one summer day during the War, we waited between trains; we were going home with her, with my mother, to her old home in the Ottawa Valley.[19]

We are told here that this is a story at least partly about disease, negation, waiting, and war. But the pronouns offer a perceptual counterpoint. It is a story about a narrator 'I' who establishes immediately her own context, three times repeated: 'With her ... with her ... with her.' When, at the end of the story, she articulates openly the burden and the worth of this connection, we have been prepared:

The problem, the only problem, is my mother. And she is the one of course that I am trying to get; it is to reach her that this whole journey has been undertaken. With what purpose? To mark her off, to describe, to illumine, to celebrate, to *get rid*, of her; and it did not work, for she looms too close, just as she always did. She is heavy as always, she weighs everything down, and yet she is indistinct, her edges melt and flow. Which means she has stuck to me as close as ever and refused to fall away, and I could go on, and on, applying what skills I have using what tricks I know, and it would always be the same.[20]

We are taken back to 'Memorial' and its assertion: 'Illness and accidents. They ought to be respected, not explained. Words are all shameful.'[21] We are taken back to all the recognitions of the past and of its vitality in reflective minds. We are taken back to 'Material' and its observation of the way in which daily experience assaults and invigorates the artist's way of seeing. But we are also made aware of the process of communication that has taken place.

Something I've Been Meaning to Tell You this book is titled. Possibly the communication *to you* does not take place in some circumstances, because the focus is on *I*. To contemplate *I*, however, is to contemplate the 'meaning' of *I*, the processes by which *I* derives, formulates, and communicates meaning. The rhetoric of each story is the rhetoric of a personality. And the personality of the book as a whole can be appreciated by listening even more faithfully to the words of the title. Beneath the surface message of 'Something I've Been Meaning to Tell You' sounds another observation, an inversion of the first: 'To Tell You Something I've Been Meaning.' To appreciate the variation is to appreciate the two lexical inferences of the word 'meaning,' both of which are integral to Munro's book. The surface structure establishes a sense of halted *intention*: this is countered by the deep structure's declaration of *significance*. The two in concert thus give voice to the book's several struggles, and epitomize the tensions (caused by the disparate personalities and by the disparate perceptions they bring to the shared moments in their lives) which it has been the author's effort to record. As the stories modulate their way toward their final revelation, readers are led from their first conception of the book's subject – that which the plots convey: the simple failure to communicate – to the realization that there is another meaning present, lodged in the processes of language, and that there is a teller of meaning, whose words convey more than they seem actually to utter. If we listen closely to those words, we start to hear their multiple messages; we move then as vigilantly as possible into Alice Munro's perceptual landscapes, which we begin to begin to understand.

7 Pronouncing Silence:
Katherine Mansfield's 'At the Bay'

In her long short story 'At the Bay' (1922), Katherine Mansfield takes the reader through twelve numbered sketches, twelve cross-sections of moments in the life of the Burnell family, one summer day near Wellington. The twelve fragments do not exactly connect into a temporal cycle, though they are arranged chronologically – the first in 'Very early morning' and the last 'Late – it is very late'[1] at night. Nor do they ultimately accumulate into a unified analysis of a single person or a representative stratum of society. Though there are sharply realized figures and social reverberations aplenty, *unity* does not seem to be the story-writer's aim. While there is an organic character to the work, this character derives from the internal fragmentation, not from a false determination of wholeness. In fact the illusion of orderly progress, or false wholeness, also contributes to the story's effect, for it is an illusion that the story attempts methodologically to unmask, with implications for the lives and literary voices of Mansfield's culture and the men and women in it.

It has become conventional to think of Mansfield as a literary rebel, one who took the Poe-based notions of short story structure, unity, and plot development and overturned them. Yet critical commentary long struggled to identify the dominant character of her style and themes, as though by naming it 'intense' or 'poetic' or 'personal' or 'feminist,' the Mansfield mode could be reabsorbed into the literary mainstream, perceived as a variant of what was accepted as the 'norm' (Engish? masculine? ordered? whole?) rather than as something radically different in kind. Such comments more often reveal the expectations of critical fashion than they isolate the degree to which form *is* meaning in a Mansfield story. Recurrent attempts, moreover, to identify Kezia Burnell (or her mother Linda or her unmarried Aunt Beryl Fairfield or her grandmother) as *the* central character of 'At the Bay' reinforce the expectations of a unity-centred criticism. The Fairfield name (Mansfield was born Kathleen *Beauchamp*) asserts some autobiographical dimension to the story's origins, but then to claim Kezia as the centre and to transform the story into a memoir or an idealization of innocence and childhood is to falsify the narrative texture. In Mansfield's control over form lies a different kind of communication entirely, one pronounced through *ellipsis*, in both its meanings.[2]

The twelve sections divide the narrative events into relatively even-lengthed sketches:

I   The animate sound of the sea breaks the morning silence, followed by the movement of sheepdog, sheep, and shepherd past Mrs Stubbs' shop, Leila the milk-girl's *whare*, and the Burnells' cat Florrie.

II Stanley Burnell rushes out to swim, only to be disappointed that his brother-in-law Jonathan Trout is there before him.

III Stanley has breakfast, prepares for work, and leaves, drawing his three daughters (Isabel, Kezia, Lottie), Beryl, Mrs Fairfield, Linda, and Alice the servant girl into commotions that centre on him.

IV The three girls head to the beach, where they play with their cousins, Pip and Rags Trout; while Kezia controls the action until they meet the boys, the two boys take over afterwards.

V   At 11 a.m., women and children have the beach to themselves; the boys swim unhesitatingly, the girls after making compromises with others; Beryl leaves the family unit to swim with 'sophisticated' Mrs Harry Kember, who admires Beryl changing, then swims away like an animal.

VI Beside her baby son, Linda dreams — of the garden, of her Tasmanian home, of Stanley's courtship, of her dread of pregnancy — and the boy turns over.

VII The tide has gone out; Mrs Fairfield talks to Kezia of her dead son, and then cajoles Kezia into good spirits again when she begins to worry about death.

VIII Alice goes to tea with Mrs Stubbs, looks at the shop-owner's photos of her dead husband, and wants to be back in her own kitchen.

IX In the washhouse the five children play a card game, the rules of which require them to pretend to be animals; they tell stories while day fades, and are frightened when Jonathan appears to take the boys home.

X   Jonathan talks to Linda about age, aspiration, insect law, and lost opportunity, and then leaves.

XI Florrie opens her eyes; Stanley returns, full of apologies for not having said goodbye to Linda that morning, causing another commotion.

XII Beryl dreams of romance with Harry Kember; then Harry Kember actually invites her into the garden for a rendezvous; she accepts, then withdraws; the sound of the sea fades into stillness.

And the apparent movement of the story from stillness and sea-sound to sea-sound and stillness establishes a sense of cyclic pattern which the recurrent references to age, death, law, time, and the world's plan would seem to reinforce. What the story form makes clear, however, is the irony of such thematic deference to regulation: the patterns exist because they are accepted, but not necessarily because they are acceptable. And the story's shaped but unspoken challenge to the reader is to hear the underlying connection between this formal inference and the sketched portraits of domestic life and expectations.

Repeatedly, the story asks not just that the reader listen to sounds, but that the reader mark how sounds break durations of silence: sound, that is, makes us aware not just of itself but also of the expressiveness of silence, of the *presence* of silence. Hence speech makes us aware of the unsaid, and action of what has not taken place: the effect of the form is oblique, drawing attention to a present *other*, while articulating a fencer's mask of daily routines. Each of the twelve sections alludes somehow to broken silence, the recurrent pattern echoing the formal effect of there being story sections in the first place (narrative moments breaking intervening silence). For example:

I The passive and copula structures of the first paragraph modulate into a 'Perhaps if' clause, only to have unstated possibility truncated by the active sounding of the sea as paragraph two begins.
II Stanley's active noises further rupture the silence, except that he is egotistically unaware of his impact, and complains that Jonathan's 'mania for conversation' irritates him 'beyond words.'
III While Stanley organizes the women around him, their voices are disembodied, not part of them; when he leaves, they change.
IV Conversation breaks silence; speech holds power; children promise 'not to tell.'
V Beryl longs to hear what Mrs Harry Kember is 'going to say.'
VI With Linda, the boy 'didn't believe a word she said,' but when Linda finds words that express a different register of what she feels, he turns away.
VII Sound from an unknown source interrupts a reverie on the inexpressible events in the unknown depths of the rock pools; Kezia interrupts her grandmother's reverie; then insists on her saying 'never' – 'But still her grandma was silent' – until they both forget 'what the "never" was about.'

214   Dreams of Speech and Violence

> VIII The jangle of Mrs Stubbs's bell breaks the silence of Alice's walk along the road, and once inside the shop, Alice has to take meaning from Mrs Stubbs's oblique glances and vocabulary.
> IX In the washhouse the children can make noise without people interrupting them, yet imagined noises none the less frighten them, first into silence and then into shrieks.
> X The silent reverential reverie between Linda and Jonathan (truncated 'story,' soundless sea) is broken by Jonathan's 'shadowy' declaration '"It's all wrong ... I'm old".'
> XI The sound of Stanley returning from his absence signals the renewed commotion of his presence.
> XII Voices (her own and Harry Kember's) punctuate Beryl's romantic dream, till the she wrenches free, the sea-sound fades, and silence is retrieved once more.[3]

Throughout, there is a power attached to speech, whether it is Isabel exerting it over Lottie, Pip and Rags over the girls, Beryl over Kezia, Mrs Harry Kember over Beryl, Mrs Stubbs over Alice, Stanley over everyone (so he believes), or Jonathan (so Stanley irrationally suspects) over Stanley. Throughout also, however, there is greater mystery and potential power held in reserve in the intervening silences, not awaiting naming (hence containment by the existing conventions of language) so much as it awaits expression and release. The fragments of story, consequently, ask to be read not as portions of a named entirety but as punctuations in the unnamed rhythms of duration.

There are signs throughout the opening section of the story that the author is concerned with background as much as foreground – but it would be a mistake to accept 'background' either as a simple pastoral setting (early morning, the sheep, the sleepy sea) or as the implied hierarchical social structure (agrarian, landowning; the *whare*, the shop), though clearly section I establishes both these elements as a preface to the narrative. The breaking of silence and the sheepdog's dismissal of 'a silly young female'[4] introduce other motifs. But the most visible feature of the opening paragraph is that of negation. By her deliberate structures, Mansfield draws attention to absences, absences which are paradoxically as present and as rich with effect as the things which positive speech claims to be real:

The sun was not yet risen, and the whole ... was hidden ... The ... hills ... were smothered. You could not see ... The sandy road was gone ... there were no white dunes ... there was nothing to mark which was beach and where was the sea ... Big drips hung ... and just did not fall ... It looked as though ... Perhaps if you had waked up in the middle of the night you might have seen ... [5]

Pronouncing Silence

At which point the story breaks into sounds and events. Mansfield stresses the contrast further when she begins section II with time, Stanley, bold strokes, sound, and a string of active verbs:

A few moments later the back door ... opened, and a figure in a broad-striped bathing suit flung down ... cleared ... rushed ... staggered ... and raced for dear life ... Splish-splosh! First man in as usual! He'd beaten them all again. And he swooped ... [6]

Stanley's movements are to no particular avail, it turns out, for Jonathan is there already, and the comedy of Stanley's petulance over Jonathan's presence inversely comments on the effect of his own presence on the women in 'his' household. As the section draws to a close, Mansfield technically reiterates her point: Stanley has rushed into the sea, claiming it in the name of practicality, as territory for himself, by right, whereas Jonathan strives to relax into the waves, discovering expression through negation ('You couldn't help feeling ... not to fight ... that was what was needed ... To live ... "why not?"')[7] which only dissatisfies him because he is unable to sustain it against time.

The open contrast between the two men reinforces the effect of the technical contrasts that are lodged in the sentence patterns and the imagery. But the fact that the story, though it begins in soundlessness, turns at once to the speech and activities of men before it addresses itself to the lives of the central characters, all women, also says something inferentially about the lives these women lead. They are founded in silence, yet framed by men, whose Adamic habit is to rush about naming the world for themselves and for women, as though by right and as though the women had no power of voice of their own. The negative-positive dichotomy implies a further dilemma: for if the women articulate themselves only as 'not-men,' then they retain their dependence upon a system that hears male speech (power) as normative, and they define themselves only vis-à-vis their male relationships.

What section III establishes is the women's covert independence. Stanley fumes about time and asks after his son, but Beryl interacts only to the degree she deems necessary. Linda holds her silence as much as possible until Stanley leaves, at which point: 'Oh, the relief, the difference it made to have the man out of the house. Their very voices were changed as they called to one another; they sounded warm and loving and as if they shared a secret.'[8] The point is that they defer to Stanley's speech (even Alice), but do not acknowledge power in it, whereas he by contrast always connects his speech with power; by not saying goodbye to Linda, for example, he means to punish her – and tries all day to salve his conscience – yet Linda has scarcely noticed the absence of speech, for she does not connect the fact of statement with her (or his) feeling of affection. In another context, when Jonathan speaks of women in the formal cadences of medieval romance, that has no meaning either: 'Linda was so accustomed to Jonathan's way of talking that she paid no attention to it.'[9] It is only in silence, and fragmentary utterance, and broken thought that they reach a bond of understanding. The interruptions to orderly sequence enact for them a kind of counterpart to the interrupted lives they lead: in large part waiting lives, taking *time out* for childbirth and marriage, or occupying time's backwaters, awaiting others' recognition.

On another level, that is, the women severally demonstrate the degree to which they live in a world bounded by male speech and are none the less absorbed in the value system it declares. Beryl, for example, can find satisfaction neither by deferring to male authority nor by competing with it in its terms, and part of the problem of the isolation she feels in the household is that she sees these as her only two options, and so divides herself from the other women, from her mother most specifically. She masquerades as Stanley, so to speak, ordering Kezia around — and Kezia in turn responds just as Beryl does to Stanley: recognizing the source of the sound of voice but only superficially responding to it. That Kezia does not respond at all when Isabel adopts the same imperative stance towards her — and that she turns to help Lottie instead — does not indicate her freedom from Beryl's dichotomy, although it does suggest the possibility of another alternative. Mrs Fairfield's ability to connect both with William and with Kezia furthers the notion. Yet Mansfield leaves this possibility largely unexplored.

Beryl, by contrast, portrayed at length within the text, strives to locate freedom outside the family and in the company of the Kembers, but is defeated by her learned expectations of speech and power. Instead of the understanding she hopes for, Beryl finds in Mrs Harry Kember (this version of her name clearly indicating her assumed, acquired identity) the same kind of predatory claim to ownership over her that she finds in men. She shrinks from Mrs Harry Kember's oblique lesbian advance, longs to hear Mrs Harry Kember *speak*, and recognizes aghast that in the water Mrs Harry Kember looks 'like a horrible caricature of her husband.'[10] In recording this sequence of reactions, Mansfield underlines the complex syllogisms of Beryl's predicament: language is power; language is male; male language cannot express female understanding; therefore a female using male language acquires power only to the degree she becomes a surrogate male; but a surrogate maleness produces only a surrogate power, neither of them real; therefore language does not represent power or reality for a female; except that in reality the system that equates power with male language still exists. The very power that repels her, consequently, is what she is attracted to, and the verbal boundary of her own expectation is what denies her fulfilment.

In this context the much-challenged eighth section of the story,[11] in which

Alice visits Mrs Stubbs, functions less as a satiric portrait of the Lower Classes than as a reinforcement of the story's glimpses of language and power. Beryl, watching Alice head off down the road, condescendingly presumes her to be headed to a bush assignation; she is wrong, inasmuch as she projects the sexual terms of her own mixed aspirations onto all other women. Though Alice's terms are slightly different — she seeks company and aspires to Society (the parallel is with Beryl seeking out Mrs Harry Kember) — the results are something the same. Metaphorically, the two women seek speech-as-expression, and are deflected into retreat when they find speech-as-power containing them instead. Like Lottie in the subsequent card game, Alice has difficulty remembering the rules; other people always make them up, and circumstances appear constantly to shift just at the moment that she grasps freedom or language or meaning.

Alone on the road, for example, Alice suddenly fears silence, which she transforms into a threat of someone unknown (male?) watching her — so she speaks in order to overpower fear, but realizes 'that was hardly company.'[12] The language she wants to control does not serve her, and the silence that should serve her (as at best it serves Linda and Mrs Fairfield) she fears and misinterprets. Mrs Stubbs's shop sign, however, is cast in the possessive mould, and when Alice enters Mrs Stubbs's parlour and presence, speech deserts her; she struggles to express 'manners,' and suffers 'a curious difficulty in seeing what was set before her or understanding what was said.'[13] Mistaking Mrs Stubbs's solecisms for control over the rules, she rises only as far as a pale mimicry, which catches her out as surely as did her pretend-power speech on the road:

'It is a nice style, isn't it' shouted Mrs Stubbs; and Alice had just screamed 'Sweetly' when the roaring of the Primus stove died down, fizzled out, ceased, and she said 'Pretty' in a silence that was frightening.[14]

Mrs Stubbs's elliptical stories of death, disease, and her husband further manipulate Alice. Mansfield's tone is comic, but underlying the surface texture there is a desperation on Alice's part that is no match for Mrs Stubbs's apparent mastery of the speech-and-power confrontation. Hence when Mrs Stubbs mentions Freedom, Alice immediately desires it, no more and no less than Beryl had done. That she should locate it in 'her own kitching' ('She wanted to be back in it again')[15] simply records the dimensions of her retreat. She surrenders to the authority of speech, and accepts as possessive control ('*her own*') the role by which others have defined her. Mansfield's focus is not on the class reverberations of this decision so much as on the importance for women of language as a sign. The fact that this language projects mixed signals only corroborates for them its unfamiliarity. The challenge then is to give that which is native and familiar some measure of recognizable authority.

The shift from Alice's outing to the children's card game seems less abrupt when this distinction between legislation and authority is realized. When Lottie runs into trouble remembering what to do, the children's reactions epitomize the verbal attitudes of the social world around them. Kezia is quietly contradictory, and tells Lottie she does, too, want to play: '"It's quite easy",' Isabel 'said exactly like a grown-up, "Watch *me* ... and you'll soon learn".' And Pip, with a male version of Isabel's egocentricity, empowered by the presumption of possession, hands one card over to Lottie saying, '"There, I know what I'll do. I'll give you the first one. It's mine, really, but I'll give it to you".'[16] It is not the portrayed fact of card-playing that is Mansfield's concern here (hence her story does not tell some idyllic version of childhood fancy) but the implied instruction in role-playing, which is consequential in ways Mansfield rejects. In the game the children all turn into animals. Pip declares himself to be a bull, Rags a sheep, Isabel a rooster (her gender-crossing claim to surrogate power amply illustrated by her choice); Lottie is called a donkey when she cannot decide for herself, and although later offered the chance to be a dog instead, she utters 'Hee-haw' anyway; only Kezia battles to be different (a bee), maintaining her choice even though the others claim that an insect is not an animal *in their terms*.

As other elements of the story make clear — Jonathan's regretful meditation to Linda, for example — being an insect does not free a person from the external rule of power and time. In its paradigm, Jonathan's plaint describes Beryl's and Alice's problem as well as his own: '"I'm like an insect that's flown into a room of its own accord. I dash against the walls ... windows ... ceiling, do everything on God's earth, in fact, except fly out again" into the "dangerous garden, waiting out there, undiscovered, unexplored".'[17] Claiming power, however, turns one even more demonstrably into an animal. Mrs Harry Kember 'turned turtle ... and swam away ... like a rat'; Mrs Stubbs's 'soft, fat chuckle sounded like a purr'; Harry Kember himself, 'quick as a cat,' came through the open garden gate and 'snatched' Beryl 'to him.'[18] Such identifications make Mrs Fairfield's seemingly affectionate epithets for Kezia ('my squirrel ... my wild pony')[19] at the very least problematic. For there is another set of suppressed and misleading syllogisms operating within the story's text: in ('wild') nature (the 'vast, dangerous garden'), animals exert power; in nature, power is natural; therefore natural law orders affairs naturally; in society, men and language exert power; therefore the power of men and language is natural and operates by natural law.

Clearly Mansfield argues the invalidity of this presumption, ridiculing it in the actions (if not the person) of Stanley Burnell, and declaring it to be a social convention, whatever authority it possesses being of another kind. Kezia's 'wildness' perhaps demonstrates the degree to which she has not yet been tamed by language, the degree to which she still perceives it as an 'easy' game. But if that is so, the story would seem to suggest that like others she will come to the point of using language as power, consequently turning herself into mockman (or animal), preying on those weaker (less fluent) than herself. (This is a conclusion with even more complex reverberations if the story is read as autobiographical memoir.) Compounding the model which the story presents is the fact that — while some women do 'master' the domains they claim — the 'victims' in the story are either female or those males who, like Jonathan, rebel against the (Presumed-to-be-male) social rules. Women, in other words, can be victims of other women, not just of animal-men. Kezia's wildness, then, if it is to be distinguished from predatory power, has to be understood in some other way: not as the articulated language of natural law, but as the unarticulated language of natural rhythm.

Yet within the world the sharpness of this distinction is arbitrary, perhaps illusory. Natural rhythms are everywhere alluded to in the story: tidal rhythms most recurrently, diurnal ones more formally, rhythms of bloom and decay, of death and birth, in the imagery of insect and garden. It is a body of rhythm that is Kezia's to inherit, and it is a pattern to which the ebb and flow of the story structure contribute, establishing narrative structure as a separate pulse of communication from the lines of semantic definition. The story's focus is not on one character alone, but on the (sometimes broken) kinship of women that derives from these simultaneous modes of 'language.' Linda, for example, rejects ownership but not love, lives by absenting herself creatively into silence as well as by parrying present speech. Other characters dream in verbal cliché, their silence no more effective than their fear. Still others lose themselves in affectation or regulation.

Technically the story breaks past 'closed' narrative form, but where is the freedom it locates for the characters? The story-teller uses speech as well as silence in order to establish the effective rhythm of silence. But the story nonetheless closes in irony. Beryl's withdrawal from experience is no more fulfilling than an embrace of Kember's reality would have been: she is defined by her inability to see past these dual options to the alternatives that her kinship promises. She continues to locate freedom through romantic fancy (hence in speech); hence she surrenders to social paradigm and the irony of its design of women's roles: marriage, spinsterhood, servitude, shop. The freedom that she and Alice appear to reach for is only to own or be owned. Even Linda's animate passivity seems an ultimately inadequate single model. It is the force of kinship in concert that the rhythms finally promise, but against the power of society's inertia, claims for a close identification between art and life are likely to oversimplify. There is irony, therefore, in the very fact of using speech to set the rhythms of a different kind of communication in motion. Yet here the story-teller also asks for the negative image to be read; she attempts to shape speech by intervals of silence, so that the open form will reshape the presumptions of speech and challenge its triple bias of order, plan, and power.

8 Saying Speech:
Frank Sargeson's 'Conversation with My Uncle' and Patricia Grace's 'A Way of Talking'

Frank Sargeson's 'Conversation with My Uncle' (1935) and Patricia Grace's 'A Way of Talking' (1975) represent not only a forty-year determination among New Zealand writers to locate an authentic New Zealand speech but also the persistence in New Zealand literary form of an attempt to use a written mode to document the textures of a fundamentally oral culture. That said, we must acknowledge the differences between the two writers: Sargeson is male and pakeha, Grace female and Maori; Sargeson's story presumes a written culture as an historical notion, against which to assess the variant of the spoken word, and Grace's story re-establishes the force of an oral civilization, against which pakeha attitudes have made historical and judgmental inroads. Yet in both cases the author's attention is less on narrative history than on narrative act: the stories are 'about' communication or the failure thereof, but such a 'subject' is of less consequence than the stories' verbal rhythms themselves, through which actual communications occur even while the words on the surface declare communication's impossibility. Textual arrangement thus inverts textual statement, adding an extra dimension to the surface story. And what appears in each case to be a slight sketch (Sargeson's is scarcely 500 words long, and Grace's about 2,000), thereby acquires an extra resonance, social as well as verbal: social *because* verbal, in a society made clear by its apprehension of speech.

Sargeson's sketch is the monologue of a man whose uncle is in business; the uncle has aspired to politics but settles for position, wears a hat to look good and attract deference, does not read (except for an occasional thriller), cannot imagine the life of the disadvantaged or conceive of the effects of economic disparity, and deflects criticism by the sheer impassiveness of his own self-containment. The nephew despairs of him. And nothing else apparently happens.

Clearly at one level the story is a mid-Depression indictment of an economic system, one that refuses to share wealth and power, perhaps because it lives by absolutes, never questioning the moral rightness of the status quo. Sargeson suggests that such a system is dead without knowing it. In saying this, however, he does not on the surface imply that its official authority is in any immediate danger of waning. Public attitude seems still to give the uncle deference. Hence the author appears to be exposing and perhaps protesting a social irony and nothing more. Yet the story is fundamentally revolutionary – not for its economic position but for its verbal one – because the verbal irony that the story enacts effectively transfers power from the uncle (and the world he represents) elsewhere.

The word on which the story hinges is the title word 'conversation.' It announces the oral nature of the story's activity – the narrator is a 'speaker' not a 'writer' – and it also establishes in verbal terms the process of sharing (conversation requires both a speaker-listener and a listener-responder) which the uncle cannot value. He neither speaks nor listens to effect. But the nephew (the story's speaker) does both. And yet – and this is Sargeson's revolutionary point – he does so most subversively when he appears most to be ordinary and plain.

The illusion of the ordinary man derives both from vocabulary and sentence form. The nephew's sentences are simple or fragmentary (the patterns sometimes linked by co-ordinate conjunctions), conveying the sense that the statements are of uniform importance, and factual as well. There is almost no subordination. The words in the story are predominantly short, idiomatic, vernacular, relying on interjection ('Oh, Lord!'), and reaching towards latinate abstraction only twice: in the words 'monopolise' and 'asceticism,'[1] which stand out from the other words and so focus the story's point. Either as denotative descriptions or as buried metaphors, the two words highlight what happens when conditions are forcedly unequal; they at once give a name to the uncle's implied authoritarian ambition (and also that of his wife, who insists on his hat and his position) and specify the narrowing that such ambition involves him in, a narrowness at once social (pyramidal), physical, and intellectual. These two words, moreover – and the power of judgment they represent – belong in this story to the common man, the man with common sense, the man whose ordinariness does not preclude intelligence.

What seems at first to be a simple sketch in the laconic mode thus turns into a formal exposition of insight into power. What the nephew is talking about is his uncle's one-sidedness, the difficulty he represents to the younger man just because of his failure to comprehend the presence or perspective of others. The nephew casts his reflection as a seemingly random series of comments on his uncle's appearance, work, habits, and reactions to his visits. Separately disconnected, each individual point adds to the portrait of a shallow man.

Sargeson's character's term is 'commonplace.'[2] But it is less the cumulative effect that matters textually than the inferential argument of the rhetoric. The nephew's apparently casual sentences in fact recurrently fasten on stances of speech, which in sequence reveal Sargeson's essential concern for the inherent power of authentic speech and (conversational) exchange.

There is a running argument, that is, lodged in the linguistic stances and linguistic identities of the pronouns, verbs, and prepositions that structure the story's six paragraphs, an argument that can be tabulated as follows:

My uncle wears	(she says its the thing)	(His position is / He is)
He grumbles	(who doesn't?)	
I admit	(people don't look)	(They look)
It's difficult to have a talk with		
If you tell him	(he'll see you)	(it chills you)
He's often told me	(you see)	
It's very difficult to have a talk with		
It doesn't interest him to listen	(to what you've got to say)	(than to look)
He loves the sound of his own voice		
I know	(I hope)	
He never reads		
I've tried talking about		
Once I asked him	(suppose)	
He said	(never)	(He can't suppose)
I said	(say)	
He said	(no)	
I asked him	(he repeated the words)	
He didn't understand	(I had to leave)	(He was)
I've tried talking to		(He is)
He eats	(He is)	(His wife says)
I say		
He says	(He looks)	(we don't want)[3]

Clearly there is a lot of *saying, grumbling, admitting, telling, talking,* and *asking* going on, but little listening and no responding. There is *talking to* and *talking about* but no actual *talking with* — that is, no 'conversation,' no interaction. Indeed, the uncle scarcely acts at all, so fixed is he in stasis: and his identity is equated with his position, given form by what the shadowy background 'she' says for him (the woman, as is typical in Sargeson's work, a curiously oppressive figure) and more accurately evoked by his absolute negatives and his self-absorption. In the midst of it all: *He can't suppose*. He deals in looks and sounds but never in possibilities or meanings. Hence his life is all on the surface, unidimensional, unburdened and unchallenged by imagination, and he is seemingly willing to allow the static surface to define for him the limits of reality.

All of this happens, moreover, *in the nephew's words*. One of the ironies Sargeson thus manages to dramatize is that the plainest of all apparent (ie, surface) realities – the 'inarticulate' common man's common tongue – is capable of a highly charged rhetorical sophistication. That the singular 'I,' repeatedly 'trying' to communicate 'with' authority, should turn by the end into a communal 'we,' opposing it ('we don't want'), gives political militancy to this revelation. It transforms plain speech into covert political power, capable of challenging the status quo because in story form ('suppose') it turns away from its vain attempts to talk with the uncle in order to hold a conversation with the reader instead. Reader becomes Listener; and the active listener, engaged in communication, hears the rhetoric that invites him (or her) into community. Still, that said, Sargeson leaves the narrator inside his text without *realized* power. The power rests *latent* in the common speech, awaiting a hearer as much as a speaker before it can become effective, and Sargeson's story turns into a parable of sorts about the plight of the New Zealand artist as well: a parable of the writer who seeks the plural dimension of speech and society but who runs up against his community's suspicion of imagination, who uses local idiom to effect change but who is then received as a simple reflector of surfaces and surface truths.

In parallel fashion, Patricia Grace's 'A Way of Talking' also makes use of a narrator more sensitive than her status-holding antagonists, and of a story-teller's rhetoric of speech, which connects speech with social power. Grace's overt concern is with conscious and unconscious verbal racism, and with her Maori characters' need to retrieve self-respect, something they do by learning what control they already possess over utterance and by learning also not to apologize for not being other than who they are. As with Sargeson, Grace uses her story to map artistic territory as well. Sargeson concerns himself with the economic stereotypes that dictated class differences; Grace focuses on the racial ones. But their common concern is to claim the force of common speech as a medium of social reform and the need for there to be an active listener to turn such speech into a rhetoric of effective action.

The basic structure of the story is simple. The narrator, a young Maori woman named Hera (Sara) about to be married, tells of her sister Rose's return from the city for her wedding. After an evening of family laughter and gossip, the two sisters together go to a local pakeha dressmaker named Jane Frazer for a fitting. Rose (Rohe), the verbal one, is abrupt when Jane says something condescending about Maori. The sisters return home, to laughter and a family meal, with Hera having acquired greater insight into her sister's life and emotional experience. Yet such a summary sentimentalizes the narrative and does disservice to the artistry with which Grace controls the story's textures. Hera's declared illumination is only the surface sign of there having been an effective 'way of talking'; through the rhetoric of its own progress, the story probes the texture of various kinds of communication, asking the careful listener to hear the covert messages of speech and action as well as the overt ones, and to respond accordingly.

In variant forms, the words 'talk' and 'say' completely permeate the text, so much so that when the word 'silence' appears[4] at the heart of the story it intensifies the reader's sense of the limits of the conventional speech being used. In direct words, communication breaks down — or at least that seems so on the surface, particularly to Hera, who places so much faith in speech. Yet it is Hera who also comes to appreciate that she has understood something from the exchange that has not been spoken aloud — and it is she who tells the story — which leads the reader to seek meaning in the *way* of talking rather than in strict semantic definition.

The story opens with Hera recounting Rose's return home. Hera is pleased that her smart sister at the university is unchanged, that she comes home full of funny stories, mimicry, and family affection. And in this first of four important rhetorical stages in the story, the narrator speaks in simple sentences, fragments, inversions, and vernacular vocabulary, making repeated use of Maori words and Maori verbal structures, conveying an illusion of equipoise — and possibly even inviting the unwary reader to hear the structures as the 'Maori' stereotypes of an earlier New Zealand prose:

She's just the same as ever Rose. Talks all the time flat out and makes us laugh with her way of talking. On the way home we kept saying, 'E Rohe, you're just the same as ever … Rose is the hard-case one in the family, the kamakama one, and the one with the brains.

Last night we stayed up talking … Nanny, Mum, and I had tears running down from laughing; e ta Rose we laughed all night.

At last Nanny … said, 'Time for sleeping. The months steal the time of the eyes.' That's the lovely way she has of talking, Nanny, when she speaks in English.[5]

It is clear that the camaraderie is real, but also that any 'lack of change' is an illusion. Next morning, the text advises us, change and time and movement thrust themselves upon the characters, and change is represented in the local community by the presence of Mrs Frazer, whom Rose does not know. It is clear also that Hera (who 'looked for words' to describe Jane, and chooses neutral ones: '"She's nice".')[6] anticipates tension between her sister and the dressmaker, because of unstated class distinctions based on race and English articulateness. Furthermore, motivated at this point more to perpetuate illusions than to engage with change (the fact that 'alteration' takes place at a dressmaker's is a buried pun that I am not at all sure is unintentional), Hera looks for ways to preserve the status quo. She suppresses criticism; she derives vicarious satisfaction from her sister's articulateness. And she takes pride in the passive fact that her sister *appears to be accepted* by Jane for 'her entertaining and friendly ways.'[7]

The rhetorical situation abruptly changes when Jane, who 'often says the wrong things without knowing,'[8] observes that her husband has 'been down the road getting the *Maoris* for scrub cutting.'[9] There follows the revelatory clipped exchange in which Rose and Jane alternately name names and utter silences, their biases and their hurt pride becoming as articulate as their previous masks of liberal convention:

'Don't they have names?'
'What. Who? ... '
'The *people* from down the road whom your husband is employing to cut scrub.'
Rose was talking all Pakehafied.
'I don't know any of their names ... '
'Do they know yours?'[10]

And so on. The scene culminates when Hera, roused to speech, bursts out 'Rose you're a stink thing' (an epithet powerful only in the fact that it punctures Hera's silence) and Rose replies (in a form that is 'not our way of talking'): 'Don't worry Honey she's got a thick hide.'[11] In that instant Hera begins to appreciate the layers of mask Rose wears, the layers of hurt she has learned in the city, and the degree to which her speech defends the one and deflects the other. In the sudden alienation from her sister, Hera discovers further knowledge of her, and in so doing sheds her ritualized assessments of her sister's abilities, her own, and the connection between them.

The story's third rhetorical stage begins when Rose and Hera start talking to each other again in voices that more approximate their old ones. Hera, unaccustomedly voluble, reflects on the bias with which a Maori can voice the word *pakeha*; Rose counters with a sardonic comment that it's 'fashionable' for a pakeha to have a Maori 'friend,' averring that fashion overrules embarrassment in such a society. The arch exchange breaks into critical mimicry:

Then I heard Jane's voice coming out of that Rohe's mouth and felt a grin of my own coming. 'I have friends who are Maoris. They're lovely people ... They're all so *friendly* and so *natural* and their house is absolutely *spotless*.'[12]

For Hera, the clichés of toleration ('friendly,' 'natural') thus become articulate and lose their intimidating power, and as the two women near home, the story enters its concluding stage and their language breaks into persiflage:

Rose started strutting up the path. I saw Jane's way of walking ... Rose walked up Mum's scrubbed steps, 'Absolutely spotless.' She left her shoes in the porch and bounced into the kitchen. 'What did I tell you? Absolutely spotless. And a friendly natural woman taking new bread from the oven.'[13]

The conscious mimicry defuses the danger inherent in all that was before represented by Hera's silent imitative deference. 'What did I tell you?' Rose asks, in her put-on voice. The answer is: a great deal. But not if it is taken at face value; and the story draws to a close by technically reinforcing this fact. It records the banter that constitutes the family's dinnertable conversation: all ironic, but entirely secure, its real meaning within the family unerringly inferred. Though at the story's end Hera still finds it difficult to use words to convey what she knows, she is also determined to let Rose know – somehow – that she understands not only what she says but also why she says it as she does. In other words, like the ironic verbal exchanges, Rose's confrontative communication also serves as an indirect revelation of experience. Reality is at variance from appearances, whether it lies in the clichés of fashion, the stereotypes of cultural permanence, or the determined independence in Rose that Hera long mistakes for strength. Hence the reality the reader infers from the story redefines strength, removing it from the apparent fluency of pakeha *style* (whether informed or not) and relocating it in the communal understanding of the *family* (whether narrowly or widely defined).

The story itself thus becomes a fifth rhetorical dimension of Grace's record of social discourse. If it is ironic that Hera the story-teller should be declaring her determination still to find a way to tell her understanding, when she already possesses words of reflection and participates in the community that gives her life its most coherent meaning, it is also part of Grace's intent. The story enacts the form of indirect revelation that is its substantive topic. Like Sargeson, Grace is in search of a listener as much as a reader, someone who by hearing can turn an utterance into a shared exchange. One writer writes of a family divided by its speech, the other of a family whose understanding grows from its appreciation of oblique meaning. The families are as emblematic as they are realistic portraits, authorial angles on inertia. For both writers, the chief interest resides in the forms of effective language, and for both, one of the achievements of effective story-telling is to break the language of social structure past its inhibiting love affair with the stasis of convention.

9 **Unsaying Memory:** Maurice Duggan's 'Along Rideout Road that Summer'

In 1984, shortly after she announced her retirement from national politics, the New Zealand feminist Marilyn Waring wrote 'A Letter to My Sisters' for *The New Zealand Listener*; in it she tabulates such changes as had taken place in New Zealand's women's lives over the previous decade – and those that had not – and she quotes at one point from the Indian writer Salman Rushdie, because, she says, he sums up 'this period for our country':

'We live in an age in which the people who control history, who control reality, are increasingly telling lies about it. Politicians have understood it. In order to control the future, it is necessary to control the past. And it is the people who control the memories of nations that control its destiny ... [Hence] an act of memory becomes a political statement ... So we find memory politicised in an age when controls tamper with history. So fiction become[s] truth, while politicians tell us lies.[1]

I preface these reflections to my comments on Maurice Duggan's 1963 story 'Along Rideout Road that Summer' because they seem relevant to both its subject and its method. The narrative concerns a seventeen-year-old boy, Buster O'Leary, who rebels against his puritan and political parents and flees twelve miles away to a Maori rangatira's farm, where he hopes to find food, sex, and happiness. Fanny, Puti Hohepa's fifteen-year-old daughter, is available, languid, and willing, and for a time at least Buster does find work (hence food) and sex. But the third prospect eludes him. Reality – or memory – intervenes, and in a tizzy of prejudice and anger, so do his parents. Duggan casts the narrative, moreover, as memoir, formally underscoring the fact that his authorial concern is as much with the legitimacy of arranging facts (Buster's memory, the politician's myths, the artist's craft) as with the narrative events Buster records. There is some ambivalence about the moment of memory, although certainly Buster as story-teller is years older than Buster as character. The repeated interrupter 'Gentlemen' suggests a beery club anecdote; the deliberate, formal language, frequently punctured, suggests that Buster has acquired a mask of sophistication to separate himself from the realities of the remembered vernacular and to guard himself against its attractions; the tense of one phrase alone – 'To my dying day I have treasured that scene and all its rich implications'[2] – even suggests a deathbed memory, whether uttered aloud or spoken silently in the mind, to the mind. Whatever the case, Buster's story is riddled with self-justifications. His act of memory is political, in other words, arranging events to justify his life, while his very manner of telling (and his continuous need to justify) reveals his continuing limitations and the basic unacceptability of many of his actions even to himself.[3]

The story opens with what appears to be the leisurely stretch of the practiced raconteur, fondly recollecting and jocularly exaggerating his wayward youth:

I'd walked the length of Rideout Road the night before, following the noise of the river in the darkness, tumbling over ruts and stones, my progress, if you'd call it that, challenged by farmer's dogs and observed by the faintly luminescent eyes of wandering stock, steers, cows, stud-bulls or milk-white unicorns or, better, a full quartet of apocalyptic horses browsing the marge. In time and darkness I found Puti Hohepa's farmhouse and lugged my fibre suitcase up to the verandah, after nearly breaking my leg in a cattle-stop. A journey fruitful of one decision – to flog a torch from somewhere. And of course I didn't. And now my feet hurt; but it was daylight and, from memory, I'd say I was almost happy.[4]

The teller allows for his youthful naïveté and indiscretion with the most innocent of missteps – the *fibre* suitcase, the stumble in the cattle guard – and the move from darkness to light appear to corroborate the promise of a tale of a scapegrace pilgrim's progress. But the careful reader sees more, recognizes the guilefulness of the story-teller's practice, and the self-deception and self-revelation that the author builds at once into Buster's words. Buster's ego comes out in his focus on 'I' and 'my,' his eagerness for ratification in 'of course' (the first of many 'of courses,' all of them designed to engage the reader in complicity, and all of them presuming to justify Buster's failure to act and his failure to listen) Buster is concerned to find speech (hence connection) but dubious about its possibility or effectiveness ('followed the *noise*,' '*if* you'd call it that,' 'I'd say *almost*'), and his most fundamental preoccupations, sex and death, are evident in his punning speech, his imagery, and the suspended communication of his fragmentary sentence structures. His language, in other words, is contrived to substantiate the image he has of himself, and it is ironically this same language which reveals the nature and source of his own dis-ease.

The apparent hyperbole of the apocalyptic horses, for example, is thematically functional. Standing '*on the marge*' at the climax of a listed series of sexual animals (the neutral *stock*, the neutered *steer*, the passive *cow*, the potent *stud-bull*, the metaphoric and imaginary and extinct *unicorn*), they offer death and revelation as the twin results of sexual aspiration. For Duggan, such a result is itself a form of sexual metaphor, a declaration of the transitory character of the life of the flesh and the intermittency of the fulfilment it provides; but in the puritan recesses of Buster's memory, death and revelation also promise punishment for the very sexuality that once led to his rebellion and that now perpetuates his exile. Hence instead of ever bringing him fulfilment, his sexuality brings him only to the suppressed snickers of his self-conscious male jocularity – the *tumbling*, the *ruts*, the *conjunctions* (he later specifies, about coupling with Fanny: '*And* in the end, beginning my *sentence* [another pun] with a happy *conjunction*, I held her *indistinct, dark head*').[5] In his words, the reader recognizes what Buster does not: his failure to escape his past and his false reconstruction of it, the reasons for his thinly masked despair.

Buster's rebellion could be attributed to adolescence and nothing more, were it not for the kinds of detail Duggan allows him to remember about his parents and his childhood. It is a middle class family, the father a banker, the mother active in social action groups, both of them keen on discipline and propriety and more sternly attentive (at least in the boy's mind) to their son's sexuality than to their own. Buster exaggerates; so, in his telling of them, do they. For them, sexuality is sin, and for sin the mother champions retributive justice (Buster's words are *flogging, lynching, castration*); perhaps defensively, the father closes others off, and more or less absentmindedly keeps to himself (Buster contemptuously calls him a 'pillar of our decent, law-abiding community, masonic in his methodism, brother, total abstainer, rotarian and non-smoker, addicted to long volleys of handball, I mean pocket billiards cue and all,' a sneer that makes his later discovery that the tractor he himself drives on the Hohepas' farm is 'brand-name Onan out of Edinburgh so help me'[6] more than the simple bar-room jest it initially seems to be). Buster is not unlike his father. What (therefore) dismays him most is the degree to which his parents reverse the conventional gender roles of his society. It is his mother who has the 'masculine hand';[7] his father is passive and ineffectual, in anger turning himself only into a mock-hero. The language tells us so. When he walks in on Buster and Fanny *in flagrante delicto*, his *footballer's* kick is to get a bra strap off his foot; *armies* march through his voice to no conquest of his own; and when he leaves, silent, the light 'lovely and *fannygold* over the pasture,' his *soles* sound like *rim-shots* on the boards:

The mad figure of him went black as bug out over the lawn, out over the loamy furrows where the *tongue* of ploughed field *invaded* the *home* paddock, all *my doing*, spurning in his violence anything less than this direct and abrupt *charge* towards the waiting car.[8]

Buster feels an inexpressible kinship with him at that moment, but hides it in his own determination to be the hero himself and reclaim what he takes to be the natural order of things.

Buster-the-storyteller recognizes some of the cockiness of this attitude; facts (even fictional ones, Buster says) are necessary. As hero, Buster-the-character is just a town boy on a tractor, his knightly armour a Hell's Angel jacket, and his courtly speech nothing more than the contextually comic inarticulacies of the 'crumpy' vernacular. But by this means, Duggan joins his concern for speech with his overt themes of sexuality and race in order to transform a simple story of adolescent rebellion into a complex one of social attitude and psychological constraint. Buster's desire for power is predicated on his hierarchical expectations of human relationships (man over woman, pakeha over Maori). The first of these he asserts as a matter of possessive right; the second he hides in sentimentality (praising the spontaneous naturalness of Maoridom) and in the language of romance, distinguishing conventionally between images of 'light' and 'dark,' identifying himself with 'Kubla Khan,' and equating sexuality ('Fanny') with the 'fannygold' landscape he invades.

In both cases, moreover, it is through the word itself that the biases of expectation become apparent. Putting down his father, Buster attacks his speech, failing to recognize his involvement in the same set of prejudices: 'Maori girls, Maori farms, Maori housing: you'd only to hear my father put tongue to any or all of that to know where he stood, solid for intolerance.'[9] Even Buster's later turn against 'Puti Hohepa and his *brat*'[10] does not awaken him to his racist presumptions – or all his ability to distinguish the clichés of national myth ('this lovely smiling land,' 'a unique social experiment'[11] from the *fact* of the rangatira's dispossession from his inheritance. But the terms he has used when he first leaves home – announcing that he has done so without *consulting* his father or *telling* his mother – reveal the relationships he desires: egalitarian consultation among men, authority towards women. They are precisely what he does not have (his father is asleep with the newspaper smothering him, words lying unfruitfully on his face, and his mother is away somewhere being articulate about revenge); the silence they later offer is as 'stony'[12] as the stones and ruts that trip him up along Rideout Road, and in his desperate search for speech lies his sublimated quest for the power that has eluded him.

Speech becomes a substitute sexuality, in some sense, but it becomes a substitute violence at the same time. The trouble is, the speech Buster acquires – the florid ornament of his later years – serves to reinforce his sexual uncertainty as much as to assert any real power: hence, while his articulateness declares his superficial difference from his father, it more fundamentally just translates his father's self-centredness, his respectable isolation, onto another plane. For Buster to remember his rebellion as a triumph of freedom and even ('almost') happiness is illusory, then; his words unsay this comic memory and tell indirectly a story of barriers and defeat instead.

The form the story takes is thus doubly functional: it is the medium of memoir, by which the old man connects with his youthful self and his quest for connection, and it is also the mode of expression which epitomizes and perpetuates his lingering disenchantment. 'Romantic love,' he sardonically observes at one point, 'was surely the invention of a wedded onanist with seven kids.' He finds words like 'Darling' and 'love' to be mere 'fundamental toffee,' and the phrase 'your-mother's love' an 'obscenity uttered in mixed company.'[13] He speaks of Fanny's 'flank,' turning her metaphorically into a bovine animal, without distinction. But these and the sexual puns express the attitudes of his own 'decent' old age; they are not the vocabulary of the lad of the crumpy 'Yair.' He seems to delight in sexual innuendo – the *ruts*, the *tumbling*, the cigarette *makings*; the summer *thickening and blazing*; Fanny smoking cigarettes, *her brown fingers moving on the white cylinder*; his father *putting tongue to Maori*; *straight mate, pearl diving, spilling darkness and sin* upon the floor; and so on – but this is scarcely erotic. It is as though Buster can live life only indirectly, only in memory and words. Further, while his memories try to celebrate the youth he once was, his words put him down, satirizing his vernacular. Concurrently they reveal a deep-seated misogyny – a distorted puritanism – that puts women down even more, as though by so doing he might yet claim some distantly conceived notion of authority and independence. Hope he has given up, dismissing it bitterly in old wives' language as an adolescent 'habit that does you no good, stunts your growth, sends you insane and makes you, demonstrably, blind.'[14] Condescendingly apologizing for using the word 'thighs' – 'forgive me, madam,'[15] he adds in parentheses (it is the one occasion, amid all the references to 'gentlemen' and 'mates,' when Buster acknowledges the possibility of a female listener, and it reveals his presumption that she, whoever she is, will find risqué even an innocent mention of a body part) – but he never balks at saying 'ballocky,' 'bloody,' or 'dark delta.' He never, that is, refrains from using speech in order to try to draw the ire of women and so make himself (among 'mates') look superior. But in so doing he reiterates his isolation; he turns his speech – his flight away from the real connections of the world – into a kind of verbal ego-stroking, as unproductive and as solitary as the spilled seed of his father's anger.

'... Ah, my country!' he muses, 'I speak of cultural problems, in riddles and literary puddles, perform this act with my own entrails.'[16] Indeed he does. And on other occasions he provides clues to his own performance that are also Duggan's commentary on his own story, a covert 'exegesis' to his own silences and 'cryptic utterances,' of the sort Buster can not get Fanny ever to say about her father's quiet reproof.[17] 'No, the problem, you are to understand, was one of connexion ... of how to cope with the shock of the recognition of a certain discrepancy between the real and the written.'[18] It's one of 'translation' as well, and a 'debate fraught with undertones, an exchange ... [both] fulsome ... and ... reserved ... '[19] But connection and translation and exchange all presume the existence of a second party, an interlocutor, lover, listener, community, friend.

It is precisely on this issue that the story finally fastens. Duggan may query the receptive sensitivities of any audience that continues to be burdened by its national clichés and its ingrained biases, but that does not deprive his art of its speaking power. For Buster such a distinction is less clear. He seems, finally, to withdraw from commitment, and to fasten so closely on himself as to deprive himself of the very power of connection. He turns away from his parents, and cannot have them back; he leaves Fanny and the farm under cover of darkness, unwilling to face Puti Hohepa again; the specks of phosphorus on his watch '*pricked* out the hour: one,'[20] and once again the innuendo emphasizes his solitary preoccupation with himself. 'Buster, is Fanny pregnant?' Puti Hohepa has asked him; 'I don't know,'[21] he answers, showing himself despite his experience to be ignorant of life and its potential. Still just 'almost happy,' he hitches a ride on a hearse, 'through the tail-end of summer,'[22] and the story closes.

But who is it spoken to? The 'gentlemen,' 'mates,' and 'madam' Buster interrupts his narrative to address may indicate the continuing need of an aging man (writer? roué?) to seek connection.[23] But if the story is a deathbed remembrance (a view which the closing mention of the hearse sustains), then they are simply the illusory judges to whom he – vainly – tries to justify his life. It remains himself he is talking to. And it is himself who is still unable to hear. Ah, my country, I speak in puddles, writes Duggan (puzzles, riddles, a portmanteau: ripples). Entering the story through the teller's frame, the reader, however, is asked to be aware both of the story's comedy and of the edges of comedy. Having acquired speech, Buster has learned how to entertain, learned showmanship. But in doing so he has only reinforced his limitations, and Duggan shows him to be both pleased and confounded by what he himself takes to be growth: confounded because, despite his pleasure in words, words alone never absolutely satisfy him. The reader, attentive to the filters of Duggan's text, recognizes the implications: the narrative history is false memory; the social truth rests more securely in the author's fiction. But a further irony then waits to be drawn: the fiction – a fabric of words – cannot ultimately substitute for life. The reader has to translate it into active history, and making the translation is what remains so difficult.

PART FOUR
EPILOGUE

10 In other words, that is to say, so to speak

In some sense the most appropriate conclusion to a book of this kind would be to avoid concluding: that is to say, to avoid imposing a boxed summary on the subject and so giving the illusion of a fixed result. One of my running arguments has been that Canadian and New Zealand writers have, generation by generation, sought ways of structuring stories so that they might break free from received conventions of speech and form, hence break formally free from the shaping social conventions that were lodged in their inherited language. This process is ongoing, and the form of their stories still individually changing. To discern a fixed pattern in what they have done would therefore falsify their accomplishment, and to conclude in any way by suggesting numbered categories of national practice would be an arbitrary critical gesture and an unsatisfactory attempt to make the little anarchies of a fluid art serve the rule of measurement instead.

It is true that in both societies writers have adapted the techniques of report to the art of narrative, extending conventional definitions of short story generic form; it is true also that this process of adaptation has been part of a twinned process of affirming and masking reality, as though in these societies fiction were only palatable as truth and truth as fiction. Repeatedly, Canadian writers have experimented with cumulative fragmentation, as though by adding perspective to perspective they could alter the dimensions of conveyed experience, asserting (through each individual story) the particularity of separateness and (through the artful whole of a broken story sequence) the acquired and perhaps artificial unity of multiple voices. For their part, New Zealand writers have more characteristically operated within verbal frames, breaking through the apparent uniform containment such frames imply by fragmenting the internal structure of their stories into moments of inferential communication, moments of active silence containing halting speech.

In some sense Canadian writers have claimed history by reshaping space, and New Zealand writers named their separateness by reshaping memory. The *inferential* nature of New Zealand narratives is also instructive, relying as it does on the interpreting talents of the *story listener*, the story reader, to hear the real communication taking place. In Canada, the more accustomed pattern is that of *implied* narrative, the onus being on the *story-teller* to indicate where the story lies (in all senses of this word), a task which most tellers accomplish indirectly, suggesting levels of authentic narrative lying below the surface report: lying in the society, so to speak, though just out of reach of a conventional vocabulary. Conveying their perception by form if not openly by speech, such tellers declare the validity of the implied story, whatever appearances might suggest to the contrary.

These are mere tendencies, generalizations based on recurrence, open to each writer's — and each story's — individual refutation. But while extrapolating such observations into national boundaries around the genre would be fallacious, it is nevertheless possible to observe in these case studies of the story in Canada and New Zealand how writers in two former colonies have taken an art *form* and turned it to their own emerging cultural needs. The narrative indirectness is a form of orderly violence against received order (whether imperial, European, Protestant, or male), permitting an alternative history its own voice and, for a duration at least, so long as it stays alive, its own narrative.

Though it does not bind a reader to political exegesis, any narrative, that is, invites a reader into a set of verbal and hence cultural presumptions. A converse is also true: that the political ramifications of any shift in cultural attitude invites a reader into narrative form. Narrative form is a *way of telling*, an active process; hence it offers a means of encapsulating a cultural point without enclosing it, and in this context an indirect means of critical summary.

* *

One of the difficulties of indirect literary form on the page is that it depends for its effectiveness as much on the reader as on the writer. In speech there is often less of a problem. An irony spoken is apparent from an artificial hitch in the voice, from the pause that waits for the listener's response, but an irony written down is apparent only from context, apparent only if the reader listens for cadence and echo, invests the written language with the dynamism of speech sound. Yet it is not sound alone that determines meaning, even in an open form. There is meaning in structure, pattern, continuity, and in disruptions to structure and pattern and continuity. With repetition, moreover — and over time, lodged in place — these disruptions sometimes come to constitute a new pattern, a way of shaping into literature a body of experience that a writer sees and a culture possibly shares.

241 In other words ...

But one of the paradoxes of literary reception is that often it lags behind both cultural fact and authorial insight. What seems a rupture often only is so from the perspective of the reader schooled to expect a different set of cultural presumptions or the formal patterns which express those presumptions. What too often goes unnoticed is the fact that such 'schooled' presumptions and patterns are not – somehow 'consequently,' *because* 'schooled' – universal norms of taste and quality. To combat such inertia is one problem; to differentiate a new form from an old one is another, particularly when the new one looks to the outsider like an odd version of a familiar form rather than a coherent, consistent recombination of elements from a number of sources; and to try to articulate the validity of the 'new' form is a third: the challenge being to make such terms as 'oblique,' 'discontinuous,' or 'indirect' into positive descriptions of a legitimate intellectual and cultural alternative rather than let them rest as indications of an aberrant departure from 'normal' design.

What complicates the matter even further is the implicit moral judgment involved in such a distinction – in the implied equivalence between 'familiar' design and 'art *as it should be*,' as though moral security rested in the literary status quo of another time and even another place. It is, none the less, this hidden connection between language and social morality which gives art its political potential and which makes an author's handling of form a means of confirming a political cause or conversely of challenging sociopolitical conventions which run counter to the author's belief or perception. It is also the reason some authors fail to reach the audience they would most like to. Always their task is twofold: to find a way of lodging matter in their manner of expression, and then to find a reader sensitive to method and hence open to its argumentative implications.

I have been concerned in this book to explore ways in which the art of the short story in two 'new' English-speaking societies, Canada and New Zealand, at once reflects these concerns and communicates some particular efforts to resolve the dichotomy perceived in these societies between language and life. They are not the only two societies in which these efforts have taken place (in some ways they simply epitomize the disruptions of twentieth-century experience); their solutions are not the only ones possible; nor are they fixed; nor is the short story the only genre in which such adaptations of form to culture might be seen. I make no claim for social distinctiveness here, only for the emergence of characteristic but unenclosed patterns of expression, through which a reader might be able to perceive some of the priorities and values and deep concerns of each separate and still changing culture. Still changing: *changing still*. Paradox, pun, irony, and oxymoron recur as features of the emerging style in this context: they are techniques which ask for double-hearing. Changing 'still.' They use the inherited forms of an inherited language in ways that invite the reader to break past a static structure: not only to listen to an apparently direct version of reality but also to hear a version that simultaneously or cumulatively runs counter to it – an 'unofficial' one in some sense, which is more 'authentic' (dishonest narrators are common) – *and to deduce the nature of the connection that links the surface mask with the character it covers.*

In some cases characters find themselves burdened by the structures of class, in others the assumptions of gender, in others the bias of region: recurrently they seek the power that is denied them for lack of a language of their own. It is not just a question of confrontation between formal standards and the vernacular. These characters speak, write, appear to communicate, yet we come to understand that their 'official' words are paste. When the only language they possess appears to deny them self-possession, they adopt masks, become mimics, sometimes surrender to the authority of Elsewhere; but the most innovative authors do battle, animating the silences and laconic idioms that punctuate and disrupt formal speech, until the unheard phrases themselves are heard, invested with meaning. That is to say, they use language, in *other words*: so to speak. Characters and authors alike live with the past, as does Laurence's Vanessa MacLeod, but with something of their own to say, seeking a way of their own to shape their saying. Hence literary form becomes an *other*-dimension of vocabulary, through which understood experience becomes articulate and present experience acquires a voice.

In New Zealand and Canada, history has variously been seen as a frame within which to delineate in miniature the cultural character, or as a linked set of present moments, distributed across space and (therefore) across time. To the degree that it reflects and records history, the art of short fiction in these two societies devises forms of linguistic structure to accord with these separate national images. There were, and continue to be, writers in both places whose commitment to civilization is inseparable from their commitment to tradition in literary form as well as in social attitude and mythology. For them, life lies in romance. For others art and culture are acts of process and observation rather than of pattern and reception. For them, art lies in life; and their literary forms, the sketch and the *Rahmenerzählung*, turned by the end of the nineteenth century into an art of fragmentary documentary. The earliest of these writers, shaping their prose so that it could convey 'reality,' contrived an appearance of order – or, at greater remove, an illusion of continuity with the past – but they sought at the same time a way to acknowledge the singularity of the present. The history of the art form in the two societies thus becomes in part a history of verbal responses to – and ultimately correlatives for – the fragmentary character of culture and time, the momentary security of systems of governance and value.

Though they both inherited attitudes to race, language, politics, religion, and law from Protestant Imperial Britain, the two societies had, by the time of Mansfield in New Zealand and D.C. Scott in Canada, embarked on separate courses – courses which World War I intensified, directing one into its outlined (hence stratified) egalitarianism (hence its coded battle between men and women) and the other into its dalliance with Catholic Quebec and its love affair with the language of American continentalism. Yet both social structures, so established, involved illusions of continuing order even in the face of change, cloaking disparities of selected kinds but nevertheless pretending to realism, engaging citizens (some of them writers) in self-satisfaction and cliché; both consequently provoked their more analytic writers to challenge the conventional view of what was portrayed as life and the legitimacy of the language that so distorted what they perceived as truth. Concerned to sound alternative perspectives – those marked by region, gender, economics, religion, ethnicity: political all – such writers rebelled verbally, not simply against inherited tradition or inherited images of civilization but against what they saw as restrictive pattern, pattern which falsely perpetuated itself (and was falsely extended) beyond its legitimate moment. The formal art of the short story thus became a means of recording at once an evolving culture and a fragmenting culture, as though growth and division were inseparable, as though speech were impossible without violence, at least to the presumptions of conventional form. But the *illusion* of order: that, too, was part of the cultural reality under observation, and the language of conventional narrative, invoking a secure response, was an inherent part of the illusion – employed as technique and at the same time undermined.

* * *

In comments he delivered to a late 1970s Christchurch conference of writers and critics – called 'Pearl Button's Boxes and the Way to Baton Rouge' – Vincent O'Sullivan called attention to this link between speech and fracture. He talked, like Robert Chapman and W.H. Pearson before him, of the strong Protestant ethos in New Zealand that cut writers off from their society, of an upbringing that gives them a society in which they never feel at home – and he might have been talking of Canada as well. He talked of New Zealand as a collective culture in which individual men are isolated from each other, struggling towards private and solitary reconciliation with their society. He talked of their fascination, both literary and social, with the 1951 wharf strike and the two world wars. Further: when the official version of society is of an egalitarian peacetime in which as individuals they cannot find community, they locate their real community (still a community *of men*) in times of upheaval.

Whatever else violence carries with it, O'Sullivan noted (with measured, deceptive nonchalance), it represents at least the possibility of something new. Not necessarily of something better. Not of something more civilized, more humane, nor even, perhaps, more accurate as a social paradigm (women are still left out of the picture, and women writers have repeatedly both in New Zealand and in Canada shaped language to counter the way women have been politically defined): but at least a crazing of the official mask. When life enacts lies, fictions, fiction comes to embody truths. Language, O'Sullivan added (moving on to talk of Janet Frame), then becomes a kind of revenge on life, the writer's equivalent to war. With authorial finesse, language shapes the truths of peoples's experience in a world that speaks their own but 'foreign' tongue, and so invites readers' recognition of themselves in the fracturing of received speech and official form.

* * * *

Yet there remains that uncertainty – the authorial uncertainty – about being heard, which becomes the very subject of literature as well as its frequent motivation. The isolation of artists from the society they so clearly see – the (often merely passive) discrimination against the discriminating – this is a recurrent theme as well as a fact of life. And the unreceptiveness of the very audience the artist seeks is one of the reasons that artists so repeatedly try to ratify the self through speech. It's a way of ratifying the artist's position and the reconstitutive power of artistic purpose. This response is only partly attributable to the remnant ethos of Calvinist mores in Canada and New Zealand – only partly the effect of occupying a role that society once rejected: that of the fiction-purveyor, the 'liar,' in a milieu preoccupied with the truth (equated with the 'documentary' reality) of empirical appearances. It also derives from the particular individuality of each good writer's imagination and turn of phrase, and is compounded by the willingness of their respective societies to accept absolute determinations of experience, even when these definitions, or limitations, come in and through a language not their own.

What results is a kind of literary fault-line between writer and reader, between writer's craft and reader's expectation – the reader seeking a confirmation of order which ends with the author's narrative closure, and the writer its reconstruction, which will end with the audience still seeking. Subverting both the factual character of report and the fictional character of story, such writers seek to retrieve truth from convention, and retrieve documentary from empirical control. By indirect means, by inference and implication (relying on the reader's oblique understanding or the teller's oblique narrative), they disrupt form as a means to remeasure reality. In the possibility of alternative narrative options lies for them the promise of alternative social choices. But for readers to follow them into such choices depends on their willingness to refuse 'foreign' norms as universally applicable; that in turn requires each reader to embrace uncertainty awhile, to listen for the stories that indirection and interruption tell, and to accept the broken, open – and to that degree 'violent' – forms of narrative as legitimate processes of reclaiming a valid history and constructing a valid speech.

APPENDIX

Short Story Terminology

Allegory an extended metaphoric structure used in prose, poetry, and drama, whereby the characters and events within the narrative equate on a one-to-one basis with specific referential meanings outside the text, as in Bunyan's *Pilgrim's Progress*.

Anatomy a term used to refer to (1) a dissection of society, or of some intellectual notion (eg, melancholy); and (2) an elaborate, often comic, narrative form that derives from Menippean satire, organizing catalogues, diagrams, and the free association of themes into an encyclopedic rendering but coherent vision of the world.

Anecdote a short, simple, plotless narrative emphasizing a single episode; it is often humorous, sometimes scurrilous, and frequently claims to be the truth about a famous person.

Animal tale a term referring at one level to any story about animals or using animals as characters; conventional usage usually retains it for the (often anthropomorphic) stories of real-life animal behaviour (eg, those of Roberts and Seton) which developed in the late nineteenth century, thus distinguishing the term from *beast fable* and *bestiary*.

Apologue a *fable* generally of the *beast fable* sort; the term has lately expanded to refer also to contemporary works of fiction (eg, the novels of Solzhenitsyn) which emphasize a main thesis or communicate a direct statement about a way of life.

Autobiography a written version of the writer's own life; open to subjective bias, it is often referred to in contemporary criticism as a form of *fiction*.

Beast fable a *fable* in which the main characters are animals.

Bestiary a literary form of the Middle Ages in which the behaviour of real or imagined animals (such as the phoenix and unicorn), was the basis for an *allegory* of Christian doctrine.

Biography a written version of a person's life, sometimes recounting simple chronological facts, sometimes seeking to reveal private ambitions and motivations.

Character a term that refers to (1) a person depicted in a poem, play, or prose work; (2) the personality of such a person; and (3) a seventeenth-century prose form that presents not a portrait of an individual but an arrangement of qualities that typify a kind of personality.

Conte a French term with no exact English equivalent; roughly comparable to *tale*, it frequently uses *parable* or *fable* form, or tells of fantastic happenings.
Conte fantastique a deliberately constructed conte which combines elements of *folk-tale* form with a deliberately morbid portrayal of everyday life.
Conte populaire the French equivalent of the German *Märchen*.
Cuento the Spanish equivalent to *tale*.
Cycle a group of poems or stories or tales, not necessarily circular in structure or implying any circular view of theme (eg, of history), which are related by their common concern with a central event or person; cycles were frequently developed, or added to, by successions of writers, though in modern practice individual writers have emulated the form by deliberately writing a related succession of novels, stories, poems, or plays.
Detective story a form of *mystery story* which emphasizes the reasoning skills by which a character solves a crime, frequently murder; the manner of storytelling ranges from urbane comedy to graphic representations of brutal violence.
Dime-store novel or **dime-store paperback** any mass circulation work of fiction, sometimes now referred to as 'drugstore novel.'
Discourse a term that refers to: (1) talk; (2) the text of a narrative.
Documentary (1) a form of writing or film-making which depends on the amassing of factual data (such as newspaper reports, transcripts, statistics, interviews) and arranges such material so as to instruct the reader / viewer or to produce a deliberate emotional effect; (2) a work of fiction which contrives to appear as a factual account, or to achieve the effect of a controlled factual record.
Dystopian fiction a story (often satiric, but sometimes simply dour or even pessimistic) that portrays life in an imaginary world in which the evil or unpleasant tendencies of the present are brought to fulfilment.
Ehrzählung the German equivalent to *tale*.
Essay a brief nonfictional prose discussion, explanation, description, or argument, focusing on a restricted topic; it may be formal or informal, witty or solemn, personal or rigorously objective, and it may include *narrative* elements, particularly as a process of illustration.
Eventyr a Norse *folk-tale*.
Exemplum a concrete narrative 'example' that medieval preachers used in the context of a sermon to illustrate a moral principle; it could be as short as an *anecdote* or long enough to be considered a *tale*.
Explanatory tale a form of *myth* or *folk-tale* which explains the origin of some natural phenomenon, or the reason for some existing pattern of behaviour.
Fable a brief story, in verse or prose, that is told to illustrate a serious moral; the moral is frequently attached to the end of the narrative, as in Aesop's *Fables*.
Fabliau a realistic, humorous, often bawdy story, popular in France and England in the Middle Ages, told to satirize human behaviour; often with a moral point, the fabliau was less serious in purpose than the *fable*.
Fabula the Russian formalist term for the basic logical pattern of any story told; cf. *sjuzet*.
Fairy-tale a story concerning the adventures of small spirits whose world sometimes

impinges on that of human beings, and who then take on diminutive human form; the term has since expanded to refer to almost any tale of magic and childlike imagination, which need not specifically mention sylphs, fairies, elves, gnomes, or similar creatures.

Fantasy a work which explores some realm of the imagination as in *science fiction, utopian fiction, fairy-tale,* or *horror story.*

Feuilleton a light work of fiction (often in serial form) which appeared as a newspaper filler.

Fiction a general term that applies to any imaginative *narrative*, though in practice it usually applies only to prose; it can be, but need not necessarily be, based on truth.

Folk-tale a short (perhaps originally rural) *narrative* handed down orally from one generation to another, embroidered by each, so that it spreads to various places, alters slightly over place and through time, and comes to have cumulative authorship; familiar (and therefore predictable) to members of a common culture, it includes stories of magic as well as stories of romantic imagination, and it can range in form and subject from *myth* and *legend*, to *fable, tall tale,* and *fairy-tale.*

Formula tale a story which is (1) a cumulative memory game (eg, of the sort: 'My aunt went to market, and took with her a [series follows, to be incrementally repeated by successive speakers]'), or (2) a suspenseful story of the campfire sort, that ends in a shout ('Boo!') rather than with a plotline resolution. These uses of the word 'formula' should be distinguished from the pejorative use, which implies a hackneyed plot or a lack of artistry on the part of the author.

Framed miscellany a collection of various literary forms (usually in prose or verse, or both) contained by an enclosing narrative; roughly equivalent to *Rahmenerzählung.*

Frame-story a story within a story, a *narrative* told within the context of an enclosing narrative; the two consequent lines of plot may or may not be directly interrelated.

Framework-story a *frame-story.*

Geschichte the German equivalent to *history.*

Gest a medieval tale of war or adventure, encountered more often in German than in English critical usage.

Geste the French equivalent to *gest.*

Ghost story a *mystery story* in which much of the suspense derives from the presence of supernatural spirits.

Histoire the French equivalent to *history.*

Historia the Spanish equivalent to *history.*

History loosely, any chronologically arranged story; more specifically, a factual record or account of people or events of the past.

Horror story a *tale* which introduces episodes designed to excite the reader's sense of fear and repugnance.

Initiation story a story in which the central character loses some aspect of innocence or naivete, but in the process acquires knowledge, wisdom, insight, experience, or an adult role in his or her culture; the focus is usually on the process of change or the moment of realization rather than on the events that lead to the change or the consequences that follow it.

Istoriya the Russian equivalent to *history*.

Jest loosely, a *joke*; more specifically, a form of *anecdote* popular in the sixteenth century; witty, generally bawdy, sometimes satiric, often ending with a moral, it thus relates both to the *exemplum* and to the *fabliau*.

Joke a brief funny story, often anecdotal, the point of which is its ability to amuse, not its narrative sophistication.

Kindermärchen that form of *Märchen* which is told to children ('Hansel and Gretel,' for example) and which derives from folk sources.

Kunstmärchen that form of *Märchen* which an artist has deliberately composed, emulating the form that derives from folk sources.

Kurzgeschicte the German equivalent to *short story*.

Landscape-essay a form of descriptive *sketch* which tries to evoke the character or quality of a particular scene.

Legend a term which refers to (1) a narrative and eulogistic life of a Christian saint; and (2) a story handed down from generation to generation, deriving usually from history and from the life of a heroic figure, and thus serving to record some feature of national character or to epitomize some feature of cultural value.

Local colour story a story designed to portray the character of life in a particular topographic or cultural region, accurate in surface detail, and often written in dialect, but generally more concerned to portray the ambience of a place than to use place as a basis for exploring some more general aspect of human behaviour.

Love story a story about affection or passion; the term is frequently restricted to mass circulation stories of this type, hackneyed in execution.

Magazine story a term used pejoratively to refer to a mechanically written, clichéd, or stereotypical story aimed at a popular market and published in a mass circulation magazine.

Märchen a German term for which there is no exact English equivalent: generally translated as *fairy-tale* or 'household tale' or 'wonder tale,' it is an episodic *narrative* that takes place in some imaginary world of marvels.

Metafiction a work of fiction which takes itself in particular, or more generally the process of fictional communication, as its main subject.

Mystery story a story (variously of thrills, adventure, crime, and espionage) in which the plot encourages suspense by withholding explanations until the end, but provides clues to suggest the possibility of logical resolution; more generally, a story within which there is no rational explanation for the events that take place. The term *mystery play* must be kept distinct; while a *mystery story* can be dramatized as a play, the term *mystery play* (from the French *mystère*,) refers to a form of medieval scriptural drama which is based upon a biblical story.

Myth loosely, an untruth; more specifically, a term which refers to: (1) a story or group of stories, anonymous in origin and religious in function, which accounts for the beliefs of a particular culture by referring to the actions of supernatural figures (gods, heroes, muses, nymphs, and the like); (2) by extension, any commonly held cultural belief which encodes (not necessarily accurately) the culture's self-image; and (3) the recurrent pattern of such myths, as employed by a writer (often deliberately) to structure a psychological analysis of human behaviour.

Narrative loosely, plot; more generally, a term which applies to (1) any sequence of events that takes place within a story or is implied by a story; and (2) the telling of a story, ie, the act of narration.

Narrative poem a poem that tells a story, the two basic forms being the 'ballad' and the 'epic' (the 'metrical romance' is sometimes considered a third form, and sometimes treated as a variety of epic); specific formal practice varies with time and place, leading to such categories as the Scandinavian *saga*, the Old French 'chanson de geste,' the dactyllic Greek 'epyllion,' the oral blank verse Russian 'bylina' or 'starina,' and the 'mock epic.' In practice, the form has been able to absorb characteristics of didactic, pastoral, and meditative verse as well.

Natursage the German equivalent to *explanatory tale*.

Nouvelle a French term with no exact English equivalent; a longer *short story*, generally highly structured, with an emphasis on the complexity of character.

Novel an extended fictional *narrative*, in prose, which in English developed in the eighteenth century and has subsequently altered extensively in subject and nature; often thought to focus on plot, character, action, or society, or to have emerged as a generic form when there was a need to use fiction to represent reality, there appear in practice to be no effective constraints of such kinds on what the form can do.

Novela the Spanish equivalent to both (1) *novel* and (2) an inserted *tale* within a novel (the latter is an archaic use).

Novelette (1) a term sometimes used to describe a long *short story* or a short *novel*, like Conrad's 'Heart of Darkness'; (2) more generally it is used pejoratively, to describe a medium-length work of pulp fiction (ie, a melodramatic romantic fiction, conventional in structure and stereotypical in characterization and subject.)

Novella (1) a term used in English to refer to a medium-length (c.15,000 – 50,000 word) prose fiction, which usually has attributes both of the longer form of the *novel* and the shorter form of the *short story*; originating as a *tale* told within the context of a longer work, or as one of a series of tales assembled into a longer work, the term has subsequently been claimed both as an equivalent to the French *nouvelle* and as a substitute term to embrace both medium-length fictions and short stories; (2) the Italian equivalent to the French *nouvelle*.

Novelle the German equivalent to the French *nouvelle*.

Nurse novel any hackneyed romantic *novel*, the term based on those with a cast of medical characters.

O. Henry story a brief, highly plotted *short story* with a surprise ending.

Oral tale (1) a tale communicated by word of mouth; primarily a myth, *legend*, or *folk-tale* in currency before it was recorded on the page, or told within an oral culture (eg, West Africa); loosely, any spoken story, including *jokes* and *yarns*.

Parable a story, usually *allegorical*, which teaches a moral lesson or illustrates a principle about moral behaviour.

Pen portrait a *sketch*, usually in the briefest outline form that will still convey some sense of the personality or the characterizing attributes of its subject.

P'ing hua a seventeenth-century Chinese popular tale, often fantastic in subject but always realistic in tone, marked by the narrator's colloquial presence.

Pourquoi story an *explanatory tale*.

Povest' the Russian equivalent to the French *nouvelle*.

Prose poem a rather vague term used to describe: (1) a prose work that makes marked use of figurative language and regular rhythm (sometimes called 'polyphonic prose'); and (2) a poem which uses a prose format and makes marked use of prose rhythms or speech cadence.

Racconto the Italian equivalent to *tale*.

Rahmenerzählung a linked collection of a variety of fictional forms (eg, *tale*, *sketch*, *fable*, *anecdote*, *yarn*, *sentimental tale*); the 'link' is usually in the form of a framing narrative.

Rasskaz the Russian equivalent to *tale*.

Récit a French term with no exact English equivalent; a very short story, usually presenting a glimpse of one moment in a life, often historical or autobiographical in mode.

Roman the French, Russian, and German equivalent to *novel*.

Romance a term used to describe: (1) a chivalric story; (2) a poetic narrative epic; (3) a mass circulation *love story*; (4) a long work of fiction, which focuses on exotic or distant settings, traces the thrilling or mysterious exploits of larger-than-life characters, uses lofty language, invokes supernatural events (making no sustained claims on credibility), and seeks by such means to express some transcendent philosophic truth; in a shorter compass, some of these same attributes appear in the *tale*.

Romanzo the Italian equivalent to *novel*.

Saga (1) a term that originally referred to a Swedish heroic *tale*, derived from *legend* or *history*, but in English generally refers to any narrative of heroic exploits or marvellous and perilous undertaking; (2) in an extended meaning (as in Galsworthy's *Forsyte Saga*) it applies to any work of family history conceived on a grand scale.

Sage a German term for a *narrative legend* that derives from local *history*, as in the stories about Ichabod Crane, Robin Hood, or the Pied Piper of Hamelin.

Schwank the German equivalent to *jest*.

Science fiction a general term that describes fiction which explores imaginative realms of space-fantasy and scientific or technological possibility, in practice referred to as *sci-fi* and *sf* respectively.

Sci-fi story a *science fiction* story which emphasizes fantasy creatures of outer space, extraterrestrial invasions, etc.; used by *sf* devotees as a term of contempt.

Seansgal a Gaelic traditional story of the *Märchen* kind, oral in character.

Sentimental tale a form of *tale* that stresses emotional intensity, written in broad gestures, now considered hackneyed.

Serial (1) a *narrative*, most commonly a *novel*, published in parts in successive issues of a journal, or broadcast in successive radio or television performances, or shown as regular instalments of a film; in practice serialization affects plot structure, for each section ends both suspensefully and climactically. (2) In more general use, serial simply means 'in a series,' implying some connection among the items in the series but not necessitating any recurrence of characters or any link of plot.

SF story a *science fiction* story whch emphasizes scientific possibility or the implications of some scientific principle, exploring it through *fantasy*.

Shaggy dog story a form of anecdotal joke, which extends the story through a series of repetitious episodes, only to come to an anticlimactic, frequently punning, punchline.

Short-short story a very brief *short story* (c.250–1000 words).

Short story a sort form of prose *fiction* (usually 500–15,000 words long) which in English developed during the nineteenth century; generally it creates a unity of effect through one or more elements of plot, character, tone, theme, or style, but no restrictive rules govern its protean nature.

Short-story Brander Matthews' term for the *short story*, developed at the end of the nineteenth century and followed by a number of subsequent critics, but now generally fallen from use; Matthews used the hyphen to distinguish those prose works which fit his definition of the short story genre (ie, those which were short, ingeniously original, unified, compressed, full of action, logically structured, and if possible touched with an element of fantasy) from stories which were merely short.

Sjuzet the plot of a story as it is told; cf. *fabula*.

Skaz A Russian *sketch*, marked by the effect of the narrator's idiomatic habits of speech.

Sketch a brief prose work that usually describes a single scene or person, thus minimizing plot and emphasizing the *documentary* (hence ostensibly objective and verifiable) character of the rendering. Its restricted proportions have meant for some writers that it must rely on representative detail, for others that it can be a finished product that (although it cannot encompass the broad strokes of tragedy or comedy) will be suitable for gentle description, wry satire, or whimsy.

Storia the Italian equivalent to *history*.

Story broadly, any *narrative* sequence, which makes it a basic element in any genre (*novel, short story, narrative poem, parable*, etc.) which makes use of narrative sequence. The word is derived from the same root as the word *history*, and commonly carries the simultaneous but contrary meanings of 'truth-telling' (ie, based on the facts of history) and 'lying' (ie, fictional, and therefore deriving from the imagination).

Storybook a book of children's stories, implying happy endings.

Tale a term that refers to: (1) any told story; (2) any simple *narrative*; (3) a form of romantic *narrative* which depends on a heightened sense of emotion, broadly depicted characters, a plot line which emphasizes action or adventure, and a setting which is often exotic and unrealistic, sometimes with a view simply to be entertaining, sometimes trying more subtly to explore the psychology of motivation or behaviour.

Tall tale a *tale* in which a simple, straightforward, and direct speaker completely exaggerates facts, for comic effect, telling or the impossible accomplishments and larger-than-life features of a character (eg, Paul Bunyan, Baron Münchhausen).

Tatsuniya a traditional, didactic Hausa oral *folk-tale*.

Thriller a *mystery, detective story, horror story*, or story of dangerous adventure.

Transformation tale a *tale* (as in Ovid's *Metamorphoses* or Kafka's 'The Metamorphosis') in which a human being is turned into an object or another creature, generally to illustrate some moral principle – though not always, as in some *horror stories*.

Utopian fiction a prose portrait of a utopia (literally, 'no place'), ie, of an imagined perfect world, generally cast in the future or in a distant place.

Vignette a brief *essay, sketch*, or *story*, characterized by the delicacy and subtlety with which it depicts its subject.

Western a story, usually some form of a popular adventure, about some aspect of the life of the western U.S. cowboy, farmer, rancher, Indian, sheriff, or townspeople.

Yarn an extravagant adventure *story*, usually long, spoken, captivating to the listener, and of doubtful accuracy, but told in a matter-of-fact way.

Notes

CHAPTER ONE: CANADA, NEW ZEALAND, AND THE SHORT STORY

1 'Review of *Twice-Told Tales*,' *Graham's Magazine* (May 1842); rpt. in Charles E. May ed., *Short Story Theories* ([Athens]; Ohio Univ. Press 1978) 45–51
2 'The Short Story: The Long and Short of It,' *Poetics* 10, no. 2–3 (June 1981) 175–94
3 *The Philosophy of the Short-Story* (New York, Longman's, Green 1901)
4 For example, Blanche Colton Williams, *A Handbook on Story Writing* (New York: Dodd, Mead 1924); Douglas Bement, *Weaving the Short Story* (New York: Richard R. Smith 1931); Walter B. Pitkin, *The Art and the Business of Story-Writing* (New York: Macmillan 1923); Kenneth Payson Kempton, *The Short Story* (Cambridge, MA: Harvard Univ. Press 1954); J. Berg Esenwein, *Writing the Short-Story* (1908; rpt New York: Noble and Noble 1928); Sylvia Kamerman, *Writing the Short Story* (Boston: The Writer 1942; rev. 1946); Cecil Hunt, *Short Stories and How to Write Them* (London: Harrap 1934); Hallie Burnett, *On Writing the Short Story* (New York: Harper & Row 1983). See E.J. O'Brien, *The Dance of The Machines* (New York: Macaulay 1929), for a curious attack on the short story (characterizing it as a mechanical, instant, standardized, and therefore 'typically' American form) as part of an attack on the mechanization of America.
5 F.L. Pattee, *The Development of the American Short Story* (New York and London: Harper and Brothers 1923); H.E. Bates, *The Modern Short Story* (1941; rpt. Boston: The Writer 1956); William Peden, *The American Short Story: Continuity and Change 1940-1975* (Boston: Houghton Mifflin, 2nd rev. ed. 1975); Walter Allen, *The Short Story in English* (Oxford: Clarendon and New York: Oxford Univ. Press 1981); T.O. Beachcroft, *The Modest Art* (London: Oxford Univ. Press 1968). In 1984 and 1985, Twayne (Boston) released a multi-volume critical survey of American, English, and Irish short fiction, edited by Philip Stevick and others.
6 (Cleveland and New York: World 1963)
7 Eikenbaum's 1925 essay, translated by I.R. Titunik, appeared in *Michigan Slavic Contributions*, ed. L. Matejka (Ann Arbor: Univ. of Michigan 1968)

1–27; Pratt's essay in *Poetics* (1981); Ferguson's 'Defining the Short Story: Impressionism and Form' in *Modern Fiction Studies* 28, no. 1 (Spring 1982) 13–24. Ingram's book was published (The Hague: Mouton 1971), Reid's (London: Methuen, and New York: Barnes & Noble 1977), Bonheim's (Cambridge, Eng.: D.S. Brewer 1982), Lohafer's (Baton Rouge: Louisiana State Univ. Press 1983), and Hanson's (London: Macmillan 1985). See also Tzvetan Todorov, *Les Genres du discours* (Paris: Du Seuil 1978) esp. 44–60; and Valerie Shaw, *The Short Story* (London and New York: Longman 1983).
8 See Reid *The Short Story* 9.
9 *Ibid*. 5
10 See Chinua Achebe, 'The Novelist as Teacher' (1965); rpt. in *Morning Yet on Creation Day* (London: Heinemann 1975) 43. See also Kirsten Holst Petersen and Anna Rutherford, eds *Cowries and Kobos: The West African Oral Tale and Short Story* (Mundelstrup, Denmark: Dangaroo 1981); and Jean de Grandsaigne and Gary Spackey, 'The African Short Story Written in English: A Survey,' *Ariel* 15 (April 1984) 73–85.
11 (Boston: Houghton Mifflin 1977)
12 'The Reading and Writing of Short Stories,' *Atlantic Monthly (1949)* rpt. in May, *Short Story Theories* 156
13 'The Faber Book of Modern Short Stories' (1936), rpt in May, *Short Story Theories* 156
14 *A Beginning on the Short Story* (Yonkers: Alicat Bookshop 1950) 8
15 Foreword to *The Short Story* (New York: Devin-Adair 1941) x
16 Gillespie, 'Novella, Novelle, Novella, Short Novel?: A Review of Terms,' *Neophilologus* 51 (1967) 117–27, 225–30; Good, 'Notes on the Novella,' *Novel* 10, no. 3 (Spring 1977) 197–211. The brief notes on the terms listed derive in part from Good, Reid, and Gillespie. On the subject of the *feuilleton*, see Mukhtar Ali Isani, 'The "Fragment" as Genre in Early American Literature,' *Studies in Short Fiction* 18 (Winter 1981) 17–27. Joseph Pivato's 'The Novella and the Short Story as Canadian Genres,' *Comparative Literature in Canada* 9, no. 1–2 (1977) 5–7, calls attention to the need to distinguish the short story from the novella in Canada, using European structuralist models. Sherrill Grace, in 'Duality and Series: Forms of the Canadian Imagination.' *Canadian Review of Comparative Literature* 7 (Fall 1980) 438–51, offers a preliminary description of the formal patterns of 'duality' and 'series' that recurrently structure Canadian prose in both English and French. On the use of fragment and fracture as modes of formal 'sub-version' in women's short fiction, see Gail Scott, 'Shaping a Vehicle for Her Use: Woman and the Short Story,' in Ann Dybikowski et al., eds., *In the Feminine* (Edmonton: Longspoon 1985) 184–91
17 *The Folktale* (1946: rpt Berkeley: Univ. of California Press 1977). For an analysis of the limitations of Thompson's motif classification, see Claude Brémond, 'A Critique of the Motif,' in Tzvetan Todorov, ed., *French Literary Theory Today* (Cambridge, Eng.: Cambridge Univ. Press 1982) 125–46.
18 See Edith Fowke, *Folktales of French Canada* (Toronto: NC Press 1981), for an anthology with commentary based on the Thompson types.

19 *Structuralism in Literature* (New Haven and London: Yale Univ. Press 1974) 3
20 Bret Harte's 'The Rise of the Short Story,' *Cornhill Magazine* 7 (July 1899) 1–8, contains assertions like these: 'The short story was familiar enough in form in America during the early half of the [19th] century; perhaps the proverbial haste of American life was some inducement to its brevity ... But it was not the American short story of today. It was not characteristic of American life, American habits ... American thought ... and ... it made no attempt ... to understand [American forms] of expression ... Of all that was distinctly American it was evasive – when it was not apologetic ...

It would be easy to trace the causes ... What was called American literature was still limited to English methods and ... models ... there were American Addisons, Steeles, and Lambs ...

It was *Humour* – of a quality as distinct and original as the country ... first noticeable in the anecdote or "story" [which diminished the power of English tradition] ...

[T]he secret of the American short story [that subsequently emerged from this comic anecdotal tradition] was the treatment of characteristic American life, with absolute knowledge of its peculiarities and sympathies with its methods; with no fastidious ignoring of its habitual expression, or the inchoate poetry that may be found even hidden in its slang ... '
21 Suzanne Henning Uphaus, for example, in 'Twain and Leacock: A Cross-Cultural View,' *Centennial Review* 26, no. 2 (Spring 1982), claims that the two writers differ because of the cultural environment in which they grew up; but then overspecifies, transforming an acceptable generalization into a rigid limitation: Leacock's world is without criminals and sexuality, we are told, because of his mother's protectiveness, the British classics, the cold Canadian winter, and the 'passivity which stems from the absence of individualism and independence which suffused the American frontier' (p 137). Multiple cultural presumptions underlie these comments.
22 *Democracy in New Zealand*, trans. E.V. Burns (London: G. Bell and Sons 1914) 254
23 Bonheim, *Narrative Modes* ix
24 Poe, in May, *Short Story Theories* 49; Kostelanetz, 'Notes on the American Short Story Today' (1966), rpt. in May, *Short Story Theories* 214; McClave, introduction to her ed., *Women Writers of the Short Story* (Englewood Cliffs, NJ: Prentice-Hall 1980) 1; Rohrberger, 'The Short Story: A Proposed Definition' (1960), rpt. in May, *Short Story Theories* 81
25 'From Tale to Short Story: The Emergence of a New Genre in the 1850's,' *American Literature* 46 (May 1974) 153–69
26 Pattee, *Development of the American Short Story* 297
27 The remark has repeatedly been attributed to Artemus Ward, though V.L.O. Chittick disputes the evidence for it; see *Thomas Chandler Haliburton* (New York: Columbia Univ. Press 1924) 358–84. See, however, Ray B. West jr: 'the early hero of our folk literature was the rootless but shrewd Yankee pedlar who travelled the trails and highways of the seaboard colonies, living by his

wits and outwitting the more pretentious and settled of his countrymen ... This is the mask – the voice – through which the American has come to speak, his characteristic tone.' 'The American Short Story at Mid-Century' (1942); rpt. in Hollis Summers, *Discussions of the Short Story* (Boston: D.C. Heath 1963) 34

28 Eg, Reid, *Short Story* 30; West, 'The American Short Story at Mid-Century' 28; Eikhenbaum, 'O. Henry' 4; Hils, *Writing in General* 2; and Jose García Villa, 'The Contemporary Short Story,' *Prairie Schooner* 10, no. 2 (Fall 1936) 231–3

29 See the special issue on 'The Contemporary Australian Short Story,' *Australian Literary Studies* 10, no. 2 (October 1981), esp. Elizabeth Webby, 'Australian Short Fiction from *While the Billy Boils* to *The Everlasting Secret Family*' 147–64. Webby isolates characteristics of 'The *Bulletin* Tradition,' but then claims that the tradition of good writers (she singles out Henry Lawson, Hal Porter, and Frank Moorhouse) is the (indeterminate) tradition 'of short fiction itself, which transcends national boundaries' (p 156) – a conclusion which, though it challenges claims for national distinctiveness (she quotes Henrietta Drake-Brockman to the effect that the short story is indigenous to Australia), also evades the issue of cultural impact on literary practice. The notion of universality is perhaps most insidious as a generalization because it seems so attractive, so clearly committed to art rather than to politics; James Cooper Lawrence, for example, in 'A Theory of the Short Story' (1917; rpt in May, *Short Story Theories* 71), argued that 'The instinct for story-telling exists in substantially the same form in every race; all men recognize and insist upon the simple limitations of brevity and coherence; and hence ... it is possible for an artist to produce masterpieces whose appeal ... is truly universal. The best short stories ... are a part of the world's anthology.' Well and good, except that the initial dichotomy is false (art and politics are not mutually exclusive), and the implicit gender bias and the mistaken assumption about instinct are open to argument. The point is that, while there are certain experiences that transcend particular cultures (love, grief, jealousy, ambition, etc.), the patterns by which these experiences are expressed are culture-marked; inevitably literature reflects such concrete particular patterns as well as the experiences as they are conceived somehow 'purely,' in the abstract.

30 Reid, *Short Story* 32.

31 See Pratt 'The Short Story' 182–7, who sensibly disputes the notion of the story's built-in fragmentariness and the novel's built-in wholeness.

32 See, eg, W.J. Howard, 'Literature in the Law Courts, 1770–1800,' in D.I.B. Smith, ed., *Editing Eighteenth-Century Texts* (Toronto: Univ. of Toronto Press 1967) 78–91.

33 See Hugh Hood's comments on Stephen Leacock and E.M. Forster in J.R. (Tim) Struthers, 'An Interview with Hugh Hood,' *Essays on Canadian Writing* nos. 13 / 14 (Winter / Spring 1978–9) 42–3.

34 '"The Flash of Fireflies",' *Kenyon Review* (1968); rpt. in May, *Short Story Theories* 179–80

35 *The Frontier in American History* (New York: Holt 1920)
36 (New York: Harcourt, Brace & World 1964). On the subject of historiography in Canada and New Zealand, see Carl Berger, *The Writing of Canadian History* (Toronto: Oxford Univ. Press 1976); Robin W. Winks, ed., *The Historiography of the British Empire-Commonwealth* (Durham, NC: Duke Univ. Press 1966); and K.A. Pickens, 'The Writing of New Zealand History: A Kuhnian Perspective,' *Historical Studies* (Melbourne) 17, no. 69 (October 1977) 384–98.
37 Canada became independent in 1867, but reached its current territorial limits in 1949, when the British colony of Newfoundland joined Confederation. Canada signed the Statute of Westminster, which set up the Commonwealth, when the British House enacted the law in 1931, but did not 'repatriate' its constitution until 1982. New Zealand reached its national territorial limits at the time of independence in 1907, though Britain made the Cook Islands (Rarotonga) a New Zealand dependency in 1901 (a constitution granted internal self-government to the Cook Islands in 1965); and New Zealand held Western Samoa as a League of Nations Trusteeship until 1962. But while New Zealand refused in 1931 to sign the Statute of Westminster (because, it was argued by the government of the time, to do so would 'weaken the bonds of Empire'), it adopted in 1950 a constitution which disbanded the provinces and set up a unicameral national House.
38 *A Victorian Authority: The Daily Press in Late Nineteenth-Century Canada* (Toronto: Univ. of Toronto Press 1982) 34
39 See Dorothy Livesay, 'The Documentary Poem: A Canadian Genre' (1969) in Eli Mandel, ed., *Contexts of Canadian Criticism* (Chicago and London: Univ. of Chicago Press 1971 267–81; and Stephen Scobie, 'Amelia,' *Canadian Literature* no. 100 (Spring 1984) 264–85.
40 See Bernard Smith, *European Vision and the South Pacific 1768–1850* (Oxford: Clarendon 1960).
41 Vol. 25, p 186
42 See Ferguson, 'Defining the Short Story' 16
43 This subject is raised by a number of commentators on the literatures of the Commonwealth. See, for example, John Matthews, *Tradition in Exile* (Toronto: Univ. of Toronto Press and Melbourne: Cheshire 1962), and W.H. New, 'New Language, New World,' in C.D. Narasimhaiah, ed., *Awakened Conscience* (New Delhi: Sterling 1978) 360–77.
44 In his 1897 letter to J.F. Archibald, quoted by C. Hartley Grattan ('About Tom Collins') in Tom Collins, *Such Is Life* (1903; rpt Chicago: Univ. of Chicago Press 1948) 385
45 Introduction to *New Zealand Short Stories* (1953; rpt London: Oxford Univ. Press 1961) 5
46 'Distance Looks Our Way,' in her *Literature in Action* (London: Chatto & Windus 1972) 115
47 See W.H. New, *Among Worlds* (Erin, Ont.: Press Porcépic 1975) for a survey of recurrent images and themes.

CHAPTER TWO: CANADA – STORY AND HISTORY

1 'Poetry and Progress' (1922), rpt. in D.C. Scott, *The Circle of Affection* (Toronto: McClelland & Stewart 1947) 147, 142
2 Introduction to D.C. Scott, *In the Village of Viger and Other Stories* (Toronto: McClelland & Stewart 1973) 9
3 Susanna Moodie, *Roughing It in the Bush* (1913 edition; rpt Toronto: Coles 1974) 475
4 'Education: The True Wealth of the World,' *The Victoria Magazine* (December 1847; rpt Vancouver: Univ. of British Columbia Library 1968) 89–92
5 *Roughing It* 329
6 *Ibid.* xx
7 Michael A. Peterman, 'Susanna Moodie (1803–1885),' in *Canadian Writers and Their Works*, fiction series, I, ed. Robert Lecker et al. (Toronto: ECW 1983) 73, 87 (hereafter referred to as *CWTW*). Vernon Rolfe Lindquist, in 'The Soil and the Seed: The Birth of the Canadian Short Story in English: Haliburton, Moodie, and others; 1830–1867,' unpub. Ph D diss., UNB 1979, surveys the emergence of short fiction in early Canadian periodicals. Lindquist emphasizes Haliburton's skill at creating atmosphere, Moodie's gift for local colour, the sentimental stories of Miss Foster, Mrs Harriet V. Cheney, Mrs Eliza Cushing, Mrs Henry Giles, Rosanna Leprohon, Catharine Parr Traill, Mrs Bayley, and Mrs Maclachlan, and the satiric and adventure stories of Ned Caldwell, Andrew Robertson, H.J. Friel, Thomas Page, and the Reverend Joseph Abbot, singling out for commentary several sketches and stories from *The Literary Garland* and *The Victoria Magazine* in particular. See also Ella Lorraine Keller, 'The Development of the Canadian Short Story,' MA thesis (Univ. of Saskatchewan 1950); and Gillian Whitlock, 'The Bush, The Barrack-Yard and the Clearing: "Colonial Realism" in the sketches and stories of Susanna Moodie, C.L.R. James and Henry Lawson,' *Journal of Commonwealth Literature* 20, no. 1 (1985) 36–48.
8 *Victoria Magazine* 113
9 *Roughing It* 392
10 Peterman, *CWTW* 70; Ballstadt, 'Susanna Moodie and the English Sketch,' *Canadian Literature* no. 51 (Winter 1972) 32–8
11 *The Friendships of Mary Russell Mitford as Recorded in Letters from Her Literary Correspondents*, ed. A.G. L'Estrange (New York: Harper 1882) 206–7
12 L'Estrange, *Friendships* 212
13 *Victoria Magazine* 287
14 Introduction to *Mark Hurdlestone, the Gold Worshipper*, rpt. in *Life in the Clearings*, ed. Robert L. McDougall (Toronto: Macmillan 1959) 292
15 Rpt. in *The Sam Slick Anthology*, selected by Reginald Eyre Watters and ed. Walter S. Avis (Toronto: Clarke Irwin 1969) 147. Another influence on the shape of these serial sketches was that of the 'serial chapters' that were common in *Blackwood's Edinburgh Magazine* in the 1820s; one writer of this time with concurrent connections with Canada was John Galt, author of *Annals of*

Notes to pages 37–49

the Parish (1821) and the founder of Guelph, Ontario. See George V. Griffith, 'John Galt's Short Fiction Series,' *Studies in Short Fiction* 17 (Fall 1980) 455–62. On Haliburton see also Frank M. Tierney, ed., *The Thomas Chandler Haliburton Symposium* (Ottawa: Univ. of Ottawa Press 1985).
16 'Holding Up the Mirror,' in *Sam Slick Anthology* 261.
17 *The Clockmaker* (1871 ed., rpt. Toronto: McClelland & Stewart 1958) 49
18 'A Note on the Speech of Sam Slick,' *Sam Slick Anthology* xxii
19 Introduction to *Sam Slick Anthology* xvii
20 *Sam Slick Anthology* 223
21 (1860 edition; rpt Ottawa: Tecumseh 1978) xxi–xxii
22 *Sam Slick Anthology* 257
23 Ibid. 153–4
24 *The Old Judge* 211–12
25 Ibid. 69
26 Ibid. 274
27 In an address to the Royal Society of Canada, published in 1893 as *Our Intellectual Strength and Weakness* (rpt, with works by T.G. Marquis and Camille Roy, introd. by Clara Thomas; Toronto: Univ. of Toronto Press 1973) 30
28 'American Influence on Canadian Thought' (*The Week*, 7 July 1887); rpt. in Sara Jeannette Duncan, *Selected Journalism*, ed. T.E. Tausky (Ottawa: Tecumseh 1978) 115
29 'Colonialism and Literature' (*The Week*, 30 September 1886); Duncan, *Journalism* 105–6
30 'Outworn Literary Methods' (*The Week*, 9 June 1887); Duncan, *Journalism* 113–14
31 *Viger* 19, 43, 53
32 *Scribner's* 1 (February 1887) 236
33 P 236
34 *Dominion Illustrated Monthly* 2nd series, 1 (February 1892) 37. I am indebted to Carole Gerson's study of Scott; see 'The Piper's Forgotten Tune,' *Journal of Canadian Fiction* no. 16 (1976) 138–43.
35 *The Strange Case of Dr Jekyll and Mr Hyde* appeared in 1886, *The Picture of Dorian Gray* in 1891.
36 Scott, 'Poetry and Progress,' 134
37 Gordon Roper, Rupert Schieder, and S. Ross Beharriell, 'The Kinds of Fiction, 1880–1920,' *Literary History of Canada*, ed. Carl F. Klinck et al. (2nd ed., Toronto: Univ. of Toronto Press 1976) I 303
38 'Duncan Campbell Scott,' *Canadian Magazine* 43 (1914) 71
39 P 70
40 There was, for example, a widespread suspicion of French-Canadian 'loyalty' to Canada, an assumption that Indians were a dying race, a resentment against the presence of Asians in the country, and a dismissive attitude towards blacks. The parallels with other parts of the Empire continued strong at this point; in 1907, *The Canadian Magazine* published a New Zealander's account of his country. In 'The Britain of the South,' T.E. Taylor describes scenery

and industrial enterprise, ignores literature, and writes: 'Many shipwrecks on the rocky coast of New Zealand have afforded the Maoris opportunity for exhibiting brilliant heroism' (23, no. 5 [March 1907] 451).
41 Even as late as 1926, when national separation was again to become an issue, R.E. Gosnell was to warn against Canadian nationalism and the current standardization of education; the present generation was too soft, he observed, the best of Canadian literature was that of the past, and the cable of Empire should not be cut. 'Canadian Literature and Nationality,' *Canadian Bookman* 8, no. 1 (January 1926) 14–15
42 See, for example, Hector W. Charlesworth, 'The Canadian Girl: An Appreciative Medley,' *Canadian Magazine* 1 (1893) 186–93. Cecil Logsdail published a complementary article in the same volume, its title using an instructively different vocabulary: 'The Women of the United States.'
43 9 (July 1897) 266
44 Muddiman, 'Duncan Campbell Scott' 70–2
45 Review of *Jack Chanty* in *Canadian Magazine* 42 (January 1914) 343
46 'French Canada and Canada,' *Canadian Magazine* 14 (February 1900) 313
47 (Toronto: George Morang 1899) viii
48 See Betty Keller, *Pauline* (Vancouver: Douglas & McIntyre 1981).
49 'Canadian Short-Story Writers,' *Canadian Magazine* 4 (February 1895) 341
50 'The Trail of the Romanticist in Canada,' *Canadian Magazine* 34 (March 1910) 533
51 Rea Wilmshurst's 'L.M. Montgomery's Short Stories' provides 'a preliminary bibliography' of her work; *Canadian Children's Literature* no. 29 (1983) 25–34
52 (New York: Doubleday, Page 1900)
53 'The Three Fives,' *Canadian Magazine* 1 (April 1893) 151
54 'Two Beauties of the Backwoods,' *Canadian Magazine* 6 (January 1896) 222
55 'The Canadian Short Story,' in *Canadian Short Stories* (Toronto: Macmillan 1928) xix
56 Foreword to *Golden Tales of Canada* (1938; rpt Freeport, NY: Books for Libraries 1972) vii
57 Jacket note
58 (Toronto: McClelland & Stewart 1923) 13–14
59 'In a Steamer Chair,' *In a Steamer Chair and Other Ship-Board Stories* (1892; rpt. Freeport, NY: Books for Libraries 1970) 55
60 'The New Power,' *Canadian Nights* (1914; rpt Freeport, NY: Books for Libraries 1971) 275
61 *Ibid.* 294
62 *Ibid.* 273
63 *An African Millionaire* (1897; rpt Freeport, NY: Books for Libraries 1976) 302, 266. On Allen's career, see George Herbert Clarke, 'Grant Allen,' *Queen's Quarterly* 45 (Winter 1938–9) 487–96; Allen published his early works as 'Cecil Power,' In a letter to the *New Age* (25 August 1910), Katherine Mansfield scornfully dismissed the writings of the two Canadians, whom J.M. Kennedy

had proclaimed the 'two boldest novelists of our time,' Grant Allen and Elinor Glyn. 'Far be it from me,' Mansfield wrote, 'to repudiate Mr Allen's statement in declaring his own novels rubbish ... If Elinor Glyn is the prophetic woman's voice crying out of the wilderness of Canadian literature, let her European sister novelists lift shekelled hands in prayer that the "great gulf" may ever yawn more widely.' *Collected Letters*, I, 99.

64 Introduction to *Off the Rocks* (1906; rpt Freeport, NY: Books for Libraries 1970) n.p. Thomas Raddall's tribute to Archibald MacMechan – in his foreword to MacMechan's posthumously published *Tales of the Sea* (Toronto: McClelland & Stewart 1947) vii–xiv – indicates the continuing attraction of Grenfell's world-view. Quoting Lindsay Bennet, Raddall recalls MacMechan: '"he had a true nature that placed him on terms of equal easy friendship with men whose work was dignified by hard struggle with the elements on land or sea"'p xiv).

65 'Seton's Animals,' *Journal of Canadian Fiction* 11 (Summer 1973) 195

66 (Boston: Page 1902) 29. Subsequent publications on the animal story include anon., 'The Animal Story,' *Edinburgh Review*, 214 (July 1911) 94–118; Michel Poirier, 'The Animal Story in Canadian Literature,' *Queen's Quarterly* 34 (January & April 1927) 298–312, 398–419; William H. Magee, 'The Animal Story: A Challenge in Technique,' *Dalhousie Review* 44 (1964–5) 156–64; James Polk, *Wilderness Writers* (Toronto: Clarke Irwin 1972); and Alec Lucas, 'Nature Writers and the Animal Story,' *LHC* (2nd ed. 1976) I 380–404.

67 See, for example, John Burroughs, 'Real and Sham Natural History,' *Atlantic Monthly* 91 (March 1903) 298–304; Edward B. Clark, 'Roosevelt on the Nature Fakirs,' *Everybody's Magazine* 16 (June 1907) 770–4; C. Lintern Sibley, 'The Voyage of the Nature Story,' *Canadian Magazine* 38 (January 1912) 287–92; Joseph Gold, 'The Precious Speck of Life,' *Canadian Literature* no. 26 (Autumn 1965) 22–32; R.H. MacDonald, 'The Revolt Against Instinct,' *Canadian Literature* no. 84 (Spring 1980) 18–29; and W.J. Keith, *Charles G.D. Roberts* (Toronto: Copp Clark 1969).

68 See John Henry Wadland, *Ernest Thompson Seton: Man in Nature and the Progressive Era 1880–1915* (New York: Arno 1978).

69 'The Butt of the Camp,' *Earth's Enigmas* (1895; rpt Freeport, NY: Books for Libraries 1969) 76

70 'The Romance of an Ox-team,' *Earth's Enigmas* 161

71 'A Sanctuary of the Plains' (1894; rpt Freeport, NY: Books for Libraries 1969) 318

72 'The Plunderer' (1896; rpt Freeport, NY: Books for Libraries 1969) 203

73 Roberts, 'The Butt of the Camp' 96; Parker, 'The Patrol of the Cypress Hills,' *Pierre* 6

74 'Old Man Savarin' and 'John Bedell, U.E. Loyalist,' in *Old Man Savarin Stories*, introd. Linda Sheshko (1917; rpt Toronto: Univ. of Toronto Press 1974) 61, 53. In 'Tales of Canada and Canadians,' *Journal of Canadian Fiction* 11 (Summer 1973) 191–4, Lorraine McMullen summarizes Thomson's career.

75 *Savarin* 313–14
76 See *The Social Criticism of Stephen Leacock*, ed. Alan Bowker (Toronto: Univ. of Toronto Press 1973).
77 'An Introduction' to *Social Criticism* xxxix. While the main body of commentary on Leacock has been literary, exploring his ironic and satiric faces, there have been repeated assertions of his documentary accuracy, as in the humorous essay by Arthur Lower, 'The Mariposa Belle,' *Queen's Quarterly* 58 (1951–2) 220–6; or the parenthetical aside of Floyd S. Chalmers in his account of leaving Orillia in 1913, in his autobiography *Both Sides of the Street* (Toronto: Macmillan 1983): 'A couple of years later I got around to reading Leacock's *Sunshine Sketches* and recognized with delight some of the prominent people I had known in Orillia' (p 19). Other Orillians were less amused.
78 *Sunshine Sketches of a Little Town* (Toronto: McClelland & Stewart 1947) 3. See also Albert and Theresa Moritz, *Leacock: A Biography* (Toronto: Stoddart 1985).
  On one possible literary model for Leacock see Gerald Lynch, 'Leacock's Debt to Daudet,' *Canadian Literature* no. 107 (Winter 1985) 186–9; see also his 'Sunshine Sketches: Mariposa versus Mr Smith,' *Studies in Canadian Literature* 9, no. 2 (1984) 169–205.
79 Peter Stevens's introduction to his selection of Knister's writings, *The First Day of Spring: Stories and Other Prose* (Toronto: Univ. of Toronto Press 1976) xi–xxx, admirably surveys Knister's life and work.
80 See David Staines, comp., 'Morley Callaghan: The Writer and His Writings,' in his ed., *The Callaghan Symposium* (Ottawa: Univ. of Ottawa 1981) 111–21; and Judith Kendle, 'Callaghan as Columnist,' *Canadian Literature* no. 82 (Autumn 1979) 6–20.
81 E.S., in 'Australian Literature,' *The Week* 4 (24 November 1887) 833
82 'Looking at Native Prose,' *Saturday Night* 43 (1 December 1928) 3
83 'The Short Story in Canada,' *Saturday Night* 43 (25 August 1928) 7
84 'Morley Callaghan,' *Saturday Night* 43 (14 July 1928) 8, 11. Cf. Agnes C. Laut, 'A Letter from Canada,' *Saturday Review of Literature* 2 (2 January 1926) 466: 'Canada must rededicate her soul, not to slavish imitation of success in British and American literature but to the expression of her own high national and international aims'; Laut found this literary 'baptism ... to a new evangel' expressed in the work of Dr [A.D.?] Watson ('the Whitman of Canada ... the seer and prophet of a New World' and Robert Norwood.
85 'The Animal Story' 419
86 (Ottawa: Overbrook Press 1931) 39
87 In his introduction to *Short Stories by Thomas Murtha* (Ottawa: Univ. of Ottawa Press 1980) 21. On Murtha, see also Joy Kuropatwa, 'An Overlooked Canadian Realist,' *Brick* no. 15 (Spring 1982) 35–7.
88 *Short Stories by Thomas Murtha* 41
89 Desmond Pacey's introduction to *Tales from the Margin: The Selected Short Stories of Frederick Philip Grove* (Toronto: McGraw-Hill Ryerson 1971) esp. 5–19, surveys Grove's accomplishments in short fiction.

90 Denison, 'The Weather Breeder,' in Knister's *Canadian Short Stories* 29; Le Rossignol, *The Habitant-Merchant* (Toronto: Macmillan 1939) 13
91 'The Short Story in Canada' 7
92 (Montreal: Dodd-Simpson 1931) xii
93 (Garden City, NY: Garden City Publishing 1924) 352–62. It is worth noting E.K. Brown's brief note in 'The Causerie,' *Winnipeg Free Press* (2 July 1949) 17, cols. 7, 8: 'Anderson was only six years younger than Leacock but he belonged to a totally different literary and intellectual world. Leacock was sure of his values. He was, like most great humorists, intellectually conservative – he belonged with the nineteenth century. His very sentences are nineteenth century sentences, so were his emotions. All that Gertrude Stein could have meant for him was a chance for a great parody.
    Anderson was a groper. His sentences have the fluidity of our time, and so had his emotions. He is one of us, and Leacock is not, although Leacock may be something better.' The influence of Anderson's 'grotesques' may extend as late as 1984, apparent in Alden Nowlan's *Will Ye Let the Mummers In?*.
94 'A Talk with Morley Callaghan,' *Tamarack Review* no. 7 (Spring 1958) 18
95 Morley Callaghan, *A Native Argosy* (Toronto: Macmillan 1929) 90–1. Hoar's commentary appears in his *Morley Callaghan* (Toronto: Copp Clark 1969) 8–10.
96 *Morley Callaghan's Stories* (Toronto: Macmillan 1959) 26, 36
    A subsequent collection, including some previously unpublished stories, appeared in 1985 as *The Lost and Found Stories of Morley Callaghan* (Toronto: Lester and Orpen Dennys / Exile Editions); included are such stories as 'The Sentimentalists' 'An Enemy of the People,' and a story loosely based on the public figure of Grey Owl, called 'Loppy Phelan's Double Shoot.'
97 *Ibid.* 158, 162, 163. There are slight variations from the *Native Argosy* text.
98 'Morley Callaghan' 8
99 In *Open House*, ed. W.A. Deacon and Wilfred Reeves (Ottawa: Graphic 1931) 97
100 'A Note on Modernism,' in *Open House* 22–3
101 'The Land Is Full of Voices,' *Saturday Night* 43 (1 December 1928) 21
102 'Katherine Mansfield,' *The First Day of Spring* 428
103 *Ibid.* 434
104 Foreword to *Collected Poems of Raymond Knister*, ed. with a memoir by Dorothy Livesay (Toronto: Ryerson 1949), vii–viii
105 See Kenneth J. Hughes, introduction to Donna Phillips, ed., *Voices of Discord: Canadian Short Stories from the 1930's* (Toronto: New Hogtown Press 1979) 11–41. See also Alistair MacLeod, 'The Canadian Short Story in the 1930's, with Special Reference to Stories of Social Protest,' MA thesis (UNB, 1961), and Evelyn Joyce MacLure, 'The Short Story in Canada: Development from 1935 to 1955 with Attached Bibliography,' MA thesis (UBC 1969). MacLeod surveys the stories that appeared in *The Canadian Forum, Masses, New Frontier,* and *Queen's Quarterly*, identifying themes (the plight of factory workers, the world of the immigrant, the 'American gangster' type, ghosts, and animals),

and singling out Mary Quayle Innis, Kimball McIllroy, and Jack Parr for particular praise. On MacLeod's own stories, see Colin Nicholson, 'Signatures of Time,' *Canadian Literature* no. 107 (Winter 1985) 90–101.
106 'Literature and Society,' in *Essays, Controversies and Poems*, ed. Miriam Waddington (Toronto: McClelland & Stewart 1972) 33–4
107 On Pacey's stories see Roy Daniells, foreword to Pacey's *The Picnic and Other Stories* (Toronto: Ryerson 1958) v–ix; and two works by Frank Tierney: 'The Short Fiction of Desmond Pacey,' *International Fiction Review* 9 (Winter 1982) 3–16, and his introduction to his ed., *Waken, Lords and Ladies Gay: Selected Stories of Desmond Pacey* (Ottawa: Univ. of Ottawa Press 1974) 9–15.
108 On Raddall, see Alan R. Young, 'The Short Stories,' *Thomas H. Raddall* (Boston: Twayne 1983) 67–86.
109 'On the Air,' *The Standard Review* (Montreal) (21 February 1948) 4. I am indebted to Neil Besner for this reference, and for the commentary on Gallant's journalism and short stories in his 'Mavis Gallant's Short Fiction,' unpublished PH D diss., UBC 1983.
110 On Ross's stories see Keath Fraser, 'Futility at the Pump,' *Queen's Quarterly* 77 (Spring 1970) 72–80; Sandra Djwa, 'No Other Way,' *Canadian Literature* no. 47 (Winter 1971) 49–66; and Lorraine McMullen, *Sinclair Ross* (Boston: Twayne 1979) 23–55.
111 F.H. Whitman, in 'The Case of Ross's Mysterious Barn,' *Canadian Literature* no. 94 (Autumn 1982) 168–9, argues that the boy is mistaken in his suspicions, a view that is disputed in Marilyn Chapman's 'Another Case of Ross's Mysterious Barn,' *Canadian Literature* no. 103 (Winter 1984) 184–6.
112 On Wilson and violence, see Blanche Gelfant, 'The Hidden Mines in Ethel Wilson's Landscape,' *Canadian Literature* no. 93 (Summer 1982) 4–23.
113 'Truth and Mrs Forrester,' *Mrs Golightly and Other Stories* (Toronto: Macmillan 1961) 111
114 *Mrs Golightly* 59–60
115 *A Private Place* (Ottawa: Oberon 1975) 34
116 *Queen's Quarterly* 45 (Summer 1938) 187. *Fiction* was a publication of the Toronto Writers' Club, a collection of winners in a short story contest which the Club had sponsored in 1935, following a Toronto visit by E.J. O'Brien, who in his address to the Club had criticized the fictional content of Canadian magazines. See MacLeod, 'The Canadian Short Story in the 1930's,' 148.
117 The first printing of *A Private Place* mistakenly reverses the titles of this story and 'So Many Have Died.'
118 'So Many Have Died,' *Tamarack Review* no. 62 (1974) 14
119 *A Private Place* 23
120 *Canadian Fiction Magazine* no. 27 (1977) 102
121 *Mrs Golightly* 71
122 See Henry Kreisel, 'Has Anyone Here Heard of Marjorie Pickthall?: Discovering the Canadian Literary Landscape,' *Canadian Literature* no. 100 (Spring 1984) 173–80.

267 Notes to pages 87–98

123 See C.D. Minni, 'The Short Story as an Ethnic Genre,' in Joseph Pivato, ed., *Contrasts* (Montreal: Guernica 1985), 61–76.
124 On Thomas's method of composition, see Audrey Thomas, 'Basmati Rice: An Essay about Words,' *Canadian Literature* no. 100 (Spring 1984) 312–17. On Kreisel's stories see Neil Besner, 'Kreisel's Broken Globes,' *Canadian Literature* no. 107 (Winter 1985) 103–11.
125 'White Magic,' *Canadian Jewish Chronicle* (7 October 1932)
126 See M.W. Steinberg, introduction to his ed of A.M. Klein, *Short Stories* (Toronto: Univ. of Toronto Press 1983) vii–xix
127 *Short Stories* 116
128 *Ibid.* 117
129 *Ibid.* 287
130 *Hear Us O Lord from Heaven Thy Dwelling-Place* (Philadelphia and New York: Lippincott 1961) 13, 29, 99, 115, 175, 201. The introduction to W.H. New's *Malcolm Lowry: A Reference Guide* (Boston: G.K. Hall 1978) summarizes Lowry criticism to 1976; annual updates appear in the *Malcolm Lowry Newsletter*. Most Lowry short story criticism addresses itself to 'The Forest Path to the Spring.'
131 *From the Fifteenth District* (Toronto: Macmillan 1979) 36
132 (New York: Beaufort Books and Toronto: General 1983) 210
133 *Selected Letters of Malcolm Lowry*, ed. Harvey Breit and Margerie Bonner Lowry (Philadelphia and New York: Lippincott 1965) 28. It is instructive to contrast this position (one shared by many other writers in Canada) with that articulated by the American writer Hortense Calisher, who began publishing stories in 1948. Calisher's view is exclusive and conventional: 'A story is an apocalypse, served in a very small cup. Still, it wants to be considered in its own company only. The presence of neighbors changes it. Worlds meant to be compacted only to themselves, bump. Their very sequence can do them violence. Even when all the stories are by the same hand.' Preface to *The Collected Stories of Hortense Calisher* (New York: Arbor House and Toronto: Clarke Irwin 1975) ix. Lowry's radicalism consisted mainly of his challenge to any dogmatic acceptance of this convention about the genre.
134 Lowry, *Selected Letters* 320
135 'Canadian Short Story Anthologies: Notes on Their Function and Form,.' *WLWE* 11 (April 1972) 53–9; 'The Anthology; a Notable and Unacclaimed Achievement of Canadian Literature,' *Literary Half-Yearly* 13 (July 1972) 111–19
136 First edition (Toronto: Univ. of Toronto Press 1965) 720
137 'The English Language in Canada,' in Richard Bailey and Manfred Gorlach, eds, *English as a World Language* (Ann Arbor: Univ. of Michigan 1982) 161
138 In *Kicking against the Pricks* (Toronto: ECW 1982) 151. Donald Stephens, in 'The Contemporary Voice in Recent Canadian Short Fiction,' *Literary Half-Yearly* 13 (July 1972) 181–4, refers to the social objectivity and the questioning of nationalism in the short story of the 1960s and 1970s; see also his 'The Short Story in English,' *Canadian Literature* no. 41 (Summer 1969) 126–30. Geoff Hancock, in 'Here and Now: Innovation and Change in the Canadian

Short Story,' *Canadian Fiction Magazine* no. 27 (1977) 4–22, praises the newer forms of fiction and the impulse behind them: the desire to explore *how we live* more than *where*. Simone Vauthier's special issue of *Ranam* no. 16 (1983), entitled 'La Nouvelle canadienne anglophone' (the proceedings of a 1983 Strasbourg colloquium), contains a number of valuable comments by fourteen critics on general topics (anthology taste, second person narration, short story history) and on particular works by Laurence, Hodgins, Munro, Gallant, Wiebe, Lowry, Emily Carr, Brian Moore, and Alistair MacLeod. Comments on Thomas, Blaise, and Ray Smith also appear in *Open Letter* 3rd series, no. 5 (Summer 1976), and comments on Gallant, Laurence, Leacock, and Hodgins in Robert Kroetsch and Reingard Nischik, eds, *Gaining Ground: European Critics on Canadian Literature* (Edmonton: NeWest 1985). *Room of One's Own* 10, nos. 3–4 (March 1986), was devoted to Thomas; and two essays in *Canadian Literature* no. 109 (Summer 1986) were devoted to Thomas and Atwood: Frank Davey's 'Alternate Stories' (pp 5–14) and Barbara Godard's 'Tales within Tales: Margaret Atwood's Folk Narratives' (pp 57–84). See also *The Literary Review* (Teaneck, NJ) 28, no. 3 (Spring 1985); and J.R. (Tim) Struthers, ed., *The Montreal Story Tellers* (Montreal: Véhicule 1985).

139 Knister, 'The Canadian Short Story' xi; Weaver, introduction to *Canadian Short Stories* (Toronto: Oxford 1960) ix. Two short histories of Canadian fiction, which follow Weaver's model, are Clare McCulloch, *The Neglected Genre* (Guelph: Alive 1973), and William French, 'Once Upon a Time,' *The Review* 66, no. 2 (1982) 18–22.
140 In 'An Interview with Hugh Hood,' by J.R. (Tim) Struthers, *Essays on Canadian Writing* nos. 13–14 (Winter / Spring 1978–9) 25–6
141 'An Interview with Hugh Hood,' 52. Carole Gerson and Kathy Mezei refer to the Leacock-Hood connection in the introduction to their ed., *The Prose of Life: Sketches from Victorian Canada* (Toronto: ECW 1981) 3. This introduction (pp 1–15) is an excellent survey of the Canadian sketch and its formal implications for subsequent story structure.
142 'Amelia or: Who Do You Think You Are?: Documentary and Identity in Canadian Literature,' *Canadian Literature* no. 100 (Spring 1984) 264–85
143 (Toronto: Macmillan 1983) 239
144 See, for example, Patricia Morley, *Margaret Laurence* (Boston: Twayne 1981); and W.H. New, 'The Other and I: Laurence's African Stories,' in George Woodcock, ed., *A Place to Stand On* (Edmonton: NeWest 1983) 113–34.
145 See W.H. New, 'Text and Subtext: Laurence's "The Merchant of Heaven",' *Journal of Canadian Studies* 13 (Fall 1978) 19–22.
146 On Godfrey's stories, see W.H. New, 'Godfrey's Uncollected Artist,' *Ariel* 4 (July 1973) 5–15 and 'Godfrey's Book of Changes,' *Modern Fiction Studies* 22 (Autumn 1976) 375–85; and Lorraine M. York, ' "River Two Blind Jacks" ': Dave Godfrey's Chaucerian Allegory,' *Studies in Canadian Literature* 9, no. 2 (1984) 206–13.
147 See, for example, Louis K. MacKendrick, ed., *Probable Fictions: Alice Munro's*

Narrative Acts (Toronto: ECW 1983); Helen Hoy, '"Dull, Simple, Amazing and Unfathomable": Paradox and Double Vision in Alice Munro's Fiction,' *Studies in Canadian Literature* 5 (1980) 100–15; and Heliane Catherine Daziron, 'The Preposterous Oxymoron,' *Literary Half-Yearly* 24 (July 1983) 116–24.

148 'On Ending Stories,' *Canadian Forum* 62 (September 1982) 7, 37. See also Susan Lohafer, esp. 81–102.
149 'Academy Stuff,' in John Metcalf, ed., *The Narrative Voice* (Toronto: McGraw-Hill Ryerson 1972) 236
150 'Academy Stuff,' 239
151 (Toronto: McGraw-Hill Ryerson 1980) 4–5. On Metcalf's own stories, see Barry Cameron, 'An Approximation of Poetry,' *Studies in Canadian Literature* 2, no. 1 (Winter, 1977) 17–35; and the special Metcalf issue in *Malahat Review* no. 70 (March 1985).
152 Introduction to his ed., *Modern Canadian Stories* (Toronto: Bantam 1975) xiii–xiv
153 Preface to his ed., *The Story So Far* (Toronto: Coach House 1971) n.p. In 'Important Writers,' in his *Craft Slices* (Ottawa: Oberon 1985) 54, Bowering complains 'Canada is the only country this side of New Zealand ... that still rewards its perpetrators of realism, naturalism, the *bildungsroman* and the like.'
154 'Dinosaur,' in *The Narrative Voice* 206–7
155 'Voices,' in John Metcalf, ed., *Making It New* (Toronto: Methuen 1982) 259
156 'The Short Story: Canada,' *Kenyon Review* 30 (1968) 476–7
157 'Sober Coloring: The Ontology of Super-Realism,' in *The Narrative Voice* 96. On the stories of Hood, Blaise, and Metcalf, see Robert Lecker, *On the Line* (Toronto: ECW 1982). See also Keith Garebian, 'The Short Stories,' *Hugh Hood* (Boston: Twayne 1983) 10–53.
158 Introduction to his ed., *The Story So Far / 2* (Toronto: Coach House 1973) n.p.
159 Introductory notes to his ed., *Fiction of Contemporary Canada* (Toronto: Coach House 1980) 7
160 *Ibid.* 20–1
161 'Sober Coloring' 98

CHAPTER THREE: NEW ZEALAND – STORY AND HISTORY

1 *Lives and Letters* (London and Boston: Faber & Faber 1978) 53. At various times in her life she also lived or wrote using the names K. Bowden, K. Bendall, Matilda Berry (in *The Signature*), Lili Heron, Käthe Beachamp-Bowden, Käthi Bowden, and the nicknames Tig, Wig, Katie, Katerina, Katiushka, and Kissienska. See *The Collected Letters of Katherine Mansfield*, ed. Vincent O'Sullivan and Margaret Scott (Oxford: Clarendon 1984) I, 89, ix. Some of her poems appeared in *Rhythm* and *The Athenaeum* as 'translations' from 'the Russian of Boris Petrovsky' or under the pseudonym Elizabeth Stanley. See introductory note to Katherine Mansfield, *Poems* (London: Constable 1923) xii.

2 Preface to Thomas Bracken, *Musings in Maoriland* (Dunedin and Sydney: Arthur T. Keirle 1890) 16–18
3 See T.M. Hocken, 'The Beginnings of Literature in New Zealand: Part II, the English Section – Newspapers,' *Transactions and Proceedings of the New Zealand Institute* 34 (1901) 99–114; and Judith Mary Wild, 'The Literary Periodical in New Zealand,' MA thesis, Victoria University of Wellington 1951.
4 'A few words to the public' 1, no. 1 (August 1862) 1
5 *The New Zealander* (10 September 1862); Wild, 'The Literary Periodical' 8
6 Anonymous review, bound with the cheap edition reprint of *Bush Life in Australia and New Zealand* (London: Swan Sonnenschein 1893)
7 (London: Sampson Low, Marston, Low, & Searle 1874) iii
8 *Ibid.* 21
9 *Ibid.* 90
10 (London: Griffith and Farran 1862) 199
11 (Auckland: W.C. Wilson 1861) 4
12 *Distant Homes* 62
13 *Ibid.* 25
14 *Ibid.* 128
15 (London: Sampson Low, Marston, Searle, & Rivington 1881) v–vi
16 Preface to *Shadows on the Snow: A Christmas Story* (Dunedin: William Hay [1865] n.p.
17 Quoted in Eleanor Farjeon, *A Nursery in the Nineties* (London: Victor Gollancz 1935) 64
18 *Shadows on the Snow* 64
19 (Dunedin: Otago Daily Times 1880) 39
20 (Melbourne: George Robertson 1875) preface, n.p.
21 (Dunedin: James Horsburgh 1889) 38
22 *We Four* 28, 10
23 'Anno Domini 2000,' 1, no. 6 (April 1889) 243
24 In Philip Mennell, ed., *In Australian Wilds and Other Colonial Tales and Sketches* (London: Hutchinson 1889) 129 Mennell's introduction observes: 'All save one of the pieces here included have for their basis incidents of life and adventure, not in Australia alone, but in the great dependencies of New Zealand and British North America ... The extreme similarity of life and habitude in all the widely separated sections of Greater Britain is nevertheless ... most striking ... ' (p 1) Farjeon was a second New Zealander in the collection. The Canadian contribution is by India-born, Montreal-educated Edward Jenkins, who held a substantial European reputation as a popular writer. 'The Settler's Tragedy: A Legend of Muskoka,' is a tale of the families Wellbeloved and Bytheway, one of which dies a horrible death, the other living to tell of it over dinner. The Australians – Tasma, C. Haddon Chambers, and Edmund Stansfield Rawson – more typically tell yarns. One of Chambers' three works closes the anthology with tale-teller's irony: 'Of the truth of the whole story I can vouch. I had it from the maniac himself.' (p 196)
25 (London & Edinburgh: Sands & Co., n.d.) 45

Notes to pages 123–31

26 9, no. 5, p 416
27 6, no. 5, p 383
28 6, no. 5, p 364
29 'In Praise of New Zealand English,' *The Reader's Digest* (February 1970) 26. Cf. Ngaio Marsh, 'It's Not What We Say ... ,' *New Zealand Listener* (14 October 1978) 23
30 *A Christmas Cake in Four Quarters* (London and New York: Frederick Warne 1887) 262
31 Eg, Clara Eyre Cheeseman, 'Colonials in Fiction,' *New Zealand Illustrated Magazine* 7, no. 4 (January 1903) 273–82.
32 (London: Hutchinson 1899) n.p.
33 1, no. 1 (July 1889) 2
34 1, no. 4 (October 1889) 238
35 9, no. 5 (February 1904) 400; referring to the story 'Chris of All-Sorts'
36 11, no. 3 (December 1904) 232–3. 'G.B. Lancaster' was the pen name of Edith Joan Lyttleton.
37 'A Book and its Writer: Poe's Tales of the Grotesque and Arabesque,' *New Zealand Illustrated Magazine* 11, no. 3 (December 1904) 216
38 *Where the White Man Treads* (Auckland: Wilson & Horton, 2nd ed., rev. 1928) 73
39 Foreword to the 1st edition, n.p.
40 'Hira,' *Maoriland Stories* (Nelson: Alfred G. Betts 1895) 89
41 *Maoriland Stories* 8
42 See *Triad* 16, no. 5 (1 August 1908) 16–20.
43 'Obiter Dicta' 16, no. 4 (1 July 1908) 3
44 Quoted in Jean Stone, *Katherine Mansfield* 13–14. Stone also admirably traces Harold Beauchamp's involvement in his daughter's early correspondence with journal editors, and some of the reasons that led to her subsequent return to London in 1908. Mansfield had, by this time, also published several stories in the Queen's College school magazine; some of these are collected in Antony Alpers' 1984 edition of Mansfield's stories.
45 The journal of that trip was later published as *The Urewera Notebook*, ed. Ian A. Gordon (London: Oxford 1970). 'Give me the Maori and the tourist,' she wrote, 'but nothing in between' (p 61), praising Maori and English and disparaging 'the third rate article' – ie, the colonial and the Maori imitation Englishman.
46 Ian Gordon notes, for example, Tom Mills's 1912 review of *In a German Pension* in the *Feilding Star*, which recalls that Mansfield had written 'some things' for the *Star* Saturday supplement before she left for England – items now apparently lost. See *Urewera Notebook* 98–9.
47 The standard biography is Antony Alpers' excellent *The Life of Katherine Mansfield* (London: Jonathan Cape 1980), which takes account of many of these versions of the writer, and supersedes earlier biographies by Sylvia Berkman, Jeffrey Meyers, and others. See also John Carswell's *Lives and Letters* for a particular account of Mansfield's intellectual connections with A.R. Orage, Beatrice Hastings, J.M. Murry, and S.S. Koteliansky.

48 See, for example, her journal entries attacking the vocabulary of D.H. Lawrence's *The Lost Girl*; her story 'The Fly'; her declaration that 'Je ne parle pas français' is 'a cry against corruption'; and her assertion in 1919 (responding to Virginia Woolf) that artists are 'traitors' if they do not take the war into account, pretend that the war has not occurred, or fail to seek 'new expressions, new moulds for our new thoughts and feelings.' *The Letters and Journals of Katherine Mansfield: A Selection*, ed. C.K. Stead (Harmondsworth: Penguin 1977) 209, 98, 147. Alpers has pointed out (p 273) that the more sexually explicit, unexpurgated version of 'Je ne parle pas français' (Heron Press 1920) makes Mansfield's glimpse of 'corruption' even clearer.

49 'Trivial' was her recurrent term of dismissal, even for those of her own published works with which she was later impatient. See *Letters and Journals* 180–1, concerning *Bliss*.

Alpers and Beachcroft both stress the influence of Theocritus on the shaping of Mansfield's dramatic or conversational satires. It is also possible to see parallels between the Mansfield of 'Epilogue II: Violet' (1913), for example, and the Stephen Leacock of *Acadian Adventures with the Idle Rich* (1914); both writers parody the fatuousness of idle behaviour and the frivolousness of the romantic language which adorns it with the illusion of substance. Mansfield's further point, of course – as in 'The Little Governess' and elsewhere – is that such language deceives women by leading them to mistake the true designs of men and the real design of the world.

50 *Letters and Journals* 111
51 *Ibid.* 236. 'Elizabeth' was born Mary Annette Beauchamp.
52 *Ibid.* 239
53 *Ibid.* 213
54 *Collected Stories of Katherine Mansfield* (1945; rpt. London: Constable 1964) 330–1
55 *Letters and Journals* 229
56 *Ibid.* 179–80
57 *Collected Stories* 706
58 *Ibid.* 787
59 *Letters and Journals* 46
60 *Ibid.* 186
61 *Ibid.* 260; cf. her journal entry for 24 January 1922: 'I can't say how thankful I am to have been born in N.Z., to know Wellington as I do, and to have it to range about in' (p 252).
62 *Collected Stories* 32
63 *Letters and Journals* 26
64 *Ibid.* 81, 137, 183. Cf. her comments on 'Poison': 'The story is told by the man who gives himself away and hides his traces at the same moment' (p 202)
65 See *Letters and Journals* 234
66 *Ibid.* 285, 284
67 *Ibid.* 213
68 *Ibid.* 259

69 *Ibid.* 137. I am indebted to Lorraine Robson for suggesting the alternative reading of the end of 'The Garden Party.'
70 *Reluctant Editor* (Wellington: Reed 1969) 29. The *Listener* began in 1939, under Oliver Duff's editorship.
71 Holcroft, *Reluctant Editor* 23–4
72 See, for example, the extended feuds in the correspondence columns of the *New Zealand Listener*; the subject of New Zealand speech, in the autumn issues of 1940, produced the following exchange: 'Let us have a little less vocal regimentation and a little more announcer-individuality' ('Circumflex,' 12 April, p 10); 'one can hardly expect a person brought up on beer to appreciate champagne' ('F.C. Beckett,' 26 April, p 34); 'in the name of all that is worthwhile in dialect, language, literature and culture generally, let us exorcise this demon of uniformity' ('C.,' 17 May, p 30); 'If people in the Dominion prefer their own rendering of the language they have a perfect right to do so, but in fairness let them remember that it is a corruption of pure British speech' ('Visitor,' 31 May, p 12). Every year produced further comment: on 24 September 1954, 'I am an Englishman who has been in New Zealand for just over two years ... [T]he thing that amazes me is the fact that the great majority of New Zealanders are completely unaware that they themselves have a strong "local" accent; and it is a horrible accent ... This letter is written in a friendly spirit ... but I believe that the BBC has set the standard for the whole English-speaking world ... ' (p 5).
73 *Red Funnel* (1 December 1905) 385–6
74 C.A.M.L. Wheeler, 'Mavourneen,' *Pataka*, ed. John Kington (Auckland: K System, n.d.) 29
75 9, no. 3 (March 1937) 165
76 To a lesser degree, the fourteen sketches, meditative essays, conversations, and indirect narratives that constitute Alice F. Webb's *Miss Peter's Special and Other Stories* (1926) also present an insider's record of women's rural experience.
77 *The New Zealander* (London: J.M. Dent 1928) 22
78 *The Poet's Progress* (London: Faber & Faber 1930) 40
79 'Literature in New Zealand,' *The Bookman* (February 1930); bound with R.A.K. Mason, 'New Zealand Literature: Critical Methods Condemned' 13
80 'Katherine Mansfield,' *New Zealand Artists Annual* 1, no. 3 (1928) 69, 71
81 *The Road to Erewhon* (Auckland: Beaux Arts 1976) 77
82 'Mansfield: How Stands She Today?,' *New Zealand Listener* (11 October 1968) 9
83 'Oak Not Ash' (pseud.), writing 'Katherine Mansfield,' *New Zealand Listener* (2 March 1951) 5
84 Published 7 October 1966, the editorial was reprinted in Holcroft's *Graceless Islanders* (Christchurch: Caxton 1970) 34. The tenor of his comments permeates much of the sociocritical commentary of Bill Pearson and R.M. Chapman as well. See Pearson's 'Fretful Sleepers,' *Landfall* 6, no. 3 (1952) 201–30, and Chapman's 'Fiction and the Social Pattern,' *Landfall* 7, no. 1 (1953)

26–58. Both these essays ably analyse the value system of the 1950s and its implications for writers, but by the 1970s the social structure and writers' reactions to it had substantially altered; the reader must be wary not to accept the analyses in them as categorical absolutes. There is a history of some cautious attitudinal change. Oliver Duff's *New Zealand Now* (1941), for example, sees less need than either Pearson or Chapman to be concerned with the New Zealand identity; aware of some differences between New Zealand and the UK, Duff nevertheless also considers the notion of New Zealand citizenship to be a dubious proposition.

Earlier still, Alan Mulgan's *Home: A Colonial's Adventure* (1927) begins with presumptions about New Zealand's Englishness, presumptions that closer acquaintance with England rapidly challenges, and the book's closing reacquaintance with New Zealand constitutes an important step in the emergence of a new stage of New Zealand cultural nationalism. As far as other influences on New Zealand's national self-image are concerned, it is hard to underestimate the impact of the two world wars, not only because of the contribution and sacrifice that were involved (the rhetorical image of the gallant fighting unit overlaps with that of the pressured rugby scrum), but also because of the reluctant shift in political reliance that took place in the 1940s: from the UK, which left the South Pacific, to the United States, which then entered it.

85 'Some Aspects of N.Z. Art and Letters,' *Art in New Zealand* 6, no. 4 (June 1934) 218, 216

86 'Fun of the Ordinary,' *New Zealand Listener* (3 February 1956) 14. Cf. the anglophile Oliver Duff's less enthusiastic review of David Ballantyne's *The Cunninghams*: 'It is a picture of New Zealand by a New Zealander working with an American brush' (*New Zealand Listener* [1 April 1949] 10). Terry Sturm has admirably surveyed Anthony's career in his introduction to Anthony's *Follow the Call* (Auckland: Auckland Univ. Press & Oxford Univ. Press 1975) vii–xli.

87 See eg, the issues for 17 December 1943 (on Canadian radio); 23 June 1944 (on Canada's plentiful supply of paper, its ignorance of New Zealand, and its eagerness to clarify its post-war relationship with England); 14 February 1947 (on Canadian art: 'It took Canadians more than a hundred years to see the world, even their own world, with Canadian eyes,' p 32); 19 August 1949 (on overheated Canadian houses); 22 June 1951 (on Canada's 84th birthday); 4 April 1952 (on James Michener's drawing a likeness between New Zealand and Canada); 30 October 1953 (on Canadian music); 11 January 1957 (on Reuben Ship's play *The Investigator*); 8 August 1958 (on Stephen Leacock). Increasingly during these years, however, the *Listener* testifies to the importance of radio as a medium for New Zealand short fiction, and fastens its attention on New Zealand practice more than on foreign models.

88 *A History of New Zealand Fiction ... from 1862 to the Present Time with Some Account of Its Relation to the National Life and Character* (Dunedin and Wellington: Reed 1939) 26.

89 31 May 1946, p 5

90 (25 October 1940) 19
91 'Under the Sun,' *New Zealand Listener* (27 October 1944) 21.
92 (Wellington: Reed 1975) 93–6
93 *More than Enough* 50–1
94 Reminiscent of Allen Curnow's poem 'The Unhistoric Story' (1941), which avers that New Zealand's is a history of 'something different, something nobody counted on.' See *A Small Room with Large Windows* (London: Oxford 1962) 7–8.
95 In 'New Zealand: Frank Sargeson and Colloquial Realism,' *The New English Literatures* (London: Macmillan 1980), Bruce King goes so far as to argue that 'the imitation of the "people" does not offer sufficient material and technical interest to make an artistic tradition. If it is necessary to liberate a new national literature from foreign dominance ... it is also necessary to go beyond the sketch, the short story, the life of the poor ... to larger literary forms and more complex material' (p 149).
96 'The First Wasp,' in *The Puritan and the Waif* (Auckland: H.L. Hoffmann 1954) 4, 5
97 'Back to the Desert,' in *The Puritan* 7, 11
98 'The Persistence of Realism: Dan Davin, Noel Hilliard and Recent New Zealand Short Stories,' *Islands* no. 20 (December 1977) 182–200
99 'The Making of a Book,' *Landfall* no. 108 (December 1973) 283.
100 *Ibid*. 276
101 'New Zealand,' *Kenyon Review* 31 (1969) 70
102 'The Making of a Book' 281
103 *All Part of the Game: The Stories of A.P. Gaskell*, ed. R.A. Copland (Auckland: Auckland Univ. Press & Oxford Univ. Press 1978) 15, 60, 161
104 Translated from *Letras e Artes* by Mrs S.R. Nathan and J.C. Reid, as 'Literary Life in Erewhon,' *New Zealand Listener* (18 February 1949) 16
105 'Back to the Desert,' *The Puritan and the Waif* 16
106 See W.H. New, 'Entering the Shadow: New Zealand Short Fiction in the 1970's,' *Pilgrims* 8 n.s. (Summer 1980) 73–9.
107 *Islands* no. 21 (March 1978) 214
108 'Violence in Drama and Literature,' *New Zealand Listener* (16 May 1969) 13; my italics
109 'Three Encounters Thirty Years Ago,' *Islands* no. 21 (March 1978) 303
110 'The Narrative Technique of Frank Sargeson,' in *The Puritan and the Waif* 58
111 'A Note on the Work of Colin McCahon,' *Landfall* no. 16 (December 1950) 338
112 'Class of Our Own,' *New Zealand Listener* (5 January 1980) 6
113 See Patricia Grace: *Waiariki* (1975), *The Dream Sleepers and Other Stories* (1980); Hone Tuwhare: *Making a Fist of It: Poems and Short Stories* (1978); Witi Ihimaera: *Pounamu Pounamu* (1972), *The New Net Goes Fishing* (1977). Albert Wendt's emergence in the 1960s indicates the appearance of a separate Samoan literature in English as well. Educated in New Zealand, Wendt also began to publish there – in the *Arts Festival Yearbook* for 1962 and 1963 and elsewhere – before returning to his homeland; but he cannot be claimed by

either of these facts to figure any way but tangentially in New Zealand literary history. Longman Paul published his collection of eight stories and a novel, *Flying-Fox in a Freedom Tree* in Auckland in 1974. Like some of the Maori writers, he makes use of Polynesian myth and of English fabular form, sometimes combining these formal features with a sharp exposé of racism, but this practice shows a common attempt to deal with an oral heritage and an urban experience rather than an *identity* of culture. For one thing, Samoan is the majority culture in Western Samoa, and the Samoan language actively in use.

114 *Farvel and Other Stories* (Wellington: Victoria Univ. Press with Price Milburn [1980]) 31. The book as a whole is not, however, consistently comic, and in other passages comments on the pressures of discrimination. Its main purpose is to detail a young girl's acquisition of language – a phrase that is to be understood in two ways: her formal learning of English and her emotional learning of her now multiple cultural inheritance. By casting her stories in the characteristic modes of earlier New Zealand writers, and yet altering them to her own purpose, du Fresne lays claim structurally to a New Zealand literary tradition, in the process making it her own to modify. See W.H. New, 'Yvonne du Fresne,' *Landfall* no. 136 (December 1980) 374–9.
115 'Only a Matter of Grammar,' *The Full Circle of the Travelling Cuckoo* (Christchurch: Whitcombe & Tombs 1967) 28
116 As in 'One of the Titans,' *Full Circle* 71
117 (London and Toronto: J.M. Dent 1930) v–viii
118 (21 December 1945) 25
119 In 'The best yet,' *N.Z. Listener* (15 September 1984) 68, Davin acknowledges the assistance of Sargeson and Eric McCormick in the preparation of the first Oxford anthology.
120 'Short Stories: An Essay,' in *The Gypsies* (Wellington: Victoria Univ. Press with Price Milburn 1978) 110
121 (Christchurch: Caxton 1942) 46
122 'Strange Tale of the Manners Street Model,' *Free to Laugh & Dance* 38
123 (London: Oxford 1953; rpt 1961) 7
124 Drawing on Helen Shaw's 1980 essay 'Some Theories and Aims' (*Pilgrims* 8 [1980] 58), Lawrence Jones traces the contemporary dream-fantasy logic of writers like Russell Haley back to Shaw. Shaw writes: 'During recent years I have not been so concerned to present an extrovert outside view of life, defined as a story of realism, rather, to generate in a story or explode through it a kind of prose-poem or fragmentary poetry, out of a situation of characters, as their spoken and unspoken thoughts surface, overlap, interact. Interior and exterior must be fused, and at the same time there should be shown all the colours and fragments of things and of thinking in movement, moving not inert, in an active state to be absorbed by a reader who finds empathy towards the story.' Such a statement appears to fuse, as Duggan does, the premise of Mansfield and the early Sargeson. Fantasy, fragmentation, and a sense of motion in New Zealand fiction go back in different form beyond Shaw to Gilbert,

Mansfield, Lapham, and Lady Barker, in whose work the fantastic serves variously to subvert and to escape from empirical documentary. See 'The Inside Story: Helen Shaw, Russell Haley, & the Other Tradition,' *Islands* 31–2 (June 1981) 120–35.
125 'Klee, the Swallower,' *Numbers* 3, no. 2 (September 1959) 40
126 *The Edge of the Alphabet* (London: W.H. Allen 1962) 46
127 See, eg, Erik Schwimmer, 'The Oxford Approach,' *Numbers* no. 6 (March 1957) 28, and Norman Simms, 'Editorial: A Statement of Beliefs,' *Cave* no. 4 (1977) 296.
128 Rpt. from *The New Zealand Listener* (27 October 1973) in Bill Manhire, ed., *N.Z. Listener Short Stories* (Wellington: Methuen 1977) 146–9
129 See Janet Frame, 'Beginnings,' *Landfall* no. 73 (March 1965) 45.
130 *The Lagoon and Other Stories* (Christchurch: Caxton 1961) 50
131 *The Lagoon* 58
132 *Ibid.* 92–3
133 *Snowman Snowman* (New York: Braziller 1963) 68–9
134 'The Short Stories of Maurice Duggan,' *Landfall* 25 (March 1971) 68
135 Introduction to Maurice Duggan, *Collected Stories* (Auckland: Auckland Univ. Press & Oxford Univ. Press 1981) 13
136 'Short Stories of Maurice Duggan' 52. See also H.W. Rhodes, 'Maurice Duggan,' in his *New Zealand Fiction since 1945* (Dunedin: John McIndoe 1968) 38; Lawrence Jones, review of *Summer in the Gravel Pit*, *Landfall* 19, no. 3 (September 1965) 289; Dan Davin, 'Telling What Was Real,' *New Zealand Listener* (12 September 1981) 100–1
137 *Immanuel's Land* (Auckland: Pilgrim Press 1956) 99
138 *Collected Stories* 359
139 Printed in C.K. Stead's 'Notes on Texts and Publishing Matters,' *Collected Stories* 378
140 *Immanuel's Land* 12, 33
141 *O'Leary's Orchard and Other Stories* (Christchurch: Caxton 1970) 134–5
142 *Ibid.* 73
143 See Lawrence Jones, 'Craft Interview with Owen Marshall,' *Landfall* 38 (June 1984) 226–41
144 *All the Dangerous Animals Are in Zoos* (Auckland: Longman Paul 1981) 72. On contemporary trends, see Lydia Wevers, 'Changing Directions: The Short Story in New Zealand,' *Meanjin* 44 (September 1985) 352–6. Subsequent anthologies include Marion McLeod and Bill Manhire, eds., *Some Other Country: New Zealand's Best Stories* (Wellington: Unwin / Port Nicholson Press, 1984); Marion McLeod and Lydia Wevers, eds., *Women's Work: Contemporary Stories by New Zealand Women* (Auckland: Oxford, 1985); and Michael Morrissey, ed., *The New Fiction* (Auckland: Lindon Publishing, 1985). The last contains a particularly useful theoretical introduction.
145 *Dangerous Animals* 34. Rpt. in Stead's *Five for the Symbol* (Auckland: Longman Paul 1981)
146 *Dangerous Animals* 35

147 *The Shirt Factory* (Wellington: Victoria Univ. Press with Price Milburn 1981) 39
148 *Dandy Edison for Lunch* (Dunedin: John McIndoe 1981) 129
149 'The Maori in Literature,' in Michael King, ed., *Tihe Maori Ora: Aspects of Maoritanga* (n.p.: Methuen 1978) 82
150 (Auckland: Heinemann 1977) 146. See also Miriama Evans, 'The Politics of Maori Literature,' *Meanjin* 44 (September 1985) 358–63.
151 See John Beston, 'An Interview with Witi Ihimaera,' *WLWE*, 16 (April 1977) 118, 125; and David Young, 'An End to the Silence,' *NZ Listener* (7 June 1986) 24–25.

CHAPTER FOUR: ALTERING CYCLES

1 'Canadian Short-Story Writers,' *Canadian Magazine* 4, no. 4 (February 1895) 338–9. Brodie was apparently commenting on the manuscript; six of the sketches had appeared in *Scribner*'s between 1887 and 1893, but not all ten.
2 'Duncan Campbell Scott,' *Canadian Magazine* 43 (1914) 72
3 See his letters to E.K. Brown, collected as *The Poet and the Critic*, ed. Robert L. MacDougall (Ottawa: Carleton Univ. Press 1983) 144–5; the notes (p 256) include the complete text of Sandwell's 23 June 1945 *Saturday Night* review.
4 Carole Gerson draws attention to this aspect of his realism in 'The Piper's Forgotten Tune,' *Journal of Canadian Fiction* 16 (1976) 138–43.
5 Raymond Knister's 1928 anthology includes 'Labrie's Wife,' from *The Witching of Elspie*; Ryerson Press later released 'Paul Farlotte,' from *In the Village of Viger*, to anthologies by Desmond Pacey and Robert Weaver,; other anthology selections have since followed.
6 See *The Poet and the Critic* 250.
7 *Ibid.* 112, 114
8 *More Letters of Duncan Campbell Scott* (2nd series), ed. Arthur S. Bourinot (Ottawa: the Editor 1960) 88
9 *The Poet and the Critic* 139
10 *Ibid.* 138, 254
11 *Ibid.* 185
12 (Toronto: McClelland & Stewart 1973) 12–13
13 Duncan Campbell Scott, 'The Wooing of Monsieur Cuerrier,' *In the Village of Viger and Other Stories* (Toronto: McClelland & Stewart 1973) 33
14 *Ibid.* 41
15 *Ibid.* 49
16 *Ibid.* 52
17 *Ibid.* 19, 26
18 *Ibid.* 75
19 *Ibid.* 77

CHAPTER FIVE: NO LONGER LIVING THERE

1 Critics have fastened primarily on the social and personal revelations of the

book. Clara Thomas emphasizes the autobiographical nature of the quest, in *The Manawaka World of Margaret Laurence* (Toronto: McClelland & Stewart 1973); Patricia Morley stresses that the eight stories reveal a society, and suggests that the stories are representative in character – 'Horses of the Night,' for example, depicting 'social madness through the personal disorder of one casualty' (p 118) – in *Margaret Laurence* (Boston: Twayne 1981) 109–19; Frank Birbalsingh summarizes what he calls the 'pattern of victimization and endurance within a doomed world order,' in 'Margaret Laurence's Short Stories,' *World Literature Today* 56, no. 1 (Winter 1982) 30–6; and George Woodcock focuses on the authenticity of the portrait of emotional relations and the prairie Depression, in 'Jungle and Prairie' (1970, rpt. in his ed., *A Place to Stand On* (Edmonton: NeWest, 1983) 229–31.
2 *A Bird in the House* (Toronto: McClelland & Stewart 1970) 3
3 *Bird* 59. See also Michael Darling, '"Undecipherable Signs": Margaret Laurence's "To Set Our House in Order",' *Essays on Canadian Writing* no. 29 (Summer 1984) 192–203, for a splendid analysis of Vanessa's maturing response to order (most notably to the illusions of order that are part of her MacLeod heritage) and of Laurence's textual skill in representing it. Two articles by Arnold E. Davidson explore various parallels between Vanessa and her father, her Grandfather Connor, and Aunt Edna, stressing Laurence's use of synecdoche and symbol as she depicts the connections between (lived, recorded) past and (real, artistic) present; see 'Unhiding the Hidden in Margaret Laurence's "The Mask of the Bear",' *Inscape* 14 (1978) 73–7, and 'Cages and Escapes in Margaret Laurence's *A Bird in the House*,' *University of Windsor Review* 16 (Fall-Winter 1981) 92–101.
4 'Review of *A Bird in the House*' (1970); rpt. in *A Place to Stand On* 233
5 Rpt. in *A Place to Stand On* 157. Laurence wrote the stories in England from 1962 on, adding the final story for the book publication.
6 Pp 156–8. Sherrill Grace finds parallels with Bergsonian time in these stories; see 'Crossing Jordan: Time and Memory in the Fiction of Margaret Laurence,' *WLWE* 16 (November 1977) 328–39.
7 'Time' 158
8 *Bird* 3
9 *Ibid.* 39, 135
10 *Ibid.* 38
11 *Ibid.* 39, my italics
12 *Ibid.* 53–4
13 *Ibid.* 59
14 *Ibid.* 89
15 *Ibid.* 128, italics mine
16 *Ibid.* 155, italics mine
17 *Ibid.* 173
18 In his introduction to the New Canadian Library edition of stories (Toronto: McClelland & Stewart 1974), Robert Gibbs notes that in the book 'the real freeing has been continuous and is still in process where the book leaves off' (n.p.).

19 *Bird* 124
20 Thomas (p 97) examines the autobiographical cast of this book.
21 *Bird* 20
22 *Ibid.* 11, 15
23 *Ibid.* 11
24 *Ibid.* 13
25 *Ibid.* 40
26 *Ibid.* 70–1
27 *Ibid.* 83
28 *Ibid.* 58
29 *Ibid.* 171, my italics
30 *Ibid.* 172
31 *Ibid.* 152
32 *Ibid.* 148, 146, 152
33 *Ibid.* 153
34 *Ibid.* 57
35 *Ibid.* 154
36 *Ibid.* 137
37 *Ibid.* 142
38 *Ibid.* 154
39 *The Tragical History of Doctor Faustus* (pp xv, 93). Ovid's 'lente currite, noctis equi' appears in *Amores* I.xiii.49, which Marlowe rendered 'Then wouldst thou cry, stay night and run not thus' in his own translation of Ovid's *Elegies*. See *Ovid's Selected Works*, ed. J.C. and M.J. Thornton (London: Dent, and New York: Dutton 1939) 6.
40 *Bird* 23
41 *Ibid.* 67
42 *Ibid.* 178
43 In 'Calling Back the Ghost of the Old-time Heroine: Duncan, Montgomery, Atwood, Laurence, and Munro,' *Studies in Canadian Literature* 4 (Winter 1979) 43–58, Catherine Sheldrick Ross exmaines the motif of the Romantic Heroine, showing how 'Jericho's Brick Battlements' both employs and reverses the compositional structures of romantic fiction.
44 *Bird* 120–1
45 *Ibid.* 126
46 *Ibid.* 36–7
47 *Ibid.* 207

CHAPTER SIX: PRONOUNS AND PROPOSITIONS

1 Alice Munro, *Something I've Been Meaning to Tell You* (Toronto: McGraw-Hill Ryerson 1974) 24
2 Quoted in John Metcalf, ed., *The Narrative Voice* (Toronto: McGraw-Hill Ryerson 1972) 22
3 *Something I've Been Meaning to Tell You* 1

4 *Ibid.* 23
5 *Ibid.* 93
6 *Ibid.* 173
7 *Ibid.* 191
8 *Ibid.* 246
9 *Ibid.* 179
10 *Ibid.* 91–2
11 *Ibid.* 67
12 *Ibid.* 66
13 *Ibid.* 61
14 *Ibid.* 117
15 *Ibid.* 199
16 *Ibid.* 83
17 *Ibid.* 106
18 *Ibid.* 123–4
19 *Ibid.* 227
20 *Ibid.* 246
21 *Ibid.* 221

CHAPTER SEVEN: PRONOUNCING SILENCE

1 *Collected Stories* (1945, rpt London: Constable 1964) 205, 241
2 Mansfield criticism was long confined to biographical summations and personal impressions, growing slowly to pay close attention to text. A general summary like that of C.W. Stanley is representative of early commentary: 'The Art of Katherine Mansfield,' *Dalhousie Review* 10 (April 1930) 26–41. Commentary on 'At the Bay,' moreover, was usually lodged in more general studies of theme or motif. Peter Alcock, 'An Aloe in the Garden: Something Essentially New Zealand in Miss Mansfield,' *Journal of Commonwealth Literature* 11 (April 1977) 58–64, and Don W. Kleine, 'An Eden for Insiders,' *College English* 27 (December 1965) 201–9, examine the cultural force of setting, Kleine emphasizing its restrictiveness: the 'hypnotic calm of the New Zealand fictions signifies a violent truce within the author' (p 209). Eileen Baldeshwiler, 'Katherine Mansfield's Theory of Fiction,' *Studies in Short Fiction* 7 (Summer 1970) 421–32, and C.K. Stead, 'Katherine Mansfield and the Art of Fiction,' *New Review* 4 (September 1977) 27–36, stress, respectively, her quest for 'honesty' in craft and the 'authenticity' of her use of detail.
  Fern Corin analyses closely the first section of 'At the Bay,' revealing how the prose structure and the use of detail effectively establish the story's tone, in 'Creation of Atmosphere in Katherine Mansfield's Stories,' *Revue des Langues Vivantes* 22 (1956) 65–78. Toby Silverman Zinman, 'The Snail under the Leaf: Katherine Mansfield's Imagery,' *Modern Fiction Studies* 24 (1978–9) 457–64, examines victim imagery in 'At the Bay,' and David Daiches, 'The Art of Katherine Mansfield,' *New Literary Values* (1936; rpt Freeport, NY: Books

for Libraries 1968) 83–114, applauds the effectiveness of the author's stylistic arrangement of details.

Other critics have focused on psychology and theme. George Shelton Hubbell, in 'Katherine Mansfield and Kezia,' *Sewanee Review* 35 (July 1927) 325–35, initiated a line of criticism that celebrated Kezia Burnell as a 'complete child,' a representative of the potential fullness of life, a view that is effectively countered by David Dowling, 'Aunt Beryl's Doll's House,' *Landfall* 34 (June 1980) 148–58, who finds Beryl more central to the Burnell stories, and the stories themselves more 'revolutionary' than is implied by readings which fasten on 'the wonders of childhood imagination' (p 157). Stead refers to 'At the Bay' and 'Prelude,' taken together, as 'The Four Ages of Woman' (p 32). André Maurois, 'Katherine Mansfield,' *Poets and Progress*, trans. Hamish Miles (London: Cassell 1936) 223–45, refers to her technique as '*feminine* impressionism' (p 239). Marie Jean Lederman, 'Through the Looking-Glass: Queens, Dreams, Fears in the Fiction of Katherine Mansfield,' *Women's Studies* 5 (1977) 35–49, reads Mansfield's fictions as a web of 'attempts to liberate herself' from the dualistic conflicts of personality and 'the prevailing role and image of Woman' (p 35), and sees the doubling of characters in 'At the Bay,' 'Bliss,' and 'Prelude' (ie, the sisterhood of Linda and Beryl) as a classic Freudian 'split of the woman into the Virgin and the Whore' (p 40).

Though finding 'At the Bay' to lack 'the complexity of imagery and association of "Prelude",' Marvin Magalaner applauds Mansfield's 'artistic representation of what life is about,' focusing on the motif of freedom and the author's 'symbol' of water: *The Fiction of Katherine Mansfield* (Carbondale and Edwardsville: Southern Illinois Univ. Press, and London and Amsterdam: Feffer and Simons 1971) esp. 39–45. Saralyn Daly, *Katherine Mansfield* (New York: Twayne 1965) 92–101, reads the story as a debate between order and disorder. In their reading of the story, Clare Hanson and Andrew Gurr, *Katherine Mansfield* (London: Macmillan 1981) esp. 99–106, stress the modernist assumptions of the story ('Man's life is no more than a single day' and, conversely, 'the whole of a man's life can be revealed during the course of a single day,' p 99), the thematic unity of its narrative 'free form,' and its reliance on Bergsonian notions of time: the male characters live by 'clock time,' the women by 'real time' (p 102). Vincent O'Sullivan, 'The Magnetic Chain: Notes and Approaches to K.M.' *Landfall* 29 (1975) 95–131, offers a guide to Mansfield's broken form, associative technique, and exploration of bisexuality. Cherry A. Hankin, *Katherine Mansfield and Her Confessional Stories* (London: Macmillan 1983) 222–34, integrates a number of these issues: motifs of sea and sun, Jungian unconscious, mother-figures, and animal imagery; her focus, however, is on the theme of death, and on what she sees as Mansfield's effort to reconcile a Wordsworthian sensibility with 'her perception that nature ... shares in the attributes of a loving Christian God' (p 234).

3 *Stories* 205, 208, 212–13, 216, 220, 223–4, 227–9, 231, 234–5, 238–40, 243–5

Notes to pages 214–27

4 *Ibid.* 207
5 *Ibid.* 205
6 *Ibid.* 208
7 *Ibid.* 209
8 *Ibid.* 213
9 *Ibid.* 236
10 *Ibid.* 220
11 Anthony Alpers, for example, writes that '*At the Bay* has some weak moments ... A more serious defect occurs in the portrayal of Alice: the dislike of her which Beryl feels becomes the author's too, and distracts attention from her important role' – a role which, for Alpers, lies in her evocation of bush stillness, the symbolic form of colonial isolation. See *The Life of Katherine Mansfield* (London: Jonathan Cape 1980) 346.
12 *Stories* 228
13 *Ibid.* 229
14 *Ibid.* 230
15 *Ibid.* 231
16 *Ibid.* 233
17 *Ibid.* 237
18 *Ibid.* 220, 231, 244
19 *Ibid.* 227

CHAPTER EIGHT: SAYING SPEECH

1 *The Stories of Frank Sargeson* (Auckland: Penguin 1982) 10
2 *Ibid.* 9
3 *Ibid.* 9–10
4 *Waiariki* (Auckland: Longman Paul 1975) 3. John B. Beston's 'The Fiction of Patricia Grace,' *Ariel* 15 (April 1984) 41–53, descriptively summarizes Grace's themes; Beston finds her an ethnic writer who strives to avoid offence, an effective pastoral scene-painter rather than a strong story-teller. By contrast, Bill Pearson, 'Witi Ihimaera and Patricia Grace,' in Cherry Hankin, ed., *Critical Essays on the New Zealand Short Story* (Auckland: Heinemann 1982) 166–84, and Norman Simms, 'Maori Prose Writers: Patricia Grace,' *Pacific Moana Quarterly* 3 (April 1978) 186–99, stress the effectiveness and the limitations of her meditative and 'macaronic' style.
5 *Waiariki* 1
6 *Ibid.* 2
7 *Ibid.*
8 *Ibid.*
9 *Ibid.* 3, my italics
10 *Ibid.*
11 *Ibid.* 4
12 *Ibid.* 5
13 *Ibid.*

CHAPTER NINE: UNSAYING MEMORY

1 (26 May 1984) 21
2 'Along Rideout Road that Summer,' *Collected Stories*, ed. C.K. Stead (Auckland: Auckland Univ. Press and Oxford Univ. Press 1981) 202
3 In one detailed article on Duggan's fiction – 'The Short Stories of Maurice Duggan,' *Landfall* 25 (March 1971) 50–1 – Terry Sturm notes this same attitude in terms of race: specifically, in terms of Buster's sentimental and apparently unconscious racism. 'Buster's simplistic equation of Puti Hohepa with his own father ... is completely fallacious ... The *real* equation, which Buster never sees, is between his father and *himself*, both of whom insist on seeing the situation in a simple single dimension ... What finally emerges is that Buster's conception of "freedom" carries with it the danger of a crippling kind of irresponsibility and ignorance' (p 61).

Patrick Evans's 'Maurice Duggan and the Provincial Dilemma,' *Landfall* 36 (June 1982) 217–31, usefully extends the implications of Duggan's concern for race, religion, and language by showing how Duggan draws variously on Sargeson (the Lenihan stories and the 'that Summer' allusion in the title of 'Rideout Road') and on Mansfield (the parallel openings of 'O'Leary's Orchard' and 'The Garden-Party') in order to break past – or to try repeatedly to break past – the ethos of a provincial culture.

In 'Towards an Appropriate Language, *London Magazine* n.s. 22 (October 1982) 46–54, Trevor James reiterates the view that a certain kind of 'narrow ... piety' (p 47) lies at the back of the New Zealand writer's thwarted flight from restriction and his accompanying quest for revelation through language; James is discussing Sargeson; but the limited world he describes is the one Evans sees as the bequest left to Duggan and in turn to Janet Frame. Like Sturm, Evans sees 'Along Rideout Road that Summer' as a 'touching and comical' inversion (p 228) of the prototypical images and events of New Zealand provincial fiction.
4 'Rideout Road,' 196
5 *Ibid.* 208; italics mine
6 *Ibid.* 200–1, 205
7 *Ibid.* 200
8 *Ibid.* 203–4; my italics
9 *Ibid.* 200
10 *Ibid.* 205; my italics
11 *Ibid.* 197, 201
12 'I could say, indeed I will say, stony silence.' 'Rideout Road' 200
13 *Ibid.* 198, 199, 202, 203
14 *Ibid.* 208
15 *Ibid.* 198
16 *Ibid.* 199
17 *Ibid.* 206
18 *Ibid.* 196–7

19 *Ibid.* 196, 200, 202
20 *Ibid.* 209; my italics
21 *Ibid.* 208
22 *Ibid.* 209
23 Dan Davin reads the story as the 'mature and ironical reflections' of an older man on 'the basically simple and lyrical tale of a passing youthful love affair,' beginning with an escape from home and ending with a relieved escape from entrapment. See 'Maurice Duggan's Summer in the Gravel Pit,' in *Critical Essays on the New Zealand Short Story*, ed. Cherry Hankin (Auckland: Heinemann 1982) 160–1. It is possible, however, to see Buster's recurrent flight from women in a less engaging light.

Index

Abbot, Joseph 260
Acadian Recorder 35
Accent. *See* language.
Achebe, Chinua 15, 98
Adam, Graeme Mercer 43
Addison, Joseph 67
Adventures of Sajo and Her Beaver People, The 59
Africa 7, 15, 20, 25, 57, 79, 87, 100–1, 114, 126, 169
African Millionaire, An 56, 57
Aiken, Conrad 4
Aleichem, Sholom. *See* Sholom Aleichem.
Alford, Edna 106
Alibi 94
Allen, Grant 50, 56–8, 61, 263
Allen, Walter 5
All Part of the Game 146
All the Dangerous Animals Are in Zoos 169–70
Almost Meeting, The 88
'Along Rideout Road that Summer' 164, 165, 166, 229–35, 284–5
Amato, Renato 154, 155, 156, 160
'American Made' 72
Amores 198, 280
Anatomy of Criticism 95
'Ancient Lineage' 74–5
And the Glory 147
'And the Hilltop Was Elizabeth' 85
Anderson, Johannes C. 123, 127

Anderson, D.M. 157
Anderson, Sherwood 4, 72, 77, 98, 142, 143, 145, 265
Anderson, W.F.R. 142
Andrews, Isobel 152
anecdote 9, 14–16, 35, 41, 56, 90, 107, 116, 121, 122, 127, 129, 141, 151, 156, 167, 198, 230
animal stories 9, 41, 59–60, 68, 170
Annals of the Parish 260–1
Anno Domini 2000 123
'Annual Affair, An' 157
anthologies 24, 54–6, 65–7, 70–1, 80–1, 82, 96, 98, 105, 106–7, 138, 146, 156–8, 168, 169–70, 172
Anthology 80, 84
Anthony, Frank S. 141, 150–1
'Anyone Home?' 157
'Appetite for Flowers, An' 166
Appleby, M. 153
'Apple Mash' 159
Arabic tradition 61
Arnason, David 106
Arcadian Adventures with the Idle Rich 62–3, 272
Around the Mountain 99, 109
Ashton-Warner, Sylvia 155
Asia 87, 169, 260, 270
'At Lehmann's' 134
'At the Bay' 132, 134, 135, 136, 160, 211–20, 281–3
Athenaeum, The 130

Attaché, The 35, 36–7, 38
Atwood, Margaret 87, 100, 106, 107
Australia 5, 15, 20, 23, 25, 66, 87, 126, 128–9, 139, 141, 144, 174, 212, 258, 270
Avis, Walter 37
Aylmer, Mrs J.E. 20, 118

Baden-Powell, Sir Robert 59
Baer, Bill 169
Baeyertz, Charles Nalder 128–9
Bail, Murray 15
Bailey, Richard 98
Baines, W.M. 117
Baker, Ida 133
Baker, Louisa 125
Ballantyne, David 147, 149, 156
Ballstadt, Carl 33
'Bank Holiday' 131
Barclay Family Theatre, The 102
Baring-Gould, Sabine 42, 126
Barker, Lady (Mary Anne Stewart, Lady Broome) 20, 120–2, 124, 156, 277
Barnard, Leslie Gordon 71, 78
Barnett, John 169
Barr, Robert 43, 56, 61
Barthelme, John 202
Bates, H.E. 5
'Bath, The' 162
Bathgate, Alexander 119
Batistich, Amelia 154, 155, 156
Baucke, William 122, 127
Bauer, Nancy 106
Baughan, Blanche 20, 120, 122, 130
Baum, L. Frank 173
Baxter, James K. 144, 150, 154, 159
Bayley, Mrs 260
Beachcroft, T.O. 5
'Beau' 145
Becker, May Lamberton 55
Beggar Maid, The 104
'Beginnings' 167
'Being a Truthful Adventure' 134
'Bells of Sobor Spasitula, The' 90–1

Bension, Ariel 89
Bentley, John 167
Bentley, Richard 32
'Big Game, The' 157
Big Game, The 146
Big Season, The 172
Bilir, Kim 53
Bird, Will 79
'Bird in the House, A' 187, 192
Bird in the House, A 102, 187–200, 242
Birdsell, Sandra 106
'Birthday, A' 133
Bissoondath, Neil 106
'Black Cap, The' 132
Blackwood's Edinburgh Magazine 260
Blaise, Clark 87, 96, 103–4, 106, 107, 202
Blank, Arapera 155
'Blind, The' 157
'Bliss' 136
Bliss 130
Blue Mountains of China, The 102
Blue Review, The 130
'Blues for Miss Laverty' 166
'Boat, The' 70
'Bobolink, The' 181, 182, 183, 184, 185
Bolitho, Hector 139
Bonheim, Helmut 5, 13
Book of Canadian Stories, A 81
Borges, Jorge Luis 10, 15
Bouchette, Errol 51
Bourinot, J.G. 42
Bowen, Elizabeth 4, 8
Bowering, George 107–8, 110–11
Bowker, Alan 62
'Boy' 144, 145
Boy the Bridge the River, The 171
Bradbrook, Muriel 24
Braden, Bernie 81
Brady, E.J. 129
Brasch, Charles 147, 152, 154
Brautigan, Richard 99
'Bravest Boat, The' 93

Breathing Spaces 146
Brémond, Claude 6
Brett, Dorothy 132
Brewster, Elizabeth 102
Brodie, Allan Douglas 4, 52
'Broken Globe, The' 88
Brontë, Emily 136
Brooker, Bertram 76
Brown, E.K. 178, 179, 185
Brown, J. Edward 168
Brown Bread from a Colonial Oven 130
Brown Man's Burden 146
Buckler, Ernest 79
Bullock, Marie 152
Bullock, Michael 106
Bunyan, John 163
Burnett, Virgil 106

Caldwell, Ned 260
Calisher, Hortense 267
Callaghan, Morley 4, 55, 56, 57, 65–8, 71–8, 81, 88, 89, 98, 99, 143
Cameron, Anne 87
Canada 3–112, 116, 126, 128, 139, 141, 144, 170, 177–210, 239–45, 259, 269, 270, 274
Canada Council 96
Canadian Accent 82
Canadian Forum, The 78
Canadian Magazine, The 43, 49–50, 54, 80
Canadian Nights 56–7
Canadian Short Stories (Knister) 55, 65
Canadian Short Stories (Weaver) 81
'Cap for Steve, A' 74
Cape Breton Tales 55
Cariboo Country 81
Carman, Bliss 43, 56
Carr, Emily 61
Carrier, Jean-Guy 106
Carswell, John 114
Carter, Dyson 78
Celebration 143
'Chaddeleys and Flemings' 104
Chalmers, Floyd S. 264

Chambers, C. Haddon 270
'Champion, The' 168
Chapman, H.S. 116
Chapman, Robert 243
'Chapter' 165
'Chassidic Song' 88
Chekhov, Anton 4, 10, 77, 113, 137, 149
Cheney, Harriet V. 260
'Chief's Daughter, The' 128
Christmas Cake in Four Quarters, A 121
Christmas in French Canada 51
Circle of Affection, The 49
Clarke, Austin 87–8
Clarke, Marcus 66
class 32, 49, 71, 74, 78, 85, 88, 90, 135, 140, 155, 172, 191, 221–4, 226, 242–3
'Class of New Canadians, A' 104
Clockmaker, The 14, 35, 36, 37
Cody, Hiram 53
Cohen, Matt 108, 110–11
Cole, John Reece 147, 149, 152
Coleridge, Samuel Taylor 135, 164
'Come Ye Apart' 85
'Connection' 104
Connor, Ralph 50, 53, 56
Conrad, Joseph 4, 43
'Conversation with My Uncle' 143, 221–4, 227–8
Conversation with My Uncle 143
Cooper, James Fenimore 115
Copeland, Ann 87, 106
Coppard, A.E. 4
copyright 18, 20
Cotnoir, Louise x
Courage, James 147, 150, 152
'Cousins' 173
Cowley, Joy 155, 167
Cresswell, D'Arcy 139, 141, 144
Crowded Out! 43
'Crows, The' 152
Crump, Barry 150–1, 164, 167
Cuckoo Clock House 81
Curnow, Allen 275

Cushing, Eliza 260
'Cynical Tale, A' 108

Dale, W.S. 139
Dalziel, Margaret 162
Dance Me Outside 81
Dance of the Happy Shades 104, 207
Dancers at Night 102
Dark Glasses 109
Dark Must Yield 106
Daudet, Alphonse 264
'Daughters of the Late Colonel, The' 93, 132
Davidson, William 120, 122
Davin, Dan 24, 116, 146, 147, 149, 150–1, 154, 156–7, 158, 163, 164, 171, 285
Dawson, E.P. 157
'Day of the Sheep, The' 161
de la Roche, Mazo 55, 56
de Mauny, Erik 154
de Maupassant, Guy 4
Death Goes Better with Coca-Cola 102
'Delicate Subject, A' 128
Dempster, Barry 106
Denison, Merrill 55, 56, 65, 69, 70
Dennis, C.J. 15
Dent, John Charles 57
'Desjardins, The' 180, 182, 184
Devanny, Jean 153, 159
dialect. *See* language.
Dickens, Charles 63, 98, 120, 121
'Diffuseness' 50
Distant Homes 118
Doctor Faustus 198
documentary form 21, 30–1, 35, 48, 58–60, 92, 94, 100, 101, 109–11, 117–20, 124, 128, 131, 137, 146, 152, 160, 162, 168, 171, 239–40, 244, 264
Domett, Alfred 116
Donnell, David 106
Dove's Nest, The 130
Down North on the Labrador 58
Dragland, Stan L. 30, 179–80

Drainie, John 81
'Drink with Adolphus, A' 87
Drummond, William Henry 51, 56
Dryden, Ken 100
du Fresne, Yvonne 154, 155, 168, 169, 172, 276
Dubliners 163
'Ducharmes of the Baskatonge, The' 45–6
Duckworth, Marilyn 154, 159
Duff, Oliver 142, 273
Duggan, Maurice 146, 149, 150, 154, 157, 158, 160, 163–7, 171, 172, 229–35, 276, 284–5
Duncan, Norman 43, 53, 55, 56, 61
Duncan, Sara Jeannette 20, 43–5, 62, 87, 114

Earth's Enigmas 60
'Editing the Best' 98
Edmond, Murray 167
Edwards, Bob 81
Eikhenbaum, Boris M. 5, 16
Elizabeth and Her German Garden 132
Elliott, George 96, 103
Else, Chris 155
'En Route' 145
endings 103, 202–10
'Enemy, The' 84, 85
'Enemy of the People, An' 265
Engel, Marian 106
'Epilogue II: Violet' 272
Erskine, Albert 95
ethnicity. *See* multiculturalism.
Europe 4–5, 13, 16, 19, 23, 36, 42, 57, 67–8, 70, 79, 84, 87, 90–2, 93, 113, 116, 117, 119, 130, 133, 146, 153, 168, 169, 185
'Evening for a Fish, An' 147
Excell, Patricia 158
'Executioners' 204, 208
'Eyes' 104

fable 7, 9, 118, 158, 159, 162, 171, 182, 183, 276

Index

Fairburn, A.R.D. 139, 141, 142, 159
Fairchild, George Moore 64
fairytale. *See* folktale.
fantasy, mystery 41, 52, 53, 57, 96, 106, 117, 158–9, 166–7, 168–9, 171, 173, 180, 276–7
Farjeon, B.L. 120, 270
Farjeon, Eleanor 120
Farr, C.C. 54
Farvel 155, 168
Faulkner, William 4
Fawcett, Brian 106
Fearing, Kenneth 95
Ferguson, Dugald 117
Ferguson, Suzanne 5
'Feuille d'Album' 131
fictional form, comments on 39–40, 42, 44, 57, 67, 68, 72, 77, 85, 91, 97, 99, 100, 103–5, 107–12, 119, 120, 121, 123–4, 126–7, 128, 132, 141, 142, 143, 148, 149, 165, 166, 171, 188, 256, 266, 276
'Fight the Good Fight' 152
Figures in Light 147
'Fijian Girl and the Octopus, The' 138
Finlayson, Roderick 146, 147, 149, 155, 172
'First Day of Spring, The' 65
'Fitting Tribute, A' 167
Fitzgerald, F. Scott 4
Five for the Symbol 167
Flaubert, Gustave 10
'Flowers that Killed Him, The' 83
Flying a Red Kite 109
'Fog' 84
Foley, Martha 66
Folk Tales of the Maori 127
folktale, fairytale 9, 15, 21, 35, 41, 86–7, 90, 96, 107, 127, 128, 162, 182
Footner, Hulbert 51
'Forest Path to the Spring, The' 92
'Forgiveness in Families' 204
Foster, Miss 260
'Found Boat, The' 204, 208

Founding of New Societies, The 20
Four Stories 107
fracture, fragmentation ix, 3, 17–20, 23, 24–5, 42, 49, 72, 77, 88, 94–5, 96, 99, 102–5, 108, 110–11, 117, 120, 135, 136–7, 145–6, 149–50, 153, 156, 160–1, 164–5, 168–9, 170, 200, 206–7, 211, 214, 216, 222, 225, 229, 239, 241–5, 256, 276
fragmentation thesis 20, 25
Frame, Janet 154, 158, 159, 160–3, 172, 244, 284
frame stories ix, x, xi, 65, 120–1, 137, 149–50, 167, 173–4, 187, 204, 207, 215, 234, 239, 242
Fraser, C.A. 43
Fraser, Keath 106
Fraser, Malcolm 168
Fraser, Raymond 106
Fraser's Magazine 38
'Frau Brechenmacher Attends a Wedding' 133
Fréchette, Louis 51, 52, 64
Free to Laugh & Dance 158
Freeman, Mary Wilkins 4
Freeman, William 116, 125–6
French Canada, attitudes toward 42, 48, 51–2, 55, 85, 100, 177–86, 243, 260
Friel, H.J. 260
'Friends, Romans, Hungrymen' 90
'From Flores' 84
From the Fifteenth District 92
'From the Testament of Eurydice' 158
frontier thesis 19–20
Fruit Man, the Meat Man & the Manager, The 109
Frye, Northrop 14, 95
Full Circle of the Travelling Cuckoo, The 155
Furphy, Joseph 23

Gadd, Bernard 168
Gallant, Mavis 79, 80–1, 91–4, 98
Galsworthy, John 143

Galt, John 260–1
Game, The 100
Garber, Lawrence 106
García Márquez, Gabriel 99
'Garden-Party, The' 135, 136–7, 284
Garden Party, The 130
Garland, Hamlin 4, 14, 45
Garner, Hugh 88, 98
Gaskell, A.P. (Alexander Pickard) 146, 147, 149, 152–3, 157
Gee, Lyndall Chapple 157
Gee, Maurice 145, 168, 172
Gemini and Lesser Lights 53
Gerrard Street Mystery, The 57
Gerhardi, William 136
Gilbert, G.R. 154, 157–8, 276
Gilboord, Margaret Gibson 106
Giles, Mrs Henry 260
Gillespie, Gerald 9
Gillespie, O.N. 156–7
Girl in the Silk Dress, The 56, 68
'Girl with Ambition, A' 73, 157
Glorious Morning, Comrade, A 168
Glyn, Elinor 263
Godfrey, Dave 96, 102, 106
Goethe, Johann Wolfgang von 77
Golden Dog, The 34
Golden Tales of Canada 55
'Good Boy, A' 145
Good, Graham 9
Goodbye Harold, Good Luck 88
Gordimer, Nadine 15, 18–19
Gordon, Adam Lindsay 66
Gordon, Ian 124
Gorse Blooms Pale, The 146, 149, 150
Gosnell, R.E. 262
Grace, Alfred 122, 127–8, 129, 130, 151
Grace, Patricia 22, 155, 169, 172–3, 221, 224–8
Grady, Wayne 107
Graham, John 152
Grannan, Mary 81
Grant, A.K. 160
'Great Day, A' 144

'Greenstone Patu, The' 173
Greer, Germaine 99
Grenfell, Wilfred 53, 58, 263
Grey Owl (A.S. Belaney) 56, 58–9, 68, 265
Grey, Sir George 115, 118
Grossman, Edith (Searle) 116, 123, 127, 159
Grove, Frederick Philip 69–70
Gunnars, Kristjana 106, 107
Gurdjieff Institute 130, 136
Gurney, Mary 138
Gustafson, Ralph 80, 82, 88
Guthrie-Smith, W.H. 138
Guy, Ray 81
Gypsies, The 157

Habib, Rowley 155
Haley, Russell 149, 169, 170, 276
'Half-Husky, The' 187, 192, 195
Haliburton, Thomas Chandler 14–15, 29, 30, 35–42, 57, 95, 100, 260
Halliburton, Richard 196
Hancock, Geoff 107
'Hand of God, The' 123
Hanson, Clare 5
'Happily Unmarried' 168
Hardy, Thomas 4
Harrison, Susie Frances 43
Harte, Bret 13, 14, 43, 66, 115, 257
Hartz, Louis 20
Hathaway, E.J. 52
Hawthorne, Nathaniel 4, 10, 13, 71
Heaphy, Charles 117
Hear Us O Lord from Heaven Thy Dwelling-Place 92, 95
Heart of the Bush, The 123
Hemingway, Ernest 4, 6, 10, 65, 72, 76
Henry, O. 4, 5, 140
'Here Comes Your Canadian Father' 170
Hickman, Albert 56–7
Hilliard, Noel 140, 147, 151, 172
Hills, Rust 6–7
historical fiction 34, 40–1, 53–4, 92,

93–4, 103, 109–10, 144, 148, 158, 187–8, 198, 221, 229, 234–5, 239–40, 242
Hoar, Victor (Howard) 73
Hodgins, Jack 85, 96, 102, 106
Holcroft, Monte H. 137, 141
'Hole that Jack Dug, The' 144, 157
Holmes, A.S. 53
Home Truths 92
Hone Tiki Dialogues 127–8
Hood, Hugh 57, 96, 98, 99, 106, 109–12
Hope, Christopher 15
Horace 116
'Horses of the Night' 102, 187, 192, 195, 196–8
Horwood, Harold 80
House Full of Women, A 102
House of the Talking Cat, The 154
Household Words 121
'How I Met My Husband' 204, 205, 207
'How Pearl Button Was Kidnapped' 132
Howe, Joseph 35
Howells, William Dean 43, 56
Hulme, Keri 167
humour, satire 14–15, 32, 36–8, 41, 43, 56–7, 61–4, 81–2, 84, 88, 109, 111, 121, 125, 131, 133, 151, 158–60, 166, 167, 168, 215, 217, 232–3, 234, 257, 260, 272
'Hunchback of Port Royal, The' 55
'Hurry, hurry' 83

'I, Ozymandias' 173–4
I Saw in My Dream 144
'I Say, Wait for Me' 168
idiom. See language.
Ihimaera, Witi 155, 172, 173–4
Immanuel's Land 163
immigrant life. See multiculturalism.
In a German Pension 130, 132, 133–4
In a Steamer Chair 56
In Australian Wilds 270
'In Search of the Emerald City' 173–4
In the Village of Viger 30, 42, 45, 47–50, 55, 177–86
Indians 21, 42, 51–2, 53, 55, 67–8, 81–2, 117, 128, 179, 193, 199, 260
Ingersoll, Will 65, 69–70
Ingram, Forrest L. 5
Innis, H.A. 62
Innis, Mary Quayle 266
'Inquiry into ... the New Zealand Short Story, An' 160
Insley, Marie 152
'Insulation' 162
Investigator, The 274
Irving, Washington 15, 16, 33, 39
Islands 154, 163, 168
It Was So Late 147
'Ivars' 155

Jacobs, W.W. 4
'Jake and the Kid' 81
James, Helen 80
James, Henry 6, 10, 43, 56, 68
Jameson, Anna 20
'Jan Godfrey' 161–2
Jenkins, Edward 270
'Jericho's Brick Battlements' 187, 192
Jerome, Jerome K. 43
Jewett, Sarah Orne 4, 45
'John Scantleberry' 46–7
Johnson, Pauline 51, 52
Johnston, Basil 82, 106, 107
Jones, Lawrence 146, 164
Joseph, M.K. 171
'Josephine Labrosse' 181, 183, 184
Joy of the Worm 144, 145
Joyce, James 4, 10, 90, 103, 163
'Judy' 123–4, 126
'Juliet' 130
'Just Mary' 81
'Just Trespassing, Thanks' 146

'Karori' 132
Kendall, Henry 66
Kempe, Edward 126
Kerslake, Susan 87

Kidman, Fiona 155, 168
Kindred of the Wild, The 59
King, Audrey B. 157
Kington, John 138
Kinsella, W.P. 81–2
Kipling, Rudyard 4, 5, 127
Kirby, William 34, 181
Kirk, Norman 169
Kirkpatrick, Ernest S. 52
Kissing Man, The 103
Klein, A.M. 78, 79, 82, 89–91, 99
Klinck, Carl 97
Knister, Raymond 30, 55, 56, 65–6, 68–70, 72, 76–8, 81, 98, 100, 179
'Kosciusko' 158
Kostelanetz, Richard 13
Kreiner, Philip 106
Kreisel, Henry 79, 80, 82, 87, 88, 99
Kroetsch, Robert 22, 82, 94

La Guma, Alex 15
'Labrie's Wife' 48
Ladies & Escorts 88
Lagoon, The 161
Lamp at Noon, The 82
Lancaster, G.B. (Edith Joan Littleton) 126
Landfall 154, 162, 167
landscape. *See* nature.
Lane that Had No Turning, The 53
language, dialect, idiom, accent, speech 12, 23–4, 37–9, 47, 54, 62, 63, 68, 70–1, 81, 85–6, 93–4, 98, 101–2, 105, 124–6, 129, 132, 134, 138, 140, 142–6, 149, 151–2, 154, 155–6, 159, 162, 166, 169, 173–4, 182, 190, 194–6, 199, 201, 213–35, 239–43, 273, 276
Lapham, Henry 121, 122, 156, 277
Laurence, Margaret 96, 98, 99, 100–2, 103, 187–200, 242
Laut, Agnes C. 264
Lawlor, Pat 138, 155
Lawrence, Margaret (Greene) 67, 76

Lawson, Henry 4, 15
Lay, Graeme 169, 170
Layton, Irving 88
Le Moine, James 35
Le Rossignol, James Edward 51, 64, 70
Leacock, Stephen 36, 57, 58, 61–5, 81, 95, 99, 257, 265, 272, 274
Lee, Edmund 160
Leeming, Owen 167
'Legend of the Lost Mythology, The' 168
Leprohon, Rosanna (Mullins) 260
'Letter from Orpheus' 171
'Letter to My Sisters, A' 229
Levine, Norman 79
linked series. *See* serial composition.
Little Girl, The 130
'Little Governess, The' 134, 272
'Little Milliner, The' 178, 180, 184, 185
Literary Garland, The 31, 260
Literary History of Canada 30, 48, 97
Lives of Girls and Women 102, 207
Livesay, Dorothy 78
local colour 14, 30, 48, 115, 181, 260
Locke, Elsie 152
Logsdail, Cecil 53, 262
Lohafer, Susan 5
Loners, The 147
'Loons, The' 187, 193, 195, 199
'Looters, The' 155–6
'Loppy Phelan's Double Shoot' 265
Lowry, Malcolm 79, 87, 91–5, 100
Lucas, Alec 96, 107
'Luft Bad' 133
Lyders, E.M. 157

Macaulay, Thomas Babington, Lord 116
MacBeth, Madge 53
McCahon, Colin 152
McClave, Heather 14
McClung, Nellie 50, 87
McCulloch, Thomas 35, 37
Macdonald, Ross 88
MacDonald, Thoreau 178–9

MacEwen, Gwendolyn 107
McFarlane, Leslie 55
McFee, Oonah 106
Machado de Assis, Joaquim 4
McIllroy, Kimball 266
Mackay, Isabel Ecclestone 64
Maclachlan, Mrs 260
MacLennan, Hugh 21
McLennan, William 51–2
MacLeod, Alistair 106, 265–6
MacMechan, Archibald 263
MacMurchy, Marjory 43
McPherson, Hugo 97
McWhirter, George 106
magazine trade, newspapers 4, 6, 20, 21, 31, 34–5, 43, 80, 95, 96, 116, 121, 125–6, 130, 154
'Magsman Miscellany, The' 163, 165–6
Main-Travelled Roads 45
'Making Father Pay' 145
'Making of a New Zealand, The' 155
Man Alone 172
Man and His Wife, A 142, 143
Mandel, Eli 22
Mander, Jane 139
Maning, F.E. 117
Mannoni, O. 101
Mansfield, Katherine 4, 10, 20, 73, 77, 93, 113–15, 116, 129–37, 139–40, 142–3, 145, 149, 150, 158, 160, 168, 172, 211–20, 243, 263, 269, 272, 276–7, 284
Maori 21, 115, 117–19, 123, 127–8, 129, 135, 138, 140, 152, 153, 154–5, 156, 164, 168, 169, 170, 172–4, 221, 224–8, 229–34, 261
Maori Tales 138
Maoriland Stories 127
Maple Leaves 35
Mark Hurdlestone 35
Marlatt, Daphne 87
Marler, Robert 14–15
Marlowe, Christopher 198, 280
'Marrakesh' 204, 208

'Marriage à la Mode' 131
Marsh, Ngaio 124
Marshall, Alan 15
Marshall, Joyce 79, 82, 83, 84–7
'Mask of the Bear' 187
Masses 265
Massey Report 96
'Material' 104, 201–3, 204, 209
Matthews, Brander 4
'Mazurka Afternoon, The' 156
Me and Gus 150
Me and Gus Again 141
Memoirs of a Peon 144
'Memorial' 204, 209
'Merchant of Heaven, The' 101
Metcalf, John 87, 98, 100, 105, 106, 107, 188
Mitcalfe, Barry 154, 159, 168
Métis 187, 193
Michener, James 274
Middleton, O.E. 147, 152, 156, 168
'Milk Round' 147, 150
Millar, Kenneth 88
Mills, Tom 129
Mincher, Philip 154, 159, 169
Miracle 160, 169
miscellany. *See* Rahmenerzählung.
'Miss Brill' 131, 132–3
'Miss Minnely's Management' 61–2
Miss Peter's Special 273
'Mist Green Oats' 69, 70
Mitchell, Ken 106, 107
Mitchell, W.O. 79, 81, 82, 83
Mitford, Mary Russell 33–4
Montgomery, Lucy Maud 52
Montieth, John 155
Moodie, J.W. Dunbar 31
Moodie, Susanna 20, 29, 30, 31–5, 43, 70, 87, 100, 260
Moons of Jupiter, The 104
Moorhouse, Frank 15
'More Little Mummy in the World, The' 102
More Than Enough 143
Morley, Patricia 59

Morrieson, R.H. 154
Morrissey, Michael 168, 169
'Moslem Wife, The' 93–4
'Motor Car, The' 88
'Mr Reginald Peacock's Day' 134
Mrs Dixon & Friend 168
Mrs Golightly 83
'Mrs Pornog's Afternoon' 157
Muddiman, Bernard 48, 50, 177–8
Mulgan, Alan 116
Mulgan, John 172
multiculturalism, immigrant life, ethnicity, race 49, 61, 70–1, 79, 82, 87–8, 90, 96–7, 101–2, 117, 119, 153–6, 159, 168, 169, 171, 193, 224–8, 232, 243, 261–2, 276, 284
Munro, Alice 96, 98, 102–5, 201–10
Murry, John Middleton 130, 131, 136, 150
Murry, Richard 132, 136
Murtha, Thomas 55, 65, 66, 68–70, 72, 76
Murtha, William 68
My Heart Is Broken 92
mystery. See fantasy.

Narrative of Edward Crewe, The 117
narrative sequence. See serial composition.
Narrative Voice, The 188
Native Argosy, A 72, 74
Native Companion, The 129, 131
'Natural History' 102
nature, landscape, wilderness 32, 39, 45–6, 49, 50, 58–60, 65, 68, 72, 84, 92, 95, 102, 115, 116, 126, 127, 129, 135, 137, 138–9, 151, 168–9, 170, 179, 218–19, 232, 260, 281
Nature and Human Nature 36, 37, 38
negative exclusion, negation 100, 170, 194, 214–15, 220, 224
New Age, The 130
New Ancestors, The 102
New Frontiers 78, 90, 265
New Neighbours 168

New Net Goes Fishing, The 173–4
New Wind in a Dry Land 101
New Zealand 3–27, 72, 79, 113–74, 211–45, 259, 260, 269, 270, 274
'New Zealand Elegy, A' 170
New Zealand Illustrated Magazine 123, 126–7
New Zealand Listener 124, 137, 139–40, 141, 142, 154, 157, 162, 172, 229, 273
New Zealand Short Stories 156
New Zealanders, The 147–8, 149
newspapers. See magazine trade.
'Nineteen Hours on a Common Jury' 122
'No Man Is an Island' 152
'No. 68 Rue Alfred de Musset' 180, 183, 184
'Noah' 157
Noman 107
None Genuine Without This Signature 109
Nonsense Novels 58
North American Education, A 104
Norwood, Robert 264
'Notebook (4)' 159
'Notes on an Abstract Arachnid' 157, 163
'Nothing But the Best' 159
'Nothings' 156, 160
Novascotian, The 35
'November Fifty-six' 155
Now That April's Here 73
Nowlan, Alden 102–3, 265

O'Brien, Edward J. 66, 266
'Obstacles' 162
O'Connor, Frank 4, 5, 13, 25
O'Faolain, Sean 8
Off the Rocks 58
O'Flaherty, Liam 4
Old Judge, The 38, 39–42
Old Man Savarin 61–2
Old New Zealand 117
'Old Woman, The' 85

'O'Leary's Orchard' 284
O'Leary's Orchard 163, 166
Olive Tree in Dalmatia, An 155
On Canadian Poetry 179
'On the Bus' 151
'On Writing the Great NZ Novel' 160
Ondaatje, Michael 106
One Generation Removed 71
'One's a Heifer' 82–3
Orage, A.R. 130
Orange Tree, The 157
O'Sullivan, Vincent 149, 153, 160, 169, 171–2, 243–4
Other Lovers 146
Other Paris, The 92
'Ottawa Valley, The' 204, 205, 209
Our Village 33
Over Prairie Trails 69
Ovid 198, 280
Owen, Ivon 107

Pacey, Desmond 30, 79, 80, 81, 87
Pacific Islands 25, 138, 153, 168, 169, 259, 274
Packer, Richard 159
Page, P.K. 79, 88
Page, Thomas 260
'Painted Door, The' 82
'Pair of Socks, A' 144
'Palace of Kandahar, The' 170
parable 78, 89–90, 102, 107, 224
Parker, Gilbert 43, 51, 53, 55, 56, 58, 60, 65, 66, 181
Parr, Jack 266
Pataka 138
Pattee, Fred Lewis 5, 14, 15
'Paul and Phyllis' 85–6
'Paul Farlotte' 181, 184, 185, 186
'Pearl Button's Boxes and the Way to Baton Rouge' 243
Pearson, W.H. 243
Peden, William 5
'Pedler, The' 180, 182, 184
Pegnitz Junction, The 92
Penguin New Writing 143

Perry, Martha Eugenie 56, 68
'Persistence of Realism, The' 146
Peterman, Michael 33
Pickthall, Marjorie 55, 56, 87
Piece of Land, A 147
Pierce, Lorne 178, 179
Pierre and His People 60
Pilgrim's Progress 163
'Pirihira' 128
Plumb 145
Poe, Edgar Allan 3, 4, 6, 10, 13, 126–7, 211
Poirier, Michel 68
Pounamu Pounamu 173
Powell, Anthony 98
Pratt, E.J. 179
Pratt, Mary Louise 4, 5
'Prelude' 132, 135–6
Presence of Music, The 147, 148
Pritchett, V.S. 4
Private Place, A 84
'Professional, The' 171
Prokosch, Frederic 95
Prophet's Camel Bell, The 101
Prospero and Caliban 101
'Pure Diamond Man, The' 101
Puritan and the Waif, The 144
'Purity Squad' 157
'Putangitangi and the Maere' 128

Queen's Quarterly 80, 265

Race, The 82
'Race Day' 157
Rachel Wilde 32
Raddall, Thomas 79, 263
radio 80–1, 124, 273, 274
Rahmenerzählung, miscellany 18, 21, 34, 41, 106, 120, 122, 165–6, 182–3, 242
'Rain Child, The' 101
'Rawiri and the Four Evangelists' 128
Rawson, Edmund Stansfield 270
Real Mothers 88, 102
Rees, Rosemary 139, 153

298 Index

region, attitudes toward 12–13, 50–2, 54, 55, 64, 82, 96, 97, 102, 154, 242–3
Reid, Ian 5, 6, 9, 17
Reid, J.C. 151
religion, spiritual belief 32, 50, 53–4, 58, 89–91, 94, 95, 109, 119, 121, 123, 147, 165, 177, 178–9, 181, 198, 243, 244, 282, 284
Reservoir, The 162–3
'Return from Oz' 173
Revans, Samuel 116
Rhodes, H. Winston 144, 157, 164
Rhythm 130
Ribbon Stories 121
Richards, David Adams 102
Richler, Mordecai 79, 88
Ride Home, The 159
Riding, Jules 158
'Riley's Handbook' 163, 164, 166
Rimanelli, Giose 30, 179
'Rise and Progress of New Zealand, The' 115
Rive, Richard 15
'River, The' 170
Roberts, Sir Charles G.D. 4, 42, 50, 55, 56, 58–61, 64–5, 66, 76
Roberts, Theodore Goodridge 58
Robertson, Andrew 260
Rogers, Grace McLeod 55, 56
Rohrberger, Mary 14
romance conventions. *See* sentimentality.
Romany of the Snows, A 60
Ronai, Paulo 149
Rooke, Leon 87, 103, 107–8
Ross, Sinclair 78, 79, 80, 82
Roughing It in the Bush 31–3
'Royal Beatings' 104
Ruberto, Roberto 30, 179
Rudd, Steele 15
'Rugby as a Way of Life' 141
Rule, Jane 87
Rushdie, Salman 229
Russell, Elizabeth, Countess 132, 136

Rutherford, Paul 20
Rutledge, J.L. 54

Sacred Bullock, The 56
'Sage, The' 126
'Sale Day' 144
Sam Slick's Wise Saws and Modern Instances 35
'Samovar, The' 155
Sandwell, B.K. 66, 70–1, 78, 178
Sargeson, Frank 4, 6, 72, 114, 140, 142–7, 149, 150–2, 155, 156–7, 163, 167, 170, 172, 221–4, 227–8, 276, 284
satire. *See* humour.
Sauna Bath Mysteries, The 169, 170
Scaife, Arthur H. 53
Scars 81
Schermbrucker, Bill 87, 106
Schlunke, E.O. 15
Scholes, Robert 10
'School Picnic' 152
Schreiner, Olive 114
Schroeder, Andreas 107
Schwimmer, Erik 144, 159
Scobie, Stephen 100
Scott, Duncan Campbell 4, 20, 29–30, 42–51, 55, 57, 58, 66, 72, 95, 98, 100, 110, 177–86, 243
Scott, Margaret 172
Scott, Sir Walter 67, 98
'Sea Gull's Cry' 158
Searle, Edith 116
'Sedan' 180, 181, 183, 184, 185
Selvon, Sam 87
Send Somebody Nice 147
'Sense of Proportion, A' 162–3
'Sentimentalitists, The' 265
sentimentality, romance conventions 14, 20, 34, 41, 43, 46–8, 53–6, 59, 60–1, 65, 70, 79, 88–90, 105, 114, 117–21, 124, 125, 127, 131, 133, 138, 146, 152, 174, 179, 183, 196, 198, 225, 232–3, 242, 260, 280

serial composition, narrative sequence, linked series ix, x, 25, 41–2, 47–8, 53, 57, 59, 62–5, 69, 72, 85–6, 91, 92, 94–6, 102–3, 107, 119–21, 148–9, 150, 177–210, 239, 242, 260–1
Service, Robert 56, 128
Seton, Ernest Thompson 43, 53, 58–9
Seton, Julia 59
'Settler's Tragedy, The' 270
Shack Locker, The 52
Shadbolt, Maurice 147–9
Shadows on the Snow 120
Shaw, Helen 144, 154, 155, 157–8, 276
'She Wore Red Gloves' 158
Ship, Reuben 274
Shirt Factory, The 169
Sholom Aleichem (Rabinovitch, Sholom) 90
short fiction. *See* anecdote; animal stories; documentary form; endings; fable; fantasy; fictional form; folktale; fracture; frame stories; historical fiction; humour; language; local colour; magazine trade; negative exclusion; parable; *Rahmenerzählung*; sentimentality; serial composition; sketch; tale forms; and names of individual authors and stories.
short fiction, terms 7–9, 247–54
short fiction, theory and criticism 3–25
Short Stories (Klein) 90
Short Stories (Middleton) 147
Shorter, Clement 132
'Sick Call, A' 73–4
Siegfried, André 12–13
Sime, Jessie Georgina 65, 87
Simms, Norman 159
Simpson, Tony 139–40
'Sister of the Baroness, The' 133
Sister Woman 65
'Six Place Names and a Girl' 165
'Sixty Nine Club, The' 147
sketch 17, 21–2, 24, 30, 32–5, 39, 41, 46, 47, 57, 71, 99, 111, 117–21, 127–9, 131, 135, 143–4, 150–1, 156–7, 158, 162, 167, 179, 212, 222, 242, 268, 275
'Sketch-Plan for the Great New Zealand Novel' 159–60
Smith, Elizabeth 142
Smith, Harry James 55, 56
Smith, Ray 106, 107–8
Smith, Seba 36
Smith's Dream 169
'Snake' 170
'Snow' 69
Snowman Snowman 162–3
'So Many Have Died' 85–6, 266
'Solutions' 162
'Some Are Lucky' 147
Some Are Lucky 147
Something Childish 130, 134
'Something I've Been Meaning to Tell You' 203, 208
Something I've Been Meaning to Tell You 104, 201–10
Sons o' Men 126
Soul of the Street, The 61
'Sound of the Singing, The' 187, 189, 194
'Spanish Lady, The' 204, 205, 208
Speaking for Ourselves 156
speech. *See* language.
Spencer, Elizabeth 87
Spit Delaney's Island 102
Spivey, Anne 167
Sportsman's Sketches, A 99
'Spring Pictures' 131
St Pierre, Paul 81–2
Station Amusements in New Zealand 121
Station Life in New Zealand 121
Stead, C.K. 151, 163, 164, 167, 169, 170
Stein, Gertrude 72, 265
Steinberg, M.W. 90
Stephens, Brunton 66
Stephens, Donald 107

Stern, James 94
Sterne, Laurence 167
Stevens, John 107–8
Stevenson, Robert Louis 4, 47
Stewart, Bruce 169
Stewart's Quarterly 22
Stone, The 147
Stones, Anthony 143
Stoney, H. Butler 118
Stories About 121
Stories of New Zealand Life 122
Stories of the Land of Evangeline 55
Story, Gertrude 102
'Story for a Xmas Annual' 158
Story Teller's Story, A 72
Stout, Sir Robert 115
Stowe, Harriet Beecher 43
'Stranger, The' 73
'Strategem of Terrance O'Halloran, The' 47
Street, The 88
Strickland, Agnes 34
Strickland, Samuel 34
Sturm, Jacqueline C. 154–5
Sturm, Terry 163, 165
Styles, Catherine 152
'Suburbanisation of Esmerelda, The' 170
Such Separate Creatures 147
Summer Fires and Winter Country 147, 148
Summer in the Gravel Pit 163
Sunshine Sketches of a Little Town 62–4, 99
Survivals 171
'Susie and Perce' 69
Sutherland, John 78, 80
'Suzanne and Susanna' 68
'Swans' 161
'Swings of the Pendulum, The' 134

tale forms 9, 14–16, 20–1, 30, 41, 43, 47, 52–4, 58, 60, 61–2, 71, 102, 106, 107, 115, 116, 118–22, 125, 127, 150, 198

Tales of a Dying Race 127–8
Tales of the Labrador 53
Tales of the St John River 52
Tamarack Review 80
Tangata Ke 127
Taranaki 118
Tasma (Jessie Couvreur) 270
Tasman, Abel 117
Taylor, Graeme 65
Taylor, Meadows 53
Ten Green Bottles 88, 102
'Tell Me Yes or No' 204, 207, 228
Texidor, Greville 154, 155, 157
Thackeray, William 63
'Thanks for the Ride' 104
'That Summer' 144
That Summer 143
Theocritus 272
Thibaudeau, Colleen 88
'This Is New Zealand' 168–9
Thomas, Audrey 87–8, 102, 106
Thompson, Kent 87, 105, 188
Thompson, Stith 9
Thomson, Edward W. 43, 55, 56, 61–2, 63, 66
Thoreau, H.D. 141
Tidal Creek 146
'Time and the Narrative Voice' 188
'To Set Our House in Order, 187, 188–9, 191
Todorov, Tzvetan 5
Told by the Innkeeper 53
Tomorrow 142, 143, 154
Tomorrow-Tamer, The 101
'Towards the Mountains' 165
Traill, Catharine Parr 32, 70, 99, 260
Tracy, Mona 138
'Tragedy of the Seigniory, The' 180, 182, 184
'Travelling Nude, The' 88
Triad 122, 128–9
'Triumph of Marie Laviolette, The' 45
Turgenev, Ivan 4, 99
Turner, Frederick Jackson 19
Tuwhare, Hone 155

Twain, Mark 14, 36, 115, 257
Twist, The 56
'Two Widowers' 162

'Uncle Adam Shot a Stag' 152
United Kingdom 4–5, 11, 13, 16, 25, 29, 33, 36, 37, 38, 42, 43–4, 49, 68, 70, 79, 87, 113, 115, 117, 118, 122, 124, 126, 129–30, 141, 159, 168, 169, 170, 179, 243, 257, 259, 261, 274
United States of America 4–5, 11, 13–16, 19, 20, 23, 31, 34, 36, 37–8, 42, 43–5, 55, 57, 62, 66, 67–8, 71, 72, 87, 89, 95, 114, 115, 123, 141, 144, 169, 173–4, 179, 243, 255, 257, 262, 274
Unmarried Man's Summer, An 92
Untold Half, The 125
'Up at the Mammoth' 152
Utopia, Arcadia, non-Utopia 23, 118, 133, 168, 170, 173, 179–80, 182, 186, 197, 232

'Vain Shadow, The' 48
Valgardson, W.D. 106
Van Dyke, Henry 58
Vanderhaeghe, Guy 106
Various Persons Named Kevin O'Brien 102
Vaughn-James, Martin 106
Victoria Magazine, The 31, 32, 33–4, 260
violence ix, x, 30, 47, 68, 76, 83–5, 123, 142, 144–6, 151, 159, 173, 188, 195, 196, 232, 240, 242, 243–5
Virgo, Sean 87, 106
Vogel, Julius 115, 123
'Voyage' 165

Waddington, Miriam 79, 88
Waitaruna 119
Waiting for the Mail 122
Walk on the Beach, A 147
'Walking on Water' 204, 205–7, 208

Wallace, Frederick William 52
Wallace, Paul 56
Walsh, Henry Cecil 64
war 49, 53, 69, 79, 83, 84, 85, 93–4, 131, 147, 151, 152, 156, 157, 180–1, 183, 193, 195, 197, 209, 232, 243–4, 272, 274
Ward, Artemus 36, 257
Waring, Marilyn 229
Warm Beer 150
'Warning to New Zealand Fathers, A' 158
Watmough, David 106
Watson, H.B. Marriott 123
Watson, Sheila 106, 107
Watters, R.E. 37
'Way of Talking, A' 172, 221, 224–8
Way of the Sea, The 61
Way to Always Dance, The 102
We Four, and the Stories We Told 121
'We have to sit opposite' 84
'Weaker Vessel, The' 122
'Weather Breeder, The' 69
Weaver, Robert 72, 80–1, 98, 100
Webb, Alice F. 273
Wedde, Ian 169, 170
Week, The 43, 66
'Wellington 1940' 158
Wells, H.G. 4
Welty, Eudora 8
Wendt, Albert 275–6
West Indies 87–8
Wharton, Edith 4
When he was free and young and he used to wear silks 88
'Where Is the Voice Coming From?' 100
Where the White Man Treads 127
Where to Go? 168
Whitman, Walt 23, 115
Who Do You Think You Are? 104
Wiebe, Rudy 100, 102–3
Wild, Judith 116
Wilde, Oscar 47, 56, 129, 133
wilderness. See nature.
Wilding, Michael 15

Wilkins, F.P. 168
Will Ye Let the Mummers In? 265
Williams, William Carlos 8
Wilson, Ethel 79, 82, 83–4, 87
Wilson, Phillip 147
'Wind Blows, The' 131
Windeater Te Kaihau, The 167
'Window, The' 84
'Windows' 85–6
Winsome Winnie 58
'Winter Garden' 162, 163
'Winter Wind' 204, 205, 207, 209
Witching of Elspie, The 49
Withrow, W.H. 53
Wolfe, Morris 107
'Woman at the Store, The' 132
women, attitudes toward 37, 49, 50, 58, 65, 81–2, 84–7, 100, 102, 114, 119, 122–4, 126, 132–5, 137, 139, 141, 145, 147, 153–5, 159, 168, 170, 172–3, 183, 201–10, 211–20, 224–7, 229–34, 242–4, 256, 262, 263, 282
Wood, Susan Nugent 122
'Wooing of Hine-Ao, The' 123
'Wooing of Monsieur Cuerrier, The' 180, 181–2, 184
Woolcott, Edith G. 123, 126
Woolf, Virginia 149
Workers' Institute Libraries 34

Yates, J. Michael 106, 111
'Yellow Brick Road' 173
You Are Now Entering the Human Heart 162
You Can't Get There from Here 109–10
Young, David 106, 111

Zealandia 125, 129
Zohar, The 89
Zola, Emile 42

www.ingramcontent.com/pod-product-compliance
Lightning Source LLC
Chambersburg PA
CBHW020355080526
44584CB00014B/1022